Financing Long-Term Care in Europe

Also by Joan Costa-Font and Christophe Courbage

ECONOMICS OF INNOVATION AND NEW TECHNOLOGY, Vol. 18 (5) (*edited with A. Mina*)

THE ECONOMICS OF NEW HEALTH TECHNOLOGY (*edited with A. McGuire*)

THE GENEVA PAPERS ON RISK AND INSURANCE – ISSUES AND PRACTICE, special issue on health, Vol. 31 (4).

Financing Long-Term Care in Europe

Institutions, Markets and Models

Edited by

Joan Costa-Font

Christophe Courbage

First published 2012 by
PALGRAVE MACMILLAN

Palgrave Macmillan in the UK is an imprint of Macmillan Publishers Limited, registered in England, company number 785998, of Houndmills, Basingstoke, Hampshire RG21 6XS.

Palgrave Macmillan in the US is a division of St Martin's Press LLC, 175 Fifth Avenue, New York, NY 10010.

Palgrave Macmillan is the global academic imprint of the above companies and has companies and representatives throughout the world.

Palgrave® and Macmillan® are registered trademarks in the United States, the United Kingdom, Europe and other countries.

ISBN 978–0–230–24946–2

This book is printed on paper suitable for recycling and made from fully managed and sustained forest sources. Logging, pulping and manufacturing processes are expected to conform to the environmental regulations of the country of origin.

A catalogue record for this book is available from the British Library.

Library of Congress Cataloging-in-Publication Data
Financing long-term care in Europe : institutions, markets, and models /
   [edited by] Joan Costa-Font, Christophe Courbage.
      p.   cm.
   Includes index.
   ISBN 978–0–230–24946–2 (hardback)
   1. Long-term care insurance—Europe.   2. Long-term care of the
sick—Europe—Finance.   3. Older people—Long-term care—Europe.
   I. Costa-i-Font, Joan.   II. Courbage, Christophe.
HG9390.F56 2011
368.4′20094—dc23   2011029569

10   9   8   7   6   5   4   3   2   1
21 20 19 18 17 16 15 14 13 12

Printed and bound in Great Britain by
CPI Antony Rowe, Chippenham and Eastbourne

Contents

List of Figures

List of Tables and Box

Tables

Box

Acknowledgements

Many people deserve our thanks for their help in making this book possible. We would first and foremost like to thank the authors of the various chapters in this book. We would also like to express our gratitude to the institutions for which we both work, The Geneva Association and the London School of Economics and Political Science, for the intellectual environment they provided us with.

Last but not least, we would like to thank our colleagues, and in particular Françoise Jaffré for the time she devoted to copy-edit the manuscript of this book, and Walter Stahel for all his good advice in the final preparation of the book.

List of Contributors

Bea Cantillon Herman Deleeck Centre for Social Policy, University of Antwerp, Belgium

Francesca Colombo Organization for Economic Cooperation and Development, France

Adelina Comas-Herrera Personal Social Services Research Unit (PSSRU), LSE Health and Social Care, London School of Economics and Political Science, United Kingdom

Joan Costa-Font London School of Economics and Political Science, United Kingdom

Christophe Courbage The Geneva Association, Switzerland

Joanna Geerts Federal Planning Bureau, Belgium

Cristiano Gori Personal Social Services Research Unit (PSSRU), LSE Health and Social Care, London School of Economics and Political Science, United Kingdom

Tor Iversen Department of Health Management and Health Economics, University of Oslo, Norway

Martin Karlsson Chair of Applied Econometrics, Technische Universität Darmstadt, Germany

Simone Krummaker Center for Risk and Insurance, Leibniz University of Hannover, Germany

Anne Laferrère INSEE and CREST (Paris), France

Pierre-Yves Le Corre Swiss Re Europe SA, France

Ninke Mussche Herman Deleeck Centre for Social Policy, University of Antwerp, Belgium

Henning Øien Department of Health Management and Health Economics, University of Oslo, Norway

August Österle Institute for Social Policy, Department of Socioeconomics, Vienna University of Economics and Business, Austria

Pierre Pestieau CORE, Université Catholique de Louvain, CREPP, University of Liege, Belgium and Paris School of Economics, France

Linda Pickard Personal Social Services Research Unit (PSSRU), LSE Health and Social Care, London School of Economics and Political Science, United Kingdom

Manuel Plisson Chair 'Risques et Chances de la transition démographique', Paris Dauphine University LEDA-LEGOS, France

Gregory Ponthière Paris School of Economics and Ecole Normale Supérieure (Paris), France

Sebastian Reddemann Center for Risk and Insurance, Leibniz University of Hannover, Germany

Silvina Santana Department of Economics, Management and Industrial Engineering and Institute of Electronics Engineering and Telematics of Aveiro, University of Aveiro, Portugal

Ulrike Schneider Research Institute for Economics of Aging and Institute for Social Policy, Department of Socioeconomics, WU Vienna University of Economics and Business, Austria

Frederik T. Schut Department of Health Policy and Management, Erasmus University Rotterdam, the Netherlands

Birgit Trukeschitz Research Institute for Economics of Aging, WU Vienna University of Economics and Business, Austria

Bernard van den Berg Centre for Health Economics, University of York, United Kingdom

France Weaver University of Geneva, Switzerland

Peter Willemé Federal Planning Bureau, Belgium

Raphael Wittenberg Personal Social Services Research Unit (PSSRU), LSE Health and Social Care, London School of Economics and Political Science, United Kingdom

Andy Zuchandke Institute for Risk and Insurance, Leibniz University of Hannover, Germany

Part I
Introduction

1
Financing Long-Term Care: New and Unresolved Questions

Joan Costa-Font
London School of Economics and Political Science, United Kingdom

and

Christophe Courbage
The Geneva Association, Switzerland

1 Introduction

Europe is confronted with an ageing population. The surge of the baby-boom generation and further gain in longevity, combined with continued below-replacement fertility rates, led to a significant increase in the number of people age 65 and over in Europe. While an ageing population is undeniably a great achievement for societies with an obvious economic value (Breyer et al., 2010), it is at the same time an unprecedented challenge for societies, governments and private markets. Today's European populations are expected to live longer than previous generations, but part of these populations will live these extra years of life with some level of dependency requiring the use of long-term care (LTC). LTC is a set of services provided on a daily basis, formally or informally, at home or in institutions, to people suffering from a loss of mobility and autonomy in their activity of daily living. Although loss of autonomy may occur at any age, its frequency rises with age.

As Europeans age, social contracts ruling inter-generational household relationships are being revisited by newer generations accordingly. Both implicit and explicit contracts determining care giving duties are being reformulated to match the demands of an increasing size of old-population cohorts in need of LTC. This trend implies that newer and often highly complex schemes define the financing of LTC coverage. However, not only LTC as a risk is shaped by young contract design, it is also distinguished from other widely insured contingencies such as health and longevity by the fact that insurance expansion takes place with either implicit or explicit coordination between the public sector, the private sector and society. Without such coordination, several forms of crowding out can hamper the development of financing mechanisms (Costa-Font, 2010), and lead to a complex financing conundrum with difficult solutions.

As explained later in this book, most European countries' LTC funding schemes follows a *de facto* partnership model that involves individuals and households, market instruments as well as public insurance structures (see Costa-Font and Courbage, this book). However, the existing interactions rules governing this partnership differ from one country to another. For instance, Germany began implementing a federal social insurance programme providing LTC in 1995, Spain set up a tax-based programme to finance the needs of people with severe dependency in 2007, whilst the United States centred on promoting the purchase of private LTC insurance together and/or in partnership with an expansion of publicly funded schemes.

Importantly, the underlying evidence on cost-incentives and sources of funding in financing LTC is heterogeneous and limited, and very often dependent on country-specific institutional features. Supply of LTC is typically divided between different levels of governments, and coordination with the health systems and income replacement schemes is not necessarily well defined. For instance, informal care and family funding of LTC is the norm in Southern European countries (see Costa-Font et al., this book) and in Eastern Europe (see Oesterle, this book), public coverage for LTC is the main form of funding in Scandinavian countries (see Karlsson et al., this book), whilst different forms of market intervention are prevalent elsewhere. Recent reforms of LTC financing suggest that there is reorganization in the North and attempts at coverage expansion in the South.

LTC for the dependent elderly typically replaces individuals in their daily life duties when individuals are unable to independently undertake them. However, although prevalence of old-age dependence is growing at relatively parallel rates across European countries, entitlements to LTC insurance and availability of private providers and insurers are extremely divergent. Furthermore, as schemes to respond to the LTC need are country- and culture-specific, it makes cross-country comparison complex. This calls for a better understanding of both demand and supply factors underpinning the development of financial instruments to cover LTC risks. Publicly financed LTC has been an area of social policy responsibility in the hands of local authorities and has received limited priority compared with other welfare state pillars such as health and pensions. However, during the late 1990s and early 2000s, not only public LTC insurance has expanded in Europe but also a private sector has developed, mainly in the form of LTC insurance markets. Figure 1.1 provides the proportion of public and private spending on LTC as a share of GDP in various Organization for European Cooperation and Development (OECD) countries. Public and private spending on LTC varies strongly from one country to the other, reflecting differences in out-of-pocket spending, public coverage and insurance market development. Interestingly, Figure 1.1 exhibits a relatively higher role of the private sector

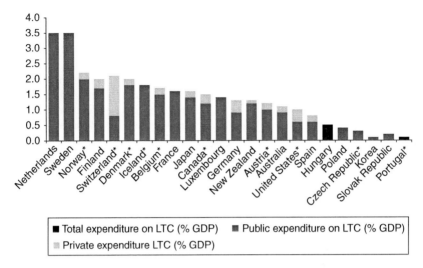

Figure 1.1   Public, private and total spending on LTC in OECD countries, share of GDP, 2007
Note: * Data for Norway, Switzerland, Denmark, Iceland, Belgium, Canada, Austria, United States, the Czech Republic and Portugal refer to nursing LTC expenditure.
Source: OECD (2009).

in countries like Spain, Germany and Switzerland where both for- or not-for-profit providers are providing LTC services. In the United States, Medicaid, a means-tested social assistance programme, is the primary source of public funding. This is especially the case of care provided at institutions, though the deinstutionalization process and the development of community service stand out as a push for further public intervention. These phenomena have ramifications into how LTC is financed, as explained in several chapters of this book.

2   The role of the government and society in LTC financing

Some dimensions of LTC are, together with health care and education, a private good that many societies prioritize, and accordingly can be classified as a 'merit good' deserving some form of government intervention. Markets alone would fail to coordinate LTC financing given the current levels of information and, hence, the difficulty to write reliable inter-temporal contracts. It is then not a surprise that the government traditionally has intervened in the financing and provision of LTC, though not all components of LTC are equally prioritized. It also explains why it is common to find higher cost-sharing than in other merit goods such as health care. In addition, the speeding up of the ageing of Western societies is a relatively recent phenomenon. Consequently, governments have traditionally ranked LTC below health and education. For the same reason, they were also confronted with a lower demand for LTC. It is also the case that LTC encompasses a set of services that were traditionally provided within the household, and governmental action could crowd out family action. In addition, the nursing home industry is dominated by for-profit facilities and government's role is therefore less pronounced when it comes to nursing home facilities.

Importantly, although LTC combines the dimension of health and social care, LTC coverage is generally a function of the health systems already in place. Yet, this does not mean that LTC is necessarily coordinated with the health system. However, it may be difficult to differentiate the health insurance system from other systems specific to LTC risk. In the face of a potential rise in LTC expenditures representing an increasing share in health budgets, several countries have decided to consider LTC as a new risk and to separate it from health care coverage more explicitly. These countries have established LTC insurance as a new branch of their social insurance system (e.g., Germany and Luxemburg).

In almost all European countries, the design of financing schemes for LTC is at the forefront of health and financial policy debates. For instance, in Britain in 2010, reforms that encompass the formation of a new government call for a new commission for the financing of LTC. Another illustration is France where the government is discussing various solutions, either creating a fifth branch of the social security to cover the LTC risks, or making mandatory private LTC insurance to complement the partial public coverage.

Generally speaking, LTC systems can fit into broad financing models that include forms of social insurance, tax-based systems and voluntary health insurance, although in practice we tend to find hybrid models. Furthermore, general institutional models might not mean much when means-testing is in place, or when countries heavily rely on cost-sharing schemes (e.g., coinsurance, copayments) to mould demand. Social insurance schemes have as an advantage that they define a general or universal eligibility to LTC, they combine cash and in-kind services and often provide more choice than tax-funded systems without hampering access as in purely market-driven systems.

One of the common institutional reforms that seems to be taking place is the regional devolution of LTC expenditures. For instance, in Spain, Autonomous Communities are responsible for the regulation of LTC (Costa-Font et al., this book). Similarly, in France, the public LTC allowance is jointly funded by both central and local governments (Courbage and Plisson, this book). In the UK, LTC is a devolved responsibility and in Scotland, unlike in the rest of the UK, the central recommendation of the Royal Commission on Long Term Care was adopted and free personal care was introduced in 2002 (Comas et al., this book).

According to a recent report by the European Commission (2008), most European countries recognize the importance of finding an appropriate balance between public and private sources of funding. The logic of mixed funding based on public–private partnership in the coverage of LTC risk seems to be the way chosen by the largest number of countries. The issue is to better understand the role of the market and its relation with public provision to cover LTC risks.

A private solution to expand LTC coverage has been the development of an insurance market for LTC. That is why, for some decades now, insurance companies have been offering contracts to cover the financial consequences of dependency and the use of LTC. Market evolution strongly depends on institutional settings, and the United States and France are currently the most developed markets. Another private solution to finance LTC is the use of home equity release.

3 Private coverage of LTC risk

3.1 Private LTC insurance

Unlike standard health insurance policies that primarily pay for the cost of health care, LTC insurance policies are long-term contracts designed to help pay for assistance (at home or in an institution) with 'activities of daily living' for individuals with physical and/or cognitive impairments. While the market for private LTC insurance should be well developed, due to the importance of the risk of dependency and the aversion of individuals to such a risk, few countries have an expanded LTC insurance market, apart from the United States and France.

A common explanation for the lack of LTC insurance purchasing is that individuals are inadequately informed about the products available and that they ignore low-frequency, high-severity events that have not occurred recently (Kunreuther, 1978). Another explanation for the limited development of LTC insurance markets includes the phenomena of moral hazard (over-consumption of care encouraged by insurance) and of adverse selection (over-representation of bad risks in the insured population), and the fact that the interaction of public insurance programmes arguably crowds out private insurance.

Since LTC is largely provided informally, mainly through family members, inter-generational factors have also been put forward to explain the rationale for taking out demand for LTC insurance (Pauly, 1990). The desire to leave a bequest seems to be a major motive for LTC insurance. However, elderly individuals with children may decide to forego the purchase of LTC insurance due to intra-family moral hazard. Indeed, parents who prefer to receive care from their children may decline the offer to purchase insurance, as this may create a disincentive for children to provide care. Intra-family moral hazard differs from classic moral hazard in the sense that it is not the policy-holder behaviour that is modified by the presence of insurance, but the caregiver's behaviour. Nevertheless, it happens that bequests can be structured so as to provide an incentive for children to care for their elderly parents. If LTC insurance were purchased, parents could increase the sensitivity of the bequest to caregiving in order to elicit attention from children (Zweifel and Strüwe, 1996).

To address the relatively low development of the market for LTC insurance, a number of proposals have been discussed to develop and make this market more accessible, in particular the combination of LTC insurance and life insurance.

3.2   Combining LTC insurance and life insurance

In recent years, new products have been developed to cover the risk of dependency, and in particular a combination of LTC insurance and life insurance into a single product. The longevity risk is usually covered through life insurance, while the risk of using LTC is covered by LTC insurance. The strategy of combining these two products in one is that risks compensate each other: healthy people with high life expectancy attracted by life insurance offset those in poor health with a short life expectancy attracted by LTC insurance. Moreover, combining these two risks in one product has two advantages. First, it reduces the phenomenon of adverse selection in the market for life insurance, since dependent people should not live long enough to qualify for long-term annuities. Second, the selection of risk is minimized because it consists only of filtering out individuals who can immediately benefit from insurance payments.

In a recent study, Murtaugh et al. (2001) have shown that combining life insurance with LTC coverage was likely to reduce the cost of both products as well as to make them more accessible to potential buyers. In particular, their model shows that under a minimum risk selection, excluding those who would be eligible to receive payments on the date of purchase, 98 per cent of 65 year-old applicants would be accepted compared with 77 per cent under current LTC insurance underwriting conditions.

If insurance is a possible way to finance LTC, other instruments also exist and in particular the concept of housing equity.

3.3   Self-insurance through housing property

Self-insurance has some specific advantages in financing LTC, as the probability of dependency can be hard to estimate with some level of certainty. Various countries are already considering housing property to finance part of LTC. This stems from the fact that a large proportion of the elderly own the place where they reside (Costa-Font et al., 2009). Financing LTC through home property is possible through the use of home equity release schemes. Such schemes are called for to provide for those who are deemed house-rich and cash-poor. More generally, the adequacy of using housing as a saving device for non-housing consumption is linked to the possibility of cash from it, with or without selling it. This home equity solutions are either close to a sale arrangement in the form of the traditional French *viager*, or to a credit operation in the form of a reverse mortgage system. A reverse mortgage is a loan secured on the value of a property which makes it possible to make liquid, or to monetize, real estate assets, without any transfer of ownership. Such schemes exist in most countries, but are only somewhat developed in the UK and the United States.

Instead of linking housing equity to LTC expenses, another possibility, as suggested by Chen (2001), would be to link the reverse mortgage, not to LTC spending, but to either life or LTC insurance. The idea is that the reverse mortgage would be used to pay insurance premiums and not LTC. The annuity to be received would be linked to the value of the house and to the level of dependency. The property would act as a safety net and would be used as financing of last resort.

However, the market for reverse mortgages has been slowed down in part due to the uncertainty surrounding housing prices and in some countries due to some level of reluctance of consumers, who expect to bequest their housing property to their children (Costa-Font et al., 2010).

4   The contents of this book

With this in mind, this book aims to address various aspects related to the financing of LTC in Europe. It has four important objectives. The first objective is to understand the institutional, economical, cultural and behavioural constraints that explain the development of models of coverage for LTC throughout Europe. The second is to develop a set of economic explanations for the development of public and private insurance for LTC. Third, the book aims at explaining the nature of business interactions and competition of different financing instruments in place. Finally, the book illustrates through various case studies how LTC is financed in Europe and what the main challenges these countries face in terms of LTC risk management.

This book consists of 15 chapters from various experts in their respective field, coming from universities, international organizations and the insurance industry.

In Chapter 2, Francesca Colombo offers an overview of public coverage mechanisms in OECD countries. More precisely, she provides a typology of public coverage for LTC. This exercise is a difficult task as in many OECD countries coverage for LTC does not follow pure models. Different approaches can apply to specific population groups or to different care cost components. This follows partly from historical and partly from societal choices about individual and collective responsibility towards care for elderly and disabled people. Bearing in mind this complexity, the author distinguishes clusters of countries with similar LTC coverage approaches. The taxonomy focuses on variation in support for personal care (whether at home or in institutions). It discusses coverage for other care services where relevant. It uses two main criteria to distinguish across country types: the scope of entitlement to LTC benefits – whether there is universal or means-tested entitlement to public funding; and whether LTC coverage is through single or multiple programmes. Three broad categories are identified as universal coverage within a single programme, mixed systems and means-tested systems.

In Chapter 3, Pierre Pestieau and Gregory Ponthiere focus on the LTC insurance market and examine the alternative explanatory factors of the so-called LTC insurance puzzle. The LTC insurance puzzle is the fact that so few people purchase LTC insurance whereas this would seem to be a rational conduct given the high probability of dependence and the high costs of LTC. The authors survey various theoretical and empirical studies of the demand and supply of LTC insurance. They discuss the vicious circle in which the LTC insurance market seems to be stuck: this market is thin because most people find the existing insurance products too expensive, and, at the same time, the products supplied by insurance companies are too expensive because of the thinness of the market. Moreover, they also show that whereas some explanations of the puzzle involve a perfect rationality of agents on the LTC insurance market, others rely, on the contrary, on various behavioural imperfections.

In Chapter 4, Pierre-Yves Le Corre also focuses on LTC insurance markets but from an industry perspective. He highlights and details the factors and structural features favouring the development of insurance solutions for LTC. He analyses the successes and failures of these insurance solutions from a commercial as well as a technical point of view. Insurance approaches implemented in various countries illustrate the topic. Finally, some perspectives are derived for the future of LTC insurance markets.

In Chapter 5, Anne Laferrère addresses the very important topic of how housing wealth can be used to finance LTC. In particular, she assesses the role of home ownership in providing self-insurance for LTC. She reviews the risks linked to old age, and how they cannot be fully assessed without taking housing into account. She presents the means to extract housing equity and also explores the complex relationships between insurance, housing, LTC and family. The idea of considering housing property to finance part of LTC stems from the fact that a large share of the elderly own the place where they reside. Home equity release schemes are called for to provide for those who are deemed house-rich and cash-poor. More generally the adequacy of using housing as a saving accumulation for non-housing consumption is linked to the possibility to cash from it, with or without selling it, depending on the types of home equity.

In Chapter 6, Joan Costa-Font and Christophe Courbage examine the interaction between the public and private sectors, together with informal care in the financing of LTC. The use of LTC by each individual is significantly different depending on a set of circumstances including the development of welfare State intervention, family ties and especially the market for services, which in turn leads to a market for the insurance of the costs of such services. All these differences explain that LTC expenditure is very heterogeneous amongst European countries. In this chapter, the authors address the role of partnership models as an alternative to the development of either State or family crowding out. The chapter contains some evidence as to how partnership alternatives work, their prospects and limitations.

The other chapters of the book provide a precise picture on how each European country organizes the financing of LTC. As mentioned earlier, LTC financing varies from one country to another and depends on both historical and societal factors. It is then important to provide a precise overview of how each country deals with the coverage of LTC risk.

In Chapter 7, Frederik T. Schut and Bernard van den Berg aim to give the background of the Dutch LTC insurance scheme, to describe current deficiencies and to discuss future prospects of LTC financing in the Netherlands. By rationing of supply and tight budgetary restrictions, the Dutch government managed effectively to control the growth of LTC expenditure, but at the expense of growing waiting lists and deteriorating quality of care. Reform plans aim to make the LTC system more efficient and consumer-directed. The authors discuss whether the proposed reforms offer a perspective on a sustainable system of comprehensive LTC insurance. They conclude that the success of the reforms depends heavily on the definition of entitlements, the accuracy of needs assessment and the feasibility of determining appropriate client-based budgets.

In Chapter 8, Christophe Courbage and Manuel Plisson describe how LTC is financed in France and discuss the possible reforms to be implemented to make the system more sustainable. They start by highlighting the specific nature of LTC as well as the demographic and cost of LTC in France. In France, there exists a long tradition of public coverage for the large risks of life, and LTC risk follows this trend. Yet, in addition to public support, a market for LTC insurance has developed and encompasses today almost 5 per cent of the population. The authors present these specificities and discuss the eventual reforms of the French system that are currently discussed by various stakeholders.

In Chapter 9, Adelina Comas-Herrera, Raphael Wittenberg and Linda Pickard address the financing of LTC in England. They aim to present a broad overview of the current organizational structures in England, to discuss the key suggested reforms and to put them in an international context. They first examine key issues relating to the current LTC system in England. They explore the problems identified in official reports on LTC and in the wider social policy literature. They discuss recent reviews and reports recommending reform of the financing system, including the proposals contained in the Labour government's Green and White Papers and the initial documents produced by the new coalition government. They argue that the current financing system in England can be characterized as a residual system where care is free only to those who cannot afford to pay for themselves, with access heavily targeted at those with the highest levels of needs and to those without informal care, and with substantial local variation in access and means-testing for home care. It is also characterized by a mixed economy of supply of care and a mixed economy of finance.

In Chapter 10, Joan Costa-Font, Christiano Gori and Silvina Santana look at the LTC financing of three Southwest European countries, namely, Italy, Portugal and Spain. The three countries under analysis face similar institutional pressure to reform their LTC system, though they differ in their objectives, needs and economic constraints. A common feature in all three countries is perhaps the structure of the family, which shares some cultural aspects. Although the political and institutional system is subject to different legacies, these countries have managed to decentralize their welfare State for some common as well as different reasons. The authors analyse the key elements of the institutional design of LTC financing systems in Italy, Portugal and Spain. They examine ongoing financial reforms in the three countries, their characteristics, actors and motivations. Finally, they discuss the differences in desired welfare policy objectives of the three systems along with the evolution of expenditure and social cohesion.

In Chapter 11, Birgit Trukeschitz and Ulrike Schneider aim to provide an in-depth view of LTC financing in Austria over and above a discussion of public funding levels and their changes over time. With a universal LTC allowance programme, subsidized LTC services for dependent persons and a new programme coping with migrant care work in private households, Austria today is one of the European Union countries addressing the issue of LTC in a substantial manner. The authors elucidate funding streams in a fiscal federalism setting and the ways in which public funding is channelled to providers of LTC services. They discuss future funding needs and measures to keep LTC spending under control. Finally, they conclude with a brief policy discussion touching on the distributional impact of LTC financing in Austria and on alternatives to the current system of LTC financing.

In Chapter 12, Andy Zuchandke, Sebastian Reddemann and Simone Krummaker address the financing of LTC in Germany. In 1995, after many years of public discussion, a mandatory social LTC insurance was implemented in Germany as the fifth pillar of the social security system. The population was then relieved of a substantial personal risk by a public insurance scheme upon the payment of contributions. The authors present an overview of the LTC system in Germany and discuss pertinent information regarding those individuals in need of care. They provide insights into the financing and expenses associated with the social LTC insurance. They also present the development of the social LTC insurance as well as current discussions on several reform options.

In Chapter 13, August Oesterle explores Central Eastern European (CEE) countries' LTC systems with a particular focus on financing, analysing the *status quo* of funding regimes, on both the macro and micro levels and the trends and challenges arising in developing more comprehensive social protection schemes towards the risk of LTC. CEE countries that have joined the European Union in 2004 and in 2007 are at the centre of the analysis in this chapter. While the international comparative literature on LTC has been substantially growing over the past two decades, there still is very little coverage of CEE countries. The author starts his contribution with an outline of the challenges LTC poses to societies in CEE. He also provides an overview of how countries in this region are currently responding to these needs and of how people perceive LTC responsibilities. An outlook and discussion of the perspectives for LTC funding in CEE closes the contribution.

In Chapter 14, Martin Karlsson, Tor Iversen and Henning Øien address the financing of LTC in Scandinavian countries, namely, Denmark, Norway and Sweden. These three countries share a common history and common political traditions, which has led to very similar systems for social care being introduced in the three countries. This goes for the division of roles and responsibilities between different public bodies, as well as for the national policy objectives that have been laid down in various pieces of legislation. Thus, all three countries pursue the general goal of providing local care services free of charge to everyone in need, independently of their financial circumstances. In this chapter, the authors describe the financing, governance and provision of LTC services in Scandinavia. The Scandinavian LTC systems have a common foundation of the universal, tax-financed and decentralized system.

In Chapter 15, France Weaver focuses on LTC financing in Switzerland. In this country, LTC financing has two main features. First, it is decentralized into the 26 cantons, and in some cantons, it is the responsibility of the municipalities. Such decentralization results in variation in LTC use and financing structure across cantons and municipalities. Second, the share of private funding – that is, private household spending – is one of the largest among OECD countries. The author's aims in this chapter are to briefly describe the LTC system in Switzerland and to present its financing structure. Most results are provided for the entire country, with some of them being reported per canton to observe regional variations. Both nursing home and formal in-home care are considered.

Finally, in Chapter 16, Peter Willemé, Joanna Geerts, Bea Cantillon and Ninke Mussche address the issue of LTC financing in Belgium. In Belgium, LTC consists of a wide range of benefits in cash and in kind, organized at the federal, regional and municipal levels, and is related to health and social service provision. Belgian LTC policy aims at helping, supporting and nursing dependent persons. While public health insurance generally covers all age categories, many LTC services in Belgium are specifically targeted at the elderly dependent population. Separate regulations exist regarding special provisions and benefits for disabled persons younger than 65 years.

All in all we hope that these contributions provide some important messages to policy makers on how best to plan the financing and the organization of LTC systems. Concerns are indeed raised about their future sustainability. However, solutions to cope with the actual trend seem to emerge as research on the topic develops further and public opinion and governments wake up to the seriousness of the situation. In particular, there is scope for the development of insurance mechanism solutions based on public and private interactions and a need to further explore the rules and limits of such partnerships in order to avoid costly overlaps and missed opportunities.

References

Breyer, F., Costa-Font, J. and Felder, S. (2010) 'Ageing, health, and health care', *Oxford Review of Economic Policy*, 26 (4), pp. 674–690.

Chen, Y.P. (2001) 'Funding long-term care in the United States: The role of private insurance', *The Geneva Papers on Risk and Insurance – Issues and Practice* 26, pp. 656–666.

Costa-Font, J. (2010) 'Family ties and the crowding out of LTC insurance', *Oxford Review of Economic Policy*, 26 (4), pp. 691–712.

Costa-Font, J., Mascarilla-Miró, O. and Elvira, D. (2009) 'Ageing in place? An examination of elderly people's housing preferences in Spain', *Urban Studies*, 46 (2), pp. 295–316.

Costa-Font, J., Gil, J. and Mascarilla-Miró, O. (2010) 'Housing wealth and housing decisions in old age: Sale and reversion', *Housing Studies*, 25 (3), pp. 375–395.

European Commission (2008) *Long-term Care for Older People* (Brussels: European Commission).

Kunreuther, H. (1978) *Disaster Insurance Protection: Public Policy Lessons* (New York: Wiley).

Murtaugh, C., Spillman, B. and Warshawsky, M. (2001) 'In sickness and in health: An annuity approach to financing long-term care and retirement income', *Journal of Risk and Insurance*, 68 (2), pp. 225–254.

OECD (2009) *Health Data 2009* (Paris: OECD).

Pauly, M.V. (1990) 'The rational nonpurchase of long-term care insurance', *Journal of Political Economy*, 98, pp. 153–168.

Zweifel, P. and Strüwe, W. (1996) 'Long-term care insurance and bequests as instruments for shaping intergenerational relationships', *Journal of Risk and Uncertainty*, 12, pp. 65–76.

Part II
Institutions and Markets

2
Typology of Public Coverage for Long-Term Care in OECD Countries

*Francesca Colombo**
Organization for Economic Cooperation and Development, France

1 Why is coverage of long-term care cost desirable?

The importance of long-term care (LTC) – that is, care for people dependent on help for daily living activities[1] – as measured by cost and utilization is growing in all high-income countries. This is a direct consequence of population ageing and, in particular, the growing number of very old people in the population. The share of the population aged over 80 years old, currently at around 4 per cent on average according to the Organization for Economic Cooperation and Development (OECD), is expected to triple to 11–12 per cent by 2050 (Figure 2.1). The sheer number of elderly that need assistance in carrying out activities of daily living is growing as a result.

Yet the actual impact of demographic trends on the demand for LTC will depend upon the evolution of functional capabilities of seniors, as well as the unit cost of care in home and institutional settings. Trends in severe disability among elderly populations do not show consistent signs of decline (Lafortune and Balestat, 2007; Bernd et al.). In addition, demographic and societal changes create upward pressures on both wages and non-labour cost in the sector. Reductions in the relative size of the working-age population create competition for attracting LTC workers, exerting demand for salary increases. With dwindling informal care supply due to higher female labour market participation and declining family size, higher demand for formal services is also emerging in some OECD countries. Importantly, the demand for more responsive, innovative and high-quality LTC services is on the rise in line with users' expectations.

All of these factors will push up the demand and cost of LTC in the coming decades. In 2007, LTC expenditure accounted for 1.5 per cent of GDP across OECD countries (OECD, 2009). European Union (EU) and OECD projections suggest that this share will at least double by 2050 (Oliveira Martins and de la Maisonneuve, 2006; European Commission and the Economic Policy Committee, 2009).

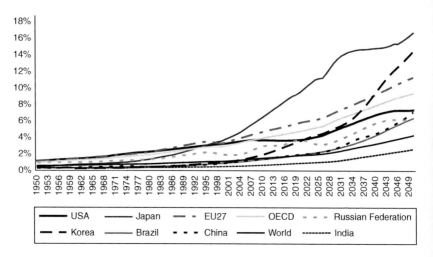

Figure 2.1   The proportion of those over 80 years old is growing rapidly all over the world (1950–2050)
Source: OECD (2009b).

In a number of advanced economies, the expected increases in LTC use and cost are pushing ahead discussions about how to improve equity and efficiency in the financing of social care systems. There are significant uncertainties in one's lifetime, about the need, duration, intensity and cost of LTC. This provides for a powerful rationale in favour of creating collective coverage mechanisms for LTC. These mechanisms can ensure protection against the potentially catastrophic cost of care, which can place a significant burden on users, more specifically those living on a low income or with high levels of dependency. They can also respond to demand for intergenerational equity and risk-pooling across today's and tomorrow societal groups. In most OECD countries, the risk of dependency is mainly pooled through publicly financed mechanisms. Private pooling mechanisms, such as LTC insurance, play a relatively small role in financing LTC expenditure.[2]

This chapter aims to inform those discussions by offering an overview of public coverage mechanism in high-income countries. After showing some statistics on financing and recipients of LTC services, the chapter clusters countries into groups with homogeneous LTC coverage systems. It then discusses some new directions and challenges ahead.

2   Who receives LTC, in what setting and at what cost?

There is significant cross-country variation in the use, organization and cost of LTC. This section provides some basic statistics. It suggests that utilization and cost of LTC follow country clusters. Although there are more users among the oldest population groups, the share of those over 80 years old is but one factor behind differences in cost of LTC systems. Other factors, such as the organization of care and the comprehensiveness of public coverage, play an important role. LTC spending has also increased faster than health spending over time.

2.1 LTC recipients concentrate among the oldest old

Users of LTC services are more prevalent among women, and are more likely to belong to the very old population group (over 80). In OECD countries, the average share of LTC recipients among this oldest age cohort is over five times the proportion of recipients aged between 65 and 79 years old. Among the oldest old, the average share of female recipients is one and a half times the male share, in their respective population groups (Figure 2.2).

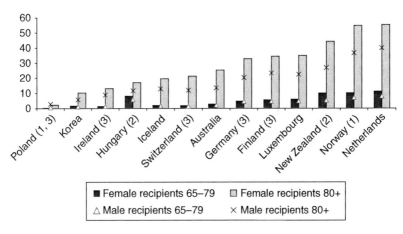

Figure 2.2 Female and male LTC recipients in OECD countries, share of respective age groups
Note: Home care recipient data are not available for Iceland, Ireland and Switzerland. Data for Australia, Ireland, Norway and the Netherlands refer to 2006; data for Korea and New Zealand refer to 2008.
(1) Data refer to different age-breakdown. The age threshold is 60 (instead of 65) and 75 (instead of 80) for Poland and it is 67 (instead of 65) for Norway. Corresponding population data are used to calculate the share for Poland. For Norway, people aged 65 and over are used to calculate the share, resulting in underestimation.
(2) Data do not refer to a specific day in the year, resulting in overestimation. Data refer to the entire year for Hungary and New Zealand.
(3) Data include care recipients who are fully paying for their care from private sources.
Source: OECD (2009a).

2.2   No place like home, yet spending in institutions remains higher

Many OECD countries have encouraged, over the past few years, the use of home care settings or adapted living arrangements for LTC needs, resulting in a larger share of home care recipients in most countries for which data are available (Figure 2.3). This shift towards home care arrangements has a number of advantages. It reflects peoples' preferences for receiving care in their home. It encourages independent living. And it reduces cost per user and reliance on expensive institutional care, particularly for recipients with lower levels of care dependency. This has been accompanied by reductions in the number of LTC beds in most OECD countries.

Even if home care outweighs institutional arrangements in terms of number of users, most of the cost of LTC originates in the institutional sector (Figure 2.4). LTC spending in institutions represents over 70 per cent of long-term nursing care.[3]

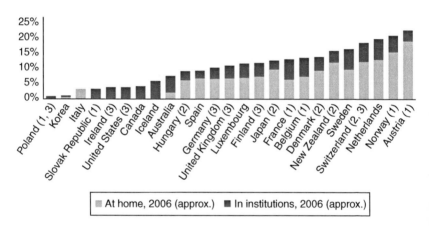

Figure 2.3   People aged 65 and over living in institutions and receiving care at home as a share of people aged 65 and over, 2007

Note: Data on home care recipients are not available for Canada, Iceland, Ireland, the Slovak Republic and the United States. Institutional recipients refer to 2003 (Canada) and 2004 (the United States). Institutional and home care recipients refer to 2003 (Austria), 2004 (Belgium, Korea and the United Kingdom) and 2006 (Australia, Japan, Sweden and Switzerland).

(1) Data refer to different age breakdown: recipients aged 60 years and over (Austria, Belgium and Poland); recipients aged 62+ (the Slovak Republic); home care recipients aged 60 and institution recipients aged 65 and over (France); recipients aged 67 and over (Norway). For Norway, people aged 65 and over are used to calculate the share, resulting in underestimation. For other countries, corresponding population data are used to calculate the shares.

(2) Data do not refer to a specific day in the year, resulting in overestimation. Data refer to a week for Denmark, a month for Japan for home care recipients, the entire year for Hungary and New Zealand and for home care recipients in the Czech Republic and Switzerland.

(3) Data include care recipients who are fully paying for their care from private sources. For the Czech Republic, only data on home care include privately funded recipients.

Source: OECD (2009a).

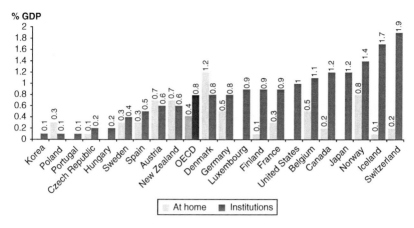

Figure 2.4 Spending on LTC at home and in institutions in OECD countries, 2007
Note: Home care includes LTC day care expenditure. Data from Japan refer to 2006, for Luxembourg and Portugal refer to 2005.
Source: OECD (2009a).

2.3 LTC spending shows rapid evolution and follows country clusters

On average, across 24 OECD countries, spending on LTC accounts for 1.5 percentage points of GDP (Figure 2.5). Per capita LTC spending ranges from almost nil in Mexico to US$1134 purchasing power parity (PPP) in Sweden. Spending on LTC is smaller – around a sixth – than spending on health care (Figure 2.6). Yet, in the past decade, it has been a sector in evolution, showing a faster upward trend than health care spending.[4] Nordic European countries, whose health spending is around the OECD average, allocate relatively large resources to LTC, unlike the United States.

Spending on LTC shows significant cross-country variation. This largely reflects differences in care needs and in the size and structure of formal LTC systems. Unsurprisingly, OECD countries with universal LTC coverage systems have a high share of recipients of LTC services and relatively high public and total LTC spending (Figures 2.3 and 2.5). Sweden shares with the Netherlands the highest spending rates – around 3.5 per cent of GDP. Other Nordic countries (Norway, Finland and Denmark) similarly rank among the highest spenders, at 2 per cent of GDP or over. Belgium, France and Japan – all of which have universal LTC insurance or universal entitlements to some LTC benefits – spend 1.6 per cent of their GDP on LTC, while Luxembourg and Canada spend around the OECD average. Similarly, the number of recipients of LTC services was high in Nordic countries – with a share of over 15 per cent of those over 65 years old in 2007 – and in other countries with universal or comprehensive LTC coverage (e.g., Austria, Germany, Japan, Luxembourg and the Netherlands).

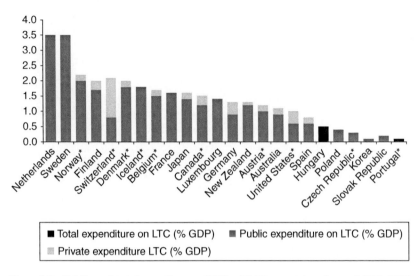

Figure 2.5 Public and total spending on LTC in OECD countries, share of GDP, 2007
Note: * Data for Norway, Switzerland, Denmark, Iceland, Belgium, Canada, Austria, United States, the Czech Republic and Portugal refer to nursing LTC expenditure.
Source: OECD (2009a).

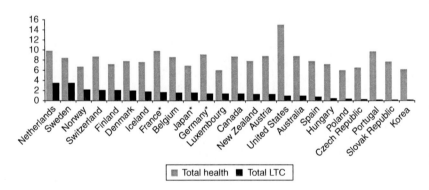

Figure 2.6 Total health and LTC spending in OECD countries, share of GDP, 2007
Note: * Data on health spending are net of LTC spending.
Source: OECD (2009a).

At the opposite end of the spectrum, Eastern and some Southern European countries, together with lower-income OECD members such as Mexico and Korea, spend relatively little on LTC and have few recipients. These countries rely predominately on informal coverage arrangements, including family-based and, in some cases, undeclared home care workers. In Korea, Italy and Eastern European countries (except Hungary), the share of the elderly receiving LTC ranged between 0.6 per cent and 3.6 per cent. In the case of

Korea – a rapidly ageing country which implemented in 2007 a universal LTC insurance system – spending is expected to grow rapidly in the future. Switzerland is a case on its own. As a whole, LTC spending in Switzerland reaches the level of Nordic countries. Such a high share is largely explained by a large private spending estimate. Switzerland spends on public LTC less than 1 per cent of its GDP (0.8 per cent), a figure comparable to public spending in Germany and Australia, but well below levels reached by Nordic countries.

There is a relatively high correlation between the share of the over-80 population and spending on LTC across OECD countries (Figure 2.7). Nevertheless, countries with a similar share of the population aged 80 and over do spend markedly different shares of their GDP on formal LTC services. This suggests that other factors – whether differences in the prevalence/need for

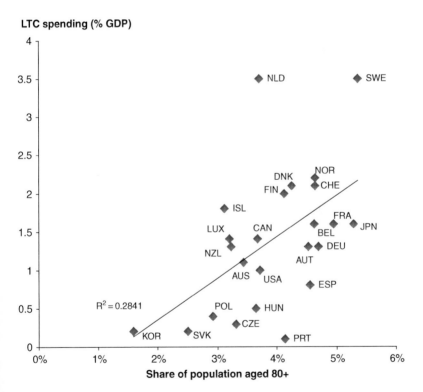

Figure 2.7 Share of the population aged over 80 and spending on LTC in OECD countries, 2007

Note: Data for Japan, Portugal and the Slovak Republic refer to 2006; data for Australia and Luxembourg refer to 2005.

Source: OECD, 2009a, b or c and 2009a, b or c. See note in references Social and Demographic Database (2009) and OECD (2009a).

care, differences in the organization or the cost structure of formal care sector, as well as differences in societal values with respect to informal care – lay behind individual country spending figures.

In terms of financing, LTC is predominantly funded from public sources (Figure 2.5) – although there is under-reporting in the private sector. Private LTC expenditure exceeds the public share only in Switzerland (62 per cent of the total), and it is relatively high in the United States (40 per cent), Germany (31 per cent) and Spain (25 per cent).

On average, the private share, at 13 per cent of total LTC spending, is a relatively lower fraction than the private share of total health spending (25 per cent). However, private LTC spending data do not cover informal payments which, by definition, do not originate from a market transaction. It is important nevertheless to bear in mind that informal care provides the bulk of care hours and its estimated economic value far exceeds spending on formal LTC systems. For example, according to a US estimate, the economic value of informal caregiving was US$375 billion in 2007[5] – three times greater than formal LTC spending. According to another estimate on Australia, the opportunity cost of income foregone as a result of unpaid informal caring was AUS$4.9 billion – equivalent to nearly 10 per cent of the total value of formal health care in Australia (Manaaki, 2009). This also suggests that reductions in the importance of informal care may have significant consequences for the growth in formal care systems.

3   Public LTC coverage in OECD countries: Three main groups

The ability of users to pay for expenses associated with LTC can create uncertainty and suffering for those unable to foot the bill or having the greatest care needs. Mechanisms for prepayment and pooling specific to LTC cost, such as LTC insurance, allowances and targeted assistance, serve two main functions. First, they help to protect disposable income and assets of users, therefore providing a safety net and preventing care-dependent people from falling into poverty. Second, they enable access to LTC services by offering compensation for the cost of such services.

Governments of OECD countries have different preferences regarding the role of the private and public sectors in financing LTC. This is partly the result of differences in the perceived 'urgency' of providing formalized coverage for LTC cost for countries with different demographic and care need structures. Partly, it mirrors institutional and historical developments, and different approaches to social protection. This is reflected in the variety of existing arrangements for prepayment and pooling for LTC cost.

There are at least three important complexities to bear in mind when analysing LTC coverage arrangements across OECD countries:

1. First, *there is fragmentation across different funding sources*. Only in a few OECD countries does LTC coverage rely on a single, specific financing

scheme. In most OECD countries, more coverage mechanisms co-exist. In some cases, fragmentation exists because public LTC benefits cover only certain age groups or a portion of the cost incurred by users. In others, responsibilities for LTC programmes cut across different ministries, agencies or institutions. Views of LTC as a health or social risk differ across countries. This has led them to set up coverage arrangements that may in part overlap with health coverage, but the health–social boundaries are not uniform across the OECD.

2. Second, *LTC policies are often decentralized.* In several OECD countries, LTC policies are either set at different government levels or local governments have large autonomy in implementing programmes, assessing need and delivering services. Often, local authorities have co-funding responsibilities. This can also be the case in systems where the legal framework is set at the central level.

3. Third, *there can be different coverage arrangements for different services and settings.* The comprehensiveness of a LTC system varies not only with respect to eligibility rules (who is or is not entitled to receive care) and the extent of private cost-sharing on public coverage, but also with the breadth of services and settings covered. LTC comprises a multiple range of services (nursing, social work, medical equipment and technologies, therapies), several providers (nurses, low-skilled carers, allied health professionals) and a mix of settings (home, institutions, community care). Reimbursement arrangements are not homogeneous across these. For example, several OECD countries feature different coverage approaches for the following:

- *Health/nursing care*, requiring medical acts typically provided by nurses (e.g., administering medication and changing dressings). Generally, they are covered under public health financing arrangements when received in hospitals or when combined with other medical care received at home. Coverage can be packaged together with personal care, particularly in LTC institutions and comprehensive LTC coverage systems.

- *Personal care*, involving help with activities of daily living (ADL) such as washing and feeding, whether at home or in institutions. Countries' coverage models vary significantly, and so does the extent to which personal care cover is tied together with the other service elements mentioned here.

- *Board and lodging* (B&L) costs (for residents in LTC institutions. They are typically not included in public LTC coverage or entitlement is subject to means-tested public support, and cost-sharing applies. This is also the case in countries where access to institutions is not conditioned to users' means. Most countries provide targeted, means-tested assistance to support the cost incurred by eligible low-income people. B&L fees can be based on income and assets (e.g., Australia, some

Canadian provinces, Finland, Korea, the Slovak Republic, some Swiss Cantons and the United Kingdom) or take only income into account (e.g., Belgium, France, Hungary, Ireland, Japan, the Netherlands, New Zealand, Norway, Poland and Sweden). Spouses' and/or children's means are often considered, but not in Sweden or Poland. In the United Kingdom, usually only the user's savings and income are considered, but the availability of informal family care may affect the likelihood of receiving public social support.

- *Domestic care, practical help*, such as cleaning and cooking and help with instrumental activities of daily living (IADL). They are typically not publicly covered, apart from selective countries with comprehensive LTC coverage (e.g., some Nordic countries).

Bearing in mind this complexity, it is still possible to distinguish clusters of countries with similar LTC coverage approaches.[6] The taxonomy focuses on variation in support for personal care[7] (whether at home or in institutions). It discusses coverage for other care services where relevant. It uses two main criteria to distinguish across country types: the scope of entitlement to LTC benefits – whether there is universal[8] or means-tested entitlement to public funding; and whether LTC coverage is through a single or multiple programmes.

Three broad categories are identified:

- universal coverage within a single programme;
- mixed systems;
- means-tested systems.

It is also possible to distinguish sub-clusters, depending for example, on: (i) whether the sources of funds are earmarked taxes/contributions or general revenues; (ii) whether the programme is or is not part of health systems; and (iii) in mixed systems, the nature of the programmes that constitute the mix. Each LTC scheme also has specific features, such as the target population group (the elderly only or the whole population), the comprehensiveness of the benefit relative to total LTC cost or the mode of administration of the benefit (whether a cash subsidy/allowance or subsidized in-kind services).

3.1   Universal coverage within a single programme

Systems with single universal LTC coverage provide *comprehensive*, publicly funded personal *and* nursing care to all individuals assessed as eligible due to their care-dependency status. The coverage is through *one system only*, whether this is separate from health systems (e.g., Nordic countries, LTC social insurance) or part of health coverage (e.g., Belgium). Benefits are adjusted to LTC need through a needs assessment. Assessment systems and dependency levels on which benefit eligibility are determined are not uniform across countries and, in some cases, across sub-national jurisdictions. They may apply to the elderly population only (e.g., Japan) or to all dependent people regardless of the age group (e.g., Germany). Co-payments, user charges or up-front deductibles apply even in universal coverage systems. They are typically subject to income thresholds, with partial or full exemption mechanisms for the poor, resulting, effectively, in a comprehensive protection of LTC cost through collective public mechanisms. It is not surprising that spending on LTC as a share of GDP and recipients of formal care services are relatively high in this group. Three main models can be distinguished.

3.1.1 Taxed-based model

Nordic countries are the most typical example. Norway, Sweden, Denmark and Finland provide universal, tax-funded LTC services as an integral component of welfare and health care services for the entire population. While the overall responsibility for the care of elderly and disabled rests with the State, a main feature of these countries is the large autonomy of local governments (e.g., municipalities, counties, councils) in organizing service provision and in financing care, including the right to levy taxes. The State typically contributes to financing by paying subsidies not earmarked either to municipalities (e.g., Finland) or to regional authorities (e.g., Denmark), adjusted to the population structure and need. Public LTC services are broad. Beside personal care support in institutions and at home, they can include, for example, help with domestic care (Denmark, Sweden), as well as the provision of sheltered housing, home adaptations, assisting devices and transport (Ministry of Health and Social Affairs of Sweden, 2007; OECD, 2008).

3.1.2 Public LTC insurance model

A second universal coverage model consists of stand-alone, dedicated insurance arrangements for LTC services. A number of countries belong to this group (Germany, Japan, Korean, the Netherlands and Luxembourg) (Table 2.1). Similar to the Nordic countries' model, service coverage is comprehensive – not just as it reaches the entire population needing care, but also for the scope of the covered services. Board and lodging in nursing homes may be covered in some countries, subject to individual co-payments.

These countries' arrangements share three main features. First, the LTC insurance is separated from health insurance, although it follows the same social insurance model. Second, participation in the scheme is mandatory for the whole or a large section (i.e., those over 40 in Japan) of the population. Third, the scheme is predominantly financed through employment-based, payroll contributions, but senior people can also be

Table 2.1 Universal LTC insurance schemes in OECD countries

	Year	Insurers/ purchasers	Financing sources	Contributions	Eligibility to benefits	Benefits
Germany	1995	Sickness funds	Payroll and income-related contributions (100%)	– 1.95% payroll tax (additional premium of 0.25% for those with no children) – Paid by all working-age and retired population. – Divided between workers and employers – 11% of the population opts out of social insurance and buy a private LTC insurance	Disabled assessed as needing LTC, regardless of age	– In-kind or cash, at user's choice – Fixed value, adjusted periodically
Luxembourg	1999	National health fund (*Caisse nationale de Santé*)	– Taxation (about 45%) – Contributions – Special tax	– Paid by working-age and retired population. – Contribution set at 1.4% of income	Disabled assessed as needing LTC, regardless of age	– In-kind and/or cash, at user's choice
Netherlands	1968	Regional insurers (private insurance companies)	– Payroll and income-related contributions – Means-tested co-payments	– Contribution rate is based on income – Paid by working-age and retired population (all citizens over 15 years old with a taxable income)	Disabled assessed as needing LTC, regardless of age	– In-kind (institution) – Cash home (personal budgets)

Japan	2000	Municipalities	– Tax (45%); – Payroll contributions (45%); – Cost-sharing (10%)	– Paid by those over 40 years old; – Individuals between 40 and 64 contribute 0.9% of wages; – Income-related contributions for those 65+	– 65+ assessed as needing LTC; – 40+ with age-related disabilities	– In-kind
Korea	2008	National health insurance (NHI) corporation	– Tax (20%); – Payroll contributions (45%); – Cost-sharing (15–20%)	– Paid by working-age population through contributions to health insurance scheme; – NHI contributions set at 5.08% of wages, 4.78% of which goes towards LTC	– 65+ assessed as needing LTC; – Younger people with geriatric diseases	– In-kind or cash

Notes: Korea: 'Long Term Care Insurance for the Elderly' (*Noinjanggiyoyangboheum*); Japan: 'Caregiving Insurance' (*Kaigo Hoken*); Germany's *Pflegeversicherung* ('Care Insurance'); AWBZ (the Netherlands). All countries' benefits provide benefits for home and institutional care. Luxembourg and the Netherlands also include home adaptation and assistive devices.
Source: OECD (2009).

asked to pay contributions (e.g., in Japan) and a share of the cost is funded out of general taxation in most countries. There are some differences in the mix of financing sources, eligibility criteria and benefit systems of these countries. For example, benefit values are fixed in Germany and have not been adjusted for inflation (which has led to a reduction in the purchasing power of LTC benefits over time), whilst they cover 90 per cent of the cost of care in Japan. In Japan, the scheme is targeted only the elderly population, while all individuals, irrespective of their age, are entitled at LTC insurance benefits in Germany and the Netherlands. Korea was the last of this group to implement LTC insurance in 2007 (Kwon, 2008).

3.1.3   Personal care through the health system

A third model is based on the coverage of LTC cost entirely through the health system. In this model, not only nursing care cost, but also help with daily activities (dressing, eating, washing and so on) are financed within the universal public health system. LTC is hence viewed as a health risk, and institutional arrangements reflect a 'medical model' of care delivery (as opposed to a welfare model), translating into the provision of care services being primarily performed by professional nurses. Belgium is an example. Belgium's public health insurance system (INAMI/RIZIV) provides for universal coverage of LTC cost, both at homes and in institutions. The reimbursement is subject to a personal contribution (i.e., *ticket modérateur*), with ceilings on out-of-pocket payments (MAF, *maximum à facturer*) and subsidies to low-income elderly people unable to meet the cost of care. In addition, at the regional level, the Flemish government implemented a compulsory dependence insurance scheme, which provides complementary cash benefits.

3.2   Mixed systems

A rather heterogeneous group of OECD countries relies on *a mix of programmes and benefits* implemented at different times and operating alongside, or a mix of universal and means-tested LTC entitlements. This results in a certain fragmentation, even if there is some degree of universality. This fragmentation can take different forms: across services governed by different programmes; across providers financed from different sources; between health and social care administrations; and across users entitled to different benefits depending, for example, on their age. Some countries have set up mechanisms to facilitate coordination across programmes, benefits or schemes and help users navigate through the system.[9]

It is difficult to give a proper account of the variety and complexity of institutional arrangements belonging to this group. The comprehensiveness of the public subsidy relative to total LTC cost varies significantly across countries and, in some cases, within countries. It can differ depending on users' care needs or the event originating the need for care. Even if entitlement to some form of LTC benefit is universal, income and, sometimes, assets of the care recipient can be taken into account to determine the subsidy level or the personal contribution to the cost of care. Often, responsibilities for provision and financing of LTC services are fragmented between social ministries, health ministries and local governments. Funding sources can include general taxes, payroll contributions and private co-payments. In addition, the universal element, benefit or entitlement may refer to one component of the care cost (e.g., home care), but not to others (e.g., care in institutions).

These systems do not cover LTC cost in their entirety. Rather they leave a share at the charge of individuals. This cost is met through different arrangements, including funding from social assistance and income support mechanisms, personal contributions and, in some countries,[10] private insurance. To the risk of oversimplification, countries can be clustered into three sub-groups, described below in decreasing order of universality of the LTC benefit.

3.2.1 Parallel universal schemes

Some OECD countries have co-existing coverage schemes, each providing universal coverage of a type of care cost. Typically, universal nursing care is financed through the health system, while universal personal care is through a separate scheme. Scotland is an example. Since 2002, all the counties of the United Kingdom have supported free nursing care for older people in nursing homes. In addition, personal care for older people, which is part of the social care system, is free in Scotland, in both institutions and at home (Bell and Bowes, 2007a, 2007b).[11] Care is funded by the local authority and subject to the assessment of care needs, but it is irrespective of users' means. The system covers help with ADL. It does not pay for accommodation costs in a nursing home, for which individuals are charged a fee. Subject to parliamentary approval, personal home care is also free in England for people with the highest needs, irrespective of their means.

Another example comes from some Southern and Eastern European countries (e.g., Italy, Czech Republic and Poland), which combine universal access to nursing homes[12] (subject to available beds) with universal, non-income-related cash allowances to cover care cost, typically at home (e.g., the *indennita' di accompagnamento* in Italy or the care allowances in the Czech Republic). The allowance covers but a fraction of the cost incurred by users and generally can be used to employ an informal carer.

3.2.2 Income-related universal benefits or subsidy

A growing number of countries opt for a universal personal care benefit but adjust the benefit amount to the recipient's income. This approach works by progressively increasing the share of the cost paid for by the public system as the income of the recipient decreases. It is sometimes referred to as 'tailored or progressive universalism' (Fernandez et al., 2009) and it is not intended to cover the full – or nearly full – cost of personal care. In the case of France, the recipient is required to complement public funding with a personal contribution as a condition for receiving the public personal care subsidy. Often, this tailored benefit applies to one care component (e.g., home vs. institutional care; personal care vs. nursing care), but different universal arrangements apply for another component of the care cost. This approach includes countries with both in-kind LTC services and cash allowances.

In Ireland, eligibility to community LTC services is universal, although access is limited by resources and can result in the targeting of services. Under the Irish 2010 *Nursing Homes Support Scheme, A Fair Deal,* all those with care needs are eligible to personal care in institutions, but everyone is required to pay for the care, based on ability to pay. This is similar to the Australian approach. Personal care is not free, although all eligible individuals are entitled to a publicly funded LTC subsidy. Recipients of residential and community aged care usually make a financial contribution to the cost of their personal care, whose amount is adjusted to the user's income and assets.

Some European countries provide income-adjusted universal cash benefits or allowances to cover personal care. Austria has a mix of universal and income-related allowances. A universal cash allowance (*Pflegegeld*) was introduced in 1993. It is provided regardless of income and assets, and its amount depends upon the level of dependency. In 2007, a new income-tested grant for the most disabled recipients was implemented to complement the universal cash allowance. The allowances do not cover the full cost of care and, for people unable to meet the remaining cost out of their pocket, public assistance comes into play. A key objective is to help individuals remain at home and live independent lives as long as possible. Another main goal is to formalize contractual arrangements between the care recipients and the caregiver, including (often undeclared) migrant carers. The law encourages care provided by family by not excluding family caregivers from entering into this kind of formal arrangement.

Another example is France. The health insurance programme (*Sécurité sociale*) pays for the health cost (*tarif de soins*) for all nursing home stays (access is based on care need). In addition, the *Allocation Personnalisée d'Autonomie* (APA) is available to disabled people aged 60 or older living either at home or in a nursing home, and involves steep income-related co-payments. For those living at home, APA provides support towards any expenses incurred in line with a personalized support plan identified by a social medical team. It can include support for both ADL and IADL services and, in some cases, the employment of a caregiver (except for their spouse or partner). For those living in a nursing home, APA offsets a portion of the personal care cost, while the remainder[13] is paid by the resident.

3.2.3   Mix of universal and means-tested (or no) benefits

In other OECD countries, two or more benefit schemes provide universal coverage for some component of LTC cost, and means-tested access (or simply, no coverage) for another component of the care cost.[14] The approaches are far from uniform across countries, but generally, *universality tends to apply to nursing care cost (either at home or in institutions) and/or to home care arrangements*. There can also be differences based on the age of the recipients, often with coverage being more generous for non-elderly disabled people.

For example, Switzerland provides universal in-kind nursing care (both at home and in institutions) through mandatory health insurance (LAMal), and in-cash means-tested disability benefits towards the cost of personal care.[15] In New Zealand, people assessed as needing home-based personal care services get these services free of charge, although care in institutions is subsidized only for eligible individuals through an income test. Most Canadian provinces provide nursing and personal care coverage without charges in home care settings (although user fees may be imposed for home support and domestic care), but have income tests for admission to nursing care facilities.[16]

Spain passed new legislation in 2006 introducing a tax-funded National Long-term Care System (Dependency Act, in force since 1 January 2007). The law guarantees a right to LTC services to all those assessed to require care, *subject to* an income and assets test. Entitlements to cash and in-kind services are slightly different, with cash allowances being universal while not all individuals might receive in-kind services. Recipients are expected to pay one-third of the total costs of services. The system is intended to provide a 'formal response' to societal and labour market changes that are reducing the supply of informal care in a context of ageing societies – and of growing need. It is expected to benefit 3 per cent of the Spanish population in the short term (a comparable percentage to that of some countries with universal benefits), and is to be phased in gradually until 2015 (Costa-Font and Garcia Gonzalez, 2007).

Finally, there are countries with less developed formal LTC provision, which provide universal coverage for institutional care but no coverage at all for home care. The Greek LTC system includes the direct provision of social services and care through health insurance funds. In theory, any disabled old person, whether insured or uninsured, has access to LTC. There are no institutional discriminations or access restrictions as long as people are legal residents of the country. On the other hand, there is limited formalized home care provision in Greece, and no public funding for home care.

3.3   Means-tested arrangements for personal care

Several OECD countries providing publicly funded LTC benefits take income and, in some cases, assets into account to determine the amount of user cost-sharing. But in a few countries, income and asset tests are actually used to set thresholds for *eligibility to any publicly funded personal care*. In these systems, only those falling below a set threshold would be entitled to a publicly funded LTC service or benefit, with care being prioritized to those with the highest care needs. The criteria for eligibility (e.g., personal and/or family income and assets; availability or not of informal care), care managers' flexibility in assessing needs and thresholds for eligibility differ markedly and may or may not overlap with social assistance norms.

This approach offers a safety net to those otherwise unable to pay for the care themselves. But safety nets can be seen as poverty programmes, rather than LTC coverage schemes, and, therefore, face challenges similar to those confronting social assistance systems. For example, they can leave elderly and disabled people impoverishing in order to become eligible to care. Setting thresholds is hard, particularly as it always implies creating a group not poor enough to qualify for public funding, and yet not rich enough to pay.

When people are required to sell their homes and use such proceeds before being eligible to public coverage, the system can be seen as unfair, particularly given older peoples' attachment to their homes. If there are no uniform criteria for eligibly across different jurisdictions, this can also lead to confusion over eligibility for public funding and reduce transparency.

There can be under-funding and under-investment in these programmes, because they are typically funded through general taxes and do not provide an entitlement to care. Especially during times of fiscal restraint, they are more vulnerable to budget cuts or cash constraints. Finally, in light of expected increase in demand for LTC, the adequacy of such an approach is called into question as many people in need of care are denied access.

The United States belongs to this category. Medicaid – the public programme for the poor[17] – is the chief public funder of LTC services. States have mandatory benefits which must be offered, including institutional nursing facility services and home health care services for individuals who are entitled to nursing facility services, but the majority of LTC services are at the discretion of the States, as are income and personal-asset eligibility requirements. Means and asset-testing is very strict. Commonly, in order for recipients to receive Medicaid coverage, participants will first have to exhaust personal resources. States may require Medicaid recipients to be responsible for a small co-payment.

England is often regarded as a means-tested system. Indeed current policy discussion about reforming LTC coverage focuses around means-tested arrangements for personal care, although it is fair to say that there are also non-contributory, non-means-tested and tax-free benefits for severely disabled people in the United Kingdom.[18] Social care is commissioned by local authorities, and is funded from a combination of central taxation, local taxation and user charges. Local authorities decide and set their own budget based on grants made from the central government, most of which are not earmarked. Access to nursing homes is both income and asset-tested. Conversely, for home care, eligible users receive an income-tested benefit, which can be granted in the form of a personal budget.

4   Challenges and trends

The analysis of public financing in OECD countries offers insights on the complexity of existing arrangements. Even more than in the case of health systems, in many OECD countries coverage for LTC does not follow pure models. Different approaches can apply to specific population groups or to different care cost components. This follows partly from historical development – many countries have added LTC benefits incrementally – and partly from societal choices about individual and collective responsibility towards care for elderly and disabled people. It is also important to remember that countries are at different stages of developing formal LTC delivery arrangements, which affects the development of mechanisms for financing LTC cost (and vice versa). In all OECD countries, family networks attend to elderly and disabled care needs, and care duties can be especially intensive where formalized LTC services and coverage arrangements have not yet developed.

There are clearly advantages and drawbacks of the different coverage arrangements reviewed here.

Comprehensive single-programme universal arrangements are good for access. They are generous in paying for the LTC cost incurred by users – in relation both to the share of the cost publicly reimbursed and the spectrum of services covered in institutional and home settings. In some cases, cover also includes the cost of support/domestic care, home adaptations and assistive devices (e.g., some Nordic countries). These systems do not discriminate access based on income or assets of users (or that of their families), although these may be taken into account to determine individual cost-sharing up to a ceiling (e.g., Norway, Sweden). Often, care provision by nurses or caregivers is regulated to ensure minimum standards for the care purchased through public funds (e.g., Japan). In addition, the separation between health and LTC budgets reduces utilization of more expensive health care services and professionals (e.g., hospital care, doctors) for LTC needs. On the downside, these systems cost a larger share of national income and domestic budgets, in line with the large number of people eligible for care and the generosity of reimbursement. Comprehensive single-programme systems may also discourage the provision of informal care, unless specific incentives, services and benefits for informal carers are designed.

The second rather heterogeneous group of countries provides access to at least a share of LTC cost for all people needing care, and, therefore, provides a stable force of financing for LTC dependent people. There is recognition that LTC can lead to catastrophic cost for users. Providing a universal entitlement is viewed as desirable both for equity reasons (i.e, sharing of cost across societal groups) and for efficiency reasons (e.g., providing insurance by pooling risks/costs). On the other hand, these systems often combine coverage through different mechanisms, benefits or entitlements. Care coordination can be costly, or a source of inefficiencies and cost-shifting incentives. Fragmentation of LTC cost across different government budgets can also mean that money from one budget may remain unspent if the budget in a different area of government is stretched – with the result of services not being delivered in adequate quantity.

Universal coverage for some share of the LTC cost does not mean that access is always prompt. There can still be deviations from the universal model due to shortage of providers in semi-urban and rural areas and of special institutions (e.g., nursing homes, institutions of rehabilitation). In some – especially in lower-income – OECD countries, service coverage is limited to what public services can provide, even when there is entitlement to some universal LTC benefit. Certain LTC services or facilities, such as home care, medical aid, technologies and therapies, may simply not be on offer and informal care arrangements substitute. Similarly, waiting lists may exist for access to nursing homes. This means that there is *de facto* targeting of access to care based on (implicit or explicit) access and prioritization rules.

The third approach – means-tested arrangements for personal care – offers a safety net to those individuals that are otherwise unable to pay for the care themselves. Typically, coverage extends to support for daily living activities, while domestic care and other LTC services (assistive devices, rehabilitation) are not covered. Board and lodging in nursing homes is typically heavily means-tested. By targeting public funds to the poor, this approach can be effective at saving cost. But it also creates cost-shifting incentives, particularly where there are universal health care services and targeted social care services. Means-assessment systems can also be administratively expensive. Importantly, these systems can result in unmet needs.

Looking over time, LTC systems in OECD countries are evolving in some common directions.

First of all, the comprehensiveness of public coverage of LTC cost is improving in many low-coverage or strict-targeting countries, but there is also greater targeting of public funding in the most generous LTC coverage systems. At the one end of the spectrum, means-tested, safety net approaches are called into question in a number of countries, mostly on grounds of fairness and growing need. As mentioned, asset-testing for nursing home access is being phased out in New Zealand, while Ireland introduced in 2010 a system of 'tailored universalism' for coverage of institutional care. Similar proposals have been made as part of the current policy debate about reforming social care coverage in England (UK Department of Health, 2009), where, despite universal disability benefits, means-tested social care leaves many people above the eligibility threshold vulnerable to catastrophic LTC spending. Even in the United States, the Congress has approved as part of health care reform the introduction of a voluntary but government-set LTC insurance programme, the so-called Community Living Assistance Services and Supports, CLASS Act.[19]

At the opposite end of the spectrum, Sweden has increased targeting of public services to the most sick and disabled (OECD, 2005). France has – at least in the medium term – set aside discussion of creating a new social security LTC pillar and is considering, among others, steeper targeting of APA. The range of services included in the universal benefit can also be the object of scrutiny in very comprehensive universal coverage countries. In Japan, for example, since 2006 the range of services for which lower-need elderly are eligible has shifted from home and institutional care benefits, to prevention and healthy ageing activities. Overall, this results in a certain convergence in the 'depth' of public coverage (share of service costs covered). Ultimately, in a context of limited public funding, there can be trade-offs between the depth of coverage and the stringency of need assessment mechanisms.

Second, coverage arrangements can be used to encourage other desirable policy goals. For example, one way to promote home care and ageing in place has been to support more universal care provided at home (e.g., Canada). Consumer choice and flexibility is another major goal of modern LTC systems. There is indeed growing demand for better tailored and more responsive care. Within both universal and safety net systems, several OECD countries have opted for providing LTC benefits in the form of cash entitlements or personal budgets, sometimes at the choice of the user (e.g., the Netherlands, Germany, Eastern European countries, Italy, England). These direct payments bring more choice over alternative providers (including in some cases between formal and informal carers) and can strengthen the role of households in the care management process (Lundsgaard, 2005). Yet, it can be more difficult to exert control over the way funds are utilized. If the value of benefits is not adjusted for cost inflation, it leads to a real loss in purchasing value of the benefit, exposing recipients to higher out-of-pocket expenses – even where benefit coverage is universal.

Third, maintaining cost growth within a sustainable path will be a key goal for the future. LTC is still a relatively small sector of the economy, but recently it has seen rapid development. Informal carers provide the bulk of care hours today. There are concerns that more generous coverage arrangements – while desirable on access ground – would lead to a significant reduction in the supply of informal care, and, ultimately, higher cost.

Furthermore, in most OECD countries, population ageing is pushing up public LTC expenditure, possibly at faster rates than the growth in government revenues. If cost grows more rapidly than the economy, this means that governments will either need to give up spending in other areas or raise contributions/taxes to pay for higher LTC costs. Alternatively, and especially in the current economic and fiscal environment, governments will need to consider ways to control future public LTC spending growth. This means that private financing arrangements may have a role in complementing public coverage, at least in some countries. While this also means that the delivery of LTC services may require reform to seek improvements in productivity, this discussion lies outside the purview of this chapter.

Notes

*Senior health policy analyst in the Health Division of the Organization for Economic Cooperation and Development (OECD). This chapter is based on preliminary analysis of the 2009–2010 OECD Project on Long-term Care Financing and Workforce. The views expressed in this chapter are those of the author and do not necessarily reflect the position of the OECD. The author is grateful to Ana LLena, Jerome Mercier and Frits Tjadens for useful comments and suggestions on the chapter.

1. Long-term care is defined as 'a range of services required by persons with a reduced degree of functional capacity, physical or cognitive, and who are consequently dependent for an extended period of time on help with basic Activities of Daily Living (ADL), such as bathing, dressing, eating, getting in and out of bed or chair, moving around and using the bathroom. This personal care component is frequently provided in combination with basic medical services such as help with wound dressing, pain management, medication, health monitoring, prevention, rehabilitation or services of palliative care. LTC services can also be combined with help with Instrumental Activities of Daily Living (IADL), such as help with housework, meals, shopping and transportation' (OECD, 2009).
2. A number of factors explain the relatively small size of the LTC private insurance market, including individuals' myopia in planning for the risk of dependency and the cost associated with it, as well as information asymmetry about the risk of needing care in the future, which generates problems of adverse selection. See, for example, Brown and Finkelstein (2007).
3. According to the System of Health Accounts, LTC includes a health and a social care component. Time-series data available in OECD *Health Data* are more complete when considering the health component (so-called, long-term nursing care).
4. Long-term nursing spending increased, in per capita terms, by an annual average of over 7 per cent in real terms, compared with an average of real per capita health spending growth of slightly over 4 per cent, across 22 OECD countries.
5. Medicare video and resource guide, available at www.medicare.gov/caregivers (accessed December 2009).
6. Countries with no or very little public LTC coverage, for example, Mexico, are not discussed.

7. This is because ADL support (personal care) is the type of care for which more variation in coverage arrangements exists across OECD countries. Reference is made to coverage for skilled nursing care and other services.
8. The term 'universal' means that all those needing LTC because of their health/dependency status would receive it, including higher-income groups, although individuals may still be required to pay a share of the cost.
9. This is, for example, the role of the *Caisse Nationale de solidarité pour l'autonomie* in France.
10. For example, private long-term insurance in France.
11. The Scottish Parliament passed the Health and Community Care Act in 2002.
12. In certain Southern and Eastern European countries, specialized nursing homes for elderly and handicapped people are part of the health system or receive a subsidy out of the health budget (e.g., the *Residenze sanitarie assistenziali* in Italy).
13. About a third of the personal care cost (Drees, 2008).
14. The 'components' in question here include nursing versus personal care or institutional versus home care.
15. LTC cash benefits are provided under the legal framework of the Law on Disability Insurance (LAI). They include disability allowances and so-called complementary benefits for old age and disability, granted to recipients affected by permanent or long-term incapacity.
16. Since 2005, the New Zealand government has been phasing out asset tests for institutional care. This is similar to a general movement in some Canadian provinces/territories to eliminate the use of asset-testing (but not income-testing) for targeting government support to residents living in LTC facilities.
17. Medicaid is a jointly funded social health insurance programme, designed as a means-tested programme to assist people with limited income to pay for medical and LTC expenses.
18. The Disability Living Allowance and Attendance Allowance are non-contributory, non-means tested and tax-free benefits, the former paid to severely disabled people who make a claim before age 65, the latter paid to those who claim from age 65.
19. The Class Act will provide only a modest benefit. Participation will be automatic for all workers, who would however retain an ability to opt out (Gleckman, 2010).

References

Bell, D. and Bowes, A. (2007a) *Financial Care Models in Scotland and the UK* (York Joseph Rowntree Foundation), http://www.jrf.org.uk/sites/files/jrf/1859354408.pdf (accessed 28 February 2010).

Bell, D. and Bowes, A. (2007b) *Free Personal Care in Scotland. Recent Developments* (York: Joseph Rowntree Foundation), http://www.jrf.org.uk/sites/files/jrf/2075-scotland-care-older-people.pdf (accessed 28 February 2010).

Bernd, B., Doyle, Y., Grundy, E. and McKee, M. (2009) *How Can Health Systems Respond to Population Ageing?* Policy Brief No. 10, European Observatory on Health Systems and Policies (Copenhagen: WHO Regional Office for Europe).

Brown, J. and Finkelstein, A. (2007) 'Why is the market for long-term care insurance so small?', *Journal of Public Economics*, 91, pp. 1967–1991.

Costa-Font, J. and Garcia Gonzalez, A. (2007) 'Long-term care reform in Spain', *Eurohealth*, 13 (1), http://www2.lse.ac.uk/LSEHealthAndSocialCare/LSEHealth/pdf/eurohealth/VOL13No1/Costa-Font.pdf (accessed 28 February 2010).

Drees (2008) 'L'allocation personnalisée d'autonomie et la prestation de compensation du handicap au 30 juin 2008', *Etudes et Resultats*, 666, October.

European Commission and the Economic Policy Committee (2009) *The 2009 Ageing Report: Economic and Budgetary Projections for the EU-27 Member States (2008–2060) Joint Report Prepared by the European Commission (DG ECFIN) and the Economic Policy Committee (AWG)* (Brussels: European Communities), http://ec.europa.eu/economy_finance/publications/publication14992_en.pdf (accessed 28 February 2010).

Fernandez, J.L., Forder, J., Trukeschitz, B., Rokasova, M. and McDaid, D. (2009) *How can European States Design Efficient, Equitable and Sustainable Funding for Long-term Care for Older People?* Policy Brief No. 11, European Observatory on Health Systems and Policies (Copenhagen: WHO Regional Office for Europe).

Gleckman, H. (2010) *Long-term Care Financing Reform: Lessons from the U.S. and Abroad* (New York: The Commonwealth Fund), February.

Kwon, S. (2008) 'Future of long-term care financing for the elderly in Korea', *Journal of Ageing and Social Policy*, 20 (1), pp. 119–136.

Lafortune, G. and Balestat, G. (2007) *Trends in Severe Disability among Elderly People: Assessing the Evidence in 12 OECD Countries and the Future Implications*, OECD Health Working Paper No. 26 (Paris: OECD), http://www.oecd.org/dataoecd/13/8/38343783.pdf (accessed 28 February 2010).

Lundsgaard, J. (2005) *Consumer Direction and Choice in Long-term Care for Older Persons, Including Payments for Informal Care: How Can it Help Improve Care Outcomes, Employment and Fiscal Sustainability?* OECD Health Working Paper No. 20 (Paris: OECD), http://www.oecd.org/dataoecd/53/62/34897775.pdf (accessed 28 February 2010).

Manaaki, T. (2009) *How Should We Care for the Carers, Now and into the Future?* (National Health Committee of New Zealand), http://www.nhc.health.govt.nz/moh.nsf/pagescm/7661/$File/caring-for-the-carers-nhc-2010.pdf (accessed 5 February 2010).

Ministry of Health and Social Affairs of Sweden (2007) *Care of the Elderly in Sweden*, Fact sheet No. 18, September (Government offices of Sweden).

OECD (2005) *Long-term Care for Older People* (Paris: OECD).

OECD (2008) *OECD Economic Surveys: Denmark* (Paris: OECD).

OECD (2009a) *Health Data 2009* (Paris: OECD).

OECD (2009b) *Labour Force and Demographic Database* (Paris: OECD).

Oliveira Martins, M.J. and de la Maisonneuve, C. (2006) *The Drivers of Public Expenditure on Health and Long-term Care: An Integrated Approach*, OECD Economic Studies, No. 42 (Paris: OECD).

UK Department of Health (2009) *Shaping the Future of Care Together* (London: The Stationery Office), http://www.dh.gov.uk/dr_consum_dh/groups/dh_digitalassets/documents/digitalasset/dh_102732.pdf (accessed 28 February).

3
Long-Term Care Insurance Puzzle*

Pierre Pestieau
CORE, Université Catholique de Louvain, CREPP, University of Liege, Belgium and Paris School of Economics, France

and

Gregory Ponthière
Paris School of Economics and Ecole Normale Supérieure (Paris), France

1 Introduction

In most Organization for Economic Cooperation and Development (OECD) countries, the era of long-term care (LTC) has arrived. More than two out of five people aged sixty-five or older report having some type of functional limitation (sensory, physical, mental, self-care disability or difficulty leaving home), and, as such, are not autonomous, and require adequate care.[1] A few years from now, the ageing trend will accelerate, fuelled by the large 'baby-boomer' generation, and the relative importance of people aged 65 or older will more than double by 2050, according to the forecasts of the European Union (2009). On the other hand, with the drastic change in family values, the increasing number of childless households and the mobility of children, the number of dependant elderly who cannot rely on the assistance of anyone is increasing.[2] Those two parallel evolutions – demographic and societal – explain why there is a mounting demand on governments and the market to provide alternatives to the family, which has been, across epochs, the largest provider of LTC services (even though those services, by being informal, remain hard to measure). One may hope that both private and social LTC insurance will grow substantially in the coming decades. But there are a number of problems that both the State and the market have to solve before they can replace family solidarity. The problems of private LTC can be coined by the concept of the LTC insurance puzzle.

There exists in the economic literature a large number of puzzles. One of the most famous of these is the annuity puzzle.[3] Accordingly, whereas economic theory says that annuities are quite valuable and that retirees ought to hold most of their portfolios in this form, empirical evidence shows that most individuals do *not* voluntarily annuitize their resources, and prefer to hold them at the risk of turning penniless if they live 'too long'. Like any puzzle, this one can be explained in part, and here are the traditional explanatory factors for keeping one's assets and not annuitizing them:

- high annuity prices, as there is a sizeable mortality difference between annuitants and the general population (adverse selection);
- the bequests motive, that is, a desire to leave wealth to one's children;
- families as (partial) substitutes for private annuity markets;[4]
- high discount rates or underassessment of life expectancy;
- uninsured medical expenditure shocks or children's income shocks; the incompleteness of *other* markets ultimately limits the purchase of life annuities.[5]

Quite interestingly, parallel to the annuity puzzle, we can also talk of a LTC insurance puzzle. Accordingly, in almost every country, very few people are insured against the risk of old-age dependence costs, and yet, as for the purchase of annuities, it would seem so rational to purchase an insurance against LTC, on the grounds that this is a protection against a risk that is sizeable and increasing.[6] This chapter is dedicated to the causes of this puzzle. As we will see, some of the causes are the same as those invoked for the annuity puzzle. Here are the causes that we will discuss:

- excessive costs (loading factors and adverse selection);
- social assistance acting as Good Samaritan;
- trust in family solidarity;
- unattractive rule of reimbursement (lump sum);
- myopia or ignorance; and
- denial of heavy dependence.

This chapter is organized as follows. Sections 2–7 present the diverse causes of the LTC insurance puzzle, explaining how these particular factors may contribute to the under development of the LTC insurance market. Throughout our survey, we also review some empirical evidence supporting those explanations, and discuss their (in)compatibility with each other. For that purpose, we refer to empirical studies on various LTC insurance markets, with a particular emphasis on the French and US markets (which are the two main markets). Concluding remarks are drawn in Section 8.

2   Excessive costs

For most individuals, the cost of LTC in the case of severe dependence appears high, if not prohibitive. Whereas the average pension of a French household is €1200 per month, the cost of a good nursing home runs much above that figure. The average cost of institutional LTC for old persons in France is currently at €35,000 per dependant per year (OECD, 2006), whereas the yearly price of a nursing home in the USA ranges between $40,000 and $75,000 (Taleyson, 2003). But then how can we explain that individuals do not insure themselves against such high costs? A first, natural explanation of the low demand for LTC insurance is merely the high cost of LTC insurance. In fact, according to Cutler (1993), 91 per cent of non-insured people (US data) find LTC insurance too costly. One factor contributing to making the insurance expensive is that elderly people tend to postpone as late as possible their purchase, so as to get better information on the appropriate policy and on its cost (Meier, 1999). Brown and Finkelstein (2004a) show, on the basis of US data, that a typical LTC insurance policy purchased at age 65 has a 0.18 *loading factor* (defined as one minus the ratio of the expected present value of the benefits over the premium).[7] Those large loading factors may explain why the covering rate of LTC insurance is so low. Regarding the *causes* of those high loading factors, Brown and Finkelstein argue that it is hard to discriminate between four causes: administrative costs, imperfect competition, asymmetric information and aggregate risk. All those causes imply a high loading factor, as well as limits in the benefits comprehensiveness (i.e., quantity rationing), which are also observed (i.e., the typically purchased policy covers only one third of expected LTC expenditures).

Note that Brown and Finkelstein also observe that loading factors differ considerably between individuals or group of individuals. They find loading factors of 0.44 for men and −0.04 for women (i.e., better than actuarially fair prices for women) with about the same rate of participation, which reveals a high within-household correlation for insurance decisions.[8]

But the cost of LTC insurance may seem even more excessive *given* some private knowledge about one's own health status. Actually, elderly people appear to have better information than the (public or private) insurance provider as to the occurrence of dependency (Norton, 2000). It has also been observed that people buying LTC insurance contracts have a *higher* probability of becoming disabled than those who do not buy such contracts (Finkelstein and McGarry, 2003, 2006, for the USA). Similarly, people who discontinue their contracts have a much lower probability of becoming disabled than those who do not (Finkelstein et al., 2005, also for the USA). This is a classic health insurance *adverse selection* problem. The existence of an adverse selection problem on the LTC insurance market is confirmed by Sloan and Norton's (1997) econometric study, which is based on two surveys for the USA (AHEAD – *Asset and Health Dynamics* – and HRS – *Health and Retirement Survey*). Sloan and Norton find a positive and statistically significant correlation between the subjective probability of entering a nursing home and the probability of purchasing LTC insurance.[9] The presence of adverse selection is also confirmed by Courbage and Roudaut

(2008) who find, on the basis of SHARE data for France (*Survey on Health, Aging and Retirement in Europe*), that there exists a positive and statistically significant correlation between, on the one hand, having a high risk of dependence (e.g., high body mass index – BMI – scores and high alcohol consumption), and, on the other hand, the purchase of LTC insurance. Hence the plausible presence of adverse selection may contribute to explaining the high LTC insurance costs and, as a consequence, the LTC insurance puzzle.

3   Social assistance acting as Good Samaritan

Besides excessive insurance costs, another widespread argument is proposed to explain the LTC insurance puzzle. According to that argument, social assistance (Medicaid in the case of the USA) would crowd out private insurance (Norton, 2000). Actually, Sloan and Norton (1997) observe in the USA a negative correlation between Medicaid availability and the purchase of private LTC insurance. According to Brown and Finkelstein (2004b), the existence of a last-resort payer like Medicaid reduces even an actuarially fair US private insurance market by two-thirds. They show that for men and women with median assets, 60 and 75 per cent of contributions, respectively, to private insurance are redundant with Medicaid. On the other hand, Brown et al. (2006) show that, if the Medicaid resource test ceiling were raised up to $10,000 per year, private insurance coverage would only increase by 1.1 per cent.[10] This latter study tends thus to qualify the size of the crowding-out effect: even though this is statistically significant, there must necessarily be other forces driving the LTC insurance puzzle. The crowding out alone cannot do the entire job.

To conclude, note that it is also important to distinguish here between two different cases of 'abuse' of social assistance.[11] On the one hand, there also exist some individuals who decide to spend all their resources while young and healthy, because they know that the State will not drop them and will act as a Good Samaritan. On the other hand, there also exist other individuals, who either hide their resources or strategically pass them to their children as *inter vivos* gifts, to be able to benefit from means-tested benefits such as Medicaid in the USA or the *allocation personnalisée d'autonomie* (APA) in France. In a number of countries, the social assistance part of LTC is managed at the local level, and even though local authorities have the legal power to reclaim part of the estate of those having benefited from LTC assistance, public authorities are reluctant to do so. But whatever the case considered, the outcome for private LTC insurance is the same: because of the existence of the State, agents have little incentive to buy a private LTC insurance, as a result of a standard crowding-out effect.

4 Trust in family solidarity

Whereas the State is often regarded as a major cause of the LTC insurance puzzle, the family is also widely cited as an alternative explanatory factor. The intuition behind that family explanation is not fundamentally different from the family explanation for the annuity puzzle. In each case, the puzzle can be solved by highlighting that the standard microeconomic argument supporting the purchase of annuities or of LTC insurance relies on a simplistic model, which may not take the richness of family life into account.

In the case of LTC insurance, buying that kind of protection seems indeed rational under some particularly defined preferences, but may not be so if one has specific family concerns. More concretely, LTC insurance reduces the cost of institutionalization, and, thus, will not be bought by elderly parents who want to be aided by their children in case of dependency (Pauly, 1990). Indeed, buying LTC insurance is paradoxically the best way to be sent to an (anonymous) nursing home, instead of being helped at home by a family member. Thus, provided the elderly person has a taste for being helped by his or her family, the incentive to buy a private LTC insurance is quite low, even in the absence of State assistance.

Note, however, that the introduction of family concerns does not, on its own, sufficient to lead to the LTC insurance puzzle. Actually, whether the parent is altruistic or not matters a lot.[12] If he is (sufficiently) altruistic, he will buy LTC insurance to avoid burdening his spouse or children in case of dependency (Pauly, 1996), even though he would prefer being helped by his children from a purely self-oriented perspective. An altruistic parent does not want to impoverish his descendants, or to cause them troubles, and, as a consequence, he is likely to buy LTC insurance. On the contrary, if the elderly person is not altruistic, he will behave strategically, and will use his estate to obtain assistance from his children, and, thus, will not purchase LTC insurance (Norton, 2000).[13]

Note that the empirical literature is far from unanimous on the role of family concerns. Sloan and Norton (1997) show that the family does not seem to play a role in the USA, as caring about the bequests left to descendants has a statistically insignificant impact on the demand for private LTC insurance. On the contrary, Courbage and Roudaut (2008), using the French SHARE data, show that being married and having children make it likelier to purchase private LTC insurance, in conformity with the theory under altruistic parents.

5 Unattractive rule of reimbursement (lump sum)

An alternative explanation of the LTC insurance puzzle may lie in the precise form of the LTC insurance *contracts* that can be found on the market. In the tradition of health care insurance, one would expect LTC insurance contracts to provide for the reimbursement of care and services costs, possibly up to a certain limit and with multiple options, including deductibles. This is less and less the case. An increasing number of insurance markets, typically the French one, provide for the payment of a monthly cash benefit, which is proportionate to the degree of dependency involved and adjusted according to the evolution of this dependency. These products are closely related to annuitized products and their limited insurability is justified by some type of *ex post* moral hazard.[14] In LTC the degree of dependency can be assessed quite objectively; what is more subjective, or at least dependent on cultural and psychological factors, is the extent of the needs of the dependant person. The perception of LTC as a risk is a very recent phenomenon, and the needs implied by a loss of autonomy are relatively vague and susceptible to widely varying interpretations depending on the social climate and the family background. For example, having difficulties in taking a bath constitutes a loss of autonomy that implies different demands for services depending on the people concerned. To avoid lengthy and costly discussions, insurance companies prefer to offer a cash benefit that people can each use in their own way, with the consequence that some individuals feel short-handed.

Whereas the form of the LTC insurance contract may seem to be an irrelevant detail for explaining the LTC puzzle, Cutler (1993) claims that the incomplete nature of the LTC insurance contract may be the major explanation of the puzzle. Cutler argues that, in the case of an LTC insurance, there exists, unlike for standard health insurance, a long delay between the purchase of the insurance and the first LTC expenditures and reimbursements. However, the risk of a rise in LTC costs per dependant person is high, and *common* to all members of a given cohort. Thus, according to Cutler, the unique way to insure oneself against a rise in LTC costs is to make intertemporal pooling (that is, on several cohorts). Unfortunately, the large *intertemporal correlation* of LTC costs makes such a division of risk difficult, if not impossible. As a consequence, the risk of a rise in LTC costs over time looks like a risk against which one *cannot* be fully insured. That theoretical rationale explains why contracts now propose lump-sum reimbursements (or numerous restrictions to reimbursement). Moreover, the fact that the LTC insurance is a quite risky business explains also the large required *premia* (and thus the excessive prices, see Section 2). But all this deters the elderly from buying a private LTC insurance, as this seems to be far from advantageous for him. This is another explanation of the LTC puzzle, which, like the previous ones, relies on the full rationality of agents, in the sense that the low demand for LTC private insurance would be, in each case, explained by rational calculations.[15] Note, however, that this explanation differs from the previous ones, as it remains true *even* in the absence of high costs, and without any family solidarity or State intervention.

6 Myopia or ignorance

The explanations of the LTC insurance puzzle that have been discussed so far do not presuppose any particular behavioural imperfection of agents on the LTC insurance market: agents are fully rational, and the underdevelopment of LTC insurance is also rational. However, various alternative explanations of the puzzle involve some kind of *behavioural imperfections*, and are thus fundamentally different from the previous ones. Let us now turn to some of these.

When considering the low amounts of purchase of private LTC insurance around the world, one cannot forget that the decision under study involves the presence of a *risk*: the risk of old-age dependency. But it is even more important to notice that individual choices – either to purchase or not to purchase LTC insurance – are not necessarily based on the *actual* risk of old-age dependency, but, rather, reveal how elderly persons *perceive* the risk of old-age dependency, which is something different.

In the LTC literature, there exist accurate empirical estimates of the risk of old-age dependency. For instance, according to Kemper and Murtaugh (1991), a person of age 65 has a 0.43 probability of entering a nursing home. That probability is also shown to differ significantly between men and women: it is merely 0.33 for men (as their wife will generally be in better health and thus will take care of them), and is above 0.50 for women. Moreover, Murtaugh et al. (1997) show that stays at nursing homes are long: 15–20 per cent of newcomers will remain more than five years. Taken together, those estimates, if coupled with the large cost of LTC, should make a large proportion of the population at risk buy LTC private insurance.

However, it is doubtful that elderly persons are informed of those figures, and can manipulate those figures cautiously when making their decision to buy LTC insurance. Agents' decision to buy or not to buy an insurance reveals their subjective probabilities of old-age dependency, and these may be significantly inferior to actual probabilities.[16]

Whereas it is not trivial to measure subjective beliefs, the data presented by Finkelstein and McGarry (2003) suffice to cast some doubt on the elderly's information and information processing capacity. According to the *Asset and Health Dynamics* survey, about 50 per cent of the surveyed population (with an average age of 79 years) reports a subjective probability of institutionalization within five years equal to 0. Such beliefs sound overoptimistic, and given the singular shape of the distribution of the subjective probability of institutionalization one may have doubts about the overall quality of these beliefs.[17]

Hence there may be a strong behavioural explanation to the LTC insurance puzzle. Whether this takes the form of some myopia, of some ignorance or of some bizarre attitude in front of risk remains to be clarified, but it seems clear that objective expected utility models with full information may not describe real choices adequately.

7   Denial of heavy dependence

Finally, let us conclude our review of possible explanations of the LTC puzzle by another, still behavioural, explanation, which also deserves to be considered here. Clearly, when discussing LTC so far, we did so *as if* the issue at stake concerned something that is common in everyday life. But old-age dependency is, by its very nature, a singular event in one's life, and, as a consequence, the insurance against LTC costs cannot be treated as a normal insurance (e.g., against domestic fires).[18]

Heavy dependence, like death, generates anxiety, and this may imply the possibility of *denial* of dependence-relevant information, interacting with intertemporal choices. Such a denial is likely to lead to time-inconsistent decisions and other 'behavioural' phenomena.[19] Repression of signals of mortality leads to under-insurance for unsophisticated individuals. Note that for forward-sophisticated individuals, the result can be reversed: they may over-insure in anticipation of future denial and seek commitment devices. Refusal to face up to the reality of dependence may help explain an inadequate purchase of LTC insurance.

Whereas that kind of explanation of the LTC insurance puzzle shares some psychological, behavioural nature with the one of Section 6 (myopia or ignorance), one should be careful before grouping these under the same heading. Clearly, while one may think about (more or less) easy ways to correct for myopia or ignorance (e.g., information campaigns, adequate taxes or subsidies), the same is not that obvious in the case of denial. A denial is not a problem of not being able to perceive things, or of not being able to collect or process the information that is necessary for the decision to be made. It is the *lack of will* to do so. This kind of behavioural imperfection seems harder to overcome. If the LTC puzzle is due to a denial of old-age dependency, then policy implications would take forms that are radically different from the ones under other sources of the puzzle, as we shall discuss below.

8   Concluding remarks

For years, researchers have been puzzled by the fact that so few people purchase lifetime annuities for their retirement portfolios. Rational theories have been proposed, but none can fully explain the small size of the actual market. This phenomenon has been called the annuity puzzle. In the same vein, one can be surprised by the very low demand for LTC insurance, which cannot be explained by traditional lifecycle theories. The market is relatively thin in most countries. We have, in this short chapter, considered a whole array of reasons, including psychological and behavioural ones, in order to solve the LTC insurance puzzle. The diversity of candidate explanations could hardly be overemphasized. Some explanations, such as excessive costs, the crowding out by the State, family concerns or inadequate contracts, rely on a full rationality of agents. Others, on the contrary, require behavioural imperfections, such as myopia, ignorance or denial. Thus some of those alternative explanations are not compatible with each other, and further empirical investigations are needed to be able to solve the LTC insurance puzzle.

But beyond a need for further empirical testing of those alternative explanations of the LTC insurance puzzle, another relevant question raised by this overview is that of *policy implications*. If we really want to have a more attractive LTC insurance market, we have to see what can be done with respect to the six factors just discussed. First, there is the issue of adverse selection. By making the insurance mandatory at a given age, or by inducing a majority of households to subscribe to such insurance, the adverse selection pitfall can be overcome. Concerning the crowding-out issue and the Good Samaritan matter, they can be avoided by enforcing the means tests and by extending them to the wealth of the family. There is no reason to fight family solidarity, but, at the same time, it is important to notice that LTC insurance can be a solution to the numerous cases where the altruism is forced. As to the phenomena of myopia or ignorance, they have to be treated separately. Ignorance can be fought by better informing people about the risk of dependence and the longevity prospects. Myopia arising from a problem of self-control and duality of selves calls for some form of mandatory programmes, exactly as does the denial of heavy dependence.

Notes

*This chapter is based on a presentation made at the *Workshop Long Term Care* on 28 May 2009 in Paris and at an ECORE seminar on 22 March 2010. We thank Luc Arrondel, Gabrielle Demange, Pierre-Yves Geoffard, André Masson and Erik Schokkaert, as well as other participants, for helpful suggestions and comments.

1. See Kemper and Murtaugh (1991) on the probabilities to enter a *nursing home* in the USA.
2. On that evolution, see the forecasts made by Duée et al. (2005).
3. Brown (2007).
4. For example, couple members who pool their retirement resources using a common budget constraint can pool mortality risk fairly effectively, and thus value annuities less than individuals who are singles.
5. The intuition behind that argument is that agents want to keep their lifetime savings as a precautionary wealth allowing them to face unexpected events against which they cannot insure, because of incomplete markets.
6. On the low proportion of people purchasing a private LTC insurance, see Brown et al. (2006) and Kessler (2007).

7. That loading factor is significantly larger than the typical load of 0.06–0.10 on acute health insurance policies (Newhouse, 2002).

8. Regarding the causes of the men/women differential in loading factors, this may come from significant gender differences in care utilization, not only due to women's higher longevity, but, also, due to the mere fact that elderly men are more likely to receive unpaid informal aid from their spouses in comparison with elderly women.

9. Naturally, one cannot exclude the existence of moral hazard explaining that correlation. However, Sloan and Norton find that family structure variables (marital status and children), which should affect the occurrence of moral hazard here, do not influence the probability of purchasing LTC insurance.

10. According to Brown et al. (2006, p. 21), this minor impact from changing eligibility criteria is due to the fact that as long as Medicaid remains a secondary payer, even without any asset limits to Medicaid eligibility, a large portion of private insurance benefits are redundant of what Medicaid would otherwise have paid.

11. Of course the term 'abuse' is value-loaded, and one may prefer to talk about a 'strategic use' of the Medicaid social insurance system.

12. See Hoerger et al. (1996) and Sloan et al. (1997) on the empirical testing of parental altruism (US data). Their results reject the strategic hypothesis, as the aid received by the elderly parent is independent from the number of children, from his or her wealth and from his or her cognitive awareness, contrary to the theory.

13. Note that this discussion presupposes that there exists no insurance that children could buy to pay for their parents' costs if necessary. Such an insurance could modify the parental strategic behaviour.

14. This type of moral hazard cannot allegedly be taken care of by the traditional co-payments or deductibles.

15. Nevertheless, there exists no consensus on the precise role played by lump-sum reimbursements as far as the LTC insurance puzzle is concerned. Actually, some works, such as Taleyson (2003) and Kessler (2007), argued that lump-sum reimbursement is a major factor explaining the dynamism of the French LTC insurance market in comparison with the US market. This claim seems hardly compatible with Cutler's analysis.

16. Regarding the formation of beliefs on the LTC risk, Courbage and Roudaut (2008) report that the fact of receiving or giving some informal help has a positive effect on the probability to purchase LTC insurance. This supports the crucial role played by subjective beliefs for the demand for LTC insurance.

17. That probability distribution has a second mode, at a level of 0.5 (for 15 per cent of the surveyed population).

18. According to Istre et al. (2001), the yearly rate of injured persons due to domestic fire is about 5.2 per 100,000, with a significant heterogeneity (higher rates for the elderly).

19. On the denial of death and its behavioural consequences, see Kopczuk and Slemrod (2005).

References

Brown, J. (2007) 'Rational and behavioural perspectives on the role of annuities in retirement planning', *NBER Working Paper* 13537.

Brown, J. and Finkelstein, A. (2004a) 'Supply or demand: Why is the market for LTC insurance so small?', *NBER Working Paper* 10782.

Brown, J. and Finkelstein, A. (2004b) 'The interaction of public and private insurance: Medicaid and the LTC insurance market', *NBER Working Paper* 10989.

Brown, J., Coe, N. and Finkelstein, A. (2006) 'Medicaid crowd out of private LTC insurance demand: Evidence from the Health and Retirement Survey', *NBER Working Paper* 12536.

Courbage, C. and Roudaut, N. (2008) 'Empirical evidence on LTC insurance purchase in France', *The Geneva Papers on Risk and Insurance – Issues and Practice*, 33, pp. 645–658.

Cutler, D. (1993) 'Why doesn't the market fully insure long term care?', *NBER Working Paper* 4301.

Duée, M., Rebillard, C. and Pennec, S. (2005) *Les personnes dépendantes en France: évolution et prise en charge*, XXVème Congrès de l'UIESP.

European Union (2009) *The 2009 Ageing Report*. Joint Report prepared by the European Commission (DGECFIN) and the Economic Policy Committee (AWG).

Finkelstein, A. and McGarry, K. (2003) 'Private information and its effect on market equilibrium: New evidence from LTC market', *NBER Working Paper* 9957.

Finkelstein, A. and McGarry, K. (2006) 'Multiple dimensions of private information: Evidence from the long-term care insurance market', *American Economic Review*, 96, pp. 938–958.

Finkelstein, A., McGarry, K. and Sufi, A. (2005) 'Dynamic inefficiencies in insurance markets: Evidence from LTC insurance', *NBER Working Paper* 11039.

Hoerger, T.J., Picone, G. and Sloan, F. (1996) 'Public subsidies, private provision of care and living arrangements', *Review of Economics and Statistics*, 78 (3), pp. 428–440.

Istre, G.R., McCoy, M.A., Osborn, L., Barnard J.J., and Bolton, A. (2001) 'Deaths and injuries from house fires', *New England Journal of Medicine*, 344, pp. 1911–1916.

Kemper, P. and Murtaugh, C.M. (1991) 'Lifetime use of nursing home care', *New England Journal of Medicine*, 324, pp. 595–600.

Kessler, D. (2007) 'The long-term care insurance market', *The Geneva Papers on Risk and Insurance – Issues and Practice*, 33, pp. 33–40.

Kopczuk, W. and Slemrod, J. (2005) 'Denial of death and economic behaviour', *B.E. Journal of Theoretical Economics*, 5 (1), Article 5.

Meier, V. (1999) 'Why the young do not buy long term care insurance?' *Journal of Risk and Uncertainty*, 8, pp. 83–98.

Murtaugh, C.M., Kemper, P., Spillman, B.C. and Carlson, B.L. (1997) 'The amount, distribution and timing of lifetime nursing home use', *Medical Care*, 35 (3), pp. 204–218.

Newhouse, J. (2002) *Pricing the Priceless: A Health Care Conundrum* (Cambridge, MA: MIT Press).

Norton, E. (2000) 'Long term care', in A. Cuyler and J. Newhouse (eds) *Handbook of Health Economics, Volume 1*, chapter 17 (Amsterdam: Elsevier), pp. 955–994.

OECD (2006) *Projecting OECD Health Care and Long-term Care Expenditures*, OECD Economics Department Working Paper (Paris: OECD), p. 477.

Pauly, M.V. (1990) 'The rational non-purchase of long term care insurance', *Journal of Political Economy*, 98, pp. 153–168.

Pauly, M.V. (1996) 'Almost optimal social insurance of LTC', in R. Eisen and P. Sloan (eds) *Long Term Care: Economic Issues and Policy Solutions* (London: Kluwer), pp. 307–329.

Sloan, F. and Norton, E. (1997) 'Adverse selection, bequests, crowding out, and private demand for insurance: Evidence from the LTC insurance market', *Journal of Risk and Uncertainty*, 15, pp. 201–219.

Sloan, F., Picone, G. and Hoeger, T. (1997) 'The supply of children's time to disabled elderly parents', *Economic Inquiry*, 35, pp. 295–308.

Taleyson, L. (2003) 'L'assurance dépendance privée: comparaisons internationales', *Newsletters techniques SCOR*.

4
Long-Term Care Insurance: Building a Successful Development

Pierre-Yves Le Corre
Swiss Re Europe SA, France

1 Introduction

Ageing creates growing long-term care needs (OECD, 2006). The financial services industry proposes financing solutions, such as savings or reverse mortgages, and more specifically insurers or reinsurers have designed *ad hoc* insurance solutions, tailored to long-term care (LTC) situations and needs.

LTC insurance has thus emerged over the last two decades as a promising area of development for the insurance industry, but only a limited number of markets have shown significant developments, such as the USA, France, Israel, Germany, Japan, Singapore and South Korea (Le Corre, 2008). Some other countries, like the UK, have not yet really succeeded in developing LTC insurance. Others, like Spain, have actively prepared a framework to develop this sector. However, insurance product approaches and frameworks differ significantly from one country to another, and success, whether commercial or financial, varies greatly between countries.

This chapter highlights and details factors and structural features which favour development of insurance solutions for LTC, thus helping to analyse successes or failures. The insurance approaches which have been undertaken in various countries illustrate the topic.

In a first step, relationships between public framework and private insurance offerings are examined. In a second step, various insurance models are described and analysed. The respective challenges, advantages and weaknesses of these models are then discussed from commercial as well as technical points of view. Finally, some perspectives are derived for the future of LTC insurance markets.

2 Public LTC scheme or private insurance market?

Building LTC programmes is an answer to structural trends and concerns, such as the ageing population, attention paid to impairments in old age,

53

progressive weakening of family support to older people and the growing cost of LTC.

2.1 Crowding out...

The existence of a public- or State-sponsored LTC system and the emergence or the development of private insurance are not independent from one another. The initial impression may be that a public programme would impede private insurance development, as evidenced by some studies (Brown et al., 2007). The Japanese situation is an illustration of this conflict. In 2000, a universal public programme was introduced, covering the whole population. Even if that system was partially financed (50 per cent) by an 'insurance' premium, co-paid by individuals over 40 and their employers, it was essentially public: financed by tax (50 per cent) and administered by municipalities. All persons over 65 were eligible for benefits without any specific condition. The implementation of this system has had a radical impact, wiping out the existing private LTC insurance market, which had grown in the 1990s: a massive lapsation hit the two million existing insurance policies.

South Korea has experienced a similar evolution. As of 2003 private LTC insurance had been developed, and products' features and prices had been approved by regulators. In a couple of years, 200,000 policies were sold. However, a public programme with features similar to the Japanese system was implemented from mid-2008. As a consequence, the development of the private insurance market was stopped.

The UK is another example of a crowding-out effect, although in a more hidden way. Despite many efforts, no significant LTC insurance market has really emerged: the number of policies has not really gone beyond 50,000. An anticipation factor may explain that people are accustomed to having all medical costs covered by the National Health Service system. For LTC needs, many people seem as well to anticipate – rightly or wrongly – that a national system may or should do the same. That does not leave much room for private insurance to develop convincing offers.

A US survey prepared for America's Health Insurance Plans (LifePlans Inc., 2007), a group representing private health insurers, has identified the belief that 'government will pay for the care' as being far more widespread among non-insured people than among insured ones. Non-buyers seem to have a far less advanced risk education and understanding than insurance buyers. The private insurance crowding out may thus materialize, even if it is based on unrealistic expectations.

2.2 ...overtaken by tough realities

Relations between public and private systems are, however, more complex. First of all, a public system may clearly state that it does not cover the whole scope of LTC needs. The German universal system, implemented in

2005 as a component of Social Security, does not provide full coverage of all needs. The system is mandatory, operating the same way as for medical expenses coverage. Even if some categories of the population – for instance, self-employed or high-income – are offered a lower price within the part of the system which is privately insured, benefits are the same for all people and are determined by the Social Security rules. Since the benefits of the public LTC framework do not cover the whole extent of needs, a private insurance system market has had room to emerge: more than one million policies, of various types – reimbursement or daily cash benefits – have been sold.

The French system is another example where significant room is left for private LTC insurance: the *Allocation personnalisée d'autonomie* (APA) public benefit is limited in amount, and many people are not eligible for full benefit. Insurers have been successful in providing additional and/or stand-alone coverage. A 20-year market experience in LTC private insurance can thus be observed: five million people are insured as at 2010. The benefits range from small amounts (e.g., €200 monthly annuity) which are generally provided through basic group coverage, to larger amounts (an average monthly annuity of €600) which are provided through individual policies. Individual insurance represents the largest part of the market premium volume (FFSA, 2010).

As a matter of fact, the limited coverage profile of public systems reflects a structural or frequent weakness: funding. Many public systems face budget deficit issues, all the more so when they aim at delivering a full or large coverage of LTC needs. In 2006, the Japanese system had to extend individual contributions from the over-40 to the over-20 population, a massive extension, thus reflecting the deepness of financial imbalance. The German system, which is based on a pay-as-you-go mechanism, had to increase mandatory contributions from 1.7 per cent to 2.0 per cent after only a few years. Further imbalance is expected: some projections show that contributions would have to be raised to 2.8 per cent in 2020, 3.2 per cent in 2040 and maybe up to 5.8 per cent in 2050 (Arntz et al., 2007). The sustainability of such funding approaches is an open question, especially since the oldest part of the population is growing at an accelerating pace. The funding limits that are met by public systems give way – or even induce an explicit invitation – to emergence of private LTC insurance.

The Singapore Eldershield LTC plan is an example worth mentioning (NTUC income, 2010). The State of Singapore has designed a programme which aims at covering all Singaporean citizens (unless they opt out) with a monthly LTC benefit. Two private insurers were selected through a first tender process held in 2002. Singaporean citizens are randomly allocated to one of the insurers. The mechanism is genuine insurance coverage. The financial balance of the system is monitored by the insurers within the limits of the tender. A new tender is planned to be held every five years. The system appears as a good combination between a State public initiative and an insurance approach. It is, however, probable that such an organized 'market solution' for LTC insurance may not be easily achievable in larger countries. It is also worth noting that the Eldershield plan does not provide full coverage: even if the benefit has been increased to SG$400 in 2007, there is significant room for private insurance products to be sold.

2.3   Magnitude of LTC costs

Average LTC costs can be compared with an average pension: they are usually two times larger in the general population, and they often reach higher levels for severe impairments. Funding those expenses is a real challenge, considering also that they are on a steep growing trend: the ageing of the population generates a volume effect, and medical progress together with improvements in the quality of care feed the growth of costs.

Most public systems cannot realistically cover entire LTC costs for the whole population, due to the funding and tolerability limits which are met by mandatory contributions or tax mechanisms. Similarly, a private insurance market can hardly pretend to providing full and comprehensive solutions at affordable prices on a large distribution base.

Coordination of public and private systems on the basis of complementary benefits appears as a realistic solution. A public system is generally necessary to provide the poorest part of the population with at least minimal coverage; a basic benefit for a larger part of the population may be envisaged in favourable circumstances. A private LTC insurance market is generally highly instrumental in providing at least supplementary coverage and most probably even stand-alone coverage for the middle class.

In the area of complementary benefits, the public framework may play a positive role: setting up a favourable, stabilized and more secured environment facilitates the provision by the private market of insurance solutions to cover LTC expenses. This is what is explored and commented on in the next section of this chapter.

3   Public system catalysing private LTC insurance

As a first answer to the challenges which are faced in developing and marketing private insurance solutions, the implementation of a public framework may bring useful enhancing items.

3.1   The public system and publicity

A public discussion or debate usually takes place when a government explores financing solutions for LTC expenses and related tackling challenges. Exploring that, through a consultation and democratic process, helps the emergence of better LTC awareness. From an insurance market point of view, it eases education in the general population on LTC cost and on the need to prepare for future possible impairment situations. When a public programme is designed and publicized, it gives a basis on which the remaining financing needs can be figured out.

Spain illustrates this situation: in 2005, a White Book for an LTC system was released (ICEA, 2005). The *Investigacion Cooperativa entre Entidades Aseguradoras y Fondos de Pensiones* (ICEA), a body providing analyses and studies on insurance matters, sponsored the publication of a study guide of mechanisms and experiences of LTC insurance systems in various countries. Many exchanges took place in 2006 within the insurance industry and in the Parliament about the development of an LTC coverage system. A legal framework was adopted in 2007, setting up a first layer of public coverage for *gran dependencia*. The whole process generated positive publicity for the future development of private LTC insurance plans.

Publicly debating about the possible implementation of an LTC public financing scheme may nevertheless generate a difficult transitory situation for the insurance market. Expectations about a future public benefit create uncertainty on the extent of the need for private insurance solutions. When an LTC insurance market already exists, such a preparation process unfortunately slows down the ongoing market development. Most of the parties, whether potential buyers, distributors or insurers, may wait for a public benefit to be fully designed, in order to know which part of the need is left for private insurance.

This is typically what has been occurring in France since 2007: the dynamic growth of the insurance market has been hampered by the announcement by the French government that LTC would become the '5th risk' within the Social Security framework. Slow progress in the preparation of such a new framework has been made until 2010, but a move forward is announced to take place in 2011. As a result of the virtual announcements of a future framework, which have been made from 2007 on, but without any concrete implementation follow-up, uncertainties have been predominant. That has *de facto* prevented many players from developing new insurance products, even if it appeared probable that the private insurance market would keep a central position for covering a large part of the needs. The heavy financial challenges, which are already met by the Social Security, do not leave much room for implementing a public universal LTC coverage.

3.2 Standardizing references

A public framework may also be useful in setting up some standard references in the area of risk definition or risk assessment criteria. It creates a reference basis for private LTC insurance products to deliver benefits consistently with that framework, as well as to qualify for a tax deduction – if any – knowing that tax deduction is generally based on compliance with the publicly defined framework.

The Activities of Daily Living (ADLs) approach is a well-known international reference which is widely used even in public systems. Some countries nevertheless use their own approach, which in turn can be used by the private insurance market for the sake of consistent understanding by prospective insurance buyers who may also have access to benefits from the public system. For instance, the *Autonomie Gérontologie Groupes Iso-Ressources* (AGGIR) grid in France (AGGIR, 1997), initially set up by the French government, has been used, despite some initial reluctance, by the private insurance market. Using the six usual ADLs and some other more detailed activities to classify people within six levels of autonomy, the AGGIR grid is more complex in its use than the sole reference to ADLs. Added to the concern the insurers have of being tied down by decisions or assessments, which may be made out of their insurance area because AGGIR is the basis for public benefit eligibility, that explains the reluctance of the insurers to rely only on the AGGIR grid. In Germany the mandatory system uses the ADLs approach, but it combines it with an assessment of frequency of help needed over 24 hours (Arntz et al., 2007); this approach is also the approach used in private insurance.

The tax environment may also play a role in the development of the insurance market. It is not certain that a tax deduction in itself is a prerequisite for an LTC insurance purchase. The French LTC insurance market illustrates the development of a sizeable individual market (more than 1.5 million individual policy-holders) without any tax deductibility of premiums; only group premiums within mandatory schemes are tax deductible, whereas the other components of group insurance are not. Tax deductibility of premiums in itself is not the primary factor for an LTC insurance market to develop.

The tax environment has nevertheless a structural role to play as a homogenizing tool for the LTC insurance market. When tax deductibility of premiums is implemented, it is based on specification of criteria for insurance policies to comply with, so that policies can be eligible for tax advantages. That set of criteria creates a reference framework which helps to structure and homogenize the landscape of insurance plans. This is very helpful for an insurance buyer to make up his mind with confidence and a good understanding of the benefit.

In the USA the Health Insurance Portability and Accountability Act (HIPAA) of 1996 (US Department of Health and Human Services, 1996) has defined criteria for federally tax-qualified policies. Criteria concerns benefit eligibility conditions based on ADLs or cognitive impairment assessment, inflation protection, non-forfeiture benefits and governance of operations, including treatment of privileged health information, consumer privacy and disclosures. The HIPAA framework has been very useful in framing the LTC insurance market in the USA.

With LTC needs being a socially sensitive topic, it is understandable that a framework should be given for insurance solutions to be built within it, so that people can buy these products with confidence. Even from a marketing point of view such a framework is globally beneficial due to the complex nature of LTC risk and to the possible sophistication of insurance solutions: through the stabilizing and clarifying effects of public framework, risk monitoring and buying decisions that can take place in a safer and reassuring environment.

4 LTC insurance: Reimbursement and cash approaches

The nature of LTC insurance benefits has a structural influence on market dynamics. The two major benefit approaches (Taleyson, 2003), reimbursement of care costs on one side and cash (denominated 'indemnity' in the USA) benefit model on the other, are discussed and compared in this section of the chapter.

4.1 Reimbursement or cash

The reimbursement approach is widely used in the USA. It is aligned with the LTC risk undertaken: payments made by the insured for the care received because of health deterioration or long-term impairment are reimbursed. Reimbursement policies repay invoices which may be of several types (e.g., nursing home bills, invoices for home care, medical care or paramedical care and so on).

The cash benefit model, which is the main approach used in France, pays a predetermined benefit when the insured needs LTC. The benefit is usually in the form of an annuity and does not depend on care services nor on the place where the insured is receiving care, whether at home or in a specific nursing facility. Freedom is left to the insured for using the cash benefit to pay the cost of a nursing home or of an assisted living facility, or to pay for home care assistance. In addition to the annuity benefit, some policies may provide a small lump-sum benefit which is paid after approval of the claim, so that the insured can finance adaptation of home equipment.

Principle and practice of the two approaches differ significantly:

- The reimbursement model is similar to a medical expenses insurance cover, hence the denomination 'Long-Term *Care*'. In its design, pricing technique, practice and monitoring this model itemizes the different types of care. After the first step, which is the recognition of care needs of an insured person according to the insurance policy criteria, the insurance scheme focuses on the expenses related to the care services which are delivered and on the repayment of corresponding invoices. This subsequently leads the insurer to administer a flow of invoices and reimbursements.
- The cash model, on the other hand, mainly focuses on the health impairment of the insured person, which is the trigger for the benefit to be paid. The critical step in claims-handling is the recognition of LTC needs, which is the recognition of an inability to perform a number of

ADLs – or, as in France – classification of the claimant according to the AGGIR grid which determines the benefit eligibility as specified in the insurance policy. Administration of cash benefits consists then only in paying an annuity as long as the insured is still alive, as in France, or is still eligible, as in the USA.

4.2   The care environment

The features of these two approaches can be related to the care environment. Reimbursement aims at delivering a comprehensive solution, directly fitting into care services and facilities. This approach has some rigidity in directing the benefits to the types of care services which have been chosen by the insured at policy inception. When needed, benefits may not match the full amount of expenses. The cash model is less ambitious: no target in reimbursement or repayment of care expenses is mentioned in the policy; it operates in a purely financial and flexible way: cash benefit can be used to pay any type of care service.

For LTC services and their funding through insurance, the care environment and public benefits structures play an important role in the shaping design of insurance policy:

- In a developed Social Security system, which already provides the older population with financing of all or several medical or paramedical care expenses, there is usually no significant additional need for insurance coverage for those types of care. Within that framework insurance need exists for nursing home or assisted living facility financing, or for caregiver services delivered at home which are often preferred to institutional care (even if they may be given informally by a family member). In this context it is understandable that insurance benefits would be cash only. The French market cash model has probably some deep roots in that care environment.
- On the opposite side, in an environment without a large or comprehensive Social Security system, a specific medical and paramedical coverage is necessary for older persons who become impaired. Insurance solutions are then designed to pay for specific medical or paramedical care expenses. In that care approach, the offer is designed within a reimbursement concept. Other costs, such as nursing home, assisted living facilities or home care are, by extension, also reimbursed by the insurance policy. The US market corresponds to that approach.

5   Simplicity and complexity challenges

The various experiences of reimbursement or cash models show some structural features of differentiation in their practice characterization, in their marketability and in their distribution approaches.

5.1   Choices and simplicity

US reimbursement products generally offer many options to purchaser's choice. Policies usually specify three types of benefits: home health care, nursing home expenses or assisted living facility. Policies can be facility only, home care only or integrated, the latter being now the most popular. The reimbursement approach leads to a detailed itemization of benefits in order to specify the types of expenses or care that can be paid within the policy. Policies also differentiate in benefit frequency, which can be daily, weekly or monthly. The benefit period is generally a pre-set number of years, which is determined by the policy-holder at issue. Inflation protection is proposed as an additional option and is, by the way, highly recommended.

Within this reimbursement approach, many choices need to be considered by the applicant, who thus has to anticipate what his or her future LTC needs will be. This introduces high complexity in marketing the insurance product and in the buying decision. Thinking in advance about so many possible LTC situations probably creates a worrying climate which is not helpful for smooth buying. For a potential insurance buyer itemization raises concerns about possible 'holes' in coverage, due to inappropriate choices or to inadequate scope of policy benefits. Multiplicity of options may be seen as a purchasing barrier. To overcome that obstacle, more in-depth education of potential insurance buyers is probably necessary but may not be sufficient.

US LTC insurance policies are mostly sold by agents and brokers who cope with the complexity of the product they sell. Due to that complexity, completing a successful sale requires a high level of product understanding and practical knowledge; it also goes through a significant investment in time, which may be seen as insufficiently rewarded by the agents in respect of the commission they earn. For many years that situation has generated post-sale issues, such as lack of understanding from the policy-holder about what she or he bought, or sometimes inappropriate purchasing. In recent years, emphasis has been put on the improvement of the selling process through training programmes for agents. The framework of the Medicaid Partnership programme has been implemented: recurring training sessions for agents are planned in order to make distribution of policies more efficient.

The cash model seems to be much simpler. Benefit is the same whatever LTC expenses are, since the cash benefit can be used for any kind of care or expense. The applicant has far fewer choices to consider when buying a policy. During the last decade on the French market most policies have been adapted to propose a possible dual level of benefit: for instance, full benefit for severe impairment, partial benefit for milder impairments. Within this framework, opting for severe impairment coverage solely or for 'severe plus milder' impairment coverage is the key choice to be made by the buyer, apart from the amount from which he or she benefits (for additional synthetic description of the French LTC insurance approach, see Eslous, 2007).

5.2   Purchasing decisions

LTC insurance is not easily sold. The magnitude of costs makes full comprehensive funding solutions through insurance rather unaffordable, even if partial funding solutions are possible through the tailoring of benefit level, which is always at the option of the individual buyer. In the group insurance area that affordability constraint often leads to the putting in place of plans with fairly small benefits. Affordability is in itself an issue which contributes to a purchasing barrier. The barrier may be reinforced by negative feelings of potential buyers, when they project themselves into their possible future LTC needs.

In this context, experience shows that a cash policy can be sold as a financial tool which provides additional funding of future costs. A cash policy does not lead the policy buyer to figure out in advance and in detail all practical LTC needs he or she may have to face in case of impairment in old age. From this perspective, a cash policy appears easier to sell.

Distribution of policies in France has been successfully done by many companies, relying on a good affinity level: for instance, young retiree clients receiving part of their pension from the organization selling the policy, or with close proximity in rural areas or regional places, have proved to be convincing client targets. On the basis of a solid relationship based on trust, selling may not require much more than financial advice, which can be delivered, for instance, through direct marketing channels, such as specialized magazines, couponing or television advertisements in direct marketing slots. In France, banks have also proved their ability to distribute LTC insurance policies: they have reached a 45 per cent market share in new production. That is consistent with financial characterization of cash policies.

More broadly speaking, it has also been confirmed by the America's Health Insurance Plans' (AHIP) survey of policy-holders (Brown et al., 2007) that the decision of buying LTC insurance is taken for asset protection. Most probably a cash approach is easier than an itemized anticipation of all the various types of situation and care needs, which may occur as a consequence of impairment. Operating through a financial presentation and perception of the insurance policy is a user-friendly approach for future possible LTC needs.

5.3   Underwriting and administration

The comparison of cash and reimbursement experiences illustrates that distribution and nature of the product cannot be considered separately; neither can underwriting and administration be considered independently of the other features.

Underwriting LTC risk may appear as a barrier to enter into the development of the insurance business. Anti-selection is a major concern when the applicant is older: buying a policy at 75 or 80 is more of a challenge than when in the early 60s. Various approaches in underwriting have been used, and they again lead to confronting the US and French models.

US policies are usually written through a full underwriting process, with a detailed questionnaire and sometimes additional investigations made by nurses. Even if questionnaires may be filled during a telephone interview, the whole underwriting process is quite complex and generates significant costs.

French underwriting practice is far simpler: a short questionnaire of five or six questions is usually enough for most applications. Only a limited number of applications deserve additional investigation through a detailed questionnaire, to be filled in with the support of a general practitioner. This simple approach is eased by the Social Security framework: a set of major diseases (*Affections de Longue Durée*, or ALD, such as cancer, diabetes, severe cardiologic pathologies, severe chronic respiratory insufficiency and so on) are recognized as deserving a 100 per cent reimbursement of medical expenses by the Social Security. Questioning about potential affection by one of these diseases is an efficient way to identify some major health issues and to investigate more in-depth in a second underwriting phase. In addition to the ALD question, only a few additional questions (no more than five) are worth being asked to identify other possible health issues. That simple and efficient approach is beneficial for all applicants. Subsequent claims experience has not demonstrated any weakness arising from that simple underwriting process, which in return is a very good asset for marketing and distribution.

Administration may also discriminate between respective complexity of cash and reimbursement policies. The US reimbursement model being based on many options and items of benefit, the subsequent administration presents the same degree of complexity. Registering, checking and paying weekly or monthly invoices of various types of care cannot be easily automated: due to multiplicity of sources of invoices and of formats, electronic transmission and treatment are practically difficult to implement. The lack of automation is a source of extra costs and of complexity, which may generate additional operational risk. Public relations, image and legal risks are also a threat, should there be some issues arising in the treatment of invoices received from claimants.

The French cash model appears to be simpler and less challenging in its administrative practice. The critical phase is when a claim is made: the assessment of impairment and the check of eligibility to benefit have to be made as efficiently and quickly as possible (although a waiting period may exist in several policies). That phase is, however, not really different from the reimbursement model. After that initial phase the annuity starts being paid and payments can easily be automated. The challenge in administration consists essentially in checking regularly that the insured is still alive: should the insured have died without the insurer being informed in due time, excess payments would be made beyond the actual claim; those excess payments would probably not be easy to recoup and they would deteriorate the financial balance of the portfolio.

The consistency concern between product design, distribution, underwriting and administration reflects the value chain of LTC insurance. This value chain also extends to technical or actuarial assessment of the insurance offer through which the solidity of the whole process can be assessed and monitored.

6   Technical challenges

LTC insurance risk has a long-tail nature: insurance exposure can frequently exceed 30 years from policy inception. Financial sustainability and profitability is therefore a central question for all stakeholders:

- policy-holders want to be sure that coverage will be maintained at a price which will not exceed their purchasing power and that will effectively deliver the expected benefits when needed;
- insurers have to ensure that they will develop and maintain a block of business fitting into their profitability criteria – thus satisfying their shareholders – and which they will be able to administer at acceptable costs;
- insurance regulators want to be sure that insurance product promises will be fulfilled in satisfactory conditions for policy-holders and in a safe approach for insurers and for the whole insurance industry.

6.1   Risk bricks

The long-tail nature of the LTC risk is technically challenging since it combines multiple technical components of risk:

- incidence of impairment, triggering the eligibility to payment of benefits, and possibly the severity of impairment, which may impact the benefit level;
- duration of impairment, depending not only on the age of the policy-holder but also more directly on the cause of impairment; for instance, impairment can be due to a cancer, in which case the insured's life expectation may be short, or it can be due to a senile dementia, in which case dependency or LTC needs may, for instance, exceed ten years;
- longevity of policy-holders: the longer they live, the higher the probability of meeting some impairment.

Pricing LTC insurance is very complex: it must combine those three risks, which interact between themselves. That is not only theoretical actuarial complexity, but also data- and experience-related work. Availability of experience data and close understanding of influence of all practical aspects of LTC are key elements for relevant and reliable pricing. Beyond the analysis of all causes of impairments and LTC needs, practical aspects also include underwriting, as well as claims-handling processes and monitoring.

From a comprehensive point of view, risk management is key in LTC insurance to preserve product viability. Several dimensions are part of risk management: within the insurer's internal monitoring framework, making the best use of actuarial and technical tools, such as data studies, pricing monitoring and a proactive reserving policy, is crucial to have a good command of insurance portfolios; upstream from the insurer's internal monitoring, the LTC risk itself can or should be addressed through health prevention approaches.

Risk understanding and follow-up are based on adequate collection of experience data. Collected data must be analysed, whether they are data of insured people in good health – tracking their mortality experience – or data of claimants, with all necessary components of claim information. Based on those analyses projections of risk and of portfolio evolution can be derived and used for reserving calculations as well as for potential pricing evolutions.

As far as data are concerned, the larger the experience basis, the better actuarial assumptions can be reliably derived from it. In that area, model simplicity probably plays a positive role: a simple model, as a cash approach, generates more uniform, more consistent and larger sets of data, whereas an itemized model, such as the US reimbursement model, generates many different sets of polymorphous data which may create aggregation and consistency issues to refine pricing and reserving actuarial assumptions.

6.2   Active pricing monitoring

Actuarial follow-up of insurance portfolio is based on data analysis to validate the original pricing assumptions which have been used. Recurrent monitoring of emerging portfolio experience and active pricing validation are necessary to refine the ability to anticipate risk evolution. This characterizes technical command of LTC insurance, which is a relatively new area as compared with other established insurance lines such as life, annuity or disability.

It is essential for LTC insurance to be able to use pricing revision. It is unrealistic to believe that prices can be guaranteed. Most insurers effectively do not propose such guarantees. The very long-term nature of risk makes it understandable: it is not easy to predict future evolutions of risk, which may be impacted by many demographic and medical factors. Life expectancy is steadily lengthening, now especially in old age, and projecting longevity is a technical challenge. Since longevity of policy-holders impacts directly and significantly claims occurrence, pricing requires prudence in the area of longevity assumptions. Medical progress may also impact claims experience:

in a positive direction through lowering risk for old people to move into impairments; in a more challenging direction – from the risk point of view – through possible stabilization of impairments, maintaining people longer than before without further health deterioration and postponing fatal ending.

Having revisable price does not prevent the running of smooth monitoring practices. That means setting sustainable prices for policies within moderately adverse variances. Sharp price increases – for instance +30 per cent or +50 per cent – are highly detrimental for the relationship of insurers to policy-holders, as well as for the overall public image of LTC insurance. It is understandable that some price increases may have to be implemented, but they need to be monitored with the long-run perspective in mind. In the short term, premium increases must also be kept within reasonable ranges. The ultimate objective is – or should be – that policy-holders keep their policies even if for the short term the insurer may be better off with policies lapsing.

The Rate Stabilization Act (US Code, 2001) in the USA has favoured smoother monitoring: it has removed minimal threshold loss ratios requirements which were prevailing until then. That change has allowed insurers to propose higher initial prices with the counterparty of limiting possible further price increases. This evolution is consistent with the very long-term nature of insurance which needs to consider as much as possible a levelling of premiums. It is necessary to keep in mind that annual risk rates are growing so steeply at old ages that in a non-levelled approach, prices at old age would not be tolerable, especially since they would apply to the oldest and probably the (financially) weakest-insured people.

Thorough technical monitoring is crucial due to the sensitive nature of risk, with health deterioration of old people often combined with some issues coming from the social setting. That is also very important to be kept in mind, because it presents affordability issues for many potential policy-holders.

6.3 Benefit period

Social aspects of LTC insurance may also raise some issues when the benefit period is limited. For instance, several US policies include defined benefit duration (e.g., three years or 700 days of care). Difficulties arise when the benefit period is reaching the end and the policy-holder still has need of assistance. US insurers have of course made efforts to prepare the insured in advance, but the actual situation to be faced then is unwelcomed hardship.

The benefit period duration issue crystallizes the challenges of LTC expenses. In a reimbursement model which ambitiously aims at funding most of the care needs, the amount of expenses is huge and creates sustainability issues. That is why US insurers, having experienced unfavourable experience with unlimited benefit periods, had to severely increase the prices of these policies. These increases made such policies generally too expensive for most applicants. In order to maintain more affordable offers, limited-duration policies were launched and some companies stopped offering unlimited benefit periods.

In a similar technical area, when insurance reimburses expenses, an inflation issue arises, especially since medical and care costs due to inflation are huge. It appears that many insurers had not correctly anticipated inflation. Without inflation protection, policy-holders do not get sufficient coverage from their insurance for expenses and are actually not fully repaid due to policy benefit limits. That is why inflation protection is now highly recommended and is effectively bought, even if it is an expensive option.

The cash model has not directly faced most of these issues. The benefit amount is selected by applicants and predefined in monetary terms at policy inception stage; no promise is included in the policy for matching whatever the amount of LTC needs. Inflation can be addressed partially through benefit revaluation, which can be done with a policy dividend technique. It is right though that this approach generally does not enable the purchasing power of the benefit to be fully maintained. That may become an issue particularly in the case of long deferral periods between inception and claim occurrence or for long claim durations. However there is no explicit matching promise, as opposed to the matching which is involved in the reimbursement approach.

As far as claim duration is concerned, the cash model used in most French policies does not limit benefit periods. Assumption of an irreversible situation is made, at least for severe impairments, and pricing is based on a lifetime annuity to be paid. Experience shows that this assumption is realistic. Technical monitoring is therefore eased under such simple assumptions, but that does not avoid having to perform detailed actuarial studies about risk factors – incidence, claims durations, longevity of policy-holders – to have a satisfactory monitoring of insurance portfolios.

6.4   Active claims assessment

Insurers may also use another monitoring tool at the claim assessment stage. Insurers receive many claim requests emanating from persons whose health has deteriorated. It is crucial for them to check closely that the health situation of the insured complies with the benefit eligibility which is stated in policy wording.

In practice, many cases reflect situations in which health deterioration is not so deep as to trigger the policy payment criteria. Assessment of ADL ability of the claimant allows verification in the most objective way. In practice a declined claim request may often simply mean that the insured is not yet so severely impaired as to qualify for policy benefits. Adequate communication to the insured should then be made, knowing that further health deterioration may happen a few months later and would then be recognized as complying with policy benefit eligibility.

Within the cash model, the ratio of number of accepted claims to total number of claims requests can be seen as an indicator for portfolio monitoring and for checking consistency with pricing. That ratio depends on the level of impairment severity for which the policy is designed. For instance, when a policy covers severe levels of impairment, a 25 per cent ratio is typically observed for stable portfolios, whereas a significantly higher ratio may indicate possible threats of deviation in portfolio technical balance.

7   Heading to future LTC insurance

The LTC insurance market is still in its infancy, despite a 25-year history since its first developments. Several experiences have taken place and many difficulties have been met, which is not surprising because of the complexity of underlying risks and of the variety of practical matters which interfere with the insurance coverage dialectics.

7.1   Further developments

Insurance offer still has some challenges to face and innovative progress to be made in order to increase its audience and availability. The following improvements can be mentioned:

- Policy-holders applying for LTC insurance at a younger age: in a level premium mechanism, the younger the age at inception, the lower the premium. This is a key factor, especially since affordability constraints are currently often encountered. Shifting to younger application ages would also be a way to reduce potential issues in underwriting, which are likely to occur frequently when applicants are in their 70s.
- Group insurance is a good solution to increase the knowledge of LTC insurance and to have people accessing it at younger ages than when buying on an individual basis. Group insurance can set up a first layer of coverage, paving the way for additional individual purchases. Group insurance does not face underwriting and anti-selection issues and it should help to improve global risk mitigation in LTC insurance portfolios.
- Developing connection and combinations between mortality, accumulation (savings) products and LTC insurance: solutions may either consist of accelerating basic benefits (typically for a life insurance policy) or in enhancing them (for annuity in the pay out phase). These combinations have the advantage of reducing potential anti-selection, providing insurers with a better mitigation of risks between LTC and mortality and increasing persistency of life/annuity business. From the insured's point of view, combined policies may be seen as limiting the 'use it or lose it' perception.

In the USA the addition of riders to life insurance or annuity products has started and should develop significantly in the years to come. France has also introduced such combinations, although still on a limited basis. In Germany, proposals have been made by the Rurup Commission (Kommission für die Nachhaltigkeit in der Finanzierung der Sozialen Sicherungssysteme, 2003) in that combination direction. The reverse mortgage technique, already widely used as an alternative funding for LTC needs in the UK and in Ireland, may also be combined with insurance to provide funding of an LTC policy with a level of benefit fitting actual needs.

7.2 Framework and regulation

For product evolution and innovations to lead successfully, the framework of LTC insurance is a central question. Stability and certainty are key factors for insured people, and regulation framework is also a structural feature for insurance products.

The US LTC insurance market has developed within the regulatory US insurance framework, which had some tight requirements such as filing for new products and rates revisions, in compliance with the regulation of each State where insurance is sold. An evolution can be seen in the US regulatory environment towards a unified insurance framework, more specifically for the implementation of a greater homogenization of LTC offer. As mentioned, the HIPAA (1996) introduced tax deductibility as a counterparty of better protection of policy-holders. More recently, both the Deficit Reduction Act (see, e.g., State of New Jersey, 2008) and the implementation of partnership programmes aim at setting some common and minimal policy standards in order to favour market development. And even more recently, the new Community Living Assistance Services and Supports (CLASS Act) (US government, 2010), which was adopted by Congress in 2010, should also have some structural effects in setting up in each State a kind of reference LTC insurance offer with cash benefits.

In France, LTC insurance has grown without stringent regulation so far: no reference reserving tables, nor any real price regulation, except through controls which may be carried out by the State Insurance Controller (ACP, *Autorité de Contrôle Prudentiel*). Convergence does occur mostly through market practices, but variety in product approaches co-exist. There are suggested ideas for the government's project announced in 2007 that are worth mentioning, namely: a more standardized platform of benefits; possible counterparty of tax deductibility; as well as some increased transparency and justification in rate increases. That typically reflects a possible move towards a more regulated market and a better protection of policy-holders.

In this perspective, the implementation of Solvency 2 within the European Union will have structural and probably beneficial effects on LTC insurance. This new regulatory framework, to be used from 2013 on, would most probably would be more demanding, not only in terms of capital requirement, but also in terms of data, of risk-monitoring work and of follow-up. Addressing a very long-tail risk, with still much to be learned in risk evolution and insured people's behaviours, the Solvency 2 framework will help to strengthen the expertise of insurance players and their command of risk, thus solidifying the reliability of LTC insurance solutions.

An increased but more tailor-made regulation makes sense, because of the very long-term nature of LTC insurance products and because of the need to ensure that private insurance can provide reliable and sustainable solutions. In a regulation framework the challenge also lies in the ability to preserve some necessary capacity for product and service innovation within the private insurance market.

Additionally and beyond financial regulation, a necessary synergy between private and public systems must be emphasized since stakes are high. Financing solutions for LTC will become more and more a stringent necessity, also because LTC costs will increase as more formal care will be used, instead of informal care with its hidden costs. Informal care capacity is shrinking in many countries, due to the delayed effect of low fertility and of a reduction in average family size; these trends have been observed in many countries, not only in European countries (Central, Eastern and Southern Europe), but also in Eastern Asian countries (China, Japan). Development of formal care is nevertheless a challenge, because it requires developing training programmes and adequate organizational networks to be able to offer reliable and efficient services. In all these areas, public impulses and framework designing will help to provide LTC needs with the appropriate environment, for all the necessary infrastructures and work resources as well as for the financial solutions which fit into them.

8   Conclusion

Being a complex combination of demographic, medical, social and financial features, LTC needs have no unique answer, whether public or private, which may be identified as the best and most efficient. Financial burden is heavy and insurance cannot pretend to offer solutions corresponding to all needs. Insurance is nevertheless an essential component, and its role will grow.

Many insurance approaches have been used. As experience increases, the reliability of the insurance model used will grow and should confirm the technical ability to monitor that risk in the long run. All kinds of tools have to be used for monitoring and risk management: pragmatic product design and risk characterization, realistic pricing, qualified distribution, efficient underwriting, reasonable but efficient claims assessment and anticipative reserving, as well as a relevant value-added interaction with the necessary financial regulation. All steps of the process bring their own added value and are part of a global consistency chain. Dynamic and anticipative monitoring in all those parts is crucial to alleviate any consistency concern which would create some deviation risk. At the insured level, a lot can be developed in health prevention to monitor LTC risk: this is an area in which insurers and reinsurers should play a decisive role.

Reimbursement and cash approaches have respective advantages and limits. Growing concern about insured people's interest and protection, as well as the necessity for insurers to develop a sustainable and profitable LTC insurance model, will drive further evolutions. Some convergence should occur between the various approaches, as well as possibly some better and more efficient integration between insurance solutions and the care services needed.

References

AGGIR (1997) grille, AGGIR, Article 6, décret no. 97 427, 28 April 1997, http://www.grille-aggir.fr/grille_aggir.php, date accessed 20 January 2011.

Arntz, M., Sacchetto, M., Spermann, A., Steffes, S. and Widmaier, S. (2007) *The German Social Long-term Care Insurance: Structure and Reform Options*, Discussion Paper Series, Bonn: Forschungsinstitut zur Zukunft der Arbeit [Institute for the Study of Labor – IZA], February.

Brown, J., Coe, N. and Finkelstein, A. (2007) 'Medicaid crowd out of private LTC insurance demand: Evidence from the Health and Retirement Survey', *Tax Policy and the Economy*, 21, pp. 1–34.

Eslous, L. (2007) *Eléments de travail sur la dépendance des personnes âgées* (Paris: Inspection Générale des Affaires Sociales).

FFSA (Fédération Française des Sociétés d'Assurance) (2010) *Les contrats d'assurance dépendance en 2009* (Paris: FFSA), April.

ICEA (2005) *El Seguro de dependencia – Guía para el desarrollo de productos de larga Dependencia en España* (Barcelona: ICEA Report).

Kommission für die Nachhaltigkeit in der Finanzierung der Sozialen Sicherungssysteme (Rürup-Kommission) (2003) *Nachhaltigkeit in der Finanzierung der Sozialen Sicherungssysteme. Bericht der Kommission* (Berlin: Bundesministerin für Gesundheit und Soziale Sicherung).

Le Corre, P.-Y. (2008) *Long Term Care Insurance: French and International Perspective*, presentation delivered at the 6th Health and Ageing Conference organized by The Geneva Association, London, 6 and 7 November.

LifePlans, Inc. (2007) *Who Buys Long Term Care Insurance – A 15 Year Study of Buyers and Non Buyers*, 1990–2005, prepared for America's Health Insurance Plans (AHIP), April.

NTUC income (2010) *Eldershield Plan*, http://www.income.com.sg/insurance/eldershield, date accessed 20 January 2011.

OECD (2006) *Projecting OECD Health Care and Long-term Care Expenditures*, OECD Economics Department Working Paper (Paris: OECD), p. 477.

State of New Jersey (2008) Long Term Care Insurance Partnership Program, Department of Banking and Insurance, Bulletin No. 08-05, http://www.state.nj.us/dobi/bulletins/blt08_05.pdf, date accessed 20 January 2011.

Taleyson, L. (2003) 'L'assurance dépendance privée, comparaisons internationales', *Newsletter Technique Vie*, 9 (Paris: SCOR), January.

US Code (2001) Long-term Care Insurance Rate Stabilisation Act, http://www.law.cornell.edu/uscode/26/usc_sec_26_00000162----000-.html, date accessed 20 January 2011.

US Department of Health and Human Services (1996) HIPAA Regulation, http://www.hhs.gov/ocr/privacy/hipaa/understanding/summary/index.html, date accessed 20 January 2011.

US government (2010) Community Living Assistance Services and Supports Act (CLASS Act): in *Patient Protection and Affordable Care* law, Title VIII.

5

Housing Wealth as Self-insurance for Long-Term Care

Anne Laferrère
INSEE and CREST (Paris), France

1 Introduction

Long-term care (LTC) insurance is about providing resources for care and services, should they be needed because of a disability, usually in very old age. A premium is paid, that is, money is put aside from current consumption, to face the risk of the expenses linked to the future need of assistance in activities of daily living. Housing wealth, by comparison, is linked to daily living in a place, consuming housing services, performing daily activities, in a particular surrounding called 'home'. If the home is owned, housing also is a form of saving. It can be used in case of need, for instance, for LTC. Due to the dual nature of housing, both consumption and investment good, and due to its indivisibility and illiquidity, the issue is how to extract housing equity to finance LTC. Financial devices, such as *vente en viager*, the sale of a home for a life annuity have existed for centuries; various forms of 'reverse mortgages' are more recent. This chapter assesses the role of homeownership in providing self-insurance for LTC. Self-insurance seems a contradiction in terms, as insurance is pooling a risk over a large population, and self-insurance does not seem adapted for a high-cost risk such as LTC. However, a more careful analysis of the risks faced in old age, and of the unique characteristics of housing as consumption good, as a place where care can be provided and as a saving vehicle may justify the oxymoron in the title of this chapter.

We review the risks linked to old age, and how they cannot be fully assessed without taking housing into account. Then we present the means to extract housing equity. Finally, we explore the complex relationships between insurance, housing, LTC and family.

2 The risks linked to old age

If very old age is defined as the age at which labour participation cannot be used as an income insurance instrument, the main economic risk of very old age is the risk of living too long and exceeding one's resources. A solution to this longevity risk is the purchase of annuities (called *assurance-vie*, insurance for life, in French). Compared with putting the same amount in a saving account, annuities offer a 'mortality premium' arising from the pooling of mortality risks and they can eliminate the longevity risk altogether.

2.1 Longevity risk, the mortality premium and the annuity puzzle

Suppose you want to insure your consumption in the next period, r is the interest rate and $m(m < 1)$ is the mortality rate between periods. By investing 1, you earn $1 + r$. With an annuity, you earn $(1 + r)/(1 - m) > 1 + r$ if you are alive in the next period, and zero in case of death. By giving up the ownership of the part of your wealth invested in annuity in case of death you get an extra income if alive. This is a winner's strategy if you do not care about leaving $1 + r$ as a bequest to your heirs (with probability m).[1] Considering this premium, why then is the voluntary additional purchase of annuities so rare? Many explanations of this 'annuity puzzle' have been put forward (Brown, 2007; Brown and Finkelstein, 2007). Alongside bequest motives, the fact that in many countries a substantial fraction of the wealth of the elderly is annuitized through social security, defined benefits or pay-as-you-go pension plans is a first rationale for so few additional purchases. Pooling risks within couples' and survivor's pensions also reduces the need for insurance. Few have pointed out that the main item of consumption, namely, housing consumption, may well turn out not to be fully insured by an annuity. In some places, the rent evolution for a tenant might exceed the general price evolution, and if the annuity, or more generally the retirement income, is poorly indexed, or indexed on a general consumer price index, a tenant is exposed to a rent risk that translates into the risk of having to move out (Sinai and Souleles, 2005). The solution would be to purchase an annuity indexed on the local rent. Such a product would be costly to design, and even if it existed, it would not eliminate the uncertainty linked to tenure insecurity, independently of the rent evolution risk. Tenure risk, the risk for a tenant to be expelled from her home is all the more important as one gets older, as psychological investment in the home and in the neighbourhood increases with the time spent in the same place. Older tenants risk losing more than younger ones in the event of an eviction, which makes moving costs higher for them.[2]

2.2 Homeownership as a 'rent annuity'

Rent risk and tenure risk combined might be one of the reasons why housing ownership is favoured over renting among the elderly: it provides perfect security of tenure and hedging against rent risk. Owning a home is an investment that provides a 'rent annuity' and hence ensures housing consumption.

In Europe many elderly tenants benefit from large security of tenure or various forms of social or public housing programmes offering rents below market price. Nevertheless, along the life cycle the proportion of home-owners culminates around age 70. On average, around 74 per cent of the current 60–69-year-olds own their home. The rate of homeownership is lower in Germany, Austria, Switzerland and the Netherlands; it is higher in the Southern countries and Belgium (Figure 5.1). Moreover, cohort effects are important, for instance, in the Netherlands where 75 per cent of the 50–59-year-olds currently own their home. Beyond detention rates, the structure of the elderly wealth is dominated by housing. Among French retirees, those in the two bottom wealth deciles have most of their savings in cash; those in the two top deciles have a somewhat diversified portfolio; all others have more than 60 per cent of their wealth in housing (Girardot-Buffard, 2009).

In theory hedging against rent risk could take any form, and a renter could be a landlord in the same area.[3] However, housing usually is held in the form of one's own home, for two main obvious reasons. Firstly and impor-tantly, to eliminate transaction cost (finding/managing tenants) and to limit the waste generated by asymmetric information and diverging incentives

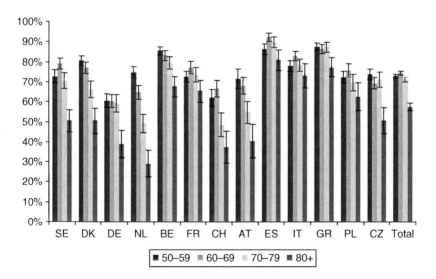

Figure 5.1 Homeownership rate by country and age group
Note: SE: Sweden, DK: Denmark, DE: Germany, NL: The Netherlands, BE: Belgium, FR: France, CH: Switzerland, AT: Austria, ES: Spain, IT: Italy, GR: Greece, PL: Poland, CZ: Czech Republic.
Source: SHARE survey, computations by Angelini and Laferrère (2008).

between tenants and landlord owners;[4] secondly, in most countries the virtual rent paid by an owner to herself is not submitted to income tax, which is an advantage to homeownership *cet. par.*

We have come up with a first reason for homeownership, that is, with a rationale for not converting the whole of the savings into annuities. For a retiring homeowner, it is cheaper and safer to ensure his housing consumption directly by going on living in his home rather than converting all his housing equity into an annuity and start renting.

2.3   Facing LTC expenditures

Another reason to hold a house in old age is linked to a second main economic risk after the longevity risk, that of a large health shock leading to the need of LTC. Health expenses in most developed countries are covered by a public insurance system that can be complemented by private insurances. Out of pocket payments for drugs, for general practitioner visits and for hospital are limited, especially for the elderly (Medicare in the US, Health branch of the *Sécurité sociale* in France). On the contrary, all forms of care and need linked to disabilities are rarely covered. Usually, health and social services are not integrated. Apart from the Scandinavian countries, Germany, Luxembourg and the Netherlands may be the only countries to offer universal LTC coverage as part of the public package.[5] The care part includes help in at least one activity of daily living (eating, bathing, dressing, walking across a room, going to bed), or at least one instrumental activity of daily living (using the telephone, handling money, shopping, taking medication, cooking). The LTC risk is important. Brown and Finkelstein (2008) estimate that the probability for a 62-year-old American woman of ever using care facilities is 54 per cent (40 for males), be it at home, or in a nursing or assisted living home. Moreover, the probability that she will have to use it for more than three years is 53 per cent (37 per cent for males).[6] The cost of such care is typically large compared with average elderly income (it is 43 per cent above the average French male pension, and 3.2 times the average female pension, according to Plisson, 2009). Confronted by such a risk of very large expenses, over a limited period of time, the prospect of a constant annuitized income over many years becomes less attractive, and keeping a buffer stock of wealth for such large expenses might be preferred.

2.4   Housing as an all-purpose vehicle?

To protect against the financial consequences of LTC risks a solution would be the purchase of long-term care insurance (LTCI). For many reasons that the other chapters in the book explore in detail such LTCI is not well developed (10 per cent in the USA).[7] Again, an additional reason might be found in the important saving that is embedded in housing. People may perceive they have enough savings to face LTC risk. Housing investment is large, and in old age might well exceed the need for an efficient portfolio (Pelizzon and Weber, 2009). Investment of elderly Europeans in risky assets such as stocks and bonds is indeed low, except in the UK and Sweden. This over-investment in housing is due in part to housing also having a consumption purpose.[8] You buy stocks or bonds to get a return; you purchase a home to have a place to live. But the optimal housing consumption of the elderly might also be exceeded when all children have left home and income is reduced on retirement or widowhood. Indeed, 56 per cent of Europeans aged 65 and above (in the countries mentioned in Figure 5.1) enjoy more than 2.5 rooms per person (excluding Poland and the Czech Republic, 60 per cent have more than 2.5 rooms per person and 46 per cent have more than four). A rational economic attitude would be to both reduce housing consumption and have a more diversified portfolio. However, some reasons can be put forward for such over-consumption and over-investment in old age. Firstly, housing transaction costs, both financial and psychological, are very high. The difference between optimal and current consumption has to be large to trigger a move (Grossman and Laroque, 1990; Gobillon and Le Blanc, 2004).[9] Secondly, a house is more than a pure investment, and even more than pure consumption. It is a place of life cycle memories linked to an area where relatives and friends live. Habits go along with an *habitation*. A dwelling is a place to inhabit, to live in, which means that life is at stake in where we reside. This makes extra housing consumption rational if 'ageing in place' is valued,[10] even at the expense of other types of consumption, and even when the house is not adapted for old age. Residential mobility of the elderly is extremely low in all countries, and the more one has stayed in a home the less likely one is to move for another home (Angelini and Laferrère, 2008). Extra housing investment is also rational in case of a bequest motive, when the parents want the house to be kept in the family.[11] Thirdly, and this is what is underlined in this chapter, the house can be seen as a store of value which can be drawn from in case of LTC need. It can be sold outright, or against annuities, or a mixture of capital and annuities to pay for a nursing home. Shore and Sinai (2005) even argue that the higher the future risk, the higher the current housing consumption level of owners. They think of a high unemployment risk for a couple, but their intuition could be extended to elderly home owners facing a large health risk and insuring it through housing (Davidoff, 2009). Hence transaction costs, the desire to age in a familiar place and to keep the home for bequest concur to over-investment and over-consumption of housing. The risk of large LTC expenditures adds weight to this somewhat irrational over-investment and over-consumption as households think they will be able to use their housing wealth in case of need. They perceive it as a good vehicle for old age self-insurance, which could explain the low level of LTC insurance. In this perception they may underestimate the costs of extracting housing equity.

3   Extracting housing equity

Homeownership, in spite of its many virtues, has some drawbacks. Housing wealth is illiquid and indivisible. If the elderly have their savings locked in a house and they do not want to leave for the reasons mentioned above, how can they draw housing equity to complement their income, or help a child immediately?

3.1   Downsizing

A passive means to release equity from a home simply is to reduce maintenance, which some elderly do (Davidoff, 2004). Another means is to let part of the home. This is frequent in Switzerland and Germany,[12] rare in other countries such as France. Downsizing, that is, selling and moving to a less expensive home, is another option. The importance of such 'trading down' at the end of the life cycle is still debated. Downsizing is rare in the absence of a shock on health or household composition such as the loss of a spouse (Venti and Wise, 2001; Bonnet et al., 2010). In spite of their low mobility rate, older households when they do move more often choose smaller than bigger homes, more often rent than buy, all the more as they grow older.[13] They also leave houses for flats, where maintenance can be more easily subcontracted, which is consistent with their anticipating a risk of disability (Angelini and Laferrère, 2008). However, as they also move closer to more expensive city centres, it is not sure that they reduce their housing expenses (Venti and Wise, 2001). As residential mobility is positively linked to income, it could mean that some immobility is constrained, and that for a minority, ageing in place is rather uncomfortable and they would be better off by moving, but are prevented from doing so by moving costs (Laferrère and Angelini, 2009).

Home equity release schemes are called for to provide for those who are deemed house-rich and cash-poor. Typically this would concern a widow who purchased the home while married, and faces large housing costs and a small pension. The survivor's pension does not compensate for the loss of economies of scale in housing consumption (Bonnet et al., 2010).[14] Individuals are not isolated, and LTC might have to be provided to one spouse, then to the survivor. Home equity release might help mitigate the consequences of the partner's mortality risk, or the partner's LTC expenses when one wants to stay in the current home. More generally, the adequacy of using housing as a saving device for non-housing consumption is linked to the possibility to obtain cash from it, without selling it. In some countries a home owner can draw equity from the house by refinancing the mortgage, drawing a second mortgage, taking a home equity loan. This is common in the USA, even if difficult for elderly low-income homeowners. It is less common in continental Europe, except in the Nordic countries or the Netherlands. All equity release systems aim at going beyond the indivisibility of housing by sharing ownership. More precisely, they are of two types, either close to a sale arrangement or to a credit operation.

3.2 Selling in *viager*

An example of sale arrangement to release equity is the traditional French *vente en viager* that has existed for centuries in many countries.[15] The contract is that of the sale of the home, while keeping the right to live in it (or get the rent) until death. It is an exchange between two individuals of an asset for a *rente*, that is, a life annuity. It is directly linked to the longevity risk (the term *viager* comes from the French *vie*, that is, life). When the seller dies, her home belongs to the buyer; nothing of it is left for her estate. *Viager* is a means to extract equity from a dwelling while going on using it, fulfilling the desire to age in place. *Viager* draws on the legal separation of full property between usufruct, kept for life by the seller, and expectant interest (*nue-propriété*) belonging to the buyer.[16] The annuity level is a function of three parameters: the value of the house, the interest rate and the seller's life expectancy. Often the seller also receives a lump-sum payment called the *bouquet*,[17] but the annuity is essential and cannot be converted into a capital. The older the seller, the higher the annuity. The annuity can be increased if the buyer does not live in the house or renounces her right to use the house, say when she enters a nursing home. In France, the law makes such annuity favourable to the seller: it is indexed on inflation, and only part of it is considered for income tax purposes. There is no tax advantage for the buyer who cannot consider the annuity as interest payment. In case the buyer cannot pay the annuity, the sale cannot be made null; the seller has only a right to the buyer's assets. In France, the number of sales *en viager* is low less than 4000 per year and is declining. The main explanation put forward for the low number of *viagers* is a bequest motive. Selling deprives the children of the inheritance of the family home. However, as for any annuity, other arguments go in the other direction. The annuity allows the parent to be independent from her children and not rely on their help. Leaving aside homes that are considered as family homes for future generations, a sale *en viager* could reconcile annuity and bequest: the *bouquet* can be given to a child (e.g. the one who takes care of the parent), and the annuity can be used to pay for professional care and be a means not to be a burden on the children.[18] Note, however, that for a parent whose only asset is the home, giving it away is losing an incentive for the children to help. It is unclear in which direction all those effects go, but selling *en viager* is overwhelmingly done by childless persons, which points to the attachment of the family to the parents' home.[19] Other explanations for the low number of *viagers* are economics (rents are not actuarially fair) and psychological. Two persons are face to face and one is betting on the date of death of the other. Also, the sale is final, whatever the date of death. To alleviate these problems and mutualize the longevity risk over larger portfolios, new forms of *viager* are currently being proposed in France, such as *prêt viager hypothécaire* (lifetime mortgage), created in 2007, or *viager intermédié partiel* (partial intermediated equity release sale) that introduce financial intermediation and are closer to a credit operation than to a sale.

3.3   Reverse mortgages: Borrow now and pay later

The main credit operation linked to home equity release is known as reverse mortgage (RM). While being very close to a *viager* sale, the RM system differs in that it is not a sale but a credit operation where the elderly borrows on her home.[20] It does not imply any transfer of ownership, contrary to a *viager*. RM also differs from mortgage refinancing or home equity loans, because no interest payment is due before the end of the contract.[21] In a regular mortgage, the debt declines as interest and principal are paid back, and the net equity in the house increases accordingly. In a RM, the debt increases with time until the end of the contract, and it is capped by the home value at the end of the contract. Net home equity declines. Such schemes exist in most countries, but are only somewhat developed in the UK and the USA. In the UK they are called lifetime mortgage, and often take the form of rolled-up interest loans ('rolled up' because no interest is paid until the end). In the USA the most common is the Home Equity Conversion Mortgage (HECM) offered by the Department of Housing and Urban Development (HUD). The credit can be a capital, a line of credit (the most common), regular annuities or a combination. It is available to all homeowners aged 62 and older. The borrower's liability is limited to the home value. As for a *viager*, the older the borrower, the higher the loan, as the expected period before repayment is shorter. The line of credit bears interest at the same rate used for the loan. As for a *viager*, there are advantages for the creditor: the credit is not considered a taxable income, and does not enter the computation of means for most means-tested benefits. When the person dies, moves or sells the home, the RM operation is closed. The person or her children can reimburse the credit in order to keep the house. This is a clear difference with *viager* where the home is irrevocably sold, whatever the date of the death. RM started slowly, but seems to be developing with baby-boomer cohorts hitting the age threshold: there were 40,000 new HECMs in 2005, more than 110,000 in 2008 according to the Federal Housing Administration.

3.4   Far from perfect instruments

The risks of RM are the same as for *viager*: longevity, interest rate and house price evolution. The longevity risk is that of the borrower living too long (in the case of the option of a payment for life). In case of adjustable interest rates or a decrease in house price the risk is that the loan is greater than the home value. Those risks, or the risk that the lender defaults, are borne by the government, but paid by premiums from the borrower. This makes for high transaction costs, up to 20 per cent of the loan principal in 1999. The transaction costs currently are so large that Caplin (2000) argues that an elderly person with an average home value above her intended bequest might want to forego RM, decrease her consumption and leave that amount as extra bequest rather than losing it in the transaction. In other words, even a moderately altruistic parent might prefer leaving the transaction cost to a child rather than to the bank or to the government. Other obstacles are linked to the stigma associated with needing a loan, procrastination and the complicated design of the product.

The main concern is that a RM might make a move more difficult in case the line of credit has already been used (Feinstein, 1996). Even if RM is in the form of an annuity, if the loan is terminated in case of a residential move,[22] HECM is not appropriate just when it is more needed, when one becomes dependent and has to move into a nursing home, and needs cash for medical or LTC expenses. Hence the whole rationale of keeping the house as a buffer for important expenses shocks may be ruined by equity release schemes. Nothing is left for such shocks. Moreover, the RM scheme itself might prevent a necessary move if moving coincides with paying back the loan.

Other obstacles to the development of RM come from the lenders' side. They stem from low origination fees, the cost of dealing with an elderly person, moral hazard in maintenance and in home sale. The risk of under-maintenance of the home is real, since the borrowers are typically house-rich and cash-poor, and old, thus less inclined to make a long-term investment.[23] Moral hazard can also play a role when the home is finally sold by a relative (who has an incentive to dissimulate part of the price) or by the probate court. It seems there is no moral hazard in the length of stay in the house of reverse mortgagers. In the USA the elderly leave their home at a rate almost 50 per cent greater than observably similar non-participating homeowners (Davidoff and Welke, 2004), but this might reverse in a period when home prices do not appreciate.

Home equity release schemes transfer the longevity risk to the provider of the mortgage, or to the purchaser of the home in case of a *viager*. How can the risk be dealt with, at a time where longevity is increasing regularly? While most papers in the mid-1990s were from the elderly perspective, stressing the need for information and counselling (Case and Schnare, 1994), now most are from the financial side of the market, and deal with the practical financial design of the product. Boehm and Ehrhardt (1994) are concerned with interest rate risk, Wang et al. (2007) suggest securitization and Szymanovski et al. (2007) recommend developing secondary markets.

3.5 House price risk

More generally, self-insuring with housing is highly sensitive to the evolution of house prices, for the elderly who has her wealth stored in a house as for the provider of housing equity (RM seller, the person who buys *en viager*). It works well when house prices go up, but can have dramatic consequences when they fall (Skinner, 1996; Khandani and Merton, 2009). The design of home equity insurance products, based on the local housing price index, is being studied and experimented upon (Goetzmann et al., 2003). The risk for a person who needs to use her stored housing wealth is to have to sell quickly, and at the time where disability reduces the fitness to handle a sale, hence the risk to get a lower price. At a macroeconomic level, the risk of a downturn in prices is increased by the baby-boom effect as many will want to withdraw cash from their house at the same time. A downturn in housing prices was announced by Mankiw and Weil (1989) for around the time of the baby-boomers' retirement age. It proved to be an error because equity release does not happen at that time in the life cycle, but it may happen later at the end of their life.

4   LTC: Who provides it and where?

A last reason for the importance of housing in LTC is that the very place where care will be provided is relevant to the choices made. By contrast, pure health expenses are less dependent on the location (general practitioners (GP) are everywhere, drugs prices are not linked to a place). Where you live commands the family help received from children, the persons who may be hired to deliver care, who will come to visit and the frequency of the visits. As many LTC public systems are managed or co-managed by local governments or agencies, their outcome and cost also depend on location.[24] The place might even command your health outcome, as being displaced from familiar surroundings is often detrimental to a disoriented person. Many put a special price on receiving the care in their home for as long as possible. Again, housing is at the core of LTC insurance and organization.

4.1   The cost of adapting homes

If home care is to be developed, homes are to be adapted. Doors have to be large enough, stairs have to be avoided. A secure and accessible neighbourhood encourages daily mobility and minimizes the risk of falls. It also facilitates the access of home care helpers. Few elderly Europeans say they live in a home that has special features to assist persons who have physical impairments or health problems: only 10 per cent of those over 70 in France, 14 per cent in Switzerland and 29 per cent in the Netherlands.[25] Even among those who have mobility problems[26] only 12 per cent live in an adapted home. It is less expensive to provide some care at home than in an institution, except when dependency problems become very heavy. The price of care and the capability of delivering it might also depend on the home quality. As adapting all homes to the needs of a dependent person is impossible, there might be a paradox in the wish to stay longer in the home than before.

Mobility might be encouraged by some incentives (one could think of home exchanges within a community if the local social network is important).

'Home' may mean the elderly person's own home, but also a child's home or a nursing home. The three types of living arrangements are possible. Among those over 80 in France, 71 per cent live on their own (41 per cent alone, 30 per cent with a spouse), 14 per cent co-reside (12 per cent with a child) and 16 per cent live in an institution.[27] It is not easy to infer the choices of future generations from past behaviours. For instance, observing that the rate of co-residence with a child is 12 per cent at age 80 and 35 per cent after age 90 hides the fact that this rate is decreasing from one generation to the next (Flipo et al., 1999). As income increases and health improves, preferences are for independent living, all the more so that a longer life expectancy means that for a given age more live as couples and fewer are widowed. According to SHARE (2006), the proportion of continental Europeans aged 80+ having no child is 12.5 per cent. The proportion co-residing with a child is less than 10 per cent in all countries, except Poland, Italy, Spain and Austria.[28]

Co-residing with children has been declining over time, but geographical proximity remains very important. In Greece, and also in Germany, more than a quarter of those over 80 have a child living in the same building. All in all, a vast majority (62 per cent) have at least one child living less than 5 kilometres away. Moreover, in old age the moves bring the families closer (Bonnet et al., 2010). Because of this proximity, the many exchanges of everyday services are easier. In that sense, for the current generations of elderly, the demise of the family is a myth.[29]

Angelini and Laferrère (2008) show that moving to a nursing home seems to take place under a triple constraint: health problems (mobility limitation), low resources and the absence of a spouse or children. This is observed in all continental European countries.[30] It is another proof of the wish to stay at home as long as possible and of the importance of the family in caregiving.

If the home is adapted in advance, costly moves (both in monetary and psychological terms) could be delayed, as care can be provided at home rather than in an institution. The relationship between LTCI and home improvement schemes needs to be studied more closely.

4.2 Family, home and LTC

Some may also forego LTCI because they plan to rely on a spouse or on their children for receiving care in their home. If the elderly put an extra value on care provided by the family, and if the family is more likely to provide care in the home than in an institution, the taste for family care would reinforce the motivation for home care, and the family might become part of LTC 'self-insurance' alongside the home and linked to it. The questions are many[31] and they involve altruism and the motivation of family transfers (see Laferrère, 1999, or Laferrère and Wolff, 2006, for a survey). From the point of view of the caregiver, it has been shown that taking care of an invalid spouse at home can be detrimental to their health, and associated with reduced well-being (Wahrendorf et al., 2006; McMunn et al., 2009). Living arrangement choices dictate who is in charge of the parents and the geography of the family might be endogenous (Konrad et al., 2002; Engelhardt et al., 2005; Engelhardt and Greenhalgh-Stanley, 2008). Public and private insurance interact. Purchasing LTCI might reduce the informal care provided by children (Zweifel and Strüwe, 1996). However, more recent studies show that residential care in an institution, professional home care and informal family care are more complements than substitutes (Bonsang, 2008).

Hence the question of home equity release and LTCI cannot be asked independently of the presence of children, nor of the public provision of LTC. Children add a transmission motive for saving. The way public care is financed and distributed, combined with rules of maintenance liability between child and parent and of estate recovery, influence LTC demand. Those rules combine with inheritance laws, and lead to a multiple actor game between parents, spouses, children, national and local communities. If LTC is means-tested and asset-tested, one would have an incentive to make *inter-vivos* gifts, rather than leave a bequest.[32] The aim might well be to have nothing left and run down the assets to become eligible for means-tested LTC benefits. In some countries the LTC benefit is not asset-tested but might by subtracted from the beneficiary's estate after death. The behavioural response to such estate recovery, *récupération sur héritage* seems huge: in France, many did not apply for *prestation sociale dépendance* (PSD) for fear of losing the inheritance, while applications for *Aide personnalisée à l'autonomie* (APA, which replaced PSD) are large because there is no such reclaiming.

The new forms of family lives complicate strategies. Do you care as much for an old step-parent as for a parent, or for the parents of an unmarried partner as for in-laws? All this has to be borne in mind when analysing the links between housing and LTC provision.

5   Conclusion

We have shown that the issue of LTCI cannot be fully understood without taking housing into account. Housing is the only asset that can be directly consumed with minimal transaction costs. In that sense, it is even more liquid than cash. It is a storage of value, which can be used, in total or partially, to help face large expenses such as those linked to LTC either by a sale or thanks to various equity release schemes. Finally, it is a place to live until the end, and, maybe receive care, a family place, a storage of memory. Its location, far from or close to children, or professional care suppliers is important. There is a good chance that the house value is linked to desired nursing home quality. Hence housing seems a good vehicle for self-insurance, and homeownership might reduce the purchase of LTCI. The continuous increase in longevity makes the investment more interesting: one lives longer in one's home and can reap more benefit in case of price appreciation. Until recently the new cohorts of elderly have been richer than former ones as pension systems were built up and women got their own pension rights. This may explain why dis-saving housing for current consumption needs is rarely seen. Most current elderly just do not need it.[33] Few are house-rich and cash-poor (Venti and Wise, 1991; Laferrère, 2006).

The future baby-boomer cohorts will face different constraints and might behave differently. A safe guess is that the current generosity of the pension system will be eroded because of increased longevity and a fall in fertility. Pensions will be lower, and consumption demand may be larger, as the first 'spoilt' post-war cohorts who enjoyed consumption as never before in history are entering 'old age'. If the enormous housing equity release of the pre-financial crisis years in the USA is to be taken as a sign of future demand, the new elderly cohort will want to cash their house equity. Much will depend on the evolution of family ties. They have been very resilient and altruism was fuelled by the welfare State (Kohli, 1999); less generosity of the welfare State might erode those intergenerational relationships. On the other hand, LTCI can be purchased to protect the home and avoid its shot-gun selling in case of need. If there were no uncertainty on who dies first, within couples LTCI should be taken up by husbands, who usually are older and have lower life expectancy than their wife, to provide for their wife and allow her to keep the house. Then housing equity release schemes would be mostly used by surviving spouses. It can be predicted that financial products helping to provide cash from home while living in it may be in demand, all the more than they are designed to save the children's inheritance and help face LTC expenses. However, some incentives to residential mobility might be encouraged for those whose housing is clearly inadequate.

Linking LTC to housing and living arrangements compels us to face the fact that the choices are interrelated. The issue is financial, and housing is an important part of income and capital; but it is also one of family relationships. A house is often the symbol of family unity and, ultimately, care has to be provided in a place where you feel 'at home'. For all these reasons, housing is an important element in the management of LTC risk.

Notes

1. It is easy to verify that $1 + r$ with probability 1 is the same as $(1 + r)/(1 - m)$ with probability $1 - m$ + zero with probability m.
2. Moving means losing the tenure discount. Tenure discount arises from two main mechanisms: firstly, rent legislation often controls the rent evolution of sitting tenants, while letting new leases free; secondly, the relation between tenant and

landlord who have built trust over time induces the landlord to ask for a lower rent from a tenant whom he knows well (Hubert, 2006).

3. Including second homes, 16 per cent of those 65+ own some other real estate, ranging from less than 4 per cent in Poland and the Netherlands, around 8 per cent in Germany and Austria, to 26 per cent in Sweden or France and 37 per cent in Greece (author's computation from SHARE data wave 2).

4. The negative renting externality mentioned by Henderson and Ioannides (1983) that makes renting more expensive than buying.

5. Cuellar and Wiener (2000). In the USA Medicare pays for some LTC if delivered in the home: 'home health care' (Engelhard and Greenhalgh-Stanley, 2008). The Netherlands has a public LTCI system which is currently being revised downward (Elbaum, 2008). Scotland has introduced free personal care.

6. In France Duée and Rebillard (2004) estimate that for the 1940–1954 cohorts reaching 60, 29 per cent of men and 52 per cent of women will need LTC for at least one year. Average duration of life in dependency (as this period of care need is currently called in France) is four years.

7. Courbage and Roudaut (2008) find a higher number for France, where 26 per cent of those 50+ claim to have an insurance covering LTC in a nursing home.

8. A favourable tax treatment also contributes to over-investment in housing, all the more that its potential inflationary effect is welcome by elderly homeowners who benefit from it at the expense of young first-time buyers.

9. A move of 'empty nesters' might also be mitigated by their anticipating the possibility of a child coming back or the next stage of having to house a child and partner for short periods of time or grand-children, or even a nurse or care provider in the more distant future. All this, added to transaction costs, deters from moving and downsizing (by diminishing the number of rooms) too brutally.

10. See Costa-Font et al. (2009) and Costa-Font et al. (2010).

11. In the absence of a financial product that would both preserve bequest and pay for LTC, see Ameriks et al. (2009) for the need and design of such a product.

12. 11 per cent of those aged 70 or more let part of their house in Germany, 15 per cent in Switzerland (author's computation from SHARE data wave 2).

13. Chiuri and Jappelli (2010) document the decline in homeownership in old age in many countries.

14. The fact that a smaller dwelling is not proportionally cheaper might be one of the main unavoidable sources of 'over-consumption' of the elderly.

15. Influenced by the Napoleonic Civil Code (France, Belgium, Italy, Spain, Poland, Germany and Austria). Home reversion schemes also exist in Finland, the UK and Ireland (Reifner et al., 2007). See Drosso (2006) for a description of the French system.

16. Such separation existed under Roman law.

17. Usually between 10 per cent and 30 per cent of the house value.

18. Just as LTCI purchase preserves bequests (Courbage and Roudaut, 2008).

19. Sale *in viager* to an heir, while not forbidden is discouraged by the tax authorities that consider the sale as a gift and tax it accordingly. The sale also has to be agreed upon by all *réservataires* heirs (those who legally cannot be disinherited, i.e., the children).

20. Some schemes lie between a sale and a credit operation: shared equity (in the line of shared appreciation mortgages; or shared equity mortgages).

21. Depending on the type of RM, no payment is due until the individual dies, moves out permanently or sells the house (in the US Home Equity Conversion

Mortgage). A fixed term can also be chosen. When one of these events occurs, the borrower or her estate is responsible for repaying the loan in full with any available funds, which may or may not include the house (Eschtruth and Tran, 2001). See also Taffin (2007).

22. It can be the case if the stay in a convalescence home exceeds some limit, which forces the borrower out of her home.

23. In a sale *en viager*, the seller becomes a renter (a tenant with no rent to pay, and who actually receives the annuity), and hence is no more in charge of heavy maintenance, nor of property tax.

24. Home health care is sensitive to public insurance payment (Engelhard et al., 2005). The description of various national care schemes is beyond the scope of this chapter. See other chapters in this volume.

25. Special features include widened doorways, ramps, automatic doors, chair lifts, alerting devices (button alarms) kitchen or bathroom modifications (SHARE survey).

26. Excluding difficulties that they expected to last less than three months, they mentioned three or more of the following: walking 100 metres; sitting for about two hours; getting up from a chair after sitting for long periods; climbing several flights of stairs without resting; stooping, kneeling or crouching; reaching or extending the arms above shoulder level; pulling or pushing large objects like a living room chair; lifting or carrying weights over five kilos, like a heavy bag of groceries; picking up a small coin from a table.

27. Estimation made by the author from the 1999 Census and from Enquête Logement (2002).

28. Author's computation. In England in 2004, 15.7 per cent of those 80+ had no child, and 7.9 per cent co-resided (computed from Table A 7 of Gjonça et al., 2006).

29. Cf. Attias-Donfut and Wolff (2007).

30. Cf. Heiss et al. (2003) for the USA.

31. Is family care cheaper than professional care? Is it better in terms of survival rate and well-being than professional care? Is it detrimental to labour force participation (Fontaine, 2009)?

32. Differential taxation of inheritance and *inter-vivos* gifts also play a role. See below our comments on *Aide personnalisée à l'autonomie* in France.

33. Because of mortality differentials, the oldest old are often the richest of their cohort; it is not without consequences on the decision to take up LTCI or enter into equity release schemes.

References

Ameriks, J., Caplin, A., Laufer, S. and Van Nieuwerburgh, S. (2009) *The Joy of Giving or Assisted Living? Using Strategic Surveys to Separate Public Care Aversion from Bequest Motives*, http://ssrn.com/abstract=982674, date accessed 12 December 2010.

Angelini, V. and Laferrère, A. (2008) 'Home, Houses and Residential Mobility', in A. Börsch-Supan et al. (eds) *Health, Ageing and Retirement in Europe (2004–2007). Starting the Longitudinal Dimension* (Mannheim: Mannheim Research Institute for the Economics of Aging), pp. 99–107.

Attias-Donfut, C. and Wolff, F.-C. (2007) 'Les comportements de transferts intergénérationnels en Europe', *Économie et Statistique*, 403–404, pp. 117–141.

Boehm, T.P. and Ehrhardt, M. (1994) 'Reverse Mortgages and Interest Rate Risk', *Journal of the American Real Estate and Urban Economics Association*, 22 (2), pp. 387–408.

Bonnet, C., Gobillon, L. and Laferrère, A. (2010) 'The Housing and Location Choices of Widows', *Journal of Housing Economics*, 19, pp. 106–120.

Bonsang, E. (2008) 'Does Informal Care from Children to Their Elderly Parents Substitute for Formal Care in Europe?' *Journal of Health Economics*, 28 (1), pp. 143–154.

Brown, J.R. (2007) *Rational and Behavioral Perspectives on the Role of Annuities in Retirement Planning*, NBER Working Paper w13537.

Brown, J.R. and Finkelstein, A. (2007) 'Why is the Market for Long Term Care Insurance So Small'?, *Journal of Public Economics*, 91, pp. 1967–1991.

Brown, J.R. and Finkelstein, A. (2008) 'The Interaction of Public and Private Insurance: Medicaid and the Long-term Care Insurance Market', *American Economic Review*, 98 (3), pp. 1083–1102.

Caplin, A. (2000) *The Reverse Mortgage Market: Problems and Prospects*, Mimeo, 1 June ('Turning Assets into Cash: Problems and Prospects', in Olivia S. Mitchell, Zvi Bodie, Brett Hammond and Steve Zeldes (eds) *Innovations in Retirement Financing*, Philadelphia, PA: University of Pennsylvania Press, pp. 234–253, 2002).

Case, B. and Schnare, A.B. (1994) 'Preliminary Evaluation of the HECM Reverse Mortgage Program', *Journal of the American Real Estate and Urban Economics Association*, 22 (2), pp. 301–346.

Chiuri, M.C. and Jappelli, T. (2010) 'Do the Elderly Reduce Housing Equity? An International Comparison', *Journal of Population Economics*, 23, pp. 643–663.

Costa-Font, J., Elvira, D. and Mascarilla-Miró, O. (2009) ' "Ageing in Place"? Exploring Elderly People's Housing Preferences in Spain', *Urban Studies*, 46 (2), pp. 295–316.

Costa-Font J., Gil, J. and Mascarilla, O. (2010) 'Housing Wealth Decisions in Old Age: Sale and Reversion', *Housing Studies* 25 (3), pp. 375–395.

Courbage, C. and Roudaut, N. (2008) 'Empirical Evidence on Long-term Care Insurance Purchase in France', *The Geneva Papers on Risk and Insurance – Issues and Practice*, 33, pp. 645–658.

Cuellar, A.E. and Wiener, J.M. (2000) 'Can Social Insurance for Long-term Care Work? The Experience of Germany', *Health Affairs*, 19 (3), pp. 8–25.

Davidoff, T. (2004) *Maintenance and the Home Equity of the Elderly*, Fisher Center for Real Estate and Urban Economics Paper 290 (Berkeley, CA: University of California).

Davidoff, T. (2009) 'Housing, Health, and Annuities', *Journal of Risk and Insurance*, 76 (1), pp. 31–52.

Davidoff, T. and Welke, G. (2004) *Selection and Moral Hazard in the Reverse Mortgage Market*, http://strategy.sauder.ubc.ca/davidoff/RMsubmit3.pdf, date accessed 12 December 2010.

Drosso, F. (2006) 'Le viager sort de l'ombre', *Les Annales de la recherche urbaine*, 100, pp. 115–120.

Duée, M. and Rebillard, C. (2004) 'La dépendance des personnes âgées: une projection à 2040', *Données Sociales, la société française*, INSEE, pp. 613–619.

Elbaum, M. (2008) 'Les réformes en matière de handicap et de dépendance: peut-on parler de "cinquième" risque?', *Droit Social*, 11, pp. 1091–1102.

Engelhardt, G.V. and Greenhalgh-Stanley, N. (2008) *Public Long-term Care Insurance and the Housing and Living Arrangements of the Elderly: Evidence from Medicare Home Health Benefits*, CRR Working Paper No. 2008–15 available at SSRN, http://ssrn.com/abstract=1360926, date accessed 12 December 2010.

Engelhardt, G. V., Gruber, J. and Perry, C.D. (2005) 'Social Security and Elderly Living Arrangements', *Journal of Human Resources*, 40 (2), pp. 354–372.

Eschtruth, A.D. and Tran, L.C. (2001) 'A Primer on Reverse Mortgages', *Just the Facts, On Retirement Issues*, Center for Retirement Research at Boston College, 3.

Feinstein, M. (1996) 'Elderly Health, Housing and Mobility', in David Wise (ed.) *Advances in the Economics of Aging*, Chapter 9 (Chicago, IL: University of Chicago Press), pp. 275–320.

Flipo, A., Le Blanc, D. and Laferrère, A. (1999) 'De l'histoire individuelle à la structure des ménages', *Insee Première*, 649.

Fontaine, R. (2009) 'Aider un parent âgé se fait-il au détriment de l'emploi?' *Retraite et Société*, 58, pp. 31–61.

Girardot-Buffard, P. (2009) 'Le patrimoine des ménages retraités', *Insee Références Les revenus et le patrimoine des ménages*, 47–58. http://insee.fr/fr/ffc/docs_ffc/ref/revpmen09d.PDF, date accessed 12 December 2010.

Gjonça, E., Tabassum, F. and Breeze, E. (2006) 'The Socio-Economic Characteristics of the ELSA Population', in James Banks, Elizabeth Breeze, Carli Lessof and James Nazroo (eds) *Retirement, Health and Relationships of the Older Population in England* (London: IFS).

Gobillon, L. and Le Blanc, D. (2004) 'L'impact des contraintes d'emprunt sur la mobilité résidentielle et le choix de statut d'occupation des ménages: un modèle simple de demande', *Annales d'Économie et de Statistiques*, 74, pp. 15–46.

Goetzmann, W.N., Caplin, A., Hangen, E. et al. (2003) *Home Equity Insurance: A Pilot Project*, Yale ICF Working Paper 03–12, available at SSRN, http://ssrn.com/abstract=410141, date accessed 12 December 2010.

Grossman, S.J. and Laroque, G. (1990) 'Asset Pricing and Optimal Portfolio Choice in the Presence of Illiquid Durable Consumption Goods', *Econometrica*, 58, pp. 25–51.

Heiss, F., Hurd, M.D. and Börsch-Supan, A.H. (2003) *Healthy, Wealthy, and Knowing Where to Live: Trajectories of Health, Wealth and Living Arrangements Among the Oldest Old*, NBER Working Paper W9897.

Henderson, J.V. and Ioannides, Y.M. (1983) 'A Model of Housing Tenure Choice', *American Economic Review*, 73, pp. 98–113.

Hubert, F. (2006) 'The Economic Theory of Housing Tenure Choice', in R.J. Arnott and D.P. McMillan (eds) *A Companion to Urban Economics* (Oxford: Blackwell Publishing), pp. 145–158.

Khandani, A., Lo, A.W. and Merton, R.C. (2009) *Systemic Risk and the Refinancing Ratchet Effect*, NBER Working Paper 15362.

Kohli, M. (1999) 'Private and Public Transfers between Generations: Linking the Family and the State', *European Societies*, 1, pp. 81–104.

Konrad, K.A., Künemund, H., Lommerud, K.E. and Robledo, J.R. (2002) 'Geography of the Family', *American Economic Review*, 92 (4), pp. 981–998.

Laferrère, A. (1999) 'Intergenerational Transmission Models: A Survey', *The Geneva Papers on Risk and Insurance – Issues and Practice*, 24 (1), pp. 2–26.

Laferrère, A. (2006) 'Vieillesse et logement: désépargne, adaptation de la consommation et rôle des enfants', *Retraite et Société*, 47, pp. 66–108.

Laferrère, A. and Angelini, V. (2009) 'La mobilité résidentielle des seniors en Europe', *Retraite et Société*, 58, pp. 87–107.

Laferrère, A. and Wolff, F.C. (2006) 'Microeconomics Models of Family Transfers', in S.-K. Kolm and J. Mercier-Ytier (eds) *Handbook on the Economics of Giving, Reciprocity and Altruism*, chapter 12 (Amsterdam: North Holland/Elsevier), pp. 17–40.

Mankiw, G.N. and Weil, D. (1989) 'The Baby Boom, the Baby Bust, and the Housing Market', *Regional Science and Urban Economics*, 19, pp. 235–258.

McMunn, A., Nazroo, J., Wahrendorf, M., Breeze, E. and Zaninotto, P. (2009) 'Participation in Socially-Productive Activities, Reciprocity and Wellbeing in Later Life: Baseline Results in England', *Ageing and Society*, 29, pp. 765–782.

Pelizzon, L. and Weber, G. (2009) 'Efficient Portfolio when Housing Needs Change over the Life-Cycle', *Journal of Banking and Finance*, 33, 11, pp. 2110–2121.

Plisson, M. (2009) 'Le marché de l'assurance dépendance', *Risques*, 78, pp. 120–125.

Reifner, U., Clerc-Renaud, S., Pérez-Carillo, E., Tiffe, A. and Knobloch, M. (2007) *Study on Equity Release Schemes in the EU*, Part III, Annexes (Hamburg: Institut für Finanzdienstleistungen e.V. Hamburg).

Shore, S. and Sinai, T. (2005) *Commitment, Risk, and Consumption: Do Birds of a Feather have Bigger Nests?* NBER Working Paper 11588.

Sinai, T. and Souleles, S. (2005) 'Owner-Occupied Housing as a Hedge Against Rent Risk', *Quarterly Journal of Economics*, 120, pp. 763–789.

Skinner, J. (1996) 'Is Housing Wealth a Sideshow?', in D. Wise (ed.) *Advances in the Economics of Aging*, NBER Project Report (Chicago, IL: University of Chicago Press).

Szymanoski, E., Enriquez, J.C. and DiVenti, T.R. (2007) 'Home Equity Conversion Mortgage Terminations: Information to Enhance the Developing Secondary Market', *Cityscape*, 9 (1), pp. 5–45.

Taffin, C. (2007) 'Le prêt viager hypothécaire', in C. Bonvallet, F. Drosso, F. Benguigui and M. Huynh M. (eds) *Vieillissement de la population et logement, Les stratégies résidentielles et patrimoniale* (Paris: PUCA, La Documentation Française), pp. 473–484.

Venti, S.F. and Wise, D.A. (1991) 'Aging and the Income Value of Housing Wealth', *Journal of Public Economics*, 44, pp. 371–397.

Venti, S.F. and Wise, D.A. (2001) *Aging and Housing Equity: Another Look*, NBER Working Paper 8608.

Wahrendorf, M., von dem Knesebeck, O. and Siegrist, J. (2006) 'Social Productivity and Well-being of Older People: Baseline Results from the SHARE Study', *European Journal of Ageing*, 3 (2), pp. 67–73.

Wang, L., Valdez, E. and Piggott, J. (2007) *Securitization of Longevity Risk in Reverse Mortgages*, Working paper, available at SSRN, http://ssrn.com/abstract=1087549, date accessed 12 December 2010.

Zweifel, P. and Strüwe, W. (1996) 'Long Term Care Insurance and Bequests as Instrument for Shaping Intergenerational Relationships', *Journal of Risk and Uncertainty*, 12, pp. 65–76.

6
Long-Term Care Insurance: Partnership or Crowding Out?

Joan Costa-Font
London School of Economics and Political Science, United Kingdom

and

Christophe Courbage
The Geneva Association, Switzerland

1 Introduction

The design of long-term care[1] (LTC) financing schemes is slowing down the transformation of protection and insurance structures that address the problems of old-age care. Most of these are not new, but highly entrenched in the organization of modern society and in State intervention in the area of welfare. However, to date there are good reasons to believe that demand triggers are markedly exacerbated by the rapid ageing of the European populations together with the transformation of family structures, and its associated norms that impinge effects on caregiving duties. The latter encompasses the redefinition of traditional intergenerational contracts in place to provide 'support for care'. However, the expansion of public insurance alone, the solution that was prevalent in the times of the so-called 'golden age of the welfare State', is not viable any more today. Indeed, public schemes face significant constraints to the expansion of welfare services that are not always perceived as welfare-improving. Similarly, current pressures to cut down excessive public expenditure do nothing but exacerbate the already tight constraints to the expansion of public insurance. On the other hand, the solution of pre-welfare State times, based on family caregiving, is not a satisfactory arrangement given the constraints of modern life unless it is complemented by State and market alternatives.

Notwithstanding existing constraints, the resulting paradox lies in that the market for LTC insurance remains stagnant in most European countries, and even fails to thrive in countries with a tradition of voluntary health insurance market purchase. As an illustration, only 1 per cent of LTC expenditures are paid by private insurance in France (Rosso-Debord, 2010).

As we explain in the lines to come, this phenomenon qualifies as that of either State or family crowding out (Pauly, 1990; Costa-Font, 2010), that is, the phenomenon whereby the existence of public insurance schemes or informal insurance arrangements through family reduce the development of private coverage. Against the evidence of crowding out, we contend that partnership models can potentially stand out to be welfare-improving. This chapter examines the interaction between the public and private sectors together with informal care in the financing of LTC. We focus on the role of partnership models as an alternative to the development of either State or family crowding out. Furthermore, we report evidence as to how partnership alternatives work, their prospects and limitations.

In the following section we provide further background to contextualize the LTC financing problem based on the coordination of State, markets and society. Section 3 recalls the broader and specific understandings of public–private partnership (PPP) arrangements. In Section 4, we briefly present the roles of both the public and private sectors in financing LTC. Finally, Section 5 provides some illustrations of PPP in financing LTC coverage and Section 6 concludes.

2 Background

2.1 The LTC financing problem

Finding a solution to the coordination processes that are necessary to resolve the provision of LTC to the old-age dependant, and the underpinning financial arrangements, is a key institutional design question in modern societies. The magnitude of the organization of LTC financing depends on the extent of demand, but also on the *status quo* and market development.

The *status quo* in a pre-welfare State world is that of the family providing care in an integrated form to its old-age elderly. However, the existing transformations of implicit family contracts cannot be assumed as valid any more, and cannot be fully anticipated today. European data show that a significant proportion of Europeans (Eurobarometer, 2007) assume that family households would take care of individuals, either because the family was at that time the unit of organization or through some form of familism, that is, the social structure form in which the needs of the family as a group are more important than the needs of any individual family member (Costa-Font, 2010). Familism remains to a certain extent important in Europe, and hence, individuals, demand for LTC services is not only based on need, but on the intergenerational transmission of preferences.[2]

In addition to family restrictions, market mechanisms are inhibited by the role of the government in providing for LTC, which some argue is systematically more efficient (Barr, 2004), if some form of social insurance is developed. Similarly, the perception that the government, due to its welfare State contract, is responsible for any need of care in old age, does exert an influence that acts against the development of products that would otherwise be perceived as welfare-improving. Expectations of State bailout of LTC needs if individual income and wealth stand below a minimum threshold are largely shared by the general population. Finally, public insurance alone might be perceived as giving rise to moral hazard, which makes full insurance suboptimal (Brown and Finkelstein, 2009). It also happens that deadweight loss of taxes also exerts an influence.

Limited demand for private insurance is in part associated with supply constraints, which include inefficient pricing explaining high mark-ups, adverse selection and moral hazard (Brown and Finkelstein, 2007). Given the novelty of LTC needs, individuals also have limited experience. Similarly, cognitive biases include 'denial aversion' of individuals to think about events that are expected to affect barely 30 per cent of individuals aged 65 and over and that are perceived as undesirable, and the systematic overestimation of low-probability, high-loss events (Kunreuther, 1978). LTC insurance is purchased by 20 per cent of more affluent individuals in the USA, and especially among those between 70 and 80 years of age (Brown and Finkelstein, 2009). Altogether, private information that individuals have on their individual need for LTC is such that it acts against their decision to purchase insurance, as premiums are perceived, perhaps due to optimism and due to overprice, as not being welfare-improving.

All these differences, namely, the extent of State or family crowding out, as well as supply and demand constraints, explain that officially, following OECD (2005) estimates, LTC expenditures range from 0.2 per cent of GDP in Portugal to 3.3 per cent in Sweden. The underpinning rationale for such cross-country differences lies in the specific interaction of the informal, public and private sectors in each country.

2.2 Interaction of public and private sectors

The interaction of the public sector, together with the market and non-market private sector, is common practice throughout Europe. For instance, in the UK the Green Paper integrates private finance proposals as complements of government activity (Mayhew et al., 2010). However, in considering the interaction of different potential providers and financial sources, one should take into consideration the set of restrictions in terms of level of information, perceptions of uncertainty, knowledge of existing providers and their quality and, finally, existing values and cultural priors that determine people's actions.

A fully free system funded by taxes can potentially pose disincentives for informal care and can arguably lead to some form of crowding out (Pauly, 1990), although there is no robust empirical evidence suggesting the existence of public insurance crowding out. However, full public coverage for LTC could provide *ex post* moral hazard problems in that individuals would expect all components of care associated with caring in old age to be publicly paid, which in turn might trigger an escalation of public outlays. Similarly, it is possible to argue that a tax-funded system would not be fair for people who have saved for their old age (Mayhew et al., 2010) and, income and wealth cost sharing would be a system that penalizes individuals' savings. The obvious advantage is that it would manage to expand the financial basis, would be simple and comprehensive as well as face lower administrative costs than other systems. Finally, whilst some components of what typically falls within services that provide LTC for the elderly are social or merit goods (e.g., financial old age security), other components (e.g., meals, hotel amenities and so on) are potentially luxury goods which weaken insurance or redistribution gains from public intervention.

In the same way, a system based on no State intervention with limited market development is likely to lead to family crowding out. Indeed, different forms of social institutions to provide a solution to the need to finance LTC are in place before markets develop. This is especially relevant in those countries where economic liberalization is a more recent phenomenon, such as Eastern Europe and Mediterranean economies. Hence, as we argue in the section to follow, partnerships stand out as an alternative to crowding out.

3 Partnership building

3.1 PPPs

PPPs are usually geared towards the creation of a social good, such as education or health, which have both a financing and provision dimension. Financing concerns how to pay for the good while provision concerns how the good will be produced or delivered. Responsibility for either dimension may be allocated partially or wholly to the public or private sectors. Public financing involves collective financing – for instance, through taxation or social insurance; private financing involves individuals or private sector bodies using their own resources. In the same way, partnerships can be integrated from non-governmental sources, such as for-profit-firms, and non-profit entities. Hence, PPPs can take various configurations, yet we will focus exclusively on the financing dimension of PPPs.

As stressed in various works, PPPs are far from new, though there is renewed interest in them due to a recent trend towards privatization. Generally speaking, private financing may come in the form of out-of-pocket spending by individuals, or it may be systematized into financial products such as insurance. Unlike contracting-out PPPs, which often derive from privatization impulses, joint-financing PPPs are set up from a desire to take advantage of multiple sources of financing. Hence PPP can be linked to various activities, whether this is in terms of insurer provider, health financing method, government support to private insurance development or government regulation of private insurers (may be similar to public insurance). In that respect, government decision in PPPs can take three forms.

Governments can prioritize the type of risks that are to be publicly financed, leaving others to be privately insured or self-paid. Second, policy makers can make explicit decisions about the permitted roles of private insurance. Third, governments can influence the structure of regulation of health delivery systems, which also shapes private insurance roles.

3.2 Social partnership

Insofar as partnerships exist between the market and State policies, one could well envisage a specific partnership between state and the family and civil society. The latter would encompass the development of arrangements that incorporate key existing informal institutions in the redelivery of public services and in the design of market products.

For instance, with regards to informal care, some countries began making payments directly to informal caregivers, such as Norway and Denmark, allowing relatives and neighbours who are providing regular home care to become municipal employees, complete with regular pension benefits. Also in Finland, informal caregivers receive a fixed fee from municipalities as well as pension payments. A number of countries with social health insurance such as Austria, Germany and Luxembourg have also started to provide cash payments to service recipients, who could then use those funds to pay informal caregivers. In Germany, the LTC fund may also make pension contributions if an informal caregiver works more than 14 hours per week. In Switzerland, time devoted to caregiving of a relative can be taken into account in the determination of the retirement and survivor benefits, as long as the caregiver and care recipient live together.

4 Financial partnerships and crowding out

4.1 Forms of interaction

The role of private insurance with respect to public insurance is not unique and depends on the institutional setting. In particular it depends first upon whether individuals buying private insurance are also eligible for part of the public insurance systems; and second, whether private insurance offers cover LTC services that are already covered by public insurance. Thus, the PPPs depend crucially on the role of private insurance and on the type of care covered.

Following the OECD (2004), private insurance can be categorized into four different roles when it comes to financing health care. Private insurance plays a leading role in financing health care in a few countries and a supporting role in many others. In countries where private insurance is the main way of financing care, this is the case because people are either not eligible for public insurance or because they have chosen to opt out of such a cover. In other countries with universal health cover for basic care, private insurance has either a duplicate, supplementary or complementary function. Duplicate coverage means that private insurance parallels some or all of the cover guaranteed by public insurance, which is typically the result of limited satisfaction of perceived quality by public health services. Supplementary cover means that private insurance offers additional services not covered by public schemes. Finally, complementary cover is equivalent to insurance complementing public insured services, which only pays a proportion of the health cost by covering all or part of the residual costs not otherwise reimbursed. While this classification applies for health insurance, it could also apply to LTC insurance.

Not only public and private insurance interact in the financing of formal care, they also interact with respect to informal care. Formal care financing works as in the case for classic health insurance. With regards to informal care, as stated before, several European countries already provide various types of public help to informal caregivers. Also, private insurers, especially in France, offer cash benefit payments in case of dependency that can be used freely to pay for both informal and formal caregivers.

4.2   Crowding out

A growing literature has addressed the issue of crowding out, that is, a phenomenon taking place when the expansion of public coverage reduces the development of private coverage. What characterizes the phenomenon is whether the public system is a primary or a secondary payer. If it is a primary payer, the public system does not take into account private insurance benefits when means-testing benefits. Instead, private insurance tends to top up the public entitlement, as happens in France. In contrast, if public insurance is a secondary payer, insurance benefits are paid first. It then often happens that people who buy insurance may be 'pushed' over the means test, even if they would have been eligible otherwise.

A classic illustration comes from the US case, and in particular Medicaid. Medicaid is a means-tested health care programme that is jointly funded by the federal and State governments and administered by the States. It is the accidental public payment for LTC, as it was originally intended to provide care for the poor. Yet, about one-third of Medicaid's budget is devoted to LTC expenses, primarily in nursing homes. Medicaid's large crowd-out effect stems from the combination of means-tested eligibility and its secondary payer status for individuals with private insurance. As a result of these two features, a large part of the premium for a private policy pays for benefits that simply replace benefits that Medicaid would otherwise have provided, a phenomenon that Brown and Finkelstein (2008) label the Medicaid 'implicit tax'. As long as Medicaid remains means-tested, private insurance, by protecting assets, reduces the probability of being eligible for Medicaid. As long as Medicaid remains a secondary payer, private insurance benefits reduce Medicaid benefits one-for-one, even if eligible for Medicaid.

To address these issues, the US Congress approved in February 2006 a legislation clearing the way for an expanded nationwide public–private LTC insurance partnership. The law authorizes changes in State law to allow individuals to purchase private LTC insurance that coordinates with Medicaid. Specifically, in States adopting the partnership approach, individuals can purchase private LTC insurance policies with the assurance that Medicaid will cover LTC costs incurred beyond the terms of the private coverage. Under the terms of the partnership, people with private LTC insurance are not required to spend their remaining assets to qualify for Medicaid. Hence this PPP between States and private insurance companies is designed to reduce Medicaid expenditures by delaying or eliminating the need for some people to rely on Medicaid to pay for LTC services.

5 Partnership illustrations in financing LTC coverage

5.1 Partnership building policies

In Europe, there exists an extended collaboration between insurance markets and the welfare State. The question to ask is which form such collaboration should take in the field of LTC. Both theoretically and in policy experience, the public sector can promote the development of LTC insurance from both the demand and supply sides. On the demand side, the government can offer tax relief on both LTC expenditure and LTC insurance premiums. Individuals can deduct a portion of their LTC expenses, including premium, of their gross income. This can take the form of either tax deductions or tax credits. Of course the effect should strongly depend on the level of price elasticity. In the same way, government could subsidize premiums for low-income subscribers, as is the case for private health insurance in various countries.

The government can act also indirectly by raising awareness about the risk of needing LTC in the future. For instance, in France, it seems that national debates associated with the search for new solutions to cover the risk of LTC need, widely covered in the press, have increased the general public's awareness of the existence of this risk. Since people are becoming more aware of the LTC risk, and they are also becoming more concerned about its financing and coverage. This has supported the development of private insurance, as stressed by Durand and Taleyson (2003). The CLASS Act in the USA, the new federal Community Living Assistance Services and Support Act, should also be an illustration of these phenomena as the federal government will spend millions of dollars to raise the awareness that people need to plan for LTC. This will undeniably contribute to inform people about the role of insurance in protecting against LTC risks.

5.2 Partnership and cost sharing

Another illustration of PPP in LTC financing could be to base the partnership on the level of severity of dependency, under which the heavy level of dependency could be dissociated from what is called moderate or 'light' dependency. The underlying idea is that the light dependency deals with a majority of individuals and can be considered more like a stage of life and regular expenses than a risk itself. Only the state of heavy dependency would be considered as a risk and would only be covered by private insurance. Light dependency could then be taken over either by a social assistance scheme for the poorest, or by individual savings accumulated over the working life for others and subject to higher levels of cost sharing. This solution is of relevance in terms of market efficiency, since heavy dependency is a risk that can be easier to identify than light dependency. In addition, moral hazard is less possible in the case of heavy dependency, while it may happen more easily in the case of light dependency.

Based on this idea, Kessler (2010) suggests even not making private LTC insurance mandatory. Any person losing autonomy would be eligible for a public LTC benefit subject to cost sharing. However, only those whose resources are insufficient would be able to benefit free of charge. For the others, a cost sharing increasing in line with the household's resources would be required in order to dissuade free-riders. This of course would necessitate a harmonization or coordination of the scale on which LTC is evaluated by both the public and private sectors. Kessler (2010) also suggests going beyond a simple tax exemption and providing a refundable tax credit which would allow all households, irrespective of their level of income and their marginal tax rate, to benefit from the same ratio of tax support. In the same way, the benefit paid in the event of LTC would also be exempt from income tax and social contributions, up to a certain limit, since it is not supposed to be a replacement income.

However, this raises at least two difficulties. First, it requires a clear distinction between heavy dependency and light dependency to be made explicit. Second, it delays the financing of dependency and curtails the coverage to the 85 per cent of cases with lighter dependency. Hence, there is scope here for forms of implicit or explicit partnership.

5.3   Government as regulator to private insurance

The existence of market failures calls for regulation to be put in place in Europe, either by national or Europeans bodies. Yet, an important reason for this regulation is to protect consumers by informing them and more generally protecting tax payers against default of an insurance company to fulfil its engagement, that is, it offers a protection against insurance insolvability. Solvency protection measures are, above all, aimed at providing incentives to firms to follow sound policies. Following Baltensperger et al. (2008), instruments of solvency regulation can include a variety of measures, such as product and price regulation, portfolio investment restrictions, mandatory (re)insurance, emergency insurance funds, capital and reserve regulation, market entry control, general supervision and inspection. Another reason for regulation is to fight against market failure due to information imperfections. The resulting phenomena of moral hazard and adverse selection have long been known in the literature as potential sources of welfare loss. Such market imperfection has a cost that needs to be borne by some parties.

However, whilst such rules protect the consumer, they can also lead to adverse effects and even increase the risk of insolvency. For instance, product regulation refers to setting up regulations governing the admissibility of a specific contract. Some of these rules may be restrictive in the sense that they can impose high costs on the market and consumers. This is also the case for specific portfolio investment restrictions.[3] It is not strange that insurance regulation tends towards a less intrusive control. Numerous national legislators have abandoned individual insurance products as the object of regulation. The focus of regulation has shifted to ensuring institutional solvency in general. The most important instrument is a generalized capital and reserve regulation, possibly supplemented by additional supervisory rules such as investment restrictions and regular inspections. More generally, this trend is reflected in Europe by the European Union's Solvency II initiative.

5.4 Government as a reinsurer for private insurance companies

For some high-loss, low-probability events, governments are more likely to act as reinsurers for private insurance companies. This is especially the case for natural catastrophic events. In such a case, the government would merely intervene to support insurance markets where their capacity would fail. One advantage is that the government has the capacity to diversify the risks over the entire population and to spread past losses to future generations. Yet the government would provide reinsurance at a lower price than the market, which could be counterproductive in terms of market efficiency. In the health and LTC insurance markets, such a solution has not been implemented yet, but this could be a possibility for the future that could fit a partnership model.

6 Conclusion

Limited market for LTC insurance lies in the imperfect partnership between family, government and markets. The existence of both State and family crowding out suggests that in the past collaboration between these bodies in different countries has not taken place or, when it has, it has not been as efficient as one might have expected. Family, government and the market have different roles in the provision and financing of LTC. While these roles may substitute each other leading to some forms of crowding out, they can also complement each other leading to partnership. The question is then to implement the right incentives to develop partnership over crowding out. This chapter has tried to provide some insights on these issues.

There are different models whereby partnerships can be established, including delisting of coverage of certain services, the introduction of different levels of dependency by need of economic means as well as through regulation or reinsurance. Evidence from all European countries reported in this book suggests that all these different systems are either implemented or available solutions to be considered seriously.

Notes

1. Long-term care refers to a variety of services which are intended to assist both the medical and social needs of people suffering from a loss of mobility and autonomy in their activity of daily living and who cannot care for themselves for long periods of time.
2. Hence, only care provided by formal providers is typically externalized to either community services financed by the State or by market mechanisms and not-for-profit organizations.
3. The exclusion or the mandatory inclusion of particular forms of assets can reduce diversification possibilities and could then even increase insolvency risk.

References

Baltensperger, E., Buomberger, A., Luppa, A., Keller, B. and Wicki, A. (2008) 'Regulation and Intervention in the Insurance Industry – Fundamental Issues', *The Geneva Reports*, No.1.

Barr, N. (2004) *Economics of the Welfare State* (Oxford: Oxford University Press).

Brown, J.R. and Finkelstein, A. (2007) 'Why is the Market for Long-term Care Insurance So Small?', *Journal of Public Economics*, 91, pp. 1967–1991.

Brown, J.R. and Finkelstein, A. (2008) 'The Interaction of Public and Private Insurance: Medicaid and the Long-term Insurance Market', *American Economic Review*, 98 (3), pp. 1083–1102.

Brown, J.R. and Finkelstein, A. (2009) 'The Private Market for Long Term Care Insurance in the United States: A Review of the Evidence', *The Journal of Risk and Insurance*, 76, pp. 5–29.

Costa-Font, J. (2010) 'Family Ties and the Crowding Out of Long Term Care Insurance,' *Oxford Review of Economic Policy*, 26 (4), pp. 691–712.

Durand, R. and Taleyson, L. (2003) 'Les raisons du succès de l'assurance dépendance en France', *Risques – Les Cahiers de l'Assurance*, 55, pp. 115–120.

Eurobarometer (2007) Special EUROBAROMETER 283, Brussels.

Kessler, D. (2010) 'Confronting the Challenge of Long-term Care in Europe', *CESifo DICE Report*, No. 2, pp. 18–23.

Kunreuther, H. (1978) *Disaster Insurance Protection: Public Policy Lessons* (New York: Wiley).

Mayhew, L., Karlsson, M. and Rickayzen, B. (2010) 'The Role of Private Finance in Paying for Long Term Care', *Economic Journal*, 120, pp. F478–F504.

OECD (2004) *Private Health Insurance in OECD Countries* (Paris: OECD).

OECD (2005) *Long-term Care for Older People* (Paris: OECD).

Pauly, M.V. (1990) 'The Rational Nonpurchase of Long-term Care Insurance', *Journal of Political Economy*, 98, pp. 153–168.

Rosso-Debord, V. (2010) *Rapport d'information sur la prise en charge des personnes âgées dépendantes*, Rapport de l'Assemblée Nationale (Paris: Assemblée Nationale).

Part III
Models

7
Long-Term Care Insurance in the Netherlands*

Frederik T. Schut
Department of Health Policy and Management, Erasmus University Rotterdam,
the Netherlands

and

Bernard van den Berg
Centre for Health Economics, University of York, United Kingdom

1 Introduction

The Netherlands was the first country to introduce a universal mandatory
social health insurance scheme (AWBZ) for covering a broad range of long-
term care (LTC) services provided in a variety of care settings. Compared
with most other Organization for Economic Cooperation and Development
(OECD) countries, coverage of LTC services is relatively comprehensive.
This comprehensive coverage might explain why, in comparison with most
other OECD countries, both total and public expenditure on LTC in the
Netherlands are high, particularly since the percentage of elderly is similar to the OECD average (OECD, 2005). This can at least partly be explained
by the relatively generous social health insurance scheme.

Nevertheless, the growth of public spending on health and LTC in the
Netherlands was fairly successfully limited until 2000 via the implementation of cost-containment policies. These policies acted essentially through
the rationing of supply, wage moderation, price controls and postponement
of investment in LTC facilities. However, increasing waiting lists and rising consumer expectations about the quality and variety of LTC services
have substantially reduced the scope for containing LTC expenditures along
these lines. Hence, the Dutch government is aiming to reform the current
LTC financing system to increase incentives for efficiency and consumer
direction.

The main aims of this chapter are (1) to describe the background, current deficiencies and proposals to reform the system of LTC financing in
the Netherlands; and (2) to discuss whether the proposed reforms can create

incentives to keep the comprehensive LTC insurance scheme sustainable in view of the ageing of the population and the expected increase in demand for LTC services.

The second section provides a short background of the Dutch public health insurance scheme. In the third section, we discuss the main features of the current public insurance scheme. In the fourth section we analyse the empirical evidence on the growth of public expenditure on LTC over the period 1985–2005. The subsequent section describes the relation between professional and informal care. Then, we specifically focus on the implications of the introduction of the personal care budgets to increase consumer direction and choice, including consequences for informal care. Subsequently we discuss the projections and determinants of future long-term expenditure growth. Next, we discuss the shortcomings of the current system of LTC financing and the proposals for reforming the system. Finally, we discuss the prospects of the reform and the questions that remain to be answered.

Since a uniform definition is lacking, we will first indicate what we mean by LTC. Often, the term LTC is used only in the context of elderly care. In this chapter, however, we use a more comprehensive definition, also including care for the mentally and physically handicapped and care for chronic psychiatric patients. This definition coincides with the types of services covered by the public insurance scheme for LTC in the Netherlands.

2   Background of public LTC insurance

The Netherlands was the first country to introduce a universal mandatory social health insurance scheme (the Exceptional Medical Expenses Act – AWBZ) for covering a broad range of LTC services provided in a variety of care settings. Whereas in the Netherlands public LTC insurance was already introduced in 1968, other countries followed only quite recently, such as Germany in 1995 (Rothgang, 2010) and Japan in 2000 (Ikegami, 2007).

Initially, the AWBZ covered primarily nursing home care, institutionalized care for the mentally handicapped and hospital admissions lasting more than a year. In due course, however, coverage was expanded by including home health care (e.g., for rehabilitation at home after hospital admission and care for the elderly with impairments, in 1980), ambulatory mental health care (in 1982), family care (e.g., home help in the case of frailty, psychosocial problems or after childbirth, in 1989) and residential care for the elderly (1997). In homes for the elderly (residential care), residents receive nursing care less frequently and intensively than residents in nursing homes. Moreover, residents in elderly homes have their own apartments, while residents in nursing homes usually share a room with one or more other residents.

It is worth noting that there is no supplementary LTC insurance market in the Netherlands. This is probably due to the fact that public LTC insurance

is quite comprehensive. In the past, several insurers have attempted to introduce supplementary LTC insurance policies, but failed because of a lack of
demand.

3 Main features of public LTC insurance (AWBZ)

The AWBZ constitutes a mandatory insurance scheme for LTC for the entire
Dutch population. Every Dutch citizen older than 15 years of age with a
taxable income has to pay an income-related contribution (up to a certain
maximum amount) that is collected through the income and payroll tax systems, along with the contributions for the other national insurance schemes
(e.g., for unemployment and disability). In addition, for most LTC services
covered by the AWBZ, income-related co-payments are required. For higher-
income groups the maximum co-payment can be so high (about €1800
per month for residential care) that private facilities are often more attractive. Income-related contributions, co-payments as well as an annual State
subsidy are collected in a General Fund (AFBZ).

Table 7.1 provides an overview of the different sources of funding of the
AWBZ in 2008. Since in the same year the total expenditures from the General Fund were €21.4 billion, there was an overall deficit of €2.1 billion
(to be compensated by an extra increase in the 2009 contribution rate).
As shown in Table 7.1, more than 75 per cent of the AWBZ is financed
directly by households, while the residual amount is paid by the State out
of general taxes. Table 7.2 provides an overview of the most important
categories of LTC users and their relative share in LTC expenditure.

Formally, the AWBZ is administered by health care insurers that provide coverage for curative health services. In practice, however, health care
insurers have delegated various responsibilities – in particular the contracting of health care providers, the collection of patient contributions and the

Table 7.1 Funding of the AWBZ scheme in 2008

Sources of funding	Payments (€ billion)	Share of total payments (%)
Income-related contributions*	13.1	68
Co-payments	1.7	9
State subsidy (from general taxation)	4.6	24
Total	19.3	100

Note: *In 2008 the income-related contribution was 12.15 per cent of a maximum of €31,589 taxable income (implying a maximum contribution of €3838 per year, exclusive of various possible
tax deductions).
Source: SER (2008), p. 31.

Table 7.2 Different groups of AWBZ beneficiaries by numbers and expenditures in 2007*

Type of LTC user	Number	Share of total number (%)	Expenditure (€ billion)	Share of total expenditure (%)
Elderly and chronically ill	360,000	69	11.4	65
Mentally handicapped persons	100,000	19	4.6	26
Physically handicapped persons	15,000	3	0.5	3
Chronic psychiatric patients	50,000	9	1.1	6
Total	525,000	100	17.6	100

Note: *Excluding about 90,000 clients with a personal care budget (expenditure €1.3 billion).
Source: SER (2008), p. 34.

organization of regional consultations – to the largest regional health care insurer. At present the Netherlands is divided into 32 care regions, and in each region a single health insurer (known as 'regional care office') carries out the AWBZ on behalf of all health insurers for all residents living in that region. Regional care offices receive a fixed budget for the administrative tasks. All LTC expenses are directly paid out of the General Fund (AFBZ). Hence, neither regional care offices nor individual health insurers are at risk of long-term expenses covered by the AWBZ scheme.

Before a person can qualify for care under the AWBZ, it is necessary to establish whether care is really required and, if so, what type of care and how much care is needed. Initially, health care providers were responsible for the required needs assessment, but in 1997 this task was assigned to regional independent needs assessment organizations, and since 2005 to a single national organization, the Centre for Needs Assessment (CIZ).[1] The idea behind this was to make needs assessment more objective and uniform and independent from the self-interest of health care providers. Notice that the access to LTC is solely based on a person's health – as in Germany and Japan – and does not depend on his income or wealth – like the Medicaid programme in the USA.[2]

Prior to 2003, the LTC benefits covered by the AWBZ scheme were defined in terms of the type of care or the type of health care provider to which people were entitled. To encourage innovation, consumer choice and an efficient substitution of LTC services, in 2003 the definition of entitlements was radically changed into seven broad functional care categories. In 2007, one of these categories – domiciliary care – was excluded from coverage and transferred to the responsibility of the municipalities under a new Social Support Act (WMO). The remaining six functional categories of LTC services that were covered under the AWBZ scheme in 2008 are summarized in Box 7.1.³

Box 7.1   Functional categories of care covered by AWBZ

1. *Personal care*: for example, help with taking a shower, bed baths, dressing, shaving, skin care, going to the toilet, eating and drinking.
2. *Nursing*: for example, dressing wounds, giving injections, advising on how to cope with illness, showing clients how to self-inject.
3. *Supportive guidance*: for example, helping the client organize his or her day and manage his or her life better, as well as day care or provision of daytime activities.
4. *Activating guidance*: for example, talking to the client to help him modify his behaviour or learn new forms of behaviour in cases where behavioural or psychological problems exist.
5. *Treatment*: for example, care in connection with an ailment, such as serious absent-mindedness.
6. *Accommodation*: for example, some people are not capable of living independent lives, but require, for example, sheltered housing or continuous supervision in connection with serious absent-mindedness. In some cases, a client's care requirements may be too great to address in a home environment, making admission to an institution necessary.

Except for the functional category 'accommodation', clients who are entitled to care have a choice of receiving care 'in kind' or in the form of a *personal care budget* (or a combination of both). The personal care budget is set at about 75 per cent of the average cost of care provided 'in kind', because the personal care budget can be spent on informal care which is expected to be less expensive than professional formal care.

4   Expansion of LTC services and expenditure, 1968–2005

The enactment and gradual expansion of AWBZ paved the way for a strong growth of both LTC facilities and public expenditure on LTC. The percentage of GDP spent on long-term services covered by AWBZ increased from 0.8 per cent in 1968 to 2.0 per cent in 1980, and further to 4.0 per cent in 2005. Part of this increase, however, is due to an expansion of AWBZ coverage.

As shown in Figure 7.1, from 1985 to 2000, the percentage of GDP spent on LTC services that were covered by AWBZ in 2000 was more or less stable, at around 3.5 per cent (in 1985, however, only 2.0 per cent was covered

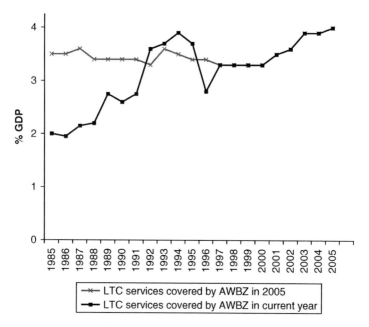

Figure 7.1   Percentage of GDP spent on LTC services covered by AWBZ in the current year and in 2005, 1985–2005*

Note: * From 1997 to 2005 the LTC services covered by AWBZ were the same as in 2005, so both lines overlap. The bubble in the dark plotted line from 1992 to 1995 is caused by a temporary inclusion of outpatient drugs in the AWBZ benefits package.
Source: Ministry of Health (2004) and Eggink et al. (2008).

by AWBZ and 1.5 per cent was financed in other ways). Hence, taking into account the expansion of AWBZ coverage, the expenditure on LTC services as a percentage of GDP has been quite constant over a considerable period of time. This is remarkable given the ageing of the population (albeit fairly moderate during that period) and the susceptibility of LTC to Baumol's cost disease due to the limited scope for productivity gains in the provision of LTC (Oliviera Martins and de la Maisonneuve, 2006). Baumol (1967) distinguished two sectors in the economy. In the first sector relatively straightforward technical innovations result in labour productivity growth, while in the second labour productivity growth seems less straightforward because of the nature of production. Examples of the latter include education and LTC. These are inevitably labour intensive because of the nature of the provided services. Despite the introduction of new technologies in the area of healthy ageing, the quality of many LTC services is likely to remain highly dependent on the input of labour. Therefore the scope of substituting capital for labour is limited.[4]

The main reason for the limited growth of public spending on LTC has been the implementation of cost-containment policies. Since the 1970s the entry and capacity of new LTC institutions has been strictly regulated. For building and major investments in facilities a licence from the government was required, and only if investments were judged to be of sufficient priority was such a licence granted. Particularly important, however, was the introduction in 1984 of a system of global budgeting for all inpatient long-term health services. In addition, especially during the 1980s, the government successfully mitigated the wages of nursing personnel. In the 1990s, prompted by an economic recession, the budgetary controls were expanded to comprise home health care and other outpatient LTC services.

The persistent rationing of supply, postponement of investments and budgetary controls resulted in growing waiting lists and a general perception of a deterioration of quality, particularly compared with the general increase in the standard of living and the rising expectations about the quality of care people would like to receive in old age. In 1999, the long waiting lists for home health care were successfully challenged in court. The court ruled that public LTC insurance entitled people to timely access to home health care, and that budgetary considerations were not a valid reason for withholding care. In fact, the court decision implied that too stringent a rationing of health services was not compatible with the 'right to care' that was guaranteed by the social insurance legislation (AWBZ).

Urged by the court decision and the mounting public and political pressure to improve access and quality of LTC services, in 2000 the government decided to lift the budgetary controls and to reimburse all extra production necessary to reduce waiting lists. Indeed, from 2000 to 2003, waiting lists were substantially reduced: for home health care by 64 per cent, for nursing homes by 39 per cent and for elderly homes by 23 per cent (Van Gameren, 2005). As a consequence, during that period the expenditure on LTC rapidly increased to more than 10 per cent per year (Figure 7.2), resulting in an increase from 3.5 to 4.0 per cent in the share of GDP spent on LTC (see Figure 7.1).

During the period 1985–2005, the average annual growth of real expenditure on LTC services covered by AWBZ was 3.3 per cent, whereas the average annual increase of GDP was about 2.7 per cent. The average difference of 0.6 per cent, however, was entirely due to the high cost of inflation during the period from 2000 to 2003.

As shown in Figure 7.3, the largest share of expenditure growth can be explained by an increase in relative prices (2.0 per cent), while about 1.3 per cent can be attributed to an increase in production.[5]

From Figure 7.3 it can be concluded that for four of the five major categories of LTC services the annual cost growth was about 4 per cent, which is well above the annual increase of GDP. This relatively high cost increase is largely compensated, however, by a relatively low cost increase of residential elderly care (on average about 1.3 per cent per year). This was caused by a decrease in production (on average −0.7 per cent per year) due to reductions in the capacity of elderly homes and a substitution towards home health

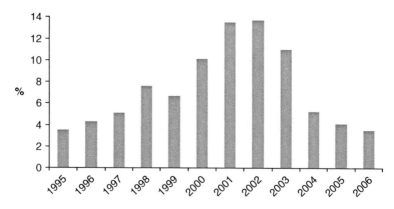

Figure 7.2   Annual growth of LTC expenditures financed by public insurance (AWBZ)
Source: IBO-werkgroep, AWBZ (2006), p. 42.

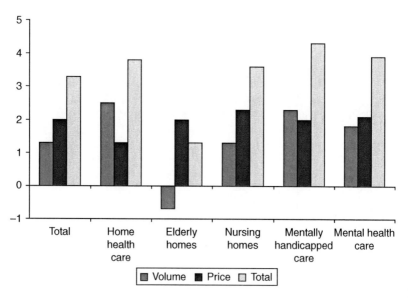

Figure 7.3   Average annual growth (%) of LTC benefits covered by AWBZ, 1985–2005
Source: Eggink et al. (2008).

care. As a result, the annual production growth in home health care is the largest among the five categories of LTC services (on average about 2.5 per cent per year). Clearly, this reflects the trend that elderly people are treated at home for a longer period.

As shown in Figure 7.4, labour productivity for all LTC services decreased by 0.3 per cent over the entire period 1985–2005, contributing slightly to

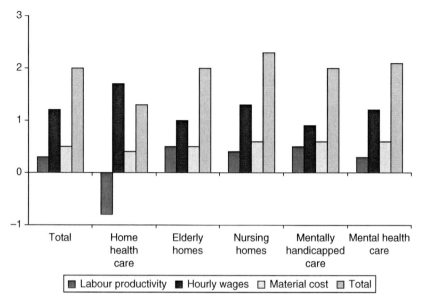

Figure 7.4 Components of the growth (%) of real prices of LTC benefits, 1985–2005
Source: Eggink et al. (2008).

the overall price increase. This corroborates the supposition that Baumol's cost disease is particularly relevant for LTC services (Oliviera Martins and de la Maisonneuve, 2006). Contrary to the general trend, labour productivity in home health care increased by on average 0.7 per cent per year during the same period. The increase in labour productivity in home health care has been particularly pronounced since 1995, and is attributed to a tightening of the budgets for home health care agencies, resulting in a relative decline in administrative and managerial personnel and the introduction of benchmarking and time management to increase the efficiency of production (Eggink et al., 2008).

Looking at the development of LTC expenditure in the period 1985–2000, supply regulation and budgetary restrictions were clearly quite effective in containing cost. The downside of the prolonged rationing policies, however, was increasing waiting lists, resulting in a growing public discontent and incompatibility with the legally established entitlements to LTC services. For this reason, in 2000, a continuation of the prevailing cost containment strategy was no longer politically feasible. On the other hand, the radical change towards an open-ended reimbursement policy proved to be no solution either, since the resulting excessive cost inflation – without accompanying incentives for efficiency – was not sustainable. In 2004 the government tried to regain control over LTC expenditure by concluding agreements with the interested associations of LTC providers to limit the growth of expenditure and to increase productivity. In addition, particularly for home health services, co-payments were increased. In 2005, the government reinstated budgetary controls by imposing regional budgets for each of the 32 regions, based on the past expenditure on LTC in each region. Regional care offices were made responsible for the allocation of these budgets and had to negotiate with regional providers about prices and maximum output levels. By reintroducing tight budget constraints, the government runs the risk that waiting lists will increase, which could again generate a conflict with the existing legal entitlement to LTC. In contrast with the late 1990s, however, there is an important safety valve: the personal care budget. Since personal care budgets do not fall under the scope of the regional budget constraints, LTC providers can exceed their budgets if they can persuade their clients to apply for a personal budget and to use this to pay the provider. Indeed, this is one of reasons for the vast increasing popularity of personal care budgets.

5 Personal care budgets and informal care

Personal care budgets were introduced in 1995 as a small-scale experiment to provide consumers with the option to buy and organize their own home health services instead of using 'in kind' services contracted by the regional care offices (Van den Berg and Hassink, 2008). Since 1995 the personal care budget scheme has been significantly expanded, both in scope and expenditure. In 2008, personal care budgets comprised about 7 per cent of LTC expenditure covered by AWBZ and were used by more than 10 per cent of LTC users. Table 7.3 provides some key figures about personal budgets in 2005.

There were several reasons put forward for the introduction of personal care budgets (Hessing-Wagner, 1990). First, personal care budgets were considered as a means to empower consumers and to motivate providers to better meet consumer preferences. During the 1990s, LTC providers were increasingly criticized for not being able to deliver the right services at the right time. Moreover, the new generation of LTC users had higher expectations and were supposed to be better able to express their preferences for LTC. By the option to opt for a personal budget rather than contracted LTC services, people would be able to arrange care according to their own preferences.

A second reason for introducing personal care budgets was to encourage the use and provision of informal care as a cheap alternative to professional formal care. Informal care is a crucial part of LTC all over the world. In the Netherlands, however, informal care plays a relatively minor role, which is partly due to the relatively generous coverage of professional formal LTC services.

Using 2004 data from the Survey of Health Ageing and Retirement in Europe (SHARE), Albertini et al. (2007) show that within Europe the annual

Table 7.3   Key data for personal care budgets, 2005

Number of budget holders		77,883
Age distribution (years)	< 18	20.4%
	18–55	32.5%
	56–65	12.6%
	66–75	14.3%
	76–80	8.7%
	> 80	11.6%
Type of health problem	Somatic	67%
	Psychogeriatric	1%
	Psychiatric	14%
	Physical handicap	14%
	Mental handicap	11%
	Sensory handicap	1%
	Psychosocial	1%
Net budget amount (in €)*	< 2500	27.7%
	2500–5000	24.9%
	5000–25,000	30.5%
	> 25,000	16.9%
Proportion of budget spent on informal care	Resident providers	21%
	Non-resident providers	17%

Note: * Net of co-payments by budget holder. The average gross personal care budget was about €14,000, of which about €1000 was paid by the budget holder out of pocket.
Source: Ministry of Health (2006).

amount of informal care per caregiver is the lowest in the Netherlands, Denmark, France and Sweden (around 300 hours) and the highest in Italy (almost 1500 hours). Also using SHARE data, Bolin et al. (2008) show that the mean hours of informal care received by single-living elderly per year in the Netherlands are among the lowest within Europe (approximately 50 hours), while in Greece, Italy and Spain the single-living elderly receive the most informal care (over 200 hours). Conditional upon receiving informal care, the amount of care received by the single Dutch elderly is also among the lowest in Europe (about 130 hours per year).

In terms of professional home care use, the opposite pattern seems to hold. Bolin et al. (2008) show that the Netherlands (together with Denmark and France) belongs to the European top level of professional home care use. Of single-living Dutch elderly, approximately 25 per cent use professional home care, while this percentage is the least in Italy (6 per cent).

Although the share of informal care in the Netherlands is lower than in most other European countries, the majority of home care is still provided by informal caregivers. Table 7.4 shows that in the Netherlands the amount of home care used in 2001 was around just 15 per cent of the total amount

Table 7.4 Hours of professional and informal home care provided per year, 2000–2003

Home care	2000		2001		2002		2003	
	Hours (×1000)	Share (%)	Hours (×1000)	Share (%)	Hours (×1000)	Share (%)	Hours (×1000)	Share (%)
Unskilled housework	13,220	22.4	13,512	21.3	12,545	18.1	12,529	16.6
Skilled housework	16,425	27.9	18,911	29.9	22,653	32.6	26,237	34.7
Total housework	29,645		32,423		35,198		38,766	
Personal care[a]	23,029	39.1	23,877	37.7	25,733	37.0	27,541	36.5
Nursing[b]	6,259	10.6	7,028	11.1	8,536	12.3	9,249	12.2
Total home care	58,933	100	63,328	100	69,467	100	75,556	100
Informal care								
All tasks[c]			375,000					

Notes:
[a]Inclusive specialized personal care.
[b]Inclusive specialized nursing.
[c]Calculated assuming that informal caregivers provide on average five hours care per day, for four days per week for 25 weeks per year.
Source: Van den Berg (2004).

of informal care provided. Nevertheless, Table 7.4 also shows the enormous growth in professional home care use (especially skilled housework) during the relatively short period 2000–2003.

The rapid expansion of personal care budgets was an effective way to encourage the provision of informal care. In 2005, 38 per cent of personal care budgets were spent on informal care, while two-thirds of budget holders use the budget for paying informal caregivers (Ramakers and Van den Wijngaart, 2005). Next to personal care budgets, the role of informal care was also increased by restricting the possibilities of substituting professional for informal care. Initially, using informal care was considered to be people's voluntary choice. Even people having a social network with potential informal caregivers could always apply to get professional care that was covered by the AWBZ. In practice, however, the needs assessment agencies increasingly took into account the amount of informal care a client already received in order to determine the amount of professional care the client could legally claim (Jörg et al., 2002). Since 2003, this practice has been formalized and strict protocols were developed regarding needs assessments taking into account the potential amount of informal care the care recipient's social network could provide.

Another way to encourage the provision of informal care was to support informal caregivers. To prevent informal caregivers getting health problems themselves, needs assessment agencies were permitted to refer caregivers to regional support centres. The support centres developed all kinds of respite care programmes, such as day care, short stays in nursing homes, holidays and informational support (see, e.g., Koopmanschap et al., 2004; Van Exel et al., 2006).

Evaluative studies point out that, as intended, personal care budgets induced a substitution of informal care for professional care, and were valued by many clients as an effective means to purchase and organize care that better met their preferences than regular care contracted by regional care offices (Ramakers et al., 2007).

However, personal care budgets also had several unintended negative effects. First, personal care budgets induced a substitution of paid care for unpaid informal care. Informal care by relatives, neighbours and friends that previously was often provided for free was becoming increasingly paid for. A study among informal caregivers pointed out that 76 per cent of caregivers would be willing to provide the same care without receiving payment, although 78 per cent indicated that getting paid nevertheless was important to them (Ramakers and van den Wijngaart, 2005). In addition, an increasing number of brokers became active, which in return for a fee offered people assistance in applying for a personal care budget. Van den Berg and Schut (2003) calculated that a substitution of paid-for by unpaid informal care from the personal care budget could result in an increase in AWBZ costs of approximately €4 billion per year (about 20 per cent of total AWBZ expenditure).[6] Counteracting the substitution of paid-for unpaid informal care was another reason for implementing the previously mentioned strict needs assessment protocols that explicitly take into account the amount of informal care the care recipient's social network could provide. According to the protocols, needs were not only based on health status or functional impairments but also on the availability of 'usual care'. For instance, the care partners provide to each other during at least three months is defined as usual care. Hence, the magnitude of the personal care budgets became explicitly dependent on the social network of the beneficiary. Nevertheless, it is unclear to what extent people can still use personal care budgets for replacing unpaid care with paid informal care. In particular, the rapidly increasing number of personal care budgets for the assistance of young people with psychiatric disorders has been attributed to the substitution of paid-for by unpaid informal care provided by their parents.

A second drawback was that personal budgets were increasingly used by home health care agencies to escape the imposed budget constraints. As a consequence, people who did not want to purchase and arrange care by themselves were more or less forced to do so in order to be able to keep the same home care provider.

It is difficult to assess to what extent personal care budgets were successful in accomplishing the aims behind their introduction. The rapidly increasing number of people opting for a personal care budget suggests that, for a substantial proportion of users of outpatient LTC, the budgets offered better opportunities to meet consumer preferences than care in kind. The problem is, however, that there is not much empirical information about the true motives of people to opt for the personal care budget. For instance, the growing demand for personal care budgets can at least partly be explained by the motivation to evade waiting lists for traditionally financed LTC and by consumer preferences to pay formerly unpaid informal caregivers. It is also unclear to what extent personal care budgets induced an efficient substitution of informal for formal care or just an expansion of paid informal care. For instance, the increasing number of parents opting for a personal care budget to provide care for their children seems to point to a substitution of paid for unpaid informal care. Moreover, for this group of clients it is unlikely that empowerment and better consumer-directed care were the main drivers to opt for a personal budget. In contrast, it seems fair to conclude that for people with long-term disabilities, personal care budgets really provide an instrument that helps them to empower themselves and to purchase care that better meets their preferences than care in kind.

6   Deficiencies of current LTC financing

Figure 7.2 showed that a *laissez-faire* policy without supply and demand constraints (as in the period 2000–2003) is likely to jeopardize the sustainability of the public LTC insurance scheme. On the other hand, a return to the stringent top-down rationing policy of the 1990s has serious drawbacks and does not seem feasible either. Faced with this dilemma, the government has temporarily opted for a mixture of both policies, half-heartedly relying on both supply constraints and arrangements to improve efficiency by increasing consumer direction and choice. For the following reasons, this inconsistent policy compromise can achieve neither cost containment nor an effective increase in efficiency.

First, the currently imposed supply constraints in the form of regional care budgets are not effective in controlling cost because they can be circumvented by opting for a personal care budget. Since personal care budgets are not included under the regional budget, the regional budget constraint is not binding. Although the government introduced a separate macro budget for personal care budgets, particularly since 2005, the demand for personal care budgets is much larger than the available funds. Rather than denying personal care budgets, the government regularly adjusts the macro budget upwards to meet the growing demand. In 2007, for instance, the government decided four times to raise the budget, resulting in a total annual budget increase of 35 per cent (Ministry of Health, 2007).

Second, the regional budget mechanism punishes providers who do a good job and consequently attract more clients than the target number of clients on which their budget is based. If these presumably efficient providers cannot effectively motivate their clients to apply for a personal care budget, they have to refuse clients or run a deficit.

Third, regional care offices do not have an incentive to allocate the regional budget to the most efficient providers, because they have a regional monopoly and are not at risk for the cost of care. Since LTC users cannot choose another regional care office, these offices have no incentive to allocate budgets to providers that best meet consumer preferences. Again, consumers may opt for a personal care budget (except for inpatient care), but this is not likely to discipline the behaviour of the regional offices because they do not benefit from having more customers. Moreover, since regional offices get a fixed budget for administrative costs, they have a financial incentive to negotiate with a limited number of large providers in order to minimize the cost of contracting. For the same reason, regional care offices have no incentive to take action against overly lenient needs assessment procedures.

Finally, the definition of 'entitlements' in terms of six functional categories (see Box 7.1) has proven to be too imprecise to provide a firm basis for uniform and unambiguous needs assessment. In particular, the number of clients that were assessed as in need of 'supportive guidance' increased dramatically, by 37 per cent, from 2005 to 2007 (Ministry of Health, 2008).

7 Proposals to reform LTC financing

In view of the serious deficiencies of the current system of LTC financing, the government asked a number of advisory and supervisory bodies[7] to draft proposals for reforming the system of LTC financing in order to guarantee a sustainable, efficient and consumer-directed provision of LTC.

This resulted in five different advisory reports, which were not all equivocal. Two reports (by the Health Care Insurance Board (CVZ) and the Council for Public Health and Health Care (RVZ)) recommended complete abolishment of the separate public long-term insurance scheme, to integrate most of the benefits covered by AWBZ into the new national Health Insurance Act for curative health services (ZVW) and to integrate benefits that are related to social support and participation into the new Social Support Act (WMO) in 2007. The main line of reasoning was that the new health insurance scheme for curative services – based on the model of managed competition (Van de Ven and Schut, 2008) – would provide much stronger incentives for efficiency and meet consumer preferences more than the AWBZ. Moreover, integrating curative and LTC into a single scheme would also provide incentives and possibilities for a better coordination of care for people with chronic diseases. Finally, the 2007 Social Support Act (WMO) provided an integrated legal framework for social and community support under the responsibility of municipalities, so the transfer of social care benefits from the AWBZ to the WMO would also enhance a better coordination of social care and welfare assistance.

The radical proposals to abolish the AWBZ scheme, however, also had serious potential shortcomings. Most importantly, it is questionable whether the model of managed competition underlying the new health insurance scheme for curative services is adequate for the provision and financing of LTC (Van de Ven and Schut, 1994). A key element of the managed competition model, which makes it possible to guarantee universal access in a competitive health insurance market, is an adequate system of risk adjustment (Van de Ven and Schut, 2008). At present, there are no appropriate risk adjusters available for LTC and it is even unclear whether adequate risk adjustment is feasible for many of these services (IBO-werkgroep AWBZ, 2006). Given the typically high level of expenditure per LTC user and the intertemporal nature of the risk, imperfect risk adjustment for these types of services may result in unfair competition among insurers and huge incentives for risk selection if insurers are obliged to charge community-rated premiums (as is the case under the 2006 Health Insurance Act). Another reason why the managed competition model may not be appropriate for LTC services is that for many of these services consumers are not able or willing to make an informed choice among health insurers that contract these services. There is substantial empirical evidence that the propensity to switch health plans substantially declines with age and the presence of health problems

(Strombom et al., 2002; Schut et al., 2003; Buchmueller, 2006). For LTC services for which the number of critical buyers is too small, competition may result in a deterioration of quality, since competitive health insurers may have an incentive to reduce quality in order to reduce cost if this does not result in a significant loss of market share (Van de Ven and Schut, 1994). Finally, the experience with both the new Health Insurance Act and the new Social Support Act is limited and it is unclear whether health insurers and municipalities are willing and able to perform as prudent purchasers of health and social services. Therefore, a major expansion of the scope of the responsibilities of health insurers and municipalities would be premature.

In view of these shortcomings, other advisory reports proposed to maintain a separate insurance scheme for several categories of LTC, at least comprising care for the mentally handicapped. Among these reports, the proposal by the Social and Economic Council (SER) is the latest and the most important (SER, 2008). The SER proposed to reform the AWBZ along the following main lines:

1. A much more precise and unambiguous delineation and definition of entitlements.
2. An improvement of the needs assessment by developing uniform protocols, benchmarking and a permanent supervision of the assessment bodies.
3. A reduction of coverage by transferring short-term rehabilitation services to the public insurance scheme for curative health services (Health Insurance Act) and by bringing the provision of social care under the responsibility of the municipalities (Social Support Act).
4. A far-reaching separation of the financing of residing and care, implying that accommodation would no longer be reimbursed by public insurance; a subsidy scheme for lower income groups to pay for the cost of accommodation; the separation of care and residing should lead to innovative combinations of residing, care, welfare and participation.
5. A replacement of provider-based budgeting by client-based budgeting. Rather than clients having to follow the money – as in the current provider-based budgeting system – the money should follow the client. Clients would have the option to choose a personal care budget (as in the current system) and arrange all care by themselves, or to choose among providers contracted by individual health insurers (that would have to replace regional care offices in 2012). Providers can increase revenues if they are able to attract more clients by offering better service (for a fixed budget per client). The client-based budgets should be based on the categorization of clients in 'care-severity packages' (ZZPs) by the needs assessment bodies. A 'care-severity package' describes the type and amount of care needed by the client. For each 'care-severity package' a budget will be calculated.

In June 2008, the government made it clear that it endorsed the main lines of the SER proposal and announced the first steps to implement its recommendations, including a more precise demarcation of entitlements and an exclusion of recovery and social support from coverage by 2009 (Ministry of Health, 2008). In a subsequent policy letter of mid-2009, the reform plans were further elaborated (Ministry of Health, 2009). In this letter the government stated to aim at abolishing the regional care offices in 2012 and instead making individual health insurers responsible for the purchasing and contracting of LTC services on behalf of their insured (next to maintaining the option for clients to choose for a personal care budget or voucher and to purchase care by themselves). However, this decision is made contingent on the possibility of making health insurers financially accountable for LTC expenses of their insured and on the feasibility of an adequate system of client-based budgeting.

8   Towards sustainable LTC financing?

Whether the proposed reform will lead to a sustainable financing and more consumer-directed provision of LTC services crucially depends on the ability to develop a clear-cut definition of entitlements, to improve the accuracy of needs assessment[8] and to develop appropriate ZZPs as a solid basis for client-based budgeting. The feasibility of these three requirements is highly uncertain. In particular, client-based budgeting may turn out to be complicated. In 2008, ZZPs had been developed for inpatient care, which from 2009 to 2011 will be phased in to determine the budgets for inpatient care LTC facilities (i.e., nursing homes, elderly homes, institutions for mentally and physically handicapped and mental care institutions). The experience with these ZZPs for financing inpatient care may make clear whether these packages can provide a firm basis for client-based financing. A key question will be whether the predictable cost variation per care package will be small enough to avoid problems of cream-skimming and misallocation of funds.[9] The first experiences with the introduction of client-based budgeting for inpatient LTC were evaluated by the Dutch Healthcare Authority (NZa, 2009). The NZa reported that it received signals from both health care providers and regional care offices of strategic upcoding (classifying clients in higher ZZPs than indicated) and risk selection (avoiding patients that are unprofitable given the ZZP, capitation payment). The main reason put forward for such behaviour was that for several ZZPs or for several patients classified within a certain ZZP capitation payments were insufficient to cover the costs. Based on the limited available data, the NZa could not determine whether upcoding and risk selection indeed occurred, but it announced it would monitor this type of behaviour and examine the accuracy of ZZP payments.

An important, yet unanswered question is how future client-based budgets should be determined: should they be based on the average cost of all providers that offer the care package? Given the increasing pressure to contain public expenditure on LTC services, the most likely outcome may be that the client-based budgets will be derived from the regional budgets (or a national budget) set by the government, using the ZZPs as relative weights for the determination of the (regional) level of the client-based budget for each care package.[10] The way of determining the budget will be closely related to another still unanswered question, namely, for which party the client-based budget should be binding. In other words, if the actual cost of providing a care package differs from the client-based budget, then who should bear the additional costs or may keep the residual: the client, the provider or the insurer contracting the provider? At present, providers receive the full ZZP capitation payments for each client they serve and neither clients nor regional care offices bear financial risk (except for the income-related co-payments clients have to pay). However, if risk-bearing health insurers replace regional care offices by 2012, it is conceivable that ZZP capitation payments will be given to the insurers, which subsequently have to negotiate prices per ZZP with various LTC providers.

In theory, the Dutch proposed reforms involve appropriate incentives to improve the sustainability of the comprehensive LTC insurance scheme. As argued, in practice the success of the reforms will depend heavily on the way entitlements are defined, an improvement of the accuracy of needs assessment and the feasibility of determining appropriate client-based budgets. For adequate client-based budgeting it is crucial that the ZZPs that are currently being developed are relatively homogeneous in terms of predicted costs, as substantial variation involves clear incentives for upcoding and risk selection.

Although the proposed reform offers a promising perspective on combining a sustainable and universally accessible LTC financing with a consumer-directed provision of care, a number of complicated issues have to be resolved. The Dutch experiences in implementing the reform may therefore provide important lessons for countries with a public insurance scheme for LTC – for example, Japan and Germany – that also struggle with the question of how to guarantee a sustainable, universally accessible and high-quality system of LTC (Ikegami, 2007; Rothgang, 2010). In addition, it may also provide important lessons for countries considering the introduction of a system of social insurance for LTC (Barr, 2010).

Acknowledgement

A previous draft of this chapter was presented at the 7th World Congress of the international Health Economics Association (iHEA) in Beijing and at the International Conference on the Policies and Regulations of Health and

Long-term Care Costs of the Elderly in Tokyo. Part of this research has been supported by a research grant to Hitotsubashi University from the Ministry of Education of Japan (grant number 18002001).

Notes

*This chapter is largely based on Schut and Van den Berg (2010).

1. In 2008, CIZ had one main office, six district offices and 30 local offices.
2. Following the recently proposed typology by Ariizumi (2008), the Dutch public insurance system can be characterized as health-based rather than a means-tested programme.
3. In 2009, two functional categories – supportive and activating guidance – were combined into a single category 'guidance'. At the same time, guidance that is aimed at social participation is excluded from coverage and brought under the scope of the Social Support Act (WMO).
4. When productivity growth in the LTC sector lags behind that in other sectors while wages grow at the same rate, relative prices of LTC *vis-à-vis* other goods and services in the economy will rise. In the case of a low price-elasticity of demand for LTC – which is likely in the presence of public insurance – the share of LTC expenditure in GDP will also increase over time.
5. Production of LTC services is measured by the Netherlands Institute for Social Research (Eggink et al., 2008) using indicators of production (e.g., admissions, day treatments, length of stay, number of patients and so on) weighted by the type and intensity of treatment.
6. This number was based on the assumption that a substantial proportion of informal caregivers already get paid from the personal care budget; see also Van den Berg and Hassink (2008). Their average payment is around €10 per hour. Multiplication of this average payment by the informal care hours presented in Table 7.4 makes approximately €4 billion.
7. Specifically, the Social and Economic Council (SER), the Council for Public Health and Health Care (RVZ), the Health Care Insurance Board (CVZ), the Dutch Healthcare Authority (NZa) and a governmental working group (IBO).
8. In the Japanese LTC insurance scheme, for instance, nationally uniform standardized eligibility criteria are used to determine to which services the elderly are entitled (Ikegami, 2007).
9. The determination of adequate ZZP capitation payments for outpatient LTC may be more complicated, because the need for outpatient care crucially depends on the availability of a social network of informal caregivers, which typically varies substantially across individuals.
10. Using a national rather than regional budgets may be politically attractive, because then government may avoid a socially controversial regional variation in the level of client-based budgets.

References

Albertini, M., Kohli M. and Vogel, C. (2007) 'Intergenerational transfers of time and money in European families: common patterns – different regimes?', *Journal of European Social Policy*, 17, pp. 319–334.

Ariizumi, H. (2008) 'Effects of public long-term care insurance on consumption, medical care demand, and welfare', *Journal of Health Economics*, 27, pp. 1423–1435.

Barr, N. (2010) 'Long term care: a suitable case for social insurance', *Social Policy and Administration*, 44 (4), pp. 359–374.

Baumol, W.J. (1967) 'Macroeconomics of unbalanced growth: the anatomy of urban crisis', *American Economic Review*, 57 (3), pp. 415–426.

Bolin, K., Lindgren, B. and Lundborg, P. (2008) 'Informal and formal care among single-living elderly in Europe', *Health Economics*, 17, pp. 393–409.

Buchmueller, T.C. (2006) 'Price and the health plan choice of retirees', *Journal of Health Economics*, 25 (1), pp. 81–101.

Eggink, E., Pommer, E. and Woittiez, I. (2008) *De ontwikkeling van de AWBZ-uitgaven. Een analyse van de AWBZ-uitgaven 1985–2005 en een raming van de uitgaven voor verpleging en verzorging 2005–2030* (Den Haag: Sociaal en Cultureel Planbureau (SCP)).

Hessing-Wagner, J.C. (1990) *Cliëntgebonden budget en zorg. De individualisering van geldstromen nader beschouwd* (Den Haag: Sociaal en Cultureel Planbureau (SCP)).

IBO-werkgroep, AWBZ (2006) *Toekomst AWBZ. Eindrapportage van de werkgroep Organisatie romp AWBZ*, Interdepartementaal Beleidsonderzoek 2004–2005, no. 4, Den Haag.

Ikegami, N. (2007) 'Rationale, design and sustainability of long-term care insurance in Japan – in retrospect', *Social Policy and Society*, 6 (3), pp. 423–434.

Jörg, F., Boeije, H.R., Huijsman, R., De Weert, G.H. and Schrijvers, A.J.P. (2002) 'Objectivity in needs assessment practice: admission to a residential home', *Health and Social Care in the Community*, 10 (6), pp. 445–456.

Koopmanschap, M.A., Van Exel, N.J.A., Van den Bos, G.A.M., Van den Berg, B. and Brouwer, W.B.F. (2004) 'The desire for support and respite care: preferences of Dutch informal caregivers', *Health Policy*, 68, pp. 309–320.

Ministry of Health (2004) *Op weg naar een bestendig stelsel voor langdurige zorg en maatschappelijke ondersteuning*, Letter to Parliament, DVVO-U-2475093, Den Haag.

Ministry of Health (2006) *Fact sheet personal budget AWBZ*, http://www.minvws.nl/en/folders/zzoude_directies/dvvo/2005/fact-sheet-personal-budget-awbz.asp, date accessed 3 November 2010.

Ministry of Health (2007) *Pgb in perspectief*, Letter to Parliament, DLZ/ZI-U-2811809, 9 November, Den Haag.

Ministry of Health (2008) *Zeker van zorg, nu en straks*, Letter to Parliament, DLZ/KZ-2856771, 13 June, Den Haag.

Ministry of Health (2009) *Nadere uitwerking toekomst van de AWBZ*, Letter to Parliament, DLZ/CB-U-2912189, 12 June, Den Haag.

NZa (2009) *Voortgangsrapportage Invoering ZZP's. Rapportage over de periode 1 januari 2009 – 30 juni 2009* (Utrecht: Dutch Healthcare Authority (NZa)).

OECD (2005) *Long-term Care for Older People* (Paris: OECD).

Oliviera Martins, J. and de la Maisonneuve, C. (2006) 'The drivers of public expenditure on health and long-term care: An integrated approach', *OECD Economic Studies*, 43 (2), pp. 115–154.

Ramakers, C. and van den Wijngaart, M. (2005) *Persoonsgebonden budget en mantelzorg, onderzoek naar de aard en de omvang van betaalde en onbetaalde mantelzorg* (Nijmegen: ITS/Radboud University).

Ramakers, C., de Graauw, K., Sombekke, E., Vierke, H., Doesborgh, J. and Wolderingh, C. (2007) *Evaluatie persoongebonden budget nieuwe stijl 2005–2006* (Nijmegen: ITS/Radboud University).

Rothgang, H. (2010) 'Long term care insurance in Germany: A system of permanent reform?', *Social Policy and Administration*, 44 (4), pp. 436–460.

Schut, F.T. and Van den Berg, B. (2010) 'Sustainability of long-term care financing in the Netherlands', *Social Policy and Administration*, 44 (4), pp. 411–435.

Schut, F.T., Gress, S. and Wasem, J. (2003) 'Consumer price sensitivity and social health insurer choice in Germany and the Netherlands', *International Journal of Health Care Finance and Economics*, 3, pp. 117–138.

SER (2008) *Langdurige zorg verzekerd: Over de toekomst van de AWBZ*, Publicatienummer 3 (Den Haag: Social and Economic Council (SER)).

Strombom, B.A., Buchmueller, T.C. and Feldstein, P.J. (2002) 'Switching costs, price sensitivity and health plan choice', *Journal of Health Economics*, 21, pp. 89–116.

Van den Berg, B. (2004) 'Dragen de sterkste schouders de zwaarste lasten? Een discussie over de positie van mantelzorgers ten opzichte van de AWBZ-zorg', *Tijdschrift voor Politieke Ekonomie*, 26, pp. 24–37.

Van den Berg, B. and Hassink, W.H.J. (2008) 'Cash benefits in long-term home care', *Health Policy*, 88, pp. 209–221.

Van den Berg, B. and Schut, F.T. (2003) 'Het einde van gratis mantelzorg?', *Economisch Statistische Berichten*, 88 (4413), pp. 420–422.

Van de Ven, W.P.M.M. and Schut, F.T. (1994) 'Should catastrophic risks be included in a regulated competitive health insurance market?', *Social Science and Medicine*, 39 (10), pp. 1459–1472.

Van de Ven, W.P.M.M. and Schut, F.T. (2008) 'Universal mandatory health insurance in the Netherlands: a model for the United States?', *Health Affairs*, 27 (3), pp. 771–781.

Van Exel, N.J.A., Morée, M., Koopmanschap, M.A., Schreuder Goedheijt, T. and Brouwer, W.B.F. (2006) 'Respite care – An explorative study of demand and use in Dutch informal caregivers', *Health Policy*, 78, pp. 194–208.

Van Gameren, E. (2005) *Regionale verschillen in de wachtlijsten verpleging en verzorging. Een emprisch onderzoek naar verklarende factoren*, Werkdocument 119 (Den Haag: Sociaal en Cultureel Planbureau (SCP)).

8
Financing Long-Term Care in France*

Christophe Courbage
The Geneva Association, Switzerland

and

Manuel Plisson
Chaire 'Risques et Chances de la transition démographique,'
Paris Dauphine University LEDA-LEGOS, France

1 Introduction

Like most industrialized countries, France is facing an ageing of its population which creates long-term care (LTC) needs and questions the financial coverage of LTC risks. In France, the public coverage of LTC derives from a long tradition of intervention concerning the *Sécurité sociale* (Social Security) and from a great diversity of stakeholders and sources of financing. At the national level, the public health insurance scheme deals with LTC expenses due to health care. In addition, the public pension scheme finances a significant part of living expenses. At the local level, local governments manage the *Allocation Personnalisée d'Autonomie* (APA). The APA is a public benefit allocated to people aged 60 or more, who are no longer able to care for themselves, regardless of their financial situation and place of residence. This allowance is jointly funded by central and local governments. APA can be seen as the first step towards recognition of dependency as a new risk of life, even if public coverage remains low in comparison with the financial expenses incurred by dependency.[1] The French government, confronted by the complexity of financing LTC, is planning to reform the current system. A draft law is scheduled for discussion by the parliament during the second half of 2011.

In parallel with public coverage, private LTC insurance (LTCI) has developed in France. LTCI contracts are with the individual or group and guarantee the payment of a fixed annuity benefit in the form of a monthly cash benefit. The French LTC market, with around three million policy-holders (FFSA, 2009), proves to be one of the most dynamic among the industrialized markets. Unlike in the United States, no tax incentives currently encourage the development of private LTC insurance. In France, public debates associated with the search for new solutions to cover the risk of LTC needs, which

125

are widely covered in the press, seem to have raised general public awareness of the existence of such a risk. Private insurance has largely benefitted
from this support. It also seems that the rapid growth of the French market
can be explained by the choice of the products offered. Whereas US insurers have launched products with service benefits[2] (payment proportional to
LTC expenditure), French insurers have turned to cash benefits (in the form
of annuities). Policy-holders appear to prefer the freedom of cash payments,
even if that implies the need to organize the care themselves, compared with
the simplicity of the service benefit (Durand and Taleyson, 2003).

The aim of this chapter is to describe how LTC is financed in France and
to discuss the possible reforms to be implemented to make the system more
sustainable. The following section highlights the specific nature of LTC in
France. Section 3 deals with the demography of LTC in France as well as its
cost. Section 4 presents the public coverage of LTC. Section 5 analyses the
market for LTC insurance. Section 6 discusses the possible reforms of the
French system. The final section offers some concluding remarks.

2   Specific nature of LTC in France

2.1   Dependency versus disability

The concept of LTC, as defined in the United States, has no equivalent in the
French institutional landscape. The French use the term 'dependency' rather
than LTC to mean the financial burden of care during old age. The notion
of dependency can be defined as the need for human assistance for essential
daily living activities (Duée and Rebillard, 2004). In France, dependency is
directly related to the age of individuals and applies to those over 60. For
persons under 60 years old, LTC applies to disabled or handicapped persons. Such distinction does not rely on any medical or social reality. It stems
from the peculiarities of the French public support to people in need of LTC.
In France, unlike in English-speaking countries, dependency is not defined
by the type of care required, but by the age of individuals.[3]

Such segmentation between disabled and dependent persons has two consequences. The first is that public support is different depending on the age
of the individual for the same needs. In France, public assistance allocated to
people with disabilities is much more generous than the one for dependent
persons. The second is that the segmentation of disability and dependency
according to age makes international comparisons difficult.

2.2   How to measure dependency in France?

The main tool to measure dependency in France is the *Autonomie Gerontologie
Groupes Iso-Ressources* (AGGIR) scale. The AGGIR scale determines benefit eligibility as a function of a set of daily living capabilities. The AGGIR scale is
made up of 15 items used to determine the group to which an individual
belongs depending on the level of dependency. Each item corresponds to

a daily living activity and is rated A if the subject is capable of carrying out this activity completely by himself or herself, B if the subject is only partially able and C if the subject is not capable at all. The results are computerized and each individual is categorized in one of the six GIR groups (GIR 1 to GIR 6), using an algorithm which has been defined by French legislation, GIR 1 being the highest level of dependency and GIR 6 the lowest.

The AGGIR scale is used by the French public authorities for eligibility to LTC public benefit and by some French insurers.

2.3 Sharing between private and public LTC financing

The institutional design of the French LTC financing is based on the idea of complementary systems involving public and private insurance, just like for health insurance. As an illustration, benefits paid by insurance companies are not included in the eligibility criteria for public insurance.

This institutional design differs from the Nordic systems where the totality of LTC expenditures is financed by governments. It is also different from the North American situation (Scanlon, 1992) where public support is only for the poorest via Medicaid. In the United States, the benefits paid by private insurers in case of LTC needs are usually included in the income which serves as the basis for calculating the eligibility to Medicaid (even if a new programme – the partnership approach – has been recently implemented to address these issues). While the US system is based on substitution between public assistance and private coverage, the French system, on the contrary, adopts a complementary approach.

3   The dependent population and the cost of LTC in France

Addressing the economic aspect of LTC requires looking at both the quantity, that is, the size of the dependent population, and the price of LTC. Yet, providing figures on these issues is not obvious, as will be shown in the next sections.

3.1   The size of the dependent population

Sources for measuring the size of the dependent population are provided either by national surveys or by the number of recipients of public LTC benefits. Three sources are currently available to estimate the size of the dependent population, and all of them tend to show that the dependent population in France in 2010 amounts to approximately 1 million people.

The first survey made in France was called *Handicap-Incapacité-Dépendance*[4] (HID). It was performed in two waves; firstly, in 1999 and then again in 2001. In 2001, there were about 800,000 dependent individuals (as measured through GIR 1 to GIR 4). This number could even increase to 960,000 if a broader definition of dependency were chosen. Based on this survey, it was forecast in 2006 that the size of the dependent population

Table 8.1   Survey HSM on the dependent population

	Losing autonomy	Dependent	Highly dependent
20–39	0	0	82,100 (0.5%)
40–59	980,000 (5.8%)	156,000 (0.9%)	24,000 (0.1%)
60–79	1,400,000 (13.7%)	273,000 (2.7%)	61,000 (0.6%)
80+*	661,000 (25%)	277,000 (11.2%)	62,000 (2.5%)
Total*	3,041,000	706,000	229,100

Note: *The survey HSM concerns only individuals living at home and not in a nursing home.
Source: Dos Santos and Makdessi (2010).

could increase by up to 50 per cent by 2040, representing an increase of about one and a half per cent per year (Duée and Rebillard, 2006). The projections based on this survey also show that the dependent population in 2010 would be approximately 1 million.

A second survey, called *Handicap-Santé en ménages ordinaires*[5] (HSM), was carried out in 2008. The first results were published in 2010, but relate only to dependent people living at home (Dos Santos and Makdessi, 2010). The survey is based both on Activities of Daily Life (ADL) and Instrumental Activities of Daily Life (IADL). Contrary to the HID survey, it concerns the whole population (people aged 20 and more) and not only the old people who are dependent. In this sense, it allows for a better understanding of how dependency evolves with age. It identifies three levels of dependency ranked by increasing order of dependency: 'losing autonomy', 'dependent' and 'highly dependent'. The results are provided in Table 8.1.

Since the survey does not take into account the dependent population living in nursing homes, it underestimates the overall size of the dependent population.

A second way of measuring the size of the dependent population is by looking at the number of recipients of APA, the public benefit for LTC needs. The drawback of this method is that the number of recipients depends on local government resources and is influenced by local political choices. In 2009, 1,117,000 people received the APA (Debout and Lo, 2009); 61 per cent of these beneficiaries were living at home and 39 per cent in elderly residential homes. The proportion of people moderately dependent (defined by GIR) 4 represented 45 per cent of recipients, while people defined by GIR 1 represented only 8 per cent of recipients. The proportion of GIR 1 in the population is still significantly higher for people living at home (57 per cent) than in institutions (24 per cent).

3.2   The cost of LTC in France

3.2.1   *The macroeconomic size*

In aggregate, public spending in LTC in France was close to €22 billion in 2010, which represented around 1.1 per cent of GDP (Rosso-Debord, 2010).

Private insurance finances part of LTC expenditures also but at a much lower level. In 2009, insurers paid €127.7 million as benefits, mostly in the form of annuities, cash or benefits in kind (FFSA, 2009). Adding annuities paid by mutual insurance companies, the total amount paid by insurers is close to €200 million per year. We also need to add to these figures individual spending from families. This includes the amount of co-payment related to APA, estimated at €7 billion (Vasselle, 2008) and the cost of informal care, estimated to be at least €6 billion (Davin et al., 2009). Therefore, current LTC expenditure in France may realistically represent as a whole around 2 per cent of GDP.

3.2.2   The cost in institutions

France has more than 10,000 host institutions for the elderly. They range from residences with no medical services to residences for people in need of LTC fully equipped for dependent individuals[6] and small living units. Coverage and associated costs vary greatly amongst these institutions. To the best of our knowledge, there is no specific study on the cost of LTC in institutions.[7] Our assessment relies therefore on several institutions assisting senior citizens,[8] as well as from interviews with several industry professionals.[9]

The gross cost of residential care varies between €2000 and €6500 per month in France, with a monthly average cost of around €2500.[10] This cost does not depend significantly on the level of dependency. In the case of strong dependency level, the cost in an institution is certainly lower than at home. Conversely, support at home can very well deal with a series of cases of 'light' dependency more cheaply than in a nursing home.

The cost in institutions is actually broken down into three types of costs. The first cost is for lodging, including lodging and meal expenses. This is the hotel component of total cost, and does not depend on the level of dependency. The second cost is linked to dependency. It varies between €300 and €500 per month, depending on the level of dependency. It represents the component specific to dependency and is mostly covered by public benefit (APA). The third cost is linked to care. It generally varies between €500 and €1000 and takes into account the share of cost dedicated to health, not to dependency, and is reimbursed by Social Security. Thus, it is essentially the cost for lodging that is individually paid by the dependant. Excluding the social allowances, the monthly cost paid by dependent people in institutions (the net cost) is on average €2200 in rural areas and €2900 in urban areas (Ross-Debord, 2010).

3.2.3   The cost of home help

The cost of home help is more closely related to the level of dependency of the person concerned than the cost in institutions. Ennuyer (2006) distinguishes five scenarios of costs depending on the level of dependency, ranging from the lower to the higher. Scenario 1 corresponds to the case of a person with light disabilities, needing help for shopping, housekeeping and other out-of-home activities. The time for this type of assistance is estimated at three and a half hours of home help per week for around €340 per month. Scenario 5 represents the case of a person with maximum physical and mental disabilities. This is the typical case of a person at the end of life with Alzheimer's disease. This level of dependency requires almost constant care, with a cost reaching €5300 per month. On average, the cost of dependency at home was estimated at around €1800 per month in 2010.[11]

For several years, institutional care has been favoured over home care in France. Recently, a reversal of this trend is noted. A national survey showed in 2009 that 60 per cent of persons in France would rather stay at home.[12]

3.3   Informal care and the role of children

Children can help their dependent parent by providing either care or financial help. In European families, financial transfers from children to elderly dependents tend to be very low. Based on the European survey SHARE, Wolff and Attias-Donfut (2007) estimate the proportion of persons financially helping their elderly parents as lower than 5 per cent. Actually, most of the assistance received by elderly dependants is help in kind[13] (Attias-Donfut, 1995, 1996), and like other European countries, a large part of LTC needs in France is met through informal caregivers, mainly relatives and nuclear family members (Breuil-Genier, 1999; Norton, 2000).

Informal care can be seen as a means to mitigate the financial cost of LTC since informal care, even imperfectly, substitutes formal LTC.[14] Hence, one suggested solution to slow down the increase in LTC expenditure is to promote the development of informal care. In that respect, France, like other European countries, has set up public policies to encourage and financially support informal caregivers. We will present these public policies later on.

3.3.1   A decrease in informal care?

Informal care essentially comprises personal care and home help. Due essentially to the disintegration of the family unit, the distancing of children from their parents, the increase in women's employment rates and the decrease in the fertility rate, the number of informal caregivers tends to decrease.[15] However, such a trend has to be put in perspective based on two grounds.

Firstly, the total quantity of aid received by elderly dependants does not necessarily increase with the number of children within the family (Fontaine et al., 2007). Consequently, the trend of decrease in the number of children by family does not have a direct impact on the total quantity of aid received by elderly dependants. This is not the number of children that counts but rather whether elderly dependant have a child, especially a daughter, or not.

Secondly, the recent literature on family interactions often shows the existence of negative interactions between siblings. Indeed, reduced contributions by the natural caregivers (usually daughters) are mostly compensated by a higher contribution of male siblings (Fontaine et al., 2009). In fact, recent works show that the family structure remains strong and the number of children helping their elderly parents may have never been as high.[16]

3.3.2 The cost of informal care

The cost of informal care is measured as an opportunity cost, that is, as the opportunity value of time, usually through wages. Davin et al. (2009) estimated this cost in France to be at least €6 billion in 1999 and is likely an underestimate, as stressed by the authors.

In addition, informal care leads to two indirect costs through the effect of caregiving on the labour force supply and on the caregiver's health. Regarding the effect on the labour supply, Fontaine (2009) estimates that one additional hour of informal care reduces labour supply by 20 minutes for European women aged 50–65 years. Caregivers tend to give up professional opportunities and to accept lower-paid positions or flexible working hours if it provides them with closer geographical proximity to elderly parents. If caregivers are ready to adjust their professional lives in order to help an elderly parent, however, few take the step of foregoing their jobs. Regarding the second issue, many epidemiological studies show the negative effects of caregiving on the caregiver's health.[17] Yet, results are not homogeneous. The study of Coe and Van Houtven (2009)[18] may be the most detailed research on this topic. Firstly, it shows that helping an elderly dependent parent increases the likelihood to suffer from depression, but only for married people. Secondly, it stresses that helping an elderly dependent parent tends to increase the likelihood to suffer from heart diseases, but only for single men.

3.3.3 Financial obligations towards supporting parents

In France, adult children are legally compelled to financially assist parents who have exhausted their own resources. Article 208 of the Civil Code stipulates that children are obliged to help their parents for their food needs. It shows that in France dependency has been traditionally financed by family support. Public support is rather new, as will be discussed in the next section.

4 Public support for LTC

LTC is funded by a great diversity of public institutions, which makes its estimation difficult. The public effort has been estimated for frail elderly at around €22 billion in 2010, which represents 1.1 per cent of GDP (Rosso-Debord, 2010). This estimate is based on the forecast of the budget and

Social Security financing, since many government expenditures related to dependency are listed under Social Security spending.

In reality, public expenditure for LTC is broken down into four sources:[19] 63.1 per cent is financed by health insurance of Social Security, 20.5 per cent by local governments, 14.5 per cent by the National Solidarity Fund for Autonomy [Caisse Nationale de Solidarité pour l'Autonomie (CNSA)][20] and 1.9 per cent by the State (Rosso-Debord, 2010).

4.1   The APA

The government decided in 2002 to create the APA after the failure of a previous public scheme known as *Prestation Spécifique Dépendance* (PSD). PSD was implemented in 1997 and was unsuccessful due in large part to the fact that it included a pledge on inheritance clause,[21] which discouraged many seniors who did not want to reduce the inheritance of their children. Under the APA, the pledge on inheritance clause is excluded. The APA is paid to all people in a state of dependency (as defined by GIR 1 to GIR 4) aged 60 or over, regardless of their financial situation and place of residence within France.[22] However, only those with a low income are exempted from co-payment, which can represent up to 80 per cent of the total cost. The amount of the allowance depends on the degree of dependency. This allowance is jointly funded by both central and local governments.[23] Its characteristics have made it a great success. As indicated before, 1,117,000 people received the APA in 2009 (Debout and Lo, 2009). Since its creation, the number of beneficiaries has been increasing (Figure 8.1). Note that the increase in recent years is due almost exclusively to the increase in home help.

The total expenditure for APA was €5.116 billion in 2009 (Rosso-Debord, 2010). The data in Figure 8.2 show that local government participation in APA financing is increasing.

The proportion of APA beneficiaries moderately dependent (as defined by GIR 4) reached 45 per cent of the total number of beneficiaries in 2008. Their proportion was still significantly higher at home (57 per cent) than in institutions (24 per cent) (Debout and Lo, 2009).

The average benefit is €406 per month for those staying at home and €313 for those who reside in institutions if we exclude the co-payments paid by dependent persons. The acceptance rate for first applicants is stable: on average, three out of four first APA applications at home are accepted, while this figure is nine out of ten for institutions.[24]

It is worth saying a few words on projections of total LTC cost. Such projections are confronted with a double challenge: firstly, there is a need to forecast the costs of LTC at home and in institutions independently and, secondly, it is necessary to forecast how the overall costs will be distributed between home and institutions. Both projections are necessary to provide an estimation of the global cost in the future. These developments will directly influence the contributions of various actors (the State, the departments supported by the CNSA and health insurance).

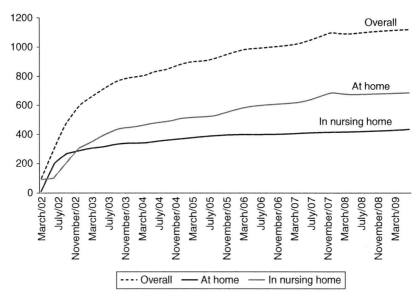

Figure 8.1 Evolution of APA beneficiaries
Source: Debout and Lo (2009).

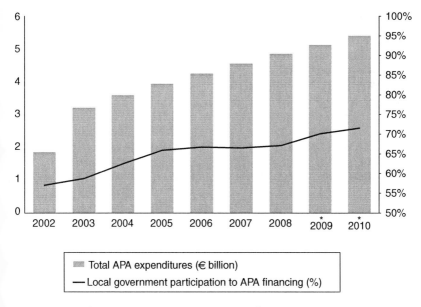

Figure 8.2 Local government participation in APA financing
Note: *Forecast.
Source: Rosso-Debord (2010).

Expenses related to APA represent only a small amount of total public assistance for dependency. Other public expenses are presented in the next section.

4.2 Other public expenditure related to the care of dependent persons

Dependent persons can also benefit from various tax deductions linked to their LTC expenses.

1. Firstly, a dependent person can benefit from a tax deduction if he or she hires a caregiver. Such tax deduction amounted to €2.101 billion in 2009 (Rosso-Debord, 2010).
2. Secondly, there exist public funds to develop informal care, either in the form of the *congé de solidarité familiale* or the *congé de soutien familial*, which both enable someone to stop working in order to help a dependent parent.
3. Thirdly, residing with a dependent parent further enables the possibility to reduce taxable income, with the dependent parent considered as a child. Finally, the caregiver child can also directly receive the APA in order to look after the dependent parent.

Finally, poor people who cannot afford to enter into a nursing home because of pensions too low and level of APA insufficient to finance the co-payment can be supported by social aid[25] to finance the cost of a nursing home. However to be eligible for this public aid, legal obligation has to be exhausted. This aid does not work for home help.

4.3 Government subsidies disadvantage middle classes

Adding up the allowances paid for dependency shows that public help is particularly unfavourable to the middle class. The amount of aid received (APA paid by the department and tax cuts) is best described through a U-curve as a function of annual income, as shown in Figure 8.3.

A dependent person, as defined by GIR 1, with a low income receives considerable help since that person's co-payment on APA is nil, even if she does not benefit from any tax exemption. The same person earning between €7756 and €28,800 in annual income receives lower public support due to the increase in the APA co-payment, which is not compensated by any tax reduction. By contrast, if that person earns over €36,000 income per year, the annual tax reduction is at maximum leverage and the total support increases until the maximum reduction of €5000 per year is reached.

4.4 The possible reforms of the APA

Local governments' budgets are becoming more and more burdened by the financing of the APA. Their financial situation is increasingly fragile. The other indirect funder of LTC, the Social Security, is not in any better shape. In addition, the APA is not always well adapted to the situation of

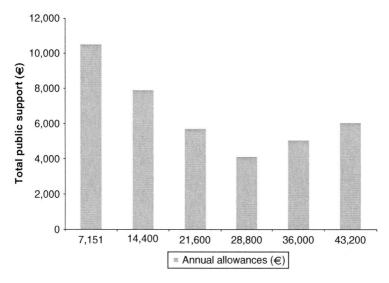

Figure 8.3 Total public support (allowance and tax cuts) received by income
Source: Cour des Comptes (2005).

dependent persons. On the one hand, for very highly dependent persons (with Alzheimer's disease, e.g.), APA is clearly insufficient compared with the cost of caregiving. On the other hand, if we consider that a person in GIR 4 is lightly dependent, APA for GIR 4 people could be seen as too high compared with the cost of caregiving.

In this context, several possible reforms of the APA have been launched by a special commission of the French Senate (Vasselle, 2008) The objective of the reforms is twofold: firstly, to help more people who are most in need; and secondly, to allow for voluntary pledge on inheritance clause.

So as to increase help for people most at need, the commission suggests raising the maximum level of APA for targeted populations, particularly for single persons and people with neurodegenerative diseases. Currently, the maximum level of APA for GIR 1 dependency is €1208.94, which has proven insufficient for this type of situation. The increase in the maximum level of APA could be offset by a decrease in the maximum APA for GIR 4 dependency at €518.55. The underlying idea is to help those most in need and help less those in 'light' dependency. Since a large proportion of dependent people have neurodegenerative diseases, this reform would also need to improve the AGGIR scale to better take into account the specificity of such diseases.

Another area of investigation would be to reinstate a pledge on inheritance clause in order to improve the tax balance of the local government. But unlike the PSD, pledging on inheritance would be freely chosen. The reform would offer higher-income persons the choice between a 50 per cent

APA rate or a full APA rate, but 'pledged' on the part of their inheritance above €150,000.[26] The amount of the 'pledge' would be subject to a maximum of €20,000. It would be repaid afterwards to the local government that paid the APA. According to the Senate commission, this device could yield €800 million in 2012. The measure should fully operate for persons with modest income but high assets. Conversely, it should play a small role for people with high incomes, for which APA pays, after deduction of cost sharing, only a very small amount (and which is asked to benefit only for certain advantages such as tax and social advantages).

5   The LTCI market in France

The insurance market currently covers a small part of LTC (FFSA, 2009). However, even though it is still recent, the French market proves to be one of the most dynamic amongst the industrialized countries. As such, it is interesting to ask to what extent the insurance market could be an important funder in the future as it is for health, and whether supply or demand factors could prevent the insurance market from playing a greater role. These questions are closely related to the notion of insurability of LTC risks and more specifically on whether dependency is a risk, whether this risk is sufficiently well defined (especially in France) and whether we can measure it. While the answer to the third question should not vary between countries, the first two answers can vary widely depending on the institutional context.

5.1   The insurability of LTC risks

5.1.1   *Is dependency a risk?*

Dependency is a risk and not a stage of life. An important proportion of people die without being dependent. The prevalence of dependency in France is rather low. Only 6.7 per cent of the population aged 60 or more is dependent. Moreover, the likelihood to become dependent (between GIR 1 and 4) before dying for a 65-year-old cohort is 15 per cent (Rosso-Debord, 2010). The incidence of dependency seems very low compared with the incidence of getting retired.

Moreover, long periods in dependency are rare. On average, people live in dependency for four years (Debout and Lo, 2009). Only 6 per cent of men and 16 per cent of women reaching the age of 60 live more than 5 years in a state of dependency (Debout and Lo, 2009). Many people are dependent for only a few weeks or months at the end of their lives (e.g., at the final stage of a deadly disease). However, when the pathology at the origin of the dependence is not evolutionary (in the case of a person affected by a severe stroke and who is very diminished but with no risk on his life expectancy), heavy dependence may last for many years. It so happens that the extent of the financial cost in case of dependency is affected by a great uncertainty on both the degree of dependency and on its duration. We are therefore well within the ground of a relatively rare risk but potentially very costly.

The characteristics mentioned above on the risk of dependency might disqualify the use of personal savings to protect against this risk, for two main reasons. Firstly, the use of personal savings does not allow pooling of risk and does not reduce the uncertainty faced by individuals. Secondly, in order to provide full protection against the risk of LTC in case of heavy dependency for many years, the savings effort would be detrimental to current consumption. Anyway, many people would not have the necessary income to assume such an effort.

In practice, the lack of insurance would weigh heavily on the middle class in France. Indeed, persons belonging to the poorer layers of the population would be supported by mechanisms of social assistance. On the other hand, the very wealthy, even in cases of high dependency, would manage to finance LTC costs without reducing current assets.

5.1.2 Is LTC risk sufficiently well defined?

Analysing the insurability of the risk of dependency presupposes a good definition of this risk. However, such a precise definition is not that obvious.

There is, in practice, a continuum of states of dependency. Hence, the definition of the threshold of incapacity from which dependency exists is partially arbitrary. The allocation of the APA is defined by the AGGIR classification based on daily living activities. Only persons classified from GIR 1 to GIR 4 are eligible for an allowance.

In practice, private insurers in France are often using the AGGIR classification supplemented with other criteria using the ADL or IADL, such as the Katz scale, to define the degree of dependency. The combination of several criteria is used to define more precisely the level of dependency,[27] but also to prevent insurers from being too reliant on a single criterion related to an official definition such as AGGIR.

Heavy dependency is actually easier to define, and the criteria used by private insurers to characterize total dependency are generally closely related. However, in the case of partial dependency, the definition is blurred and the criteria used are far from being homogeneous among the different insurance companies. This 'light' level of dependency (as defined by GIR 4)[28] causes problems for insurers because moral hazard is more likely. In fact, a non-dependent individual could be incited to become lightly dependent in order to receive free services which are useful even for non-dependent individuals (cooking, house cleaning, shopping and so on). In this case, it will be difficult for the insurer to prove that this individual would be autonomous without any insurance.

5.1.3 Assessing the risk of dependency

The risk of dependency from the insurer's point of view can actually be broken down into three risks: an occurrence risk, a dependency duration risk and a cost of care risk.

The main difficulty in assessing the dependency risk is that it is an intertemporal risk deferred in time. Individuals are likely to become dependent only after some decades once they have contracted insurance. Offering an assessment, and a pricing, of this risk means that insurance companies are able to forecast on a 15–20-years horizon the risk of becoming dependent, the length of dependency and the future costs of LTC.

Predicting probabilities of transition between three or four states of dependency is very complex (Taleyson, 2003). As an illustration, depending on whether an efficient treatment against Alzheimer's disease (representing a high proportion of dependent people) becomes available, the total number of dependent people could be very different. It would be illusory to believe that insurers are able to estimate accurately the evolution of the average probability of entering into dependency, and the average life expectancy when in a state of dependency.

In addition, the average cost of care is very difficult to model. US studies have shown that over a long period of time, the cost of care in institutions were not stationary and that the confidence interval estimates of these costs were very wide (Cutler, 1993). Studies in France confirm this hypothesis of non-stationary costs. However, we observe that if we focus on home care, the confidence intervals of the evolution of these costs are lower (Plisson and Nouet, 2007). In practice, formal care at home is provided by relatively unskilled personnel. The future evolution of the average cost of care will be correlated with the wages of unskilled jobs, whose long-term trend is difficult to predict with a good confidence interval. As regards care in institutions, other criteria may also strongly influence the costs (price of real estate, health regulations, number of helpers and so on).

5.2 The products offered

The insurance product currently proposed in France is a cash benefit product, in the form of an annuity. The insured decides when signing the contract how much cash he will receive if he were to become dependent. For this product to work well, it is still necessary for the insured to assess the exact amount of his pension in the future, his future level of dependency and the future cost of home help. While the first prediction can be made with reasonable confidence intervals, uncertainty is high when one considers the last two points. It follows that the risk on the level of dependency and the risk on the cost of care are to be partially borne by the insured.

5.2.1 *Waiting periods and deductible periods*

So as to prevent moral hazard and especially adverse selection, insurers protect themselves through waiting periods and elimination periods.[29]

Implementing a waiting period means that the benefit in case of dependency can only be received after a certain period has elapsed after the subscription of the contract. This waiting period is usually one year when the dependency is due to illnesses other than mental illnesses, and three years in the case of mental pathologies (Alzheimer type). These waiting periods are rather long. However, dependency usually occurs at a later stage in life and the issue of waiting periods can be solved with an incentive to start a LTC contract earlier (around age 50, e.g.). These waiting periods are primarily designed to fight against adverse selection. If adverse selection in the French market cannot already be detected with confidence (Legal and Plisson, 2008), it is likely to develop in the future with the likely availability of improved genetic screening tests for neurodegenerative diseases (Oster et al., 2009). Therefore, these waiting periods are often more important for neurodegenerative diseases (three years) than for physical dependencies.

Moreover, most policies have a 'deductible period', typically 30 to 100 days in length, which is the number of days a person must be in dependency before insurance payments commence; this is analogous to a deductible in other insurance contracts. During this time, relatively high levels of cost can be incurred (several thousands euros). That being said, the existence of a deductible period does not preclude the crucial role of LTCI to ensure that LTC costs are covered for a very long time.

5.2.2   Choice of indemnity level in case of dependency

The risk associated with the future monthly LTC cost in practice remains with the insured because the latter chooses the amount of the indemnity and the level of premium adjusts accordingly.

Insurers set minimum and maximum indemnity levels. In some cases, a maximum indemnity is high enough to ensure good coverage (at least given the cost of LTC today), but this is not always the case. In a recent study of contracts amongst the most popular in France today (Dufour-Kippelen, 2008), a maximum indemnity from €900 to €3865 per month was reported in case of total dependency. It is clear that an indemnity of €900 only partially covers the cost of heavy dependency.

Beyond this issue, the choice of the indemnity by the subscriber is efficient only if one assumes that the insured has a good understanding of the level of his needs in case of dependency. The average indemnity selected in case of total dependency is about €600 per month, which is notoriously inadequate to cope with heavy dependency. It is clear that LTCI only allows for partial coverage of LTC risks.

5.2.3   Indexation clauses limiting the extent of guarantees

Most contracts in France include an indexation of indemnity (and therefore of premiums to ensure financial equilibrium) to protect against inflation, often based on the Consumer Price Index (CPI) or the 'AGIRC point'[30] (evolving like inflation). However, if the minimum wage varies more rapidly than the CPI (which has been the case in the past), the amount of the indemnity may grow more slowly than the cost of intervention of professional carers. In addition, a maximum adjustment is often provided (5 per cent or 10 per cent per year) that would be problematic if inflation were to return to levels found in the 1970s. Finally, a number of contracts impose that the revaluation should take place after the first dependency payment has occurred, that is, potentially many decades after the initial choice of the indemnity level by the subscriber. If there was no regular reassessment of the level of the indemnity (through higher premiums, of course), it could well yield a lower value once dependency occurs.

5.2.4   *Distribution of products as part of group contracts*

A significant amount of LTCI in France is contracted through group contracts (although the risk is minimal given the age of employees). LTC coverage is often an additional guarantee to health insurance. What often happens is that coverage stops when the employees leave the company upon retirement, since either they cannot afford it anymore[31] or because they are not aware of it.

5.3   The market for LTCI in France

The first LTCI contracts were marketed in the mid-1980s by the insurance company AG2R. However, until the late 1990s, the market remained relatively small. In the early 2000s, as shown in Figure 8.4, the French market experienced strong growth, particularly due to new entrants, mainly bank insurers who developed marketing or cross-selling products through their banking client network. The number of persons covered by a LTCI contract in 2009 was approximately 3 million, 2 million being covered by insurance companies and about 1 million by mutual insurance or pension institutions (FFSA, 2009).

It is worth stressing that the market remains highly concentrated. Among approximately the 30 companies in this market, 4 accounted for 76 per cent of the total premiums in 2008 and 83 per cent of persons covered. In terms of product distribution, banking groups seem more dynamic. Indeed, for two-thirds of those covered in late 2008, the LTC contract was subscribed through a network of banks (FFSA, 2009).

Amongst the 2 million people having insurance, 60 per cent were covered by an individual contract, the remainder being covered by group contracts through their employers. There is a noticeable difference in the level of contributions and benefits between individual and group membership, as shown in Figure 8.5. This difference could be explained by at least two reasons: firstly, subscribers of group contracts are younger, which allows for the same level of service to pay a lower premium; secondly, group contracts often do not consider the LTC risks as the principal risk. These are

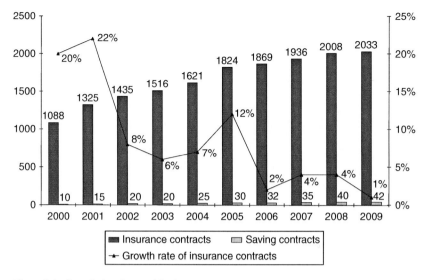

Figure 8.4 Population insured by insurance companies
Source: FFSA (2009).

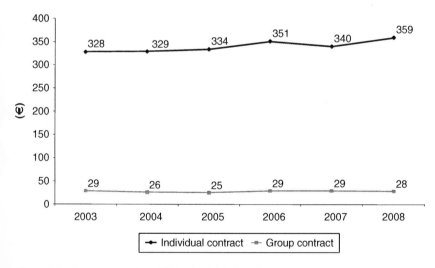

Figure 8.5 Average premium (€) by individual and year
Source: FFSA (2009).

complementary benefits to a health or pension insurance, that is, the level of coverage selected in case of dependency is much lower than a LTC contract.

Yet, the demand for LTCI would seem relatively small in comparison with the importance of the risk of dependency and the aversion of individuals to such a risk. Several theoretical arguments have been proposed to explain the decisions whether to purchase LTCI. The most common explanatory factors include: information asymmetry phenomena, intergenerational factors, bias in risk perception, the role of the State as insurer of last resort, the family structure, access to informal care and the amount of inheritance to leave to children. For a detailed analysis of the arguments for the low demand for private LTCI, please refer to Chapter 3 in this book. There is also another suggestion for this low development that is much more contextual. In 2006, the French government announced a major reform of LTCI that is still to come. This uncertainty creates a form of waiting period for the population, but also for insurers who need to know the new institutional framework before proposing new products. This explanation is particularly relevant to interpret the low dynamism of the market since 2006.

There exist few empirical studies on the market for LTCI in France. Courbage and Roudault (2008) based on the SHARE survey show that altruism plays a significant role in the demand for insurance covering LTC. The authors show that the French insurance market for LTC is not limited by potential phenomena of intra-family moral hazard[32] as defined by Zweifel and Struwe (1998). A second study based on company data shows that there is no adverse selection in the French market when using standard tests of adverse selection (Legal and Plisson, 2008).[33] This apparent lack of adverse selection can be explained by low market maturity. However, many signs suggest that phenomena of compensation between different dimensions of adverse selection exist (Plisson, 2009).[34] As observed in the United States, it seems that the phenomenon of adverse selection on the probability of loss is compensated by the fact that those most risk averse have a higher level of coverage. They also invest more in prevention, reducing their likelihood of becoming dependent (Finkelstein and McGarry, 2006).

6   Possible reforms of the French system: Which project for the 'fifth risk'?

There is nowadays a strong will in France to consider LTC risks as a fifth risk of life that needs to be covered by society, in parallel to the four risks of life already covered by Social Security, which are illness, old age, family and recovery. The ways the fifth risk will be covered are still in discussion and different proposals have emerged.

It is therefore relevant to study the different institutional forms that the financing of LTC risk can take and to highlight some advantages and disadvantages.

6.1   Universal Social Security

One proposal is to create a fifth branch of Social Security to cover LTC risks. This can have different interpretations. For some, the fifth branch means nearly total public coverage of the LTC risk, as Social Security does in the case of health risk. The fifth risk branch would result in an overall upgrading of benefits, and the LTCI market would play a marginal role. It would be the government's responsibility to increase the Social Security contribution rates accordingly, which may create public opposition. It would also be the government's responsibility to ensure equality between generations and phasing in of benefits and contributions.

For others (including elected officials and local governments), the fifth branch would mean a simple transfer to the Social Security of the funding supported so far by local governments in order to relieve their budget. The fifth risk branch would not necessarily mean a change in the level of allocation or in the allocation criteria, but a new mode of financing. This debate may be of interest to local governments but may not be necessarily an issue for users.

An obvious argument in favour of full support by the Social Security comes from uncertainties about the evolution of dependency, as discussed above. Confronted with this uncertainty, it should be the State responsibility to take over the entire risk. This argument has been developed by Cutler (1993). The second argument concerns the economic scale possibilities. When the same contract is applied to everybody, the average price may be reduced.

However, the project, attractive for its simplicity, raises a series of questions. Firstly, it faces limited margins of public finances that will necessarily limit the coverage that is really needed. It also causes rigidity in the system with the difficulties of coming back to the previous level of benefits. Secondly, opportunistic behaviours from the demand side of LTC, due to high public coverage, are expected to grow. A universal Social Security could increase moral hazard, in particular in the case of 'light' dependency. These behaviours could increase the total expense of LTC.

This project could also have an anti-redistributive effect going against the philosophy of Social Security. For rich people, this project would indirectly allow a more important transmission of assets between generations. If people with substantial assets were fully covered, they would not have to dip into their savings to pay for either LTC or private insurance. This anti-redistributive effect would affect different generations. It would require a full transfer from the current and future generations to the benefit of the 'post-war generation', whose size has already reached an unprecedented level. Some even see in this universal Social Security project 'the last hold-up of the baby-boom generation'.[35]

6.2 A compulsory private LTCI: An economic approach

A recent public report on the financing of LTC advocates a private compulsory insurance (Rosso-Debord, 2010). This project could be based on the same institutional design as motor insurance in France or the health insurance system in Switzerland. From an economic point of view a compulsory insurance has at least three benefits (Geoffard, 2010).

Firstly, it forces individuals to protect against LTC risk. Individuals tend to underestimate the risk of becoming dependent before dying. It is difficult for them to buy an insurance contract for a risk which will occur only in decades. Moreover, it is difficult to behave rationally in front of the LTC risk. A compulsory insurance is a means to force people to be cautious and provident. The same argument is used to justify a compulsory pension scheme, whether public or private. Forcing people to be insured is also a means to avoid opportunist behaviours – for example, people who believe that the State will always pay for them.

Secondly, it reduces market failures in the LTCI market. Asymmetric information between insurers and policy-holders is an inherent problem of all insurance markets. In particular, the 'good risks' tend not to be uninsured and the 'bad risks' tend to be insured, which entails a rationing or a destruction of the market. This adverse selection phenomenon is likely to occur for a risk which depends on health status and which will occur only in decades. Compulsory insurance is the most common way to eliminate adverse selection.

Thirdly, it creates a market for LTC services. Financing LTC is useless if elderly dependents cannot buy a quality good for LTC services at a competitive price. A compulsory insurance may develop the market for LTC services (at home and in nursing homes). It tends to increase the number of LTC providers, which should decrease the price and guarantee a good quality of service. This link between compulsory insurance and development of services is not automatic, but it has already been observed concerning health insurance.

However, compulsory insurance resolves only a part of the problem. Firstly, compulsory insurance is difficult to apply from a practical point of view. For instance, motor insurance is compulsory in France. However, many drivers drive without any insurance. Secondly, even if the LTCI were compulsory insurers tend spontaneously to segment the market. It is the law of supply and demand. Therefore, Geoffard (2010) advocates three measures required for a compulsory insurance: to regulate the price of insurance, to standardize insurance contracts and to pool the risk between insurers. If these three arguments concern the benefits of a compulsory insurance, they do not advocate for a private or a public compulsory insurance. And finally, two issues remain: a solution has to be found for people who cannot afford a private insurance, likely in the form of public subsidies, and the transition cost to set up this private compulsory insurance is high (estimated at around €1.5 billion).

6.3   Public–private partnership

Another possibility to cover LTC risk would be the development of a universal guarantee for LTC within a public–private partnership (PPP), under which the heavy level of dependency would be dissociated from what is called moderate or 'light' dependency. The underlying idea is that light dependency deals with a majority of individuals and should be considered more like a stage of life and regular expenses than a risk itself. Only the state of heavy dependency would be considered as a risk and it would only be covered by private insurance. The light dependency could then be taken over either by a social assistance scheme for the poorest, or by individual savings accumulated over the working life for others. This solution is of relevance in terms of market efficiency, since heavy dependency is a risk that can be easier to identify than light dependency. In addition, moral hazard is less possible in case of heavy dependency, while it may happen more easily in the case of light dependency.

Based on this idea, Kessler (2010) even suggests not making private LTCI mandatory. Any person losing autonomy would be eligible for a public LTC benefit. However, only those whose resources are insufficient would be able to benefit free of charge. For the others, a financial participation increasing in line with the household's resources would be required, in order to dissuade free-riders. This of course would necessitate a harmonization or coordination of the scale on which LTC is evaluated by both the public and private sectors. Households should be free to choose to participate in the LTCI market with tax incentives. For instance, the premium could be exempt from social and tax deductions. Kessler (2010) also suggests going beyond a simple tax exemption and providing a refundable tax credit which would allow all households, irrespective of their level of income and marginal tax rate, to benefit from the same ratio of tax support. In the same way, the benefit paid in the event of LTC would also be exempt from income tax and social contributions, up to a certain limit since it is not supposed to be a replacement income.

Such an option raises at least two difficulties. Firstly, it requires a clear distinction between heavy dependency and light dependency, which is not so obvious. Secondly, it delays the issue of the financing of dependency since it deals only with high dependency, which represents 15 per cent of the cost of LTC, the remaining 85 per cent being due to light dependency.

7 Conclusion

France is ageing rapidly, like most other European countries, challenging the ways LTC is financed. In France, there exists a long tradition of public coverage for the large risks of life, and LTC risk follows this trend. Yet, in addition to public support, a market for LTCI has developed and encompasses today almost 3 million individuals.

This chapter has tried to provide an analysis of the ways LTC is financed in France, focusing on both the public coverage and the private insurance market. Yet, there are other ways of financing LTC, in particular through personal savings or equity home conversion. We would like briefly to touch upon these two topics.

Indeed, one way pursued by various countries is to allow and/or to force individuals to save during their working lives in order to pay for either their LTC expenses later in life or to pay LTCI premiums so as to spread the cost of LTC over time. These savings can take the form of health savings accounts, as in China, Singapore or the United States, where savings are invested in special accounts to cover only health-care spending. These accounts are generally offered in combination with a high-deductible and tax incentives insurance. Various saving options exist: whether in the form of voluntary participation with financial incentives, or of mandatory contribution with additional contribution from the employer. These savings accounts could also take the form of the Swiss second pillar, the mandatory occupational pensions system. The funds of the second pillar are already being used to expand home ownership. They could also be used to expand access to LTC or insurance. The drawback is that such accounts do not enable risk sharing between individuals and depend on the performance of financial markets. Additionally, they can segment the pool of insurees further and make LTC risks more difficult to insure.

Another individual way to finance LTC is through home ownership. Actually, a large proportion of the elderly own their homes. This real estate asset can be used as a way to finance LTC. This is done first by downsizing, that is, moving to a smaller or cheaper home and releasing the difference as equity. Secondly, this can be done via equity home conversion or 'reverse mortgage', which approximates the notion of *viager* in France. A reverse mortgage is a loan secured on the value of a property. This type of loan enables the creation of liquid, or monetization of, real estate assets, without any immediate transfer of ownership. This concept seems to appeal primarily when it is directly linked to LTC expenses. This is well illustrated by a proposal from the French Senate suggesting that, to receive the full APA rate, persons whose wealth exceeds a certain threshold will have to pledge part of their inheritance. Chen (2001) suggests going further by linking the reverse mortgage, not to LTC spending, but to either life or LTC insurance. The idea is that the reverse mortgage would be used to pay insurance premiums and not LTC. One solution would be to link the annuity to be received to the value of the house and to the level of dependency. The property would act as a safety net and would be used as financing of last resort. Of course, a limit to home equity conversion is that this source of income is available only to property owners.[36]

As discussed in this chapter, the way LTC risk is financed in France is quite complex and relies on various supports. Both the private and the public sectors play a role. Faced with an increase in LTC needs, these roles may change in the future. The decision the government will take to organize the financing of the fifth risk will undeniably shape the future of French society.

Notes

*Helpful comments were received from Alistair MacPherson, Bernard Ennuyer, Philippe Egger, Jérôme Wittwer and Roméo Fontaine. Manuel Plisson acknowledges support from the Fondation Médéric Alzheimer.

1. Public coverage represents only 30 per cent of the average cost of LTC (Ennuyer, 2006).
2. Also called 'reimbursement insurance'.
3. Throughout the text, we will use interchangeably either LTC or dependency to refer to care for old age to people limited in their activities of daily living.
4. Meaning Handicap-Incapacity-Dependency.
5. Meaning Handicap-Health in ordinary household.
6. Called Établissement d'Hébergement pour Personnes Âgées Dépendantes (EHPAD).
7. In particular, we have neither an official survey about the distribution of this cost, nor a national survey which shows how the cost depends on geographic place, level of dependency, type of structure (profit or non-profit nursing homes) and so on.
8. Notably Age Village Association (http://www.agevillage.com, accessed 22 January 2011).
9. Including Pascal Champvert, chairman of ADPA (French Association of Nursing Homes).
10. Estimates provided by the site http://www.agevillage.com (accessed 22 January 2011).
11. This figure comes from a report produced by the French General Direction of competition, consumption and fraud. It is available at http://www.dgccrf.bercy.gouv. fr/documentation/fiches_pratiques/fiches/assurance_dependance.htm (accessed 22 January 2011).
12. Le Monde Argent (2009).
13. Which means non-financial.
14. The literature on the determinants of informal LTC largely focuses on the links existing between informal care and formal care (see, e.g., Van Houtven and Norton, 2004, 2008; Bolin et al., 2008; Bonsang, 2009). Results are not unanimous and depend on the causal sense of the relationship and on the type of formal care considered.
15. See Gisserot (2007) and Rosso-Debord (2010), p. 45.
16. See the Vasselle (2008) report, p. 148, which reports the results of Simone Pennec about this issue.
17. See Sorensen et al. (2002) and Brodaty et al. (2003).
18. This study is based on American data and not on French or European data. The results could be different in a European context.
19. Using 2005 figures.
20. This fund was created in 2003, following the heatwave of summer 2003 in France, to help assist the elderly. It is financed through various taxes and transfers from the Social Security, and amounted to about €17 billion in 2008. Its role is to pool a part of the wealth between local governments.
21. People needing LTC were supported by the local government but those whose wealth exceeded a certain threshold had to pledge part of their inheritance, which was collected afterwards to reimburse part of the care expenditures.
22. For example, if they are living in a city with many shops and services close by, or isolated in the country.

23. But the main part is funded by the local government.
24. This difference is explained by the fact that people who wish to enter institutions have, on average, higher levels of dependency.
25. The social aid in France is close to Medicaid in the United States. It is reserved only for poor people.
26. If a dependent individual wants to receive the full APA amount, she or he has to accept this pledge.
27. But this choice also leads probably to a more restrictive definition of 'dependency' than in the case of APA. Hence, for many insurance policies, total dependency requires at the same time that the person is classified as GIR 1 or 2, is unable to perform three out of the four ADL and that his or her state of health is not likely to improve.
28. Some insurance companies even offer a lump sum to adapt housing in the case of dependency defined by GIR 5.
29. These mechanisms are very often used by insurers and are not specific to LTC risks.
30. AGIRC is the supplementary public pension scheme. The AGIRC point is computed to determine the total amount of the supplementary pension. The AGIRC point is thus used to update other allowances.
31. In France, the 1989 Evin Law guarantees the protection of the individual's coverage (provided they make a request and subject to any increase in premiums up to 50 per cent) to employees leaving the company only for health reasons (Article 4).
32. Intra-family moral hazard refers to the disincentive for informal caregivers to provide care to their dependent relatives in the presence of insurance coverage for formal LTC.
33. Available online at http://www.dauphine.fr/fileadmin/mediatheque/chaires/chaire_transition/pdf/Assurance_Dependance_Plisson_Legal_JESF_2009.pdf (accessed 22 January 2011).
34. Available online at http://www.dauphine.fr/fileadmin/mediatheque/chaires/chaire_transition/pdf/these_Plisson_2009.pdf (accessed 22 January 2011).
35. *Dixit* Philippe Trainar during the conference La dépendance: que sait-on vraiment? organized by the University Chair 'Risques et chances de la transition démographique', Université Paris Dauphine and Fondation du Risque, Paris, 4 December 2008.
36. For a detailed analysis of this issue, we refer the readers to Chapter 5 in this book.

References

Attias-Donfut, C. (1995) *'Les solidarités entre générations. Vieillesse, familles, Etat'* (Paris: Nathan).

Attias-Donfut, C. (1996) 'Les solidarités entre générations', Données Sociales (Paris: Insees), pp. 317–323.

Bolin, K., Lindgren, B. and Lundborg, P. (2008) 'Your next of kin or your own carer? Caring and working among the 50+ of Europe', *Journal of Health Economics*, 27, pp. 718–738.

Bonsang, E. (2009) 'Does informal care from children to their elderly parents substitute for formal care in Europe?' *Journal of Health Economics* 28, pp. 143–154.

Breuil-Genier, P. (1999) 'Caring for the dependent elderly: More informal than formal', *INSEE Studies*, 39, September, pp. 1–25.

Brodaty, H., Green, A. and Koschera, A. (2003) 'Meta-analysis of psychosocial interventions for caregiviers of people with dementia', *Journal of the American Geriatrics Society*, 51, pp. 657–664.

Chen, Y.P. (2001) 'Funding long-term care in the United-States: The role of private insurance', *The Geneva Papers on Risk and Insurance – Issues and Practice*, 26, pp. 656–666.

Coe, N.B. and Van Houtven, C.H. (2009) 'Caring for mom and neglecting yourself? The health effects of caring for an elderly parent', *Health Economics*, 18 (9), pp. 987–990.

Costa-Font, J. and Rovera-Forns, J. (2008) 'Who is willing to pay for long term care insurance in Catalonia?', *Health Policy*, 86, pp. 72–84.

Cour des Comptes (2005) *Les personnes âgées dépendantes*, November.

Courbage, C. and Roudaut, N. (2008) 'Empirical Evidence on Long-term Care Insurance Purchase in France', *The Geneva Papers on Risk and Insurance – Issues and Practice*, 33, pp. 645–658.

Cutler, D. (1993) 'Why Doesn't the Market Fully Insure Long Term Care?', NBER Working Paper no. 4301.

Davin, B., Paraponaris, A. and Verger, P. (2009) 'Entre famille et marché: déterminants et coûts monétaires de l'aide informelle reçue par les personnes âgées en domicile ordinaire', *Revue Management & Avenir*, 2009/6 – , 26, pp. 49–62.

Debout, C. (2010) 'La durée de perception de l'APA: 4 ans en moyenne', *Etudes et Résultats*, no. 724 (DREES: Paris), April.

Debout, C. and Lo, S.H. (2009) 'Les bénéficiaires de l'APA au 30 juin 2009', *Etudes et Résultats*, no. 710 (DREES: Paris), November.

Dos Santos, S. and Makdessi, Y. (2010) 'Une approche de l'autonomie chez les adultes et les personnes âgées: Premiers résultats de l'enquête Handicap-Santé 2008', *Etudes et Résultats*, no. 718 (DREES: Paris), February.

Duée, M. and Rebillard, C. (2004) 'La dépendance des personnes âgées: une projection à long terme', *INSEE, série des documents de travail de la Direction des Études et Synthèses Économiques*, no. G2004/02.

Duée, M. and Rebillard, C. (2006) 'La dépendance des personnes âgées: une projection en 2040', *Données sociales – La société française*, 7, pp. 613–619.

Dufour-Kippelen, S. (2008) 'Les contrats d'assurance dépendance sur le marché français en 2006', *Etudes et Recherche*, no. 84 (DREES: Paris), December.

Durand, R. and Taleyson, L. (2003) 'Les raisons du succès de l'assurance dépendance en France', *Risques – Les Cahiers de l'Assurance* 55, pp. 115–120.

Ennuyer, B. (2006) *Repenser le maintien à domicile: Enjeux, acteurs, organisation* (Paris: Dunod).

FFSA (2009) *Les contrats d'assurance dépendance en 2008 (aspects quantitatifs)*, May.

Finkelstein, A. and McGarry, K.M. (2006) 'Multiple dimensions of private information: Evidence from the long term care insurance market', *American Economic Review* 96 (4), pp. 938–958.

Fontaine, R. (2009) 'Aider un parent âgé se fait-il au détriment de l'emploi?', *Retraite et Société*, 58, pp. 31–61.

Fontaine, R., Gramain, A. and Wittwer, J. (2007) 'Les configurations d'aide familiales mobilisées autour des personnes âgées dépendantes en Europe', *Economie et statistique*, Programme National Persée, 403 (1), pp. 97–115.

Fontaine, R., Gramain, A. and Wittwer, J. (2009) 'Providing care for an elderly parent: Interactions among siblings?', *Health Economics*, 18, pp. 1011–1029.

Geoffard, P.-Y. (2010) 'Quelle assurance contre le risque dépendance?', in *Le choc des génération? Dettes, retraites, dépendance...*, Regards croisés sur l'économie no. 7 (Paris: La Découverte), pp. 159–166.

Gisserot, H. (2007) *Perspectives financières de la dépendance à l'horizon 2025: prévisions et marge de choix*, Mission confiée à Hélène Gisserot, Procureur Général Honoraire auprès de la Cour des Comptes.

Kessler, D. (2010) 'Confronting the challenge of long-term care in Europe', *CESifo DICE Report*, no. 2, pp. 18–23.

Le Monde Argent (2009) 'Le Baromètre de la dépendance', France Info – Le Monde – Ocirp, 5 December.

Legal, R. and Plisson, M. (2008) 'Assurance dépendance, effets de sélection et anti-sélection', *Journées des Economistes de la Santé Français*, paper was presented in a conference in Paris, 4 and 5 December.

Norton, E. (2000) 'Long-Term Care', in A.J. Culyer and J.P. Newhouse (eds) *Handbook of Health Economics*, vol. 1, chapter 17 (North Holland: Elsevier), pp. 955–994.

Oster, E., Shoulson, I., Quaid, K. and Dorsey, E.R. (2009) '*Genetic adverse selection: Evidence from long-term Care Insurance and Huntington Disease*', NBER Working Paper 15326.

Plisson, M. (2009) *Assurabilité et développement de l'assurance dépendance*, PhD Dissertation, Paris Dauphine University, available at http://www.dauphine.fr/fileadmin/mediatheque/chaires/chaire_transition/pdf/these_Plisson_2009.pdf, date accessed 22 January 2011.

Plisson, M. and Nouet, S. (2007) 'L'assurabilité et la place des produits dépendance en France', *Risques* no. 72, December.

Rosso-Debord, V. (2010) *Rapport d'information sur la prise en charge des personnes âgées dépendantes*, Rapport de l'Assemblée Nationale.

Scanlon, W. (1992) 'Long-term care financing reform possible directions', *Journal of Economic Perspectives*, 6, pp. 43–58.

Sloan, F.A. and Norton, E.C. (1997) 'Adverse selection, bequests, crowding out, and private demand for insurance: Evidence from the long-term care insurance market', *Journal of Risk and Uncertainty*, 15, pp. 201–219.

Sorensen, S., Pinquart, M. and Duberstein, P. (2002) 'How effective are interventions with caregivers? An updated meta-analysis', *Gerontologist*, 42, pp. 356–372.

Taleyson, L. (2003) 'La dépendance', in J. Blondeau and C. Partrat (eds) *La Réassurance – Approche technique* (Paris: Economica), pp. 67–82.

Van Houtven, C. and Norton, E. (2004) 'Informal care and health care use of olders adults', *Journal of Health Economics*, 23, pp. 1159–1180.

Van Houtven, C. and Norton, E. (2008) 'Informal care and Medicare expenditures: Testing for heterogeneous treatment effects', *Journal of Health Economics*, 27, pp. 134–156.

Vasselle, A. (2008) *Rapport d'étape sur la prise en charge de la dépendance et la création du cinquième risque*, Rapport du Sénat, 8 July.

Wolff, F.-C. and Attias-Donfut, C. (2007) 'Les comportements de transferts intergénérationnels en Europe', *Économie et Statistique*, 403–404, pp. 117–141.

Zweifel, P. and Struve, W. (1998) 'Long term insurance in a two-generation model', *Journal of Risk and Insurance*, 65 (1), pp. 13–32.

9
From Commission to Commission: Financing Long-Term Care in England

Adelina Comas-Herrera, Raphael Wittenberg and Linda Pickard
Personal Social Services Research Unit (PSSRU), LSE Health and Social Care,
London School of Economics and Political Science, United Kingdom

1 Introduction

The financing of long-term care (LTC) has been among the most debated social policy issues in England since at least the mid-1990s (Royal Commission on Long Term Care, 1999; Brooks et al., 2002; JRF, 2006; Wanless et al., 2006, HM Government, 2010a). Underlying the debate are concerns about both the future affordability of LTC and the fairness of the current funding system. The key issue in the financing debate is how far people should fund their own care and how far they should be publicly funded, in particular whether public funds for LTC should benefit only those who cannot afford to pay for themselves (a residual model) or whether free LTC should be a universal entitlement. The debate started from before the establishment of the Royal Commission on Long Term Care (1999) and has continued, more or less unabated, since then.

One reason why the debate has been so intense is because, since 2002, there have been different systems of LTC in different parts of the United Kingdom (UK). LTC is now a devolved responsibility to the nations of the United Kingdom, and in Scotland the central recommendation of the Royal Commission on Long Term Care was adopted and free personal care was introduced in 2002. In the rest of the UK, however, free personal care has not been introduced.

The debate over LTC in England intensified further after the publication of the Wanless social care review, which argued in favour of a 'partnership' model of funding personal care, whereby the costs of care would be shared partly by the State and partly by the individual (Wanless et al., 2006). The debate over LTC continued in England with the outgoing Labour Government's publication in 2009 of a Green Paper, *Shaping the Future of Care Together* (HM Government, 2009), and the announcement of a policy of free personal care in their own homes for people with the highest needs (*Community Care*, 2009b). This was followed by the publication of a White Paper in March 2010, *Building the National Care Service* (HM Government, 2010a). The new Coalition Government, which replaced the Labour Government in May 2010, has set up a Commission on the Funding of Care and Support due to report in July 2011.

The first section of this chapter examines key issues relating to the current LTC system in England, exploring the problems identified in official reports on LTC and in the wider social policy literature. The second section of the chapter discusses recent reviews and reports recommending reform of the financing system, including the proposals contained in the Labour Government's Green and White Papers and the initial documents produced by the new Coalition Government. The chapter aims to present a broad overview of the current organizational structures in England to discuss the suggested key reforms and to put them in an international context. The chapter updates a recent article by the authors (Comas-Herrera et al., 2010).

Since responsibility for health and social care in the UK is, as already implied, devolved to the administrations for each country, this chapter concentrates on England, but references are also made to the systems in Scotland, Wales and Northern Ireland.

2   The current English LTC system

The English LTC system has been characterized as a 'safety-net' (Fernández et al., 2009) or 'residual' (Brodsky et al., 2003) system that only supports those with very severe needs who are unable to meet the costs of their care. It is also a system that has evolved incrementally from earlier systems of welfare for the poor by developing specific services to meet the LTC needs of older people and a limited relaxation of the means-tests (Ikegami and Campbell, 2002). Partly as a result of its origins, it is a complex system that most people do not understand. A review of eligibility criteria for social care in England by the former Commission for Social Care Inspection (CSCI) concluded that there is 'a lack of clarity and transparency in practice, particularly relating to the complexity of the framework, so neither professionals nor people using services are confident of their understanding' (CSCI, 2008, p. 4).

LTC in the UK is usually taken to mean help with domestic tasks, such as shopping and preparing meals, assistance with personal care tasks, such as dressing and bathing, and nursing care. There is a mixed economy of provision of care. The system relies heavily on informal or unpaid care provided by family, friends or neighbours (Pickard et al., 2000, 2007). Formal services are provided by a range of agencies including local authority social services, community health services and independent (for- and non-profit) sector residential care homes, nursing homes, home care and day care services.

There is also a mixed economy of finance. Services are financed by the National Health Service (NHS), local authorities, charities and older people themselves. While health care services are free at the point of use, social care is means-tested. There is a non-means-tested disability benefit for older people with personal care needs and a benefit for carers. The market for LTC insurance in England is minimal: only a very small number of people, just under 22,000, had private LTC insurance in 2008 (Association of British Insurers, 2009). There is currently only one provider selling LTC insurance products in the UK. The lack of enthusiasm for private LTC insurance in England has been attributed to both demand and supply side failures (see, e.g., Department of Health, 2009d).

Access to publicly funded services is mainly through an assessment of care needs coordinated by the local authority social services department. Assessment and care management aim to determine eligibility for publicly funded care and develop a care package to meet assessed needs. There has been, increasingly, an emphasis on targeting services to people with greater disabilities. A care manager may be involved in coordinating the assessment and organization of care and may have a devolved budget with which to purchase services. People assessed as eligible for a package of care can instead opt for a direct payment that they can use to buy equipment or services themselves. In 2008–2009, 495,000 older people not already in receipt of services had a completed assessment of their needs (Department of Health, 2010b). Most of the referrals (for people of all ages) were self-referrals (26 per cent), followed by referrals from secondary health services (25 per cent), from family, friends or neighbours (14 per cent) and from primary or community health (13 per cent). After first contact, 61 per cent of older people had their completed assessment within two weeks and 96 per cent within three months (Department of Health, 2010b).

Following an assessment, a person may be provided with a new service, may not be offered a service, may themselves decline any service or may have some other outcome. Some may be referred on to the NHS or housing agencies or to voluntary sector services. In 2008–2009, most older people assessed as eligible (80 per cent) received all their services within two weeks after the assessment (Department of Health, 2010b).

Eligibility criteria for publicly funded social care, arrangements for assessments and budgets are determined locally and there is great variability between local authorities. In 2002, the Department of Health published a national framework for eligibility criteria, *Fair Access to Care Services*, to address inconsistencies across the country (Department of Health, 2002). The aim of the framework was to ensure that people with similar needs would be able to achieve similar outcomes. It did not require individuals with similar needs to be given similar services. The framework provided four severity bands (low, moderate, substantial and critical) to which individuals are allocated. Councils can choose where to set their eligibility criteria within those bands.

The eligibility criteria have tightened considerably over recent years, partly as a result of budgetary constraints. Most councils only consider eligible those in the substantial and critical bands, and some only those in the critical band. The report by the former CSCI, mentioned earlier, found that despite the implementation of the eligibility framework there are still wide variations between councils (CSCI, 2008). Another report by the Audit Commission (2008) on the effects of the *Fair Access to Care Services* system on expenditure and service provision found that there were wide variations in spending on care for older people, according to how restrictive was the use of thresholds. There are concerns that the needs of people in the more moderate bands are not being met and that opportunities for prevention are being missed, leading to worse outcomes for care users and higher costs to the system (Wanless et al., 2006; CSCI, 2008; HM Government, 2009). In 2007, the Labour Government published a ministerial concordat, *Putting People First* that aims at changing the emphasis of the system towards early intervention and prevention (HM Government, 2007), and *Fair Access to Care Services* was revised (Department of Health, 2010c). The new Coalition's government document *A Vision for Adult Social Care* also puts a strong emphasis on prevention (Department of Health, 2010d).

Eligibility for publicly funded care and support takes into account the availability of informal care, so that older people with similar levels of disability do not receive the same amounts of formal service support. The revisions to *Fair Access to Care Services* in early 2010 (Department of Health, 2010c) did not alter this. Services in England are primarily directed at disabled older people who do not receive informal care, particularly those who live alone (Arber et al., 1988; McNamee et al., 1999; Evandrou, 2005). Since the majority of disabled older people in England either live with others and/or receive informal care (Table 9.1), eligibility criteria restricting formal service support primarily to those living alone or those without informal care are an important reason why many disabled older people are currently not considered eligible for publicly funded support (Table 9.2). As a consequence, unlike a number of other LTC systems in Western Europe, the LTC system in England is not 'carer-blind' (Pickard, 2001; Fernández et al., 2009). The fact that eligibility criteria take into account the availability of informal care in England has been a source of criticism of the LTC system in this country (Royal Commission on Long Term Care, 1999; Glendinning and Bell, 2008; Himmelweit and Land, 2008).

Those people who have been assessed as eligible for social care services are then subject to a means-test to establish whether their services will be funded wholly or partly by the local authority. There is a national charging regime for residential and nursing home care in England, which takes into account the income and assets (in most cases including any housing wealth)

Table 9.1 People with a functional disability in private households aged 65 and over, by marital status, household type and receipt of informal care, England, 2006

Marital status, household type and receipt of informal care	Numbers	Column %
Single, living alone, no informal care	205,000	10
Single, living alone, receives informal care	670,000	32
Single, living with child, receives informal care	160,000	8
Single, living with others, receives informal care	55,000	3
Couple, no informal care	75,000	4
Couple, receives informal care from spouse	695,000	34
Couple, receives informal care from child	100,000	5
Couple, living with others, receives informal care	110,000	5
Total disabled in households	2,068,000	100

Note: Numbers are rounded to nearest 5000. 'People with a functional disability' are defined as those having difficulties with instrumental or basic Activities of Daily Living, or needing help with one Activity of Daily Living. 'Single' refers to widowed, divorced, separated and never married people who are not cohabiting; 'couple' refers to those living in legal or de facto partnerships. *Source*: PSSRU model estimates, based on data from the 2001/2002 GHS and 2006 official population data.

Table 9.2 Estimated number of older people receiving services in a given day by service type and age, England, 31 March 2009

	Number of users	% of older population
Day care	81,000	0.96
Meals	229,000*	2.72
Local authority arranged home care	275,000	3.26
Respite care	14,000	0.17
Private home care	150,000*	1.78
Community nursing	460,000*	5.46
Direct payments	27,000	0.32
Professional support	132,000	1.57
Equipment and adaptation	223,000	2.65
Independent sector residential care	183,000	2.17
Local authority residential care	16,000	0.19
Nursing care homes	128,000	1.52
Long-stay hospital	9,000	0.11
Total in institutions	336,000	3.99

Note: * Estimates from the PSSRU LTC model, based on levels of service receipt report in the 2001–2002 General Household Survey. Note that the definition of private help used here only includes those who needed help with one or more ADLs.
Source: Department of Health (2010b). There is overlap between home-based services.

of residents. Those with assets over an upper limit, currently set at £23,250, are not eligible for local authority support. Those with assets below this level are required to contribute most of their income towards the costs of their care. The NHS makes a non-means-tested contribution for nursing costs in care homes.

Local authorities have discretion over whether and how they charge for home care services, although there are national guidelines (Department of Health, 2003) which set out common principles to which local authorities must adhere in determining how much to charge users. In particular, they must disregard a sum of income equivalent to at least 25 per cent above the level of social security income maintenance benefits.

Services are provided by local authorities and independent providers. In the last ten years there has been a rapid increase in the amount of care provided by private providers (Philpott, 2008; NHS Information Centre, 2009), and this trend is expected to continue (Department of Health, 2010b). Prices are negotiated between the local authorities and the providers, except in the case of clients with direct payments who negotiate directly with providers. People can also buy services directly from private providers, without any mediation from the public sector. There are concerns that, where the fees paid by local authorities are low, providers set higher prices for private payers, which means that, effectively, private payers are subsidizing local authority-funded services (Netten et al., 2003).

Around 335,000 older people, some 4 per cent of the older population of England, were residents in care homes in 2008. These comprise 182,000 local authority-funded residents, an estimated 120,000 privately funded residents and an estimated 35,000 NHS-funded residents. Around 650,000 older people receive local authority-funded community-based services, including some 275,000 receiving home care. An estimated 150,000 severely disabled older people (unable to conduct personal care tasks without help) purchase home care privately, with substantially larger numbers of less disabled older people purchasing private help. Further details are given in Table 9.2.

Services are heavily concentrated on the oldest old. Those over age 85 are more likely to receive all formal services than the 'younger' old, and this is particularly true of residential care (Table 9.3). Recipients of residential care are also more likely to have lived alone prior to admission to care and are less likely to have owned their own homes (Hancock et al., 2002).

In the context of a general national policy of extending individual consumer choice in the public sector (6, 2003), and in line with developments in other countries (Lundsgaard, 2005; Pavolini and Ranci, 2008), reforms are under way to give people entitled to publicly funded social care services choice and control over their care. These reforms started with the introduction of a form of cash payments called direct payments in 1997 for younger adult disabled people and the extension to older people in 2000. Direct payments are available to people who have been assessed as needing

Table 9.3   Key characteristics of recipients of domiciliary and residential care, compared with the general population of older people, Great Britain, 2002

Percentages	% all older people (aged 65 and over)	% recipients of community services*	% recipients of residential care
Aged 85 and over	12	26	52
Female	58	66	76
Living alone**	38	65	68
Owner-occupier**	68	73	43

Notes:
*Covering home care and private domestic help services.
**For people in care homes, household type and housing tenure prior to admission.
Source: PSSRU model estimates, using ONS population estimates and analyses of 2001/2002 GHS, Department of Health and PSSRU residential care survey data.

services and are eligible for publicly funded support. The level of a direct payment is calculated according to the amount of personal support needed by the individual and costed with reference to the costs of equivalent services in kind. They are commonly used by recipients to employ a personal assistant or helper to provide the support they need. The employment of close relatives living in the same household is not allowed, except in exceptional circumstances. The purchase of services from the local authority is not allowed either. The take-up of direct payments, especially among older people, has been low. Numerous barriers have been identified, including the restrictions on the use of the payments, the administrative burden of becoming an employer, lack of effective support schemes for users and reluctance of local authorities to promote direct payments (Davey et al., 2007).

In 2007, the Labour Government published a ministerial concordat called *Putting People First*, which sets out reforms to personalize social care. The document stated that 'the time has now come to build on best practice and replace paternalistic, reactive care of variable quality with a mainstream system focussed on prevention, early intervention, enablement, and high quality personally tailored services. In the future, we want people to have maximum choice, control and power over the support services they receive' (HM Government, 2007, p. 2). A fundamental component of the reform was personal budgets: an individual allocation of funding to enable individuals to make choices about how best to meet their needs, including their broader health and well-being. A person would be able to take all or part of their personal budget as a direct payment, to pay for their own support either by employing individuals themselves or by purchasing support through an agency. Others may wish, once they have decided on their preferred care package, to have the council continue to pay for this directly. It would be possible to have a combination of both the approaches. The *Putting People First* reforms aimed at reducing the barriers to take-up that direct payments had encountered. Personal budgets involved much lower demands on the individual in terms of employing and managing people (Samuel, 2009). They were also accompanied by targets and a substantial 'Social Care Reform Grant' to local authorities to help them redesign and reshape their services (Department of Health, 2009).

There has also been a large-scale pilot of a similar system called Individual Budget (IB). IBs were piloted in 13 local authorities as a new system that would bring together, for any individual, the resources from a number of different services or funding streams to which they are entitled. These resources included local authority funding for social care, community equipment and housing adaptations and other disability-related benefits (but not Attendance Allowance or NHS funding). An IB would pool these resources for any one person and the total amount would be made transparent to the individual. The IB could be used to secure a flexible range of goods and services, from a wider variety of providers than is possible with direct payments. For example, the IB could be used to pay informal carers living in the same household, or to purchase goods or services from local authorities. A national evaluation found that IB resources were typically used to pay for personal care, domestic help and social, leisure and educational activities. Most people chose to purchase conventional forms of support. The evaluation found that overall holding an IB was associated with better social care outcomes but older people reported lower psychological well-being with IBs, perhaps because they felt the processes of planning and managing their own support were burdens (Glendinning et al., 2008). The Coalition Government has wholeheartedly embraced the personalization agenda, stressing the aim of expanding the use of personal budgets (Department of Health, 2010d).

Total expenditure on LTC services for older people in England has been estimated, using the PSSRU macrosimulation model, to be around £18 billion in 2008 (or 1.66 per cent of GDP). Of this, around 30 per cent was funded by local authorities (personal social services), and 35 per cent by individuals or their families (of which 16 per cent was user charges and 19 per cent was direct private expenditures). This figure does not include the contribution of informal carers or contributions by charities.

Another important component of the care system is social security disability benefits. Attendance Allowance, and Disability Living Allowance for those who started to receive disability benefits from before the age of 65, are the main disability benefits for older people with disabilities. In 2008–2009, these benefits paid out £4.8 billion. Attendance Allowance is paid at two rates, depending on whether the older person needs assistance during the day (2008–2009, £44.85 a week) and/or night (£67.00), and is not means-tested. In 2008, 1.29 million people were receiving Attendance Allowance in England. Eligibility for Attendance Allowance is governed by the need for help or supervision, but the claimant does not actually have to be in receipt of such support. It is a compensation for disability rather than a payment to cover the costs of services. Analysis of data from the English Longitudinal Study of Ageing (ELSA) showed that only a minority (27 per cent) of Attendance Allowance claimants used either State-funded or privately funded social care. Some 29 per cent were receiving neither formal nor informal care (Wanless et al., 2006:94).

The LTC system in the UK has been characterized as one in which there is 'extensive financial support for informal care' (Lundsgaard, 2005). Financial support for informal care in this country takes the form of Carer's Allowance, a non-means-tested benefit paid to people providing long hours of informal care. The allowance, which amounts to £53.90 a week, is paid to informal carers who provide at least 35 hours, informal care per week, earn less than £100 per week, are not in full-time education and look after someone who receives qualifying disability benefits (such as Attendance Allowance). Carer's Allowance is based on a social security model of payments for care (Glendinning and McLaughlin, 1993) and is regarded by the Department for Work and Pensions as a compensation for loss of earnings, not as a wage for caring. There were approximately 510,000 recipients of Carer's Allowance in the UK in 2008 and UK expenditure on the allowance was approximately £1.3 billion in 2007/2008 (Carers UK, 2008; NAO, 2009). Carer's Allowance (and its predecessor, Invalid Care Allowance) has long been the subject of criticism in this country, primarily because of its low level and its poor coverage of heavily committed carers (Pickard, 1999; NAO, 2009). The present Coalition Government has recently published a White Paper proposing the introduction of a Universal Credit, which may involve changes to the Carer's Allowance (Department for Work and Pensions, 2010, p. 19).

In addition to social security support, there are national policies intended to provide support for informal carers in England. Indeed, there has been an increasing emphasis in government policy over the last two decades on providing support for informal carers (Pickard, 2001; Beesley, 2006). Current policies are embodied in a national strategy for carers (HM Government, 2010c). The policy emphasis in the carers' strategy is primarily on provision of support to enable informal carers to continue providing care. Since the mid-1990s, people providing substantial and regular care in England have had the right to a local authority assessment of their needs for services and, since 2001, they have been entitled to receive services in their own right (Beesley, 2006). However, only a minority of 'heavy duty' carers receive assessments and only around one in ten receive carer support services (Beesley, 2006).

3   Financing long-tem care: Key suggested reforms

The previous Labour Government considered the issue of LTC funding sufficiently important and complex to warrant the first Royal Commission for many years. The purpose of the Royal Commission on Long Term Care was to review the financing of LTC and to make recommendations about future financing. Its key recommendation, as indicated at the beginning of this chapter, was that there should be 'free' personal and nursing care, that is, the nursing and personal care components of the fees of care homes and home-based personal care should be met by the State, without a means-test, and financed out of general taxation (Royal Commission on Long Term Care, 1999). Means-testing would remain for the accommodation and ordinary living costs ('hotel' costs) covered by residential fees and for help with domestic tasks. The report of the Royal Commission also recommended that 'the Government ensure services become increasingly "carer blind"' (Royal Commission on Long Term Care, 1999, p. 90).

The Government accepted some of the Royal Commission's recommendations but only removed the means-test for nursing care in nursing homes (Secretary of State for Health, 2000). Similar decisions were adopted by the National Assembly for Wales and the Northern Ireland Assembly. However, as indicated earlier, the Scottish Executive decided that it would make personal care for older people free of charge as well (Care Development Group, 2001).

These decisions did not bring an end to the debate about how best to fund LTC. Pressure to make personal care free of charge throughout the UK remained. A left-leaning think tank, the Institute for Public Policy Research (IPPR), for example, advocated that personal care should be made free to all (Brooks et al., 2002). The Joseph Rowntree Foundation (JRF) conducted a major three-year programme on paying for LTC in the UK and argued strongly for better funding arrangements, describing the policy of free personal care in Scotland as 'promising', 'popular' and 'perceived as fair' (JRF, 2006, p. 2) The JRF, though stressing the need for fundamental reform of the system, has also suggested a number of ways in which the present system could be improved without incurring excessive costs (Hirsch, 2005; JRF, 2006).

The King's Fund set up in 2005 a review of care for older people, under the leadership of Sir Derek Wanless, to determine how much should be spent on social care for older people in England over the coming 20 years. The report of the review *Securing Good Care for Older People* was published in 2006 (Wanless et al., 2006). As indicated earlier, the Wanless review favoured a partnership arrangement 'characterised by combining a publicly funded entitlement to a guaranteed level of care, with a variable component made up of contributions from individuals matched at a given rate by contributions from the state' (Wanless et al., 2006, p. 278). Wanless proposed that the publicly funded entitlement should be two-thirds of the benchmark level of care. Users could choose whether they wanted the remaining third, with the costs being met half by the user and half by the State. The benchmark level of care is the level that is cost-effective given a cost-effectiveness threshold of £20,000 per ADLAY (i.e., the gain for one year of life of having core activities of daily living (ADL) needs improved from being entirely unmet to being fully met). A partnership arrangement on these lines would require an increase in public expenditure of some £3.5 billion.

The Wanless report advocated a partnership model because it believed that, on balance, it compared favourably to free personal care or a means-tested system.

- The Wanless report argues that the partnership model is efficient. It suggests that it produces the highest ratio of outcomes (ADLAYs) to costs of the three funding systems (Wanless et al., 2006, p. 270).
- It has strengths and weaknesses in regard to equity and fairness: 'for the guaranteed element, support is based entirely on need and not ability to pay, but the converse is largely the case for the matched element...' (Wanless et al., 2006, p. 269).
- It scores well on choice, as individuals will be able to choose the level of care they receive above the guaranteed level, albeit subject to co-payment.
- It scores as well as free personal care on dignity, as no means-testing would be required within the care system.
- It is not as strong as a means-tested system on economic sustainability, but if necessary 'the guaranteed entitlement can be scaled back to reduce costs... or the matching contribution can be reduced' (Wanless et al., 2006, p. 271); and more options for dealing with sustainability could be added.
- It is not as strong as free personal care in terms of introducing a 'carer-blind' approach, since the partnership model is not 'carer-blind', whereas free personal care is described as partially so in the Wanless review (Wanless et al., 2006, p. 246).

The Wanless review prompted renewed interest in the financing of LTC. In February 2008, the International Longevity Centre – UK set out a proposal for funding older people's LTC based around a social insurance fund for the retirement stage, into which individuals would make contributions as a lump sum, through regular instalments or as a charge on their estate (Lloyd, 2008). Barr proposes the extension of social insurance to provide mandatory cover for LTC, with the possibility of topping up either from private savings or through supplementary private insurance (Barr, 2010).

During 2008, the Labour Government ran a six-month engagement process on the care and support system in England. This involved seeking the views of the public, service users and staff. It was followed in July 2009 by the publication of a Green Paper (HM Government, 2009), which set out the then Government's proposals for ways to reform the care and support system for adults in England.

The Green Paper listed a number of problems with the current LTC system, which the proposed reforms were intended to address (HM Government, 2009, p. 8). A key problem is that many older and disabled people in England do not get any help from the State towards paying for their care and support, partly because publicly funded social care is means-tested (HM Government, 2009, p. 8). The means-test for long-stay residential care includes the value of the older or disabled person's house, which means that many older people in need of residential care have to 'sell their homes to pay for care and support' (HM Government, 2009, p. 8). In addition, State-funded care and support is often provided only when people have already developed high levels of need, therefore allowing preventative opportunities to be missed (HM Government, 2009, p. 8). Moreover, people with the same needs receive different levels of care depending on where they live; the different parts of the care and support system do not work together; the care system as a whole is confusing and the system is not tailored to people's needs (HM Government, 2009, p. 8). Problems associated with the current system are expected to be exacerbated in the coming years by the growing numbers of older people, with the Green Paper estimating that 1.7 million more adults will need care and support by 2026 (HM Government, 2009, p. 9).

The Green Paper stated the Labour Government's intention to build the first National Care Service in England. The vision was 'for a system that is fair, simple and affordable for everyone, underpinned by national rights and entitlements but personalised to individual needs' (HM Government, 2009, p. 9). The proposals extended beyond the financing system to cover prevention services; national assessment; a 'joined-up service'; information and advice; personalized care and support and 'fair funding', where everyone who qualified for care and support from the State would get help meeting the cost of care and support needs. The Green Paper discussed five possible funding options:

- pay for yourself, under which there would be no support from the State;
- partnership, where everyone who qualified for care and support would be entitled to have a set proportion of their basic care and support costs met by the State, with that proportion inversely related to the person's resources;
- insurance, which would comprise the partnership system plus insurance for those wanting to purchase it;
- comprehensive, where everyone over retirement age who had the resources to do so would be required to pay into a state insurance scheme;
- tax-funded system, which would provide free care funded from increased general taxation.

The Green Paper ruled out the first and last of these options and consulted on the other three. Because the first option was ruled out, the Green Paper was in essence proposing that 'everyone who has high levels of care and support need gets *some* of their care and support paid for by the state' (HM

Government, 2009, p. 19, emphasis added). In this sense, the underlying model advocated in the Green Paper was the partnership approach. As the Green Paper put it, 'We think that the Partnership option should be the foundation of the new system' (HM Government, 2009, p. 19). The questions then were whether, how far and by what financing mechanism the remaining costs would be met (HM Government, 2009, p. 19).

Responses to the Green Paper suggested that there was general approval for a National Care Service, but also raised a number of issues for debate (Age Concern and Help the Aged, 2009; Community Care, 2009a; *Health Service Journal*, 2009; Scope, 2009). One area of concern was the proportion of care and support needs to be met by the State in either a partnership- or insurance- based option. The Green Paper suggested that the State might meet, for example, a quarter to a third of basic care and support costs (HM Government, 2009, p. 17). This fell considerably short of the two-thirds of the 'benchmark level of care' that Wanless suggested should be met by the State (Wanless et al., 2006). Another area of contention was the Green Paper's suggestion that Attendance Allowance could be integrated into the care and support system (Age Concern and Help the Aged, 2009; Scope, 2009). A third area of potential concern was the ruling out of taxation as a means of funding the proposed National Care Service and the confinement of the funding options to contributions from older people alone (Age Concern and Help the Aged, 2009). Finally, the treatment of informal care in the Green Paper also raised concerns. Because the foundation of the proposals in the Green Paper was a partnership approach (HM Government, 2009, p. 19), and because a partnership approach is not 'carer-bind' (Wanless et al., 2006, p. 246), not all the options proposed in the Green Paper addressed concerns about the dependence of the care and support system on the availability of informal care (Glendinning and Bell, 2008; Himmelweit and Land, 2008).

The Labour Government's Green Paper was followed by a White Paper, published on 30 March 2010, just a few weeks before the 2010 UK General Election. The White Paper (HM Government, 2010a) built on the earlier Green Paper. The White Paper stated that the National Care Service would (in its own words):

- 'Be universal – supporting all adults with an eligible care need within a framework of national entitlements.'
- 'Be free when people need it – based on need, rather than the ability to pay.'
- 'Work in partnership – with all the different organisations and people who support individuals with care and support needs day-to-day.'
- 'Ensure choice and control – valuing all, treating everyone with dignity, respecting an individual's human rights, personal to every individual's needs and putting people in charge of their lives.'

- 'Support family, carers and community life – recognising the vital contribution families, carers and communities play in enabling people to realise their potential.'
- 'Be accessible – easy to understand, helping people make the right choices' (HM Government, 2010a, p. 13).

The White Paper proposed that reform would be conducted in three stages. The first stage would include free personal care at home for those with the highest needs. This had been proposed by the Prime Minister in autumn 2009 and was the subject of new legislation, the Personal Care at Home Bill. It would also include continuation of policies to extend personalization, support for carers and integration of services. The second stage, to be implemented during the 2010 to 2015 Parliament, would involve putting in place the systems and processes to make the comprehensive National Care Service a reality. This would include enshrining national eligibility criteria for social care in law, building a new quality framework, commissioning national information and advice and providing that every eligible person would be offered a personal budget. In addition, from 2014, anyone staying in residential care for more than two years would receive free care after the second year. The Government also proposed to establish a commission to help to reach a consensus on the right way of funding a comprehensive National Care Service. The third and final stage of reform, after 2015, would be 'to move to a comprehensive National Care Service for all adults in England with an eligible care need, free when they need it, whoever they are, wherever they live and whatever condition leads to their need for care' (HM Government, 2010a, p. 27).

There was little opportunity for evaluation of the proposals in the White Paper, since it was published towards the end of the outgoing Labour Government's time in office. Moreover, the White Paper did not make proposals around the funding of the new National Care Service and therefore side-stepped many of the issues, identified earlier, that had been raised in connection with the Green Paper.

The New Coalition Government which took office following the UK General Election in May 2010 decided not to implement the recommendations of the previous Government's White Paper and not to bring into effect the provision of the Personal Care at Home Act. They stated in their formal Coalition Agreement that 'We will establish a commission on LTC, to report within a year. The commission will consider a range of ideas, including both a voluntary insurance scheme to protect the assets of those who go into residential care, and a partnership scheme as proposed by Derek Wanless' (HM Government, 2010b). The new Government duly announced on 20 July 2010 the formation of a new Commission on the Funding of Care Support. Its terms of reference state that 'The Commission is asked to make recommendations on how to achieve an affordable and sustainable funding system for care and support, for all adults in England, both in the home and other settings... The approach recommended... must be consistent with the Government's deficit reduction plan as set out in the June 2010 Budget and the Spending Review, and be sustainable for the public finances in the long term in the context of an ageing society' (Department of Health, 2010e). The Commission has published the criteria by which it will assess different options for the future funding of care and support (Commission on the Funding of Care and Support, 2010). These comprise:

- Sustainabilty and resilience: ensuring the costs to the state are sustainable in the long term, and the care and support system is able to respond to demographic, economic, political and societal change.
- Fairness: for individuals, families, carers and wider society.
- Choice: offering an affordable choice to individuals, carers and families across a range of care settings, and helping people to prepare and plan for their future.
- Value for money: securing the highest quality care outcomes with the available resources.
- Ease of use and understanding: making the system as clear and simple as possible for people, supporting people to take responsibility for their future well-being.

The next step in the long debate about the financing of social care in England now rests with the Commission, which is due to publish its recommendations by July 2011. It remains to be seen whether these will command a wide range of public support and finally bring the debate to a close.

4 Conclusions

The current UK LTC system is, to a considerable extent, formed by many local systems. Health and social care are a devolved function, which means that the responsibility for health and social policy is devolved to the administrations for England, Scotland, Wales and Northern Ireland. Devolution has led to some policy divergence and key differences have arisen in the funding of social care: in particular, while Scotland has introduced free personal and nursing care, the other countries have introduced only free nursing care.

Responsibility for assessing local needs and commissioning health and social services rests currently with Primary Care Trusts (PCTs) and local authorities, respectively, in England and their equivalents in the other countries. For social care, local authorities are responsible for assessing population needs, commissioning services, setting local eligibility criteria and assessing individuals against those criteria. While there is a national system for means-testing and charging for residential care, local authorities determine locally the system for charging and means-testing for home care.

The UK system is marked by a mixed economy of supply. The system relies heavily on informal care provided mainly by close relatives. There is a wide range of providers of formal care in the public, voluntary (not-for-profit) and private (for-profit) sectors. Direct payments, which are cash alternatives to services, are now available to enable people to employ their own carers or to use for a wide range of purposes.

The system is also marked by a mixed economy of finance. Health care, including nursing care in all settings, is free at point of use, and is funded mainly from general taxation. Most social care (except for personal care for older people in Scotland) is means-tested and is funded by a combination of central taxation, local taxation and user charges. Disability benefits, by contrast, are not means-tested and are funded from general taxation. This means that the system is complex and not easily understood.

The English LTC system has now been the subject of debate for nearly two decades and there have been numerous proposals for reform. The last Labour Government proposed the creation of a new National Care Service, shortly before being replaced by a Coalition Government. The new government duly announced on 20 July 2010 the formation of a new Commission on the Funding of Care Support due to report in July 2011. Its terms of reference stated that 'The Commission is asked to make recommendations on how to achieve an affordable and sustainable funding system for care and support, for all adults in England, both in the home and other settings...The approach recommended...must be consistent with the Government's deficit reduction plan as set out in the June 2010 Budget and the Spending Review, and be sustainable for the public finances in the long term in the context of an ageing society' (Department of Health, 2010e).

The Coalition Government plans to publish a White Paper in late 2011 and their Social Care Reform Bill in early 2012. It should then become clearer whether the long debate over financing LTC in England, from the Royal Commission set up by the previous government to the current Commission set up by the Coalition Government, will have reached closure.

References

6, P. (2003) 'Giving Consumers of British Public Services More Choice: What can be Learned?', *Journal of Social Policy*, 32 (2), pp. 239–270.

Age Concern and Help the Aged (2009) *Green Paper Sets Out Reform Challenge*, available at http://www.army-acquisition.net/article/Green-Paper-Sets-Out-Care-Reform-Challenge--UK.html, 14 July, date accessed December 2010.

Arber, S., Gilbert, G.N. and Evandrou, M. (1988) 'Gender, Household Composition and Receipt of Domiciliary Services by Elderly Disabled People', *Journal of Social Policy*, 17, pp. 153–175.

Association of British Insurers (2009) *Personal communication*, 16 September.

Audit Commission (2008) *The Effect of Fair Access to Care Services Bands on Expenditure and Service Provision*, available at http://www.cqc.org.uk/_db/_documents/

Tracked%20Audit%20Commission%20report%20on%20FACS%2013%20August_
typeset.pdf, date accessed December 2010.

Barr N. (2010) 'Long-term Care: A Suitable Case for Social Insurance', *Social Policy and Administration*, 44 (4), pp. 359–374.

BBC (2009) 'Free personal care' for elderly, 29 September, available at http://news.bbc.
co.uk/1/hi/health/8281168.stm, date accessed December 2010.

Beesley L. (2006) *Informal Care in England* (London: King's Fund).

Brodsky, J., Habib, J., Hirschfeld, M., Siegel, B. and Rockoff, Y. (2003) 'Choosing Overall LTC Strategies: A Conceptual Framework for Policy Development', in WHO (ed.) *Key Policy Issues in Long-Term Care* (Geneva: World Health Organization), pp. 245–270.

Brooks, R., Regan, S. and Robinson, P. (2002) *A New Contract for Retirement* (London: Institute for Public Policy Research).

Care Development Group (CDG) (2001) *Fair Care for Older People* (Edinburgh: The Stationery Office).

Carers UK (2008) *Policy Briefing: Carers' Allowance Statistics, August 2008* (London: Carers UK).

Comas-Herrera, A., Wittenberg, R. and Pickard, L. (2010) 'The Long Road to Universalism? Recent Development in the Financing of Long-term Care in England', *Social Policy and Administration*, 44, pp. 375–391.

Commission on the Funding of Care and Support (2010) *Criteria*, available at http://www.dilnotcommission.dh.gov.uk/criteria, date accessed 6 January 2011.

Community Care (2009a) 'Public funding will not increase, DH confirms', *Community Care*, 14 July.

Community Care (2009b) 'Gordon Brown makes free personal care pledge', *Community Care*, 29 September.

Costa-Font, J. (2010) 'Devolution, Diversity and Long-Term Care Reform in the "Latin Rim"', *Social Policy and Administration*, 44 (4), pp. 481–494.

CSCI (Commission for Social Care Inspection) (2008) *Cutting the Cake Fairly: CSCI Review of Eligibility Criteria for Social Care* (London: CSCI).

Davey, V., Snell, T., Fernández, J.-L. et al. (2007) *Schemes Providing Support to People Using Direct Payments: A UK Survey* (London: Personal Social Services Research Unit).

Department of Health (2002) *Fair Access to Care Services. Guidance on Eligibility Criteria for Adult Social Care* (London: Department of Health).

Department of Health (2003) *Fairer Charging Policies for Home Care and Other Non-residential Social Services. Guidance for Councils with Social Care Responsibilities*, available at http://www.dh.gov.uk/prod_consum_dh/groups/dh_digitalassets/@dh/@en/documents/digitalasset/dh_4117931.pdf, date accessed 10 September 2009.

Department of Health (2009) *Transforming Adult Social Care*, Local Authority Circular, available at http://www.dh.gov.uk/en/Publicationsandstatistics/Lettersandcirculars/LocalAuthorityCirculars/DH_095719, date accessed December 2010.

Department of Health (2010a) *Impact Assessment of the Care and Support White Paper, Building the National Care Service, 30th March 2010*, available at http://www.dh.gov.uk/prod_consum_dh/groups/dh_digitalassets/documents/digitalasset/dh_114931.pdf, date accessed February 2011.

Department of Health (2010b) *Community Care Statistics 2008–09: Social Services Activity Report, England*. The NHS Information Centre for Health and Social Care, available at http://www.ic.nhs.uk/webfiles/publications/Social%20Care/socialcarepubs280410/Community%20Care%20Statistics%20Social%20Services%20Activity%20Report%20England%20-%202008-09%20FINAL2.pdf, date accessed February 2011.

Department of Health (2010c) *Prioritising Need in the Context of Putting People First: A Whole System Approach to Eligibility for Social Care. Guidance on Eligibility Criteria for Adult Social Care, England, 2010* (London: Department of Health).

Department of Health (2010d) *A Vision for Adult Social Care: Capable Communities and Active Citizens* (London: Department of Health), available at http://www.dh.gov.uk/prod_consum_dh/groups/dh_digitalassets/@dh/@en/@ps/documents/digitalasset/dh_121971.pdf, date accessed February 2011.

Department of Health (2010e) *First Step to Sustainable Care and Support System*, press release 20 July 2010, available at http://www.dh.gov.uk/en/MediaCentre/Pressreleases/DH_117636, date accessed December 2010.

Department for Work and Pensions (2010) *Universal Credit: Welfare that Works*, Cm 7597, November (London: Department for Work and Pensions).

Evandrou, M. (2005) 'Health and Social Care', in Office for National Statistics (ed.) *Focus on Older People* (London: The Stationery Office), pp. 51–65.

Fernández, J.-L., Forder, J., Truckeschitz, B., Rokosova, M. and McDaid, D. (2009) *How Can European States Design Efficient, Equitable and Sustainable Funding Systems for Long-term Care for Older People?* Policy Brief 11 (Copenhagen: World Health Organization Europe).

Glendinning, C. and Bell, D. (2008) *Rethinking Social Care and Support. What Can England Learn from Other Countries?* (York: Joseph Rowntree Foundation).

Glendinning, C., Challis, D., Fernández, J.-L. et al. (2008) *Evaluation of the Individual Budgets Pilot Programme Final Report.* Individual Budgets Evaluation Network, available at http://www.pssru.ac.uk/pdf/IBSEN.pdf, date accessed 6 January 2011.

Glendinning, C. and McLaughlin, E. (1993) *Paying For Care: Lessons from Europe* (London: HMSO).

Hancock, R., Arthur, A., Jagger, C. and Matthews, R. (2002) 'The Effects of Older People's Economic Resources on Care Home Entry under the UK Long-term Care Financing System', *Journals of Gerontology: Social Sciences*, 57B (5), pp. S285–S293.

Health Service Journal (2009) '"National care service" Could Pit Councils against NHS', *Health Service Journal*, 15 July.

Himmelweit, S. and Land, H. (2008) *Reducing Gender Inequalities to Create a Sustainable Care System* (York: Joseph Rowntree Foundation).

Hirsch, D. (2005) *Facing the Cost of Long-Term Care. Towards a Sustainable Funding System* (York: Joseph Rowntree Foundation).

HM Government (2007) *Putting People First: A Shared Vision and Commitment to the Transformation of Adult Social Care* (London: HMG).

HM Government (2009) *Shaping the Future of Care Together* (London: HMG).

HM Government (2010a) *Building the National Care Service*, command 7854, available at http://www.dh.gov.uk/en/Publicationsandstatistics/Publications/PublicationsPolicyAndGuidance/DH_114922, date accessed 6 January 2011.

HM Government (2010b) *The Coalition: Our Programme for Government*, available at http://webarchive.nationalarchives.gov.uk/20100919110641/http://programmeforgovernment.hmg.gov.uk/index.html, date accessed December 2010.

HM Government (2010c) *Recognised, Valued and Supported: Next Steps for the Carers Strategy* (London: HMG).

Ikegami, N. and Campbell, J.C. (2002) 'Choices, Policy Logics and Problems in the Design of Long-term Care Systems', *Social Policy and Administration* 36 (7), pp. 719–734.

Joseph Rowntree Foundation (JRF) (2006) *Paying for Long-Term Care* (York: Joseph Rowntree Foundation).

Le Bihan, B. and Martin, C (2010) 'Long Term Care policy in France: A Long Way to the Insurance Model', *Social Policy and Administration*, 44 (4), pp. 392–410.

Lloyd, J. (2008) *A National Care Fund for Long-Term Care* (London: International Longevity Centre – UK).

Lundsgaard, J. (2005) *Consumer Direction and Choice in Long-Term Care for Older Person, Including Payments for Informal Care: How Can it Help Improve Care Outcomes, Employment and Fiscal Sustainability*, OECD Health Working Papers No. 20, DELSA/HEA/WD/HWP(2005)1.

McNamee, P., Gregson, B.A., Buck, D., Bamford, C.H., Bond, J. and Wright, K. (1999) 'Costs of Formal Care for Frail Older People in England: The Resource Implications Study of the MRC Cognitive Function and Ageing Study (RIS MRC CFAS)', *Social Science and Medicine*, 48, pp. 331–341.

NAO (National Audit Office) (2009) *Department for Work and Pensions: Supporting Carers to Care* (London: The Stationery Office).

Netten, A., Darton, R. and Williams, J. (2003) 'Nursing Home Closures: Effects on Capacity and Reasons for Closure', *Age and Ageing*, 32, pp. 332–337.

NHS Information Centre (2009) *Community Care Statistics 2008 Home Care Services for Adults, England* (The Health and Social Care Information Centre), available at http://www.ic.nhs.uk/webfiles/publications/Home%20Care%20(HH1)%202008/ HH1%20Final%20v1.pdf, date accessed 4 September 2009.

Pavolini, E. and Ranci, C. (2008) 'Restructuring the Welfare State: Reforms in Long-term Care in Western European Countries', *European Journal of Social Policy*, 18 (3), pp. 246–259.

Philpot, T. (ed.) (2008) *Residential Care: A Positive Future* (Surrey: The Residential Forum).

Pickard, L. (1999) 'Policy Options for Informal Carers of Elderly People', in *With Respect to Old Age: Long Term Care – Rights and Responsibilities*, Research Volume Three of the Report of the Royal Commission on Long Term Care, Cm 4192-II/3 (London: The Stationery Office).

Pickard, L. (2001) 'Carer Break or Carer Blind? Policies for Informal Carers in the UK', *Social Policy and Administration*, 35 (4), pp. 441–458.

Pickard, L., Wittenberg, R., Comas-Herrera, A., Davies, B. and Darton, R. (2000) 'Relying on Informal Care in the New Century? Informal Care for Elderly People in England to 2031', *Ageing and Society*, 20, pp. 745–772.

Pickard, L., Wittenberg, R., Comas-Herrera, A., King, D. and Malley, J. (2007) 'Care by Spouses, Care by Children: Projections of Informal Care for Older People in England to 2031', *Social Policy and Society*, 6 (3), pp. 353–366.

Royal Commission on Long Term Care (1999) *With Respect to Old Age*, Cm 4192 (London: The Stationery Office).

Samuel, M. (2009) 'Direct Payments, Personal Budgets and Individual Budgets: Expert Guides'. *Community Care*, 8 April.

Scope (2009) *Social Care Green Paper: Ten Questions*, November, available at http://www. scope.org.uk/news/social-care-green-paper-ten-questions, date accessed December 2010.

Secretary of State for Health (2000) *The NHS Plan. The Government's Response to the Royal Commission on Long Term Care*, Cm 4818-II (London: The Stationery Office).

Wanless, D., Forder, J., Fernández, J.-L. et al. (2006) *Securing Good Care for Older People: Taking a Long-term View* (London: King's Fund).

10
Financing Long-Term Care in Southwest Europe: Italy, Portugal and Spain

Joan Costa-Font
London School of Economics and Political Science, United Kingdom

Cristiano Gori
Personal Social Services Research Unit (PSSRU), LSE Health and Social Care,
London School of Economics and Political Science, United Kingdom

and

Silvina Santana
Department of Economics, Management and Industrial Engineering & Institute of
Electronics Engineering and Telematics of Aveiro, University of Aveiro, Portugal

1 Introduction

The progressive ageing of the European population and the transformation of family care giving arrangements bring to the fore the question of how best to Finance long-term care (LTC). Particularly important is the specific financial organization of LTC systems when both social and demographic constraints compete with economic motivations to rationalize public insurance schemes. LTC provides support for old age dependants that need some health care, but primarily social care. However, Southern European countries are facing the paradox of health care being a top policy priority as in almost all European countries, whilst social care is nearly privatized or has been heavily decentralized to local authorities, and subject to means- as well as needs-testing (Costa-Font and Font-Vilalta, 2006; Gil, 2009; Costa-Font, 2010a; Santana, 2010). Private financing is primarily dominated by intra-household interactions and self Financing. The role of private financing alternatives is developing in some countries such as Spain, but is still far from taking off.

Among the different models of LTC financing, Southern European countries are particularly characteristic. The role of community services in providing care to the elderly is still in its infancy even when it has been largely prioritized in all of the three countries examined here, and the mixed economy of care has relied heavily on informal care relative to other European countries. However, modernization of caregiving and its financing differ significantly across the territory of the different States, which give rise to heterogeneity of preferences and needs, and calls for adjusting welfare governance (Costa-Font, 2010a).

Southwest European countries follow similar culture patterns such as the distrust of excessive public intervention in issues of family affairs, but in terms of expected demand and needs, exhibit significant country hetero-geneity. For instance, Italy is the country with the largest significant ageing rate in Europe (19.2 per cent) and Spain is the fifth (16.9 per cent), whilst Portugal is among the youngest countries (13 per cent) relative to the other two (Eurostat, 2008 data, consulted in June 2006). However, in terms of both male and female life expectancy at 60, Spain exhibits the highest rate (20.6 for men and 25.6 for women) followed by Italy (20.4 among men and 24.8 among women) and Portugal (19.9 for men and 23.3 for women) (Eurostat, 2008). Although the proportion of elderly in Portugal is currently below the average in Europe, it is expected to grow strongly. Between 2005 and 2030, those aged 65 years and more will increase from 16.9 per cent to 23.3 per cent and those aged 80 and more from 3.7 per cent to 6.4 per cent of the population (Eurostat, 2008). At-risk-of-poverty rate after social transfers for those aged 65 years or more was 22 per cent in 2006 (INE, 2010), above the EU15 average.

If a Southwest European model of LTC exists at all, it would be defined by the relative strength of the family, together with the privatization of old age care financing (see Table 10.1). Individuals and families are expected to find a solution to the question of old age care by themselves and the State is seen as an 'actor of last resort' and, as we explain in this chapter, steps to provide support either take the form of insufficient allowances in the case of Italy, of delegation of services planning and provision (in the con-text of protocols with the State) to private entities in the case of Portugal or of a partial reform as in the case of Spain. In Spain, perhaps the excep-tion of the countries examined, a 39/2006 Bill was passed in 2007 to grant central funding for LTC, but still leaves to regional governments the design of LTC financial structures and to families to share some of the costs. The

Table 10.1 Public LTC expenditure as percentage of GDP

	2000	2005
Spain	0.2	0.3
Portugal	0.4	0.5
Italy	0.6	0.6

Source: OECD (2008).

Spanish scheme provides an entitlement to care funded through general tax revenues, alongside regional funds and individuals' cost-sharing. Unlike in Spain, there have not been financing reforms in Italy and Portugal. However, in Portugal, a social care network based on private, non-profit organizations (*Instituições Particulares de Solidariedade Social* (IPSS)), mostly financed by the State and clients' co-payments, has been in place for a long time, and the National Network of Long-Term Integrated Care (*Rede Nacional de Cuidados Continuados Integrados* (RNCCI)), more driven to health care but also accounting for some social care services. In contrast, in Italy financial reforms have proved to be scarce and have failed to succeed (Costa-Font, 2010a). Indeed, a national reform has been under public and political discussion since the mid-1990s but has not been enacted and, nowadays, has disappeared from the political agenda. All proposals made public since the mid-1990s pursued the same aims: to increase the State public expenditure devoted to LTC, to increase the provision of in-kind services, mostly in the community and to reduce the huge inter-regional differences in the amount of public care provision.

This chapter draws evidence from three Southwest European countries, namely, Italy, Portugal and Spain. The three countries under analysis face similar institutional pressure to reform their LTC system, though they differ in their objectives, needs and economic constraints. A common feature in all three countries is perhaps the structure of the family, which shares some cultural aspects. Although the political and institutional system is subject to different legacies, these countries have managed to decentralize their welfare State for some common as well as different reasons. The percentage of total health expenditure financed by social health insurance has been low and similar in the three countries (OECD, 2008).

Therefore, one would expect these countries to follow a similar reform process of policy-making though, as we show below, this is not the case. On the other hand, the policy outcomes of LTC reform in the three countries are comparable and exhibit some heterogeneity worth studying. Finally, Italy, Portugal and Spain exhibit relatively similar economic development levels, which make them especially comparable. Our argument is that rather than a Southern model of LTC financing, we find that heterogeneous demand for funding alternatives gives rise to the development of both public and private funding alternatives. Common limits of the system lie in the relative strength of the family and the difficulty of putting forward financing reforms that encompass a redefinition of the entitlements.

The structure of the chapter is as follows. The next section is devoted to describing the key elements of the institutional design of LTC financing systems in Italy, Portugal and Spain. Section 3 examines ongoing financial reforms in the three countries, their characteristics, actors and motivations. Section 4 touches upon decision-making in LTC, and we particularly refer to the advantages it poses for policy-making. Finally, Section 5 discusses the differences in desired welfare policy objectives of the three systems along with the evolution of expenditure and social cohesion.

2 Contextualizing LTC in Southwest Europe

The structure and developments of the financing and provision of LTC very much depend on inertia and path dependence on historically entrenched institutions, as well as on the expectations conveyed by culture and on country-specific demands and needs.

Southwest European Welfare States are highly decentralized and fragmented. LTC is managed typically at the local levels, and regulated at a regional level. Care combines both cash subsidies for home and informal care with in-kind care. However, whilst in Spain care is almost entirely provided in-kind, in Italy there is a generalized State entitlement to a cash subsidy, *indennità di accompagnamento*. In Portugal, IPSSs are directly State-financed alongside user co-payments most of the time in the context of protocols established with the Social Security (*Segurança Social*), and dependent people opting for staying at home may apply for a cash subsidy additionally to home support. Similarly, in all three countries the family is still the main caregiver of its older members, especially in rural areas (Duarte and Paúl, 2006/2007; Costa-Font, 2010b).

LTC was identified as one of the gaps in Portuguese National Health System coverage. Therefore, the RNCCI was created by Law no. 101/2006 within the scope of the Ministry of Health and of the Ministry of Labour and Social Solidarity, based on existing institutions. In Italy the long-awaited national LTC reform, under public and political discussion since the mid-1990s, has not been enacted, as previously stated. The State expenditure devoted to LTC has actually increased over time, but not as an outcome of a change of direction in policy. In fact, the percentage of older people receiving the 'companion payment' – a payment available to severely disabled people, regardless of their age, based solely on an assessment of their needs – rose from 5.5 per cent to 9.5 per cent. In contrast, Spain did exhibit a major funding reform of the system which, as we explain in Section 4, covers a 'basic care package', complementary care packages being regionally provided and financed. Yet, although the new programe started to operate in 2007 as explained in Section 4, its full implementation will gradually take place until 2015.

Figure 10.1 compares Italy and Spain to show similar residential care patterns of use explained by similar demand pressures although, as Table 10.2 shows, availability of beds in nursing homes has expanded as well. However, in Spain a high percentage (60 per cent) of these beds is privately owned and the effect of public expansion of welfare does not always converge. Still, important regional heterogeneity remains in part due to the extent of civil societal involvement in sorting out social needs before the welfare State was

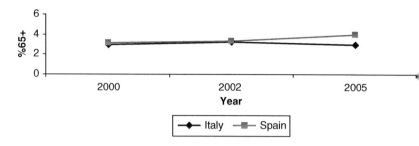

Figure 10.1   Elderly in residential care in Italy and Spain, 2000–2005

Table 10.2   LTC beds in nursing homes, per 1000 population aged 65 years and over

Country	2001	2002	2003	2004	2005	2006
Italy	14.5	15.7	16.3	16.0	16.5	17.4
Spain	16.7	n.a	n.a	n.a	18.9	21.3
Portugal	n.a.	n.a.	n.a.	n.a.	n.a.	n.a.

Source: OECD Health Data (2008), Version: December 2008.

set up as a generalized insurance institution. These arrangements are partially reflected today by an uneven privatization across the countries, being legacies of a pre-welfare past.

3   The system organization

3.1   Spain

The financing system is formally defined as 'universal' and access to LTC considered a 'subjective right'. Funding is shared between the central government and the autonomous regions. The Spanish parliament approved a 'National LTC System' that covers immigrants under certain conditions, partially operative from January 2007, though not totally operative until 2015. Potential users are assessed at the local level, using the same instrument throughout the whole country. If they qualify as eligible, they are classified according to three levels of dependency. The gradual introduction of the system was designed as follows: in 2007, individuals with dependency Levels 3 received care; in the period between 2008 and 2010 care was ensured for people with Level 2 dependency, and finally in the period between 2011 and 2015, the system will also reach the people with Level 1 dependency. Elderly who are eligible can choose between services in-kind and benefits in cash. In 2008, elderly with Level 3 dependency could receive €406–507 a month in cash, or €609–812 a month as services in-kind.

The funding of the system is split in half between the State and the regions. This programme covers a 'basic package' which is intended to be accessible for anyone everywhere; complementary packages are provided and financed by the regions and the profile of these packages depends on their own choices. The institutional structure of Spain consists of three levels: the State, the 17 regions (Autonomous Communities (ACs)) and the municipalities. For both social and health care the State is in charge of the overall aims while the actual policies are designed by the regions. The provision of health services is carried out by the regions' local offices whereas the provision of social services is assured by the municipalities. Each region has a specific statutory law that covers the provision of publicly financed LTC. At the national level there is a Secretary of State for Health and a Secretary of State for Employment and Social Affairs (responsible for social services). Also at the regional level there is usually a minister in charge of health and another one responsible for social care. A central agency provides support for the elderly (IMSERSO), and in most cases civil servants in each specific region are in charge of supervision. The main instruments at the State level have been, until 2008 (see below), the so-called 'gerontology plans', structural plans covering the entire country that assessed the needs for services in accordance with forecasts of the numbers of disabled. However, they have had very little, almost negligible influence. Publicly paid social care is mainly financed by taxation and regional resources are derived from the financing grants received from the central government. Local resources are derived both from regional funding to the municipalities and from local taxes.

Residential care accounts for the largest share of individuals over 65 (3.8 per cent), and 60 per cent refers to nursing homes in 2004.The provision of residential care is mainly in the hands of the private sector, and recent trends seem to suggest that despite the fact that new nursing home centres have been created with public funding, the number of people who attended private profit and non-profit centres expanded from 73 per cent in 1999 to 80 per cent in 2004. However, the financing of the system still remains mainly in the hand of the public sector, about 60 per cent of nursing homes being publicly financed and in 2004 about 18 per cent of the total number of beds were contracted out by the public sector. Public home care is managed by municipalities, and financed roughly at 50 per cent by them, at 30 per cent by ACs and 20 per cent by the State.

3.2 Italy

The institutional structure of Italy also consists of three levels: the State, the 20 regions and some 8000 municipalities. For health care the State defines the overall aims and the regions design the policies, whereas for social care there are no rules at the national level, the regions providing a few guidelines and most of the design being up to any single municipality. As in Spain, at the national level there is a Secretary of State for Health and a Secretary of State for Employment and Social Affairs (responsible for social services). Also at the regional level of responsibility there is usually a minister in charge of health and another one responsible for social care.

There are two main publicly funded home care services for the elderly in Italy: integrated domiciliary care and home help. Integrated domiciliary care (*Assistenza Domiciliare Integrata* – ADI), which – in theory – should make both home help (social care) and home health care (home nursing, physiotherapy, specialist and GPs' visits) available to the user at home. ADI encompasses in turn a wide range of care inputs and the packages of care provided can be substantially different from one another; 3.3 per cent of older people receive ADI.

Home help is provided by the municipalities, while home health care is provided by the Local Health Authorities – *Aziende Sanitarie Locali* (ASLs), which are also in charge of coordinating the overall provision of ADI. Evidence at a national level, along with other findings of several projects, is consistent in showing that the overall majority of ADI users receive only health care inputs. Municipalities provide home help, the services included in this kind of care are of a family/domestic nature (housework, bathing and toileting, feeding, laundry, accompanying and so on) to allow the persons who are not self-sufficient to keep his or her habits in the home environment. Home help is received by 1.8 per cent of the older people. Overall, 5.1 per cent of the people aged 65 and over receive home care (home help + ADI). Residential care includes a huge variety of institutions. Residential care institution types vary widely among the regions, both in their denominations and features. Overall, the users of residential care amount to 3 per cent of the older people.

The most important public input, both in terms of expenditure and of the number of older people affected, is a national scheme, named *indennità di accompagnamento* ('companion payment'). It is a payment made available to severely disabled people (i.e., those who find themselves unable to walk without the permanent help of a companion or are not able to carry out the activities of daily living need continuous assistance and are not in residential care), regardless of their age, based on an assessment of their needs and paid irrespectively of the claimant's financial conditions. It amounts to €480 per month. There is no control over its actual use and no care plan is made. *The indennità* is completely detached from the provision of in-kind services. It is funded by the State and the eligibility criteria are the same for the whole country. It is received by 9.5 per cent of the older people.

Table 10.3 shows the percentage of people aged 65 and over receiving public care and those receiving privately paid care (almost entirely from migrant workers) from the early 1990s onwards; please note that the users of the companion payment and those receiving private care often overlap as the former is commonly used to pay for the latter. The trends clearly stand out. The percentage of older people in residential care has remained more or less

Table 10.3 Older people users of LTC, percentage of people aged 65 and over, Italy

	Early 1990s	Early 2000s	Late 2000s
Public care			
Residential care	2.9	3	3
Home care (services in-kind)	2	3.8	5.1
Companion payment	5.0	5.5	9.5
Private care			
Elderly receiving privately paid care at home	n.a.	7	7

Source: Official data and Gori (2011).

stable (i.e., the number of beds has increased only enough to match the rise in the number of older people). The percentage of older people in home care has steadily risen (mostly in ADI, currently 3.3 per cent out of 5.1 per cent); the intensity, nevertheless, is slowly decreasing as the average yearly hours per user have dropped from 26 to 22 between 2001 and 2007. The number of users of the companion payment rose from 5.5 per cent (2001) to 9.5 (2009), that is, by 72 per cent in 8 years. This amount of money is often used – as previously stated – to employ migrant care workers, who work in 7 per cent of households with older people.

The rapid growth in the percentage of older people receiving the companion payment – even if its design did not change at all – is due to several reasons. The most important consists in the growth of the number of migrant workers. Over the last decade, the number of migrant workers has risen enormously and the *indennità* is the main benefit that can be used by families to remunerate them. There is, in fact, a tax allowance to support privately paid care, but it amounts to only some 10–15 per cent of the *indennità* and, in addition, the tax allowance can be used only for formal employment while the companion payment can be received even if the assistant is not regularly employed (as is often the case). The need to pay for migrant care workers has pushed an increasing number of families to look for public economic support and, in turn, to apply for the companion payment.

Along with this, the increase in the elderly population has played an important role. Within those aged 65 and over, the speed of increase was particularly high in the group of those aged 75 and over (+23 per cent from 2002 to 2009) who – within the older people – are the main users of the companion payment. Also the scarcity of services in-kind (and the low intensity of home care) has been another driver, along with the fact that – until 2009 – the companion payment was financed by the State, with no budget ceiling while the regions (through their Local Health Authorities) had to decide whether or not the claimants could receive it. As the regions did not pay for it, they had an incentive to accept the applications; this system is currently under reform (Gori, 2011).

3.3 Portugal

The institutional structure in Portugal consists of three levels, both in health and social care. The national government develops the legislative framework for health and social policies and redistributes tax income to the regional public authorities responsible for health and social provisions.

The Ministry of Health is responsible for developing health policy and overseeing and evaluating its implementation. The five Regional Health Administrations (RHAs) are responsible for the regional implementation of national health policy objectives and coordinating all levels of health care. They work in accordance with principles and directives issued in regional plans and by the Ministry of Health. They supervise the development of strategic guidelines, coordinate all aspects of health care provision, supervise the management of hospitals and primary health care, and the establishment of agreements and protocols with private bodies and liaise with government bodies, *Misericórdias*, other private non-profit-making bodies and municipal councils (Barros and Simões, 2007). They are also in charge of the development of the National Network of Continued Integrated Care (RNCCI). Below the RHAs are the Primary Care Trusts (*Agrupamentos de Centros de Saúde* (ACES)), which have been created in the context of an on-going reform of the primary care sector in Portugal. ACES are public services constituted by a number of functional units, with administrative autonomy. They may contain a range of Family Health Units, Community Care Units, Personalized Health Care Units, Shared Assistance Resources Units and traditional health centres together with the Public Health Unit, the Management Support Unit and a Clinical Council, respectively, for every ACES. For the purposes of health care provision, boundaries are based on geographical proximity rather than administrative areas, so the definition for the purposes of the Ministry of Health is not exactly co-terminous with administrative boundaries (Barros and Simões, 2007). The Ministry of Labour and Social Solidarity is responsible for social benefits such as pensions and unemployment and incapacity benefits. Support is provided in each region through *Segurança Social* (Social Security), in the form of money and the large majority of support services for elderly and dependent people. However, *Instituições Particulares de Solidariedade* Socia (IPSS)l – Solidarity Private Institutions) which are non-profit and non-public institutions for social solidarity, and among them *Misericórdias*, have been the main providers of these services, most of the time in the context of protocols established with *Segurança Social*. They act at the local level, deciding on the eligibility for services and setting prices, according to available legislation and the economic and social condition of the user. Protocols are signed annually between the ministry responsible for the *Segurança Social* and the three unions representing

IPSSs. A typical agreement defines a value per client per month, including for home care.

The social network created by IPSS has been in place for a long time. By the end of 2008, 72 per cent of the providers were non-profit-making organizations. From 1998 to 2008, the number of owners of social facilities increased by 58.1 per cent, stabilizing in the year 2008. The number of facilities has increased by 41 per cent in the same period, reaching 8602 in 2008. From these, 85 per cent were operated under the non-profit-making status. Around 52 per cent provided services to the elderly population, yet it is not clear how many beds in these units may be classified as 'nursing home' beds. In fact, *Carta Social* refers only to residential homes (*Lar e Residência para Idosos*), the Domiciliary Support Service (*Serviço de Apoio Domiciliário* (SAD)) and day centres (*Centro de Dia*). The concept now applies to units with contracts with the RNCCI.

In 2007, 71,663 persons received services from the SAD, about 0.7% of the total population (Ministério do Trabalho e da Solidariedade Social, 2009). The Domiciliary Support Service represents high utilization rates, reaching 89.3 per cent in 2007. From 1998 to 2007, the SAD had the highest growth rate (79.3 per cent) in terms of number of facilities, followed by day centres (40.6 per cent) and residential homes for the elderly population (33 per cent). In the case of the SAD, the number of places available more than doubled, corresponding to a growth rate of 111 per cent (Ministério do Trabalho e da Solidariedade Social, 2009). However, due to demographic, social and epidemiologic trends, institutionalization has been expanding as a solution to provide the elderly and dependent people the adequate care they require.

Collaboration between the two ministries has improved in recent years, leading to the implementation of the RNCCI, an emblematic joint project. Municipalities, on the other hand, are relatively absent from the process of care. No formal evidence exists on the subject, but 'it is possible to make a conjecture that the involvement of the municipalities in health promotion and improvement programmes has not expanded beyond a few specific projects' (Barros and Simões, 2007, p. 26).

In Portugal, the RNCCI, mostly based on pre-already existing institutions, was created by Decree Law no. 101/2006 within the scope of the Ministry of Health and the Ministry of Employment and Social Solidarity. It brings together teams providing LTC, palliative action and social support with members coming from hospitals, health centres, local and district social security services, community services, local government and the Solidarity Network. Geographically, the network is organized at three levels of coordination (central, regional and local) aiming at improved governance and equity of access. Structurally, it is based on establishing protocols with existing institutions, designated according to the kind of services they provide as *Unidade de Convalescença* – UC (Convalescence Unit), *Unidade de Média*

Duração e Reabilitação – UMDR (Medium-Term and Rehabilitation Unit), *Unidade de Longa Duração e Manutenção* – ULDM (Long-Term and Maintenance Unit), *Unidade de Cuidados Paliativos* – UCP (Palliative Care Unit) and *Unidade de Dia e de Promoção de Autonomia* – UDPA (Day Care and Autonomy Promotion Unit). It should also comprise the so-called *Equipas Domiciliárias de Cuidados Continuados e Integrados* (Domiciliary Teams of Long-Term Integrated Care). Local coordination teams are located in specific health centres. Each team might coordinate the work of teams in several health centres in different but geographically close council areas and is responsible for validating the reasons stated by the family doctor in a health centre or the discharge team in an acute care hospital for admission of each patient to the RNCCI and finding places in the appropriate unit of the network.

The RNCCI is being developed alongside a major restructuring of primary care that has led to the creation of Family Health Units in health centres and to the introduction of a system of payment by objectives for doctors and nurses choosing to adhere to this system. Another chief measure to be taken should be the creation of *Equipas Domiciliárias de Cuidados Continuados e Integrados* (Home Teams of Continuous and Integrated Care), but field implementation has not been significant so far. A first structured attempt to implement integrated domiciliary support services in Portugal was made in 1998 with the creation of *Apoio Domiciliário Integrado* (Integrated Domiciliary Support) in health centres, though with modest results.

Table 10.4 provides a basic overview of the differences in organization and demand side-pressures in Italy, Portugal and Spain. We find some similarities between the three countries based on a larger reliance on informal care and in-kind care in Spain, and more reliance on cash support in Italy. In Portugal, the 2008 mean coverage rate for home care, day care and residential care was 11.6 per cent, with wide variations through the country (Ministério do Trabalho e da Solidariedade Social, 2009).

4   Cost-sharing and other funding arrangements

Although certain LTC services – especially those related to health care – are considered as a public sector responsibility in many European Union countries, a proportion of LTC services costs (e.g., feeding costs) is unavoidably classified as an individual responsibility provided that the household has sufficient means. Hence, governments are expected to introduce cost-sharing structures through means-testing mechanisms in accordance with a household's ability to pay, and to finance LTC in full only when families are clearly unable to do so. However, there is evidence pointing out limited individuals' knowledge of their own old age dependency risks, and Eurobarometer data show that Southern Europeans have foreseen less the event of old age risks (Eurobarometer, 2007). This feature might well be envisaged as an 'information market failure' that could justify,

Table 10.4   LTC systems in Italy, Spain and Portugal

	Italy	Spain (before reform)	Portugal
Demographic trend (% 65+)	20.2 (2009)	15 (2007)	17.6 (2008) 17.9 (2009)
Informal care (%)	37	78 (2007)	n.a.
Home care coverage (%)	5.1	3.9	n.a.
Day care coverage (%)	n.a.	0.3	n.a.
Residential care coverage (%)	3	3.2	n.a.
Care allowances	9.5%	Fiscal relief for dependant	Dependency complement for those staying at home. Maybe received additional to SAD
Institutional arrangements	Companion payment – the State has the regulatory power; ADI – regions have the regulatory power; home help – municipalities have the regulatory power; residential care – the regulatory power is mostly in the regions' hands and partly with the municipalities	Social care in the hands of Local Authorities	Social care provided mostly by private organizations (non-profit and for-profit). Most of them are IPSS, institutions funded mostly by the State and clients' co-payments

unless corrected, full public support for funding LTC for old age dependants. Therefore, to avoid the costs to the public sector of possible market failures in the (self-)financing of LTC, a key issue refers to the design of means-testing schemes ensuring that people have incentives to save for their retirement (Costa-Font et al., 2010). A pre-funded tax-based system guarantees a basic coverage but may also create incentives for private sector institutions to develop financial products and/or expand capacity to deliver care. Yet, a key challenge is to enhance regional coordination and cooperation without affecting efficiency and policy innovation.

In Spain, dependent individuals are expected to co-pay in accordance with their income; those that can afford to pay for LTC will contribute up to 90 per cent of their total costs. On average, cost-sharing is estimated to account for 30–35 per cent of total costs and no tax has been associated with the funding of the system. Provision will be both public and private, and home help is the key service. Overall, the system leaves the door open to the development of complementary markets to cover co-payments for LTC and supplementary insurance. The capacity of individuals to pay for LTC services in old age is a key issue in the Spanish LTC debate. According to the 2002 Spanish Household Survey, 60 per cent of the elderly in Spain receive a public pension, 32 per cent receive a work-related pension and the average monthly pension in 2000 was €460. The 2005 survey on the Wealth of Spaniards – *Encuesta Financiera de las Familias* – reveals that housing accounts for 80 per cent of total household wealth on average, though it ranges from 88 per cent in the highest income quartiles to 68 per cent in the lowest quartiles, where about 86 per cent of the population owns its own home,[1] more than in any other European country. Housing accounts for 28 per cent of total household expenditure, also the highest proportion in Europe. Among the elderly, 74 per cent are home-owners though only 7 per cent are still paying a mortgage (Costa-Font et al., 2009).[2] Hence, the high rate of home-ownership might well be taken into account as a potential source of private LTC funding in addition to the role of insurance and public support.

Home-ownership is an important variable in determining individuals' preferences for alternatives of LTC provision and funding. Important public financial policy questions refer to elucidating whether, on the one hand, means-testing schemes take into account housing assets as the requirements for adjudicating publicly funded LTC. Indeed, some studies document evidence of old age individuals being 'income poor and housing rich' (Costa-Font et al., 2009, 2010). On the other hand, another question refers to whether individuals are willing to sell their dwellings to fund LTC. Generally, people prefer to live in their own homes as long as possible (Costa-Font et al., 2009), and individuals admitted to nursing homes were more likely to have been owner-occupiers. Hence, the development of community care along with the maintenance of means-testing might require the development of alternative financial mechanisms to allow individuals to remain at home whilst using housing assets to partially pay for LTC. Finally, given that the responsibility for social and health care in Spain is regionally spread and that preferences for LTC funding and social values may be heterogeneous, it is important to examine regional specific evidence.

In Portugal, IPSSs are funded by the Portuguese government, through *Segurança Social*, family co-payments, membership fees and donations. Co-payments from the *Segurança Social* are defined in the *Protocolos de Cooperação* (Cooperation Protocols) and consubstantiated in the corresponding cooperation agreements. Protocols take place annually between the ministry responsible for the *Segurança Social* and the three unions representing IPSSs. A typical agreement defines a value per user per month. Eligibility is not income-dependent, but the amount of client co-payment depends on the type of services requested and family income. The limit established by law is the operational cost of the service declared by the institution in the previous year. IPSSs and *Misericórdias* set their own criteria for access to the services they provide, including prices. Criteria are based on indications issued by *Segurança Social* and obligatorily stated on their *Regulamento Interno*, a public document nowadays published on the Internet. Between 1998 and 2008, State expense rose by 85.5 per cent, mirroring the effort made to increase the unitary co-payment by *Segurança Social* and the coverage rate. In 2008, provision of social care aimed at the needs of the elderly population was responsible for 40.8 per cent of the total expense (Table 10.5).

The RNCCI is financed by the health sector (around 80 per cent) and the social sector (around 20 per cent), with the costs of health care provision being paid by the Ministry of Health, while the Ministry of Labour and Social Solidarity is responsible for a possible component of social care. The patient accounts for the co-payment for social care she or he might receive, as formerly discussed, while the component of health care is free of charge. In 2008, the Ministry of Labour and Social Solidarity attributed €11 million from the profit of social gambling (e.g., lottery, lotto) to the RNCCI. The corresponding execution rate of the budget was 88.15 per cent, an increase of almost 60 per cent from the previous year. In the same year, the Ministry of Health attributed €77.7 million to the RNCCI, from which only €33.3 million were executed. The execution rate of the budget for home nursing provided by health centres previewed in the Implementation Plan (€6,100,000, to be funded by the Ministry of Health) was less than 8 per cent according to the Audit Court in 2009 (Tribunal de Contas, 2009).

Dependent people opting to stay at home may apply to the Dependency Complement (formerly, Third Person Subsidy) from *Segurança Social* and buy some services in the market. This subsidy can be received in addition to the reception of in-kind care, and its value depends on the level of dependency and on the regime covering the dependent person.

In Portugal, a study conducted during May and July 2005 (Perista and Baptista, 2007), including 30 interviews with home-owners and renters of

Table 10.5 Mean operational costs and mean co-payments from clients and the *Segurança Social* in Portugal, 2008

Elderly	Operational cost (€)	Client's co-payment (€)	*Segurança Social's* co-payment (€)
Residential homes	647.15	313.56	274.85
Day centres	209.17	71.02	79.71
Social Intercourse Centre	61.79	6.36	37.87
SAD	251.57	73.58	191.238

Source: Data from ISS extracted from ISS website (2006).

dwellings located in a municipality in the coastal centre of Portugal, showed that, for most Portuguese respondents, the dwelling is seen as a home or a refuge rather than an asset, revealing the strong emotional ties that people have with their residences. This was true both for home-owners and renters.

According to this study, using housing equity to access finance seems to happen only rarely in Portugal. Only in a few cases do the respondents regard their homes simply as a roof over their heads or as an investment. Even in the case of relationship breakdown, on only one occasion was the property sold in order to allow the ex-partner to have access to his share of the money. Home-owners referred to housing as a theoretical financial resource and 'a haven for their old age', but had never thought about taking advantage of the financial equity. In this study, almost all the home-owners reported having compulsory life insurance (a few had older contracts that did not require this insurance), but this was their only safety net, apart from the compulsory insurance against accidents at work that most people have. Only a few interviewees had taken out non-compulsory insurance policies, to cover unemployment, for instance, because of financial constraints, as they felt that their incomes were too low.

In Italy health care inputs consumed by ADI are covered by the Local Health Authorities' budgets based on capitation formula. This means that ADI services are free for users and delivered only according to the claimants' needs; no co-payments are requested from users. Residential homes can be funded by municipalities and are subject to high charges or co-payments. Middle-class people living in these institutions (or their families) tend to pay most of their fees, if not the whole cost. Similar to home help, over recent years, residential care homes have been characterized by a stricter means-testing and an increase in charges. If any health care is provided, the Italian national health services will pay only for dependent patients a daily tariff agreed on a regional level. Nursing homes, thus, are considered, in fact, to be both health and social care services. Other costs ('social care') are typically subject to means-tests, which in turn exhibit important regional variability.

Individuals receiving home help are often requested to pay a charge that is set by each municipality and varies substantially across the country. Users contribute to the financing of the service, especially in residential care. The local authorities provide funding for the care when users are not able to cover the cost of their care, and relatives are also involved in covering the costs according to the regional regulations since there are not clear national rules about user contributions.

5   Towards a common South European LTC financing model?

The reform of the financing of LTC is far from a highly ranked priority in countries where a prevalent family structure inhibits community development. The latter is explained because the default (family care) is the least cost alternative. Reform has been generally limited both in Portugal and Italy, whilst in Spain a general financial reform took place in 2007 just before the economic crises hampered growth perspectives. Hence, the implementation of the financial reform has not been as ambitious as expected and targeted highly dependent individuals primarily due to funding constraints, and has been politically manipulated (Costa-Font, 2010a). Other strategies of blame avoidance have been to include extensive cost-sharing structures and shift the blame to regional and local governments which are responsible for running the LTC system (Costa-Font, 2010b). A comparison between Portugal, Spain and Italy provides us with a set of common features that could lead us to define what can be regarded as a Southeast model of welfare based on a key and pivotal role of the family and informal care, a heavy decentralization mainly in Italy and Spain and fragmentation together with underfunding in Portugal. Finally, the scope for market instruments to provide for care is very limited due to the existence of very close substitutes to self-insure LTC, the popular perceptions that it is the responsibility of the public sector to provide last resort financing and the existence of family ties that provide a safety net and make reform less of a socially urgent feature.

It is important to understand that drivers of financial reform for LTC include the incorporation of female workers in the labour market, which curtails the availability of caregivers within the household, and the ageing of the populations, which is particularly accentuated in Southern Europe. Therefore the demand for LTC is expected to be more intense than elsewhere in Europe while social changes hinder the reproducibility of the traditional social model as they did in the past.

Limits to reform are the need to comply with cost containment pressures and, generally, the commitment to fiscal stability and austerity associated with the growth and stability pact. Other limits include the view that financing LTC should be largely paid out of savings throughout someone's life and family wealth, the resilience of an inheritance culture based on intergenerational bequests and, finally, and partly as a result of the latter, an unwillingness to redistribute.

Notes

1. http://www2.vrom.nl/Docs/internationaal/housingStats2002.pdf (accessed 17 January 2011).
2. 16 per cent are tenants and 3 per cent use other financial means.

References

Barros, P. and. Simões, J. (2007) *Health Systems in Transition – Portugal* (Copenhagen: WHO, Regional Office for Europe on behalf of the European Observatory on Health Systems and Policies).

Costa-Font, J. (2010a) 'Devolution, diversity and welfare reform: long-term care in the "Latin Rim" ', *Social Policy and Administration*, 44 (4), pp. 481–494.

Costa-Font, J. (2010b) 'Family ties and the crowding out of long term care insurance', *Oxford Review of Economic Policy*, 26 (4), pp. 691–712.

Costa-Font, J. and Font-Vilalta, M. (2006) 'Design limitations of long-term care insurance schemes: a comparative study of the situation in Spain', *International Social Security Review*, 59 (4), pp. 91–110.

Costa-Font, J., Garcia-Gonzalez, A. and Font-Vilalta, M. (2008) 'Relative income and attitudes towards long-term care financing', *The Geneva Papers on Risk and Insurance – Issues and Practice*, 33 (4), pp. 673–693.

Costa-Font, J., Mascarilla-Miró, O. and Elvira, D. (2009) 'Ageing in place? An examination of elderly peoples' housing preferences in Spain', *Urban studies*, 46 (2), pp. 295–316.

Costa-Font, J., Gil, J. and Mascarilla-Miró, O. (2010) 'Housing wealth and housing decisions in old age: sale and reversion', *Housing Studies*, 25 (3), pp. 375–395.

Duarte, M. and Paúl, C. (2006/2007) 'Avaliação do ambiente institucional – público e privado: estudo comportamental dos idosos', *Revista Transdisciplinar de Gerontologia. Universidade Sénior Contemporânea*, 1 (1), pp. 17–29.

Eurobarometer (2007) *Health and Long Term Care in the European Union*. Special Eurobarometer 283, Brussels.

Eurostat (2008) *Population Statistics*, http://epp.eurostat.ec.europa.eu/portal/page/ portal/population/data/database, date accessed 6 March 2010.

Eurostat databases (2008) (Brussels: Office of European Statistics).

Gil, A. (2009) *Custos reais das respostas sociais desenvolvidas pelo sector solidário*, Instituto da Segurança Social, IP, Departamento de Planeamento e Sistemas de Informação.

Gori, C. (2011) 'The rise of the companion payment in Italy', *Health and Social Care in the Community*, forthcoming.

INE (2010) *As Pessoas. The People. 2008* (Lisbon: Instituto Nacional de Estatistica).

ISS (2006) *Custos reais das respostas sociais desenvolvidas pelo sector solidário*, Instituto da Segurança Social IP, Departamento de Planeamento e Sistemas de Informação.

OECD (2008) Health Database (Paris: OECD).

Perista, P. and Baptista, I. (2007) 'The sense of home', in M. Elsinga, P. De Decker, N. Teller and J. Toussaint (eds) *Home Ownership Beyond Asset and Security: Perceptions of Housing Related Security and Insecurity in Eight European Countries* (Amsterdam: IOS Press BV), pp. 201–223.

Pesaresi, F. (2007) 'La suddivisione dei costi tra servizi e utenti', in C. Gori (ed.) *Le riforme regionali per i non autosufficienti* (Roma: Carocci), pp. 34–53.

Santana, S. (2010) 'Reforming LTC in Portugal: dealing with the multidimensional character of quality', *Social Policy and Administration*, 44, pp. 512–528.

Tribunal de Contas (2009) Auditoria à Rede Nacional dos Cuidados Continuados Integrados 2006–2008, Relatório no. 38/09 – 2ª S, Processo no. 51/08 – Audit Volume I.

UMIC (2009) Relatório de monitorização do desenvolvimento e da actividade da Rede Nacional de Cuidados Continuados Integrados no. 1, semestre de 2009.

WHO Regional Office for Europe (2007) European Health for All Database (offline database) (Copenhagen: WHO Regional Office for Europe), January 2007 update.

11
Long-Term Care Financing in Austria

Birgit Trukeschitz* and Ulrike Schneider**
Research Institute for Economics of Aging and Institute for Social Policy, Department of Socioeconomics, WU Vienna University of Economics and Business, Austria

1 Introduction

With a universal long-term care (LTC) allowance programme, subsidized LTC services for dependent persons and a new programme coping with migrant care work in private households, Austria today is one of the European Union (EU) countries addressing the issue of LTC in a substantial manner. In 2006, Austria spent slightly less than 1 per cent of its GDP on care for elderly people alone, ranking the country fourth in the EU-25, behind Sweden (2.4 per cent), Denmark (1.7 per cent) and Norway (1.6 per cent) (Eurostat, 2010).

Austria's policy efforts in LTC reflect the fact that in a few decades the country's population will be among the oldest in Europe. In line with some other European countries, Austria's population is ageing at an unprecedented speed and scale. Projections to the year 2030 reveal that Austria's old-age dependency ratio will be likely to exceed the EU-27 average of 40.3 per cent. At the same time, the risk of long-term dependency steeply increases past retirement age. In Austria, more than 5 per cent of the population requires substantial permanent help for living their lives: more than 420,000 people were in an approved need of at least 50 hours of LTC per month in 2008. Of these, 82 per cent were older than 60 years and 45 per cent needed more than 120 of hours care per month (BMASK, 2010b).

The vast majority of dependent persons living in private households in Austria receive help from relatives, neighbours or friends. Notwithstanding, professional care services have grown in importance over the past decades and funding for such services is a major concern for those affected by LTC as well as for policy makers. Population ageing and the policy goal of supporting LTC-dependent people impose substantial challenges on efficient, equitable and sustainable funding solutions today and in the near future.

The aim of this chapter is to provide an in-depth view of LTC financing in Austria over and above a discussion of public funding levels and their changes over time: more specifically, Section 2 reflects on public and private responsibilities in funding LTC in Austria. Section 3 elucidates funding streams in a fiscal federalism setting and the ways in which public funding is channelled to providers of LTC services. Section 4 discusses future funding needs and measures to keep LTC spending under control. The chapter closes in Section 5 with a brief policy discussion touching on the distributional impact of LTC financing in Austria and on alternatives to the current system of LTC financing.

2 The mix of private and public responsibilities in LTC provision in Austria

2.1 Principles shaping the division of private and public responsibilities in LTC provision

Being in need of LTC imposes substantial costs on dependants and their families (Fernández et al., 2009, p. 7). The direct, monetary costs of long-term dependency constitute a serious poverty risk. The financial burden of long-term dependency is particularly challenging when institutional care is required. The costs of formal LTC services easily exceed the monthly pension income of older households,[1] who are most likely to use institutional care. This is reflected by the fact that 56 per cent of the social welfare spending of Austria's provinces was paid to nursing homes in 2008 (Hauptverband der österreichischen Sozialversicherungsträger, 2009, p. 20; BMASK, 2010a, p. 105).

Clearly identifiable private insurance schemes for covering needs and costs of dependent people are under development in Austria, and the contract volume is still quite moderate. According to the Association of the Austrian Insurance Industry, approximately 40,000 contracts against these risks had been signed to summer 2008 (VVO, 2008). A number of private insurance companies offer LTC insurance, of which eight insurers present 'stand-alone' products whereas others offer coverage as a supplement to life insurance or pension insurance products. The stand-alone products differ enormously, for example, with regard to the terms on assessing LTC needs, age limits and waiting times (Arbeiterkammer Wien, 2005, pp. 18–19; Eisenmenger, 2007, p. 170; Bischof, 2009, p. 81).

Against the backdrop of demographic challenges, fragmented cash benefit systems and an underdeveloped infrastructure of LTC services, Austria introduced a comprehensive LTC system in 1993, which marks the establishment of LTC as a distinct and systematic social policy issue. The system consists of a universal care allowance scheme for persons in need of LTC, and a binding commitment of Austria's nine provinces (*Länder*) to provide a sufficient supply of professional care services (see Section 3.2 for details on the agreements between the Federal State and provinces in the area of LTC). Moreover, benefits for informal caregiving have been established in recent years (e.g., coverage of informal carer under social insurance law, respite care, family hospice system – for more detailed information, see Schneider and Trukeschitz, 2008, pp. 21ff.).

Taken together, these elements of LTC policy clearly represent the *solidarity principle* which is deep-rooted in Austrian social policy: the universal care allowance is non-means tested. This cash benefit is paid regardless of income, demographic characteristics and causes of dependency. It enhances the purchasing power of households that are confronted with long-term dependency. The level of public support increases with the level of need requirement. In a wider sense the principle of solidarity is also reflected in public interventions into the care market in order to assure adequate and sufficient service provision. Several Austrian provinces influence price setting and shape market conditions so that care services are available and more likely to be affordable by people in need of care (see Section 3.3).

However, public care allowances were never meant to cover all private costs of LTC (see Section 1 BPGG). Up until the present day, Austrian policy makers stress that LTC remains a family responsibility and that public provisions serve to complement and stabilize rather than substitute private efforts in LTC. In cases where benefits under the LTC allowance scheme and provisions by the provinces do not suffice to prevent poverty, there is still the option to receive means-tested welfare benefits. This position reflects another ingrained principle in Austrian social policy, which is the *principle of subsidiarity*. This principle is mirrored in both, private co-payments for care services (see below and Section 3.4) and in a certain threshold of hours of care required for being eligible for public cash benefits.

In what follows, we will briefly sketch out LTC cash benefits[2] and LTC services before turning to the issue of how these benefits are actually funded in the Austrian LTC system.

2.2 LTC cash benefits and services

The *universal care allowance* (*Pflegegeld*) targets persons who are (i) expected to depend on care for a period of at least six months and (ii) who required more than 50 hours of care per month (1993–2010) or more than 60 hours of care per month (for applications submitted from January 2011). The lump-sum cash benefit is granted as an entitlement, regardless of income, age or cause of dependency. It is graded into seven categories depending on the degree of care dependency. Those in the lowest category of care requirements (support needs ranging from 50 to 75 hours of care per month, or 60 to 85 hours of care for applications from 2011) are eligible for a monthly payment of €154.20; those in the highest category (180 hours of care per month and additional hardship conditions) receive €1655.80 in monthly benefits.

The Federal State funds care allowance for pensioners in need of LTC (and for people receiving related benefits which are based on Federal statutory provisions), whereas the provinces cover expenditures for care allowances for the remaining groups of people in need of LTC. Both levels of government decided to harmonize their respective entitlement laws for the LTC allowance (e.g., with regard to defining care needs, need assessment procedure and benefit levels). Nevertheless, the Austrian Court of Audit observed differences not only between the Federal Act on LTC allowance and the nine provincial laws but also between the provincial laws. It documented differences in both eligibility criteria and benefit levels that occurred over the years (Trukeschitz et al., forthcoming; for further details, see Rechnungshof, 2010). In the course of searching for solutions to cover the rise of public LTC costs, the Federal State and the nine Austrian provinces decided in spring 2011 to concentrate both legislative and administrative competences for the Austrian care allowance at the Federal level. Provinces and communities only contribute to funding. For an interim period the provinces and communities will contribute €372 million per year, which equals their expenditure on care allowances in 2010. This regulation will be in force from 2012 to the time when the new Federal law on fiscal equalization will be put in place, in 2015.

On 1 July 2007, financial support for 24-hour care was introduced. *Twenty-four-hour-care support* (*Förderung der '24-Stunden-Betreuung'*) is a benefit for dependent persons living in private households. The caregiver is either employed by the dependent person or self-employed. She or he resides in the dependent person's household and is directly paid by the dependent person. Usually the period for co-residency of the live-in caregiver is two entire weeks, until a second care worker takes over. This type of care arrangement has proliferated in Austria, and in many cases involved migrant care workers from Eastern Europe who were neither covered by social insurance nor paying taxes in Austria. Therefore, eligibility criteria for this benefit not only relate to the care client but also include two conditions relating to the care worker.

In order to be entitled to 24-hour care-support (i) the care client has to be eligible for a universal LTC allowance of level three or higher[3] and his or her condition would have to require 24-hour care support; (ii) the net income of the care client is not to exceed €2500 per month (as of 1 November 2008 assets are no longer accounted for); (iii) a care worker from Austria or another EU Member State has to be employed under proper conditions; and (iv) the care worker has to meet qualifications and process-related quality requirements. The cash benefit for 24-hour-care support amounts to €500 or €1100 per month depending on whether the personal care worker is self-employed or not.

Another important field in Austria's LTC system is to develop and sustain an adequate supply of *professional LTC services*. To this effect, the nine Austrian provinces (and their communities) maintain and fund nursing and care facilities as well as infrastructures supporting extra-mural care in the community. Users of professional care services still have to share in the cost of service provision. User fees are set by the provinces and therefore differ by region (see, for an illustration, BAG, 2009, pp. 68–69). Co-payments for home care services usually account for the income of the household.

Last but not least, the expenditure for professional care services, care devices or house-keeping is acknowledged as *tax deductible*.

The double strategy of strengthening the purchasing power of individuals in need of LTC through cash benefits and securing availability of professional LTC services by funding infrastructure triggers a variety of funding flows in Austria's LTC system (Figure 11.1).

The first strategy involves the design and management of the flow of funding from an administrative body to eligible care clients. Similarly, the second strategy entails the design of funding flows from public funding bodies to private or public providers of LTC services (see Section 3.3).

In addition to benefits and services for people in need of care, *public support for their caring relatives* has been established. In 1993, the Federal State pledged itself to organize provisions for informal carers under social insurance law (see Vereinbarung gemäß Article 15a B-VG – Pflegeversorgung). As information is crucial to informal carers and their dependent relatives, information services (an Internet platform for informal carers and a hotline) have been provided. At the beginning of the twenty-first century further benefits for informal carers were introduced at the Federal level: a family hospice leave system (2002), respite care (2004) and social insurance contributions (100 per cent and for an unlimited period) by the Federal State on behalf of family caregivers who care for persons with a dependency level of three or higher (2009). Support to informal caregivers on the provincial level is heterogeneous and fragmented (Schneider and Trukeschitz, 2008).

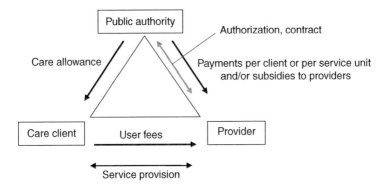

Figure 11.1 Flow of funding for LTC service provisions in Austria

2.3   Public spending on LTC

One of the most difficult tasks is to get accurate figures of current expenditures on LTC in Austria. This is true not only for private but also for public spending. Also, no consistent information on expenditure is publicly available for informal carer support.

Most accurate figures of public spending are available for the *LTC cash allowance*. In 2008, the Federal State spent €1.8 billion under the Federal Act governing LTC benefits (BPGG). Spending by the provinces on their respective care allowance schemes amounted to €0.3 billion in the same year, where part of this state-level spending is co-financed by contributions of cities and local authorities (BMASK, 2010b).

As of 30 June 2010, expenditure on the *cash benefit for 24-hour-care* amounted to another €19.6 million in 2010 where payments were made to 6058 beneficiaries (BMASK, 2010a, pp. 9, 85).

Expenditures for *LTC services* in Austria are difficult to obtain and to report. Nine provinces are responsible for LTC service provision in Austria. Although time and effort have been invested by the Austrian Ministry of Labour, Social Affairs and Consumer Protection to collect information on social care expenditure, available data are still found to be sketchy (BMASK, 2008; Rechnungshof, 2010). In 2006, the estimated expenditure on care-related social services totalled €1.33 billion and was mostly covered by the budgets of the provinces (Federal Ministry of Social Affairs and Consumer Protection, 2008, p. 64). In addition, expenditure on the Federal level for respite care reached €8.2 million in 2009 (BMASK, 2010a, p. 84).

According to these figures the Federal State (Federal LTC cash allowance, financial support for 24-hour care, support to informal caregivers) and the provinces (provinces' LTC cash allowances, financial support for 24-hour care, LTC services and support to informal caregivers) share public expenditures on LTC fairly equally.

3   Basic characteristics of the Austrian LTC funding system

3.1   Tax-based financing of LTC: Typical or atypical for Austrian social policy?

The comparative welfare State literature usually places Austria in the category of Bismarckian welfare States (see, e.g., Palier, 2008). Welfare States in this tradition started out with a strong focus on securing workers (and their families). Bismarckian systems rely on para-public social insurance to provide for major risks of life such as ill-health or old age poverty. Access to benefits is generally connected to an employment status (or a work history) and payroll taxes constitute the main funding base. Particularly in corporatist countries, payroll taxes are levied from both employers and employees. In addition, Bismarckian systems adhere to equivalence of

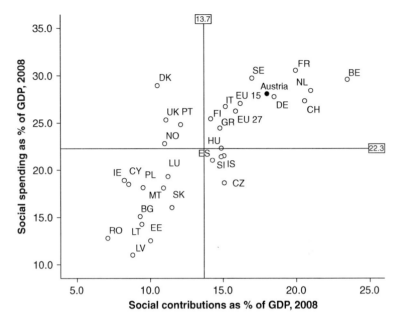

Figure 11.2 Social spending and social contribution revenues as percentage of GDP in EU countries, 2008
Source: Authors following Bonoli (1997) based on data from ESSPROS.

contributions and benefits and to the subsidiarity principle (see, e.g., Palier, 2008).

In fact, looking at a Bonoli-type classification of European welfare States (Bonoli, 1997) by social spending as a share of GDP and social contribution revenues as a share of GDP (Figure 11.2), Austria belongs to the grouping of countries with above-average social spending and heavy reliance on contribution-based funding.

Nevertheless, tax funding has always been a complementary element in Austria's welfare system, for example, in funding pensions of civil servants, health infrastructure or social assistance. LTC is one of the few social policy fields in the country's social system that is purely tax-funded. While tax-funding is not entirely new to Austria's welfare system, long-term dependency is the one and only large-scale insurable life risk for which provisions have been taken outside the traditional contribution-financed social insurance system.

There are (at least) three possible reasons for this 'not quite Austrian' funding strategy in LTC. First, the risk of long-term dependency is not as clearly related to working conditions or work hazards as are other life risks promoting the need for occupation-related insurance. Second, despite the introduction of the universal care allowance, LTC is still considered a family obligation in Austria. LTC policy might have avoided investments in tested organizational structures that could promise a larger public commitment. Thus, the given system is focused on solidarity rather than providing extensive security against a major risk of (late) life (as is the case in health policy). Third, the 1993 legislation on LTC in Austria brought about the most recent substantial addition to Austria's social system, in a period that was otherwise characterized by restructuring and retrenchment. Palier (2008) observed that welfare reforms in Bismarckian welfare States lately have embraced tax financing and benefits managed by the State, rather than traditional modes of financing.

Finally, it is important to note that from a historical point of view, tax-funding was an inherent characteristic of pre-existing programmes in support of LTC. In 1993, the universal LTC allowance scheme(s) replaced fragmented support provided at both the Federal and provincial levels. The former benefits for people dependent on support or care at the level of provinces were tax-funded. Prior to 1993, pensioners in need of care received a cash benefit (*Hilflosenzuschuss*) paid by the social insurance body. This benefit was anchored in the social pension insurance and social accident insurance systems but (tax-)financed by the Federal budget. Gruber and Pallinger (1994) concluded that with regard to this benefit the insurance principle had reduced in importance over the years.

The introduction of the Federal LTC allowance in 1993 imposed additional costs on the Federal State which were financed by restructuring Federal spending at the beginning of the 1990s. The Federal State reduced its subsidies to the Austrian Social Pension Insurance and lowered its employer's contribution to the health insurance for civil servants. It is interesting to mention that the restructuring in the Federal budget in order to finance the universal LTC allowance would have entailed a loss of revenue for the social health insurance. To avoid this loss of revenue the health insurance premiums had to be raised (1196/AB (XXI. GP), Rechnungshof, 2010, p. 40). At least as regards the financing of the federal LTC allowance, it can thus be argued that the historic perspective reveals a funding element that is *implicitly* contribution-based.

3.2   Public funding for LTC in Austria's fiscal federalism setting

As discussed in Section 2, one of the major principles in Austrian social policy is subsidiarity. According to this principle, the government should only take charge of issues that cannot be settled in the private sector. Within the public sector tasks should be approached by lower government levels whenever possible in order to account for sub-national preferences. This limits the responsibilities of the Federal State to complex, large-scale or distributional problems.

As a result, federalism is a defining feature in the Austrian social policy (see for a detailed description and analysis Trukeschitz, Schneider and

Czypionka, forthcoming). The Austrian federal constitution assigns responsibilities to both the Federal State and the nine provinces (*Länder*).[4] At the same time, the Constitution's Article 15a provides that both government levels can negotiate agreements in areas where their competences overlap. For LTC, two such 'Article 15a Agreements' exist, which clarify the division of tasks, financing responsibilities and the inter-governmental clearing of payments.

The first agreement between the Federal State and the provinces (Vereinbarung gemäß Article 15a B-VG – Pflegeversorgung) prepared the ground for the 1993 legislations on LTC allowances at both Federal and provincial level. With this first agreement based on Article 15a of the Austrian Constitution, the Federal State and the nine provinces defined responsibilities for LTC in a way which does not require any financial clearing mechanism. The agreement identified target groups of dependent people eligible for either Federal care allowance or provincial care allowance (for details, see Section 2.2). The agreement worked to harmonize the entitlements across ten distinct care allowance systems (namely, the Federal care allowance and the nine provinces' care allowance schemes). As noted in Section 2.2, legal and administrative responsibilities for the provincial long-term care allowance will be shifted to the Federal state.

The provinces pledged to provide for intramural and extramural LTC services. Each province is free to design its own policy for the care-service system – including the rules that govern the funding flows to service providers (see Section 3.3).

Fifteen years later, the Federal State and the provinces reached a second 'Article 15a Agreement' in 2008 to come to grips with 'grey labour' in the area of home care (Vereinbarung gemäß Article 15a B-VG – 24-Stunden-Betreuung). This agreement aimed at improving access to care for people in need of round-the-clock care living in private households and legalizing existing low-cost care arrangements (see Section 2). The 2009 inter-governmental agreement arranged for an additional type of cash benefit to be accommodated in existing Federal- and provincial-level care allowance laws. In this case, the funding responsibility for issuing benefits was not split up according to the enrolment eligibility of persons in either the Federal or one of the provinces' care allowance schemes. Instead, the agreement fixes a 60:40 division of costs between the Federal State and the provinces. This solution benefits the Federal level, given that the Federal LTC allowance programme covers six times the number of dependent people than the provinces' care allowances schemes. Put differently, as a result of the second 'Article 15a Agreement' on LTC the provinces currently share the cost for beneficiaries enrolled in the *federal level* care allowance programme for this specific type of care service, which blurs the dividing lines in LTC financing that had been meticulously compiled with the first contract. The agreement also entrusts the (pre-existing) 'liaison agency of the Austrian provinces' (*Verbindungsstelle der österreichischen Bundesländer*) with the yearly settlement of financial claims.

Both 'Article 15a Agreements', while clarifying the funding responsibilities do not define any specific types of revenues to be channelled into the LTC system. Each government level uses its own resources to cover its respective commitments in the area of LTC. However, tax sharing across different government levels is very common in Austria, which is mirrored in the modest 4 per cent share of provincial taxes in total provincial revenues[5] (Bröthaler, 2008, p. 176). The majority of provincial revenues are made up from their share of combined Federal and provincial taxes (*Gemeinschaftliche Bundesabgaben*), from formula-based transfers in the course of horizontal fiscal equalization and – to a lesser extent – from financing, subsidizing or equalization grants (Bröthaler, 2008, pp. 184ff.) All government levels usually adhere to the principle that all general tax revenues serve to furnish all types of tasks (*Non-Affektationsprinzip*) rather than tying specific taxes or grants to specific purposes. As a result, it is safe to assume that there are (at best) minor differences between the varying government levels and across provinces with regard to the revenue mix used to finance LTC.

In Austria, transfers from the Federal State to the provinces usually take the form of non-earmarked general purpose grants. These grants secure the provinces' general capacity to provide LTC benefits and to invest in service infrastructure (Bergvall et al., 2006, p. 128). There are no specific Federal block grants or subsidizing grants setting incentives for the development of LTC services. However, such grants are not a foreign element in Austria's fiscal equalization system, as illustrated by Federal grants supporting investments in local and regional public transport, environmental protection, agriculture or performing arts (Bröthaler, 2008, p. 185). Similarly, earmarked grants from the Federal State for provincial- or community-level investments in LTC infrastructure could increase the Federal Government's influence in service provision on sub-national government levels (Bergvall et al., 2006).

Along a similar line of reasoning, it is interesting to note that parts of the revenues from combined Federal and provincial taxes are deducted in advance (so-called '*Vorwegabzüge*') in order to secure financing for a variety of funds (disaster fund, water supply and distribution fund and so on) and special requirements (e.g., health promotion programme). A major part of the revenues for these funds and special purposes are withdrawn from the general inter-governmental revenue allocation and create additional leverage for the Federal State in supporting specific policy aims (Bröthaler, 2008, p. 177). The amount of general taxes bypassing or complementing the regular fiscal equalization process was €4 billion in 2005 (Bröthaler, 2008, p. 177), which is in the order of magnitude of Austria's total public LTC expenditure.

Austrian policy makers have embraced the idea of establishing a LTC fund as an alternative to (parts of) the current LTC funding system (see Section 5.2). One option to implement such a LTC fund is to include it in the system of advance deductions.

3.3 The design of public funding flows to LTC providers

LTC services are provided by public and private (non-profit and for-profit) providers in Austria. In looking at the design of funding flows, intra-sectoral and inter-sectoral funding flows can be discerned: *intra-sectoral* funding flows are transactions between members of the same institutional sector. In the field of LTC services intra-sectoral funding flows occur when public funds are allocated to public LTC service providers. *Inter-sectoral* funding flows are transactions between actors of different institutional sectors. In the field of LTC services funding flows from public authorities, mainly the provinces and communities, to private providers.

According to the agreement between the Federal State and the nine provinces on common measures for people in need of care (see Section 3.2), the provinces are responsible for providing sufficient and adequate care services in a spatially inclusive and comprehensive manner. As a consequence, the level and modalities of public funding of private service provision vary between the provinces and between the type of service. Public funding flows to the providers of LTC services are typically connected with LTC service utilization (payments per client or service) or take the form of subsidies to the service provider. The latter plays a minor role in domiciliary care in most provinces but is of crucial importance in covering the building costs of care homes. Different modes of public funding apply for domiciliary services and care home services. In what follows we first address regulations of provinces regarding public funding for home care, before turning to institutional care. Both types of services have in common that service providers need to be authorized to be eligible for public support and public support of their clients.

In the area of domiciliary care, intra- and inter-sectoral funding flows exist. In one province, Tyrol, domiciliary care is mainly provided by adjacent sets of collaborating communities (called *Sozial- und Gesundheitssprengel*) organised as association. Other non-profit social service providers add to the social care service supply. In the remaining eight Austrian provinces, authorized private organizations, mainly non-profit organizations, provide domiciliary care services. The corresponding inter-sectoral funding flows are predominately designed as a substitute payment per hour of care worker activity. Subsidies are the financing mode for health-related home care in the province of Vorarlberg, and are also existent (but of minor importance) in funding flows to private domiciliary home care providers in Vienna.

The substitute payment per hour of care worker activity can thus be regarded as the dominant public funding arrangement for home care in Austria. Interestingly, there are two different ways of calculating such local payments for domiciliary care clients: some provincial authorities prefer to prescribe public payments per hour of care work. In these provinces the level of public support is the same for all providers. Other provincial authorities define types of costs that LTC service agencies can claim against the provincial authority. In these provinces the level of public support depends on the cost structure of the providers and therefore varies between providers (for further information, see Trukeschitz and Buchinger, 2007b, pp. 146ff.). Organizations need to be authorized to be eligible for public support. If provinces set the price of domiciliary care, this price applies only to entities that receive public funding (either directly as subsidies or per service unit).

Public authorities that set the amount of public payments per hour of care work do so in three different ways (see Trukeschitz and Buchinger, 2007a, p. 16):

Type 1: The provincial authority fixes the market price of one hour of care work and also sets the public payment limit paid per hour of care work.

Type 2: The provincial authority sets the public payments paid per hour of care work only.

Type 3: The provincial authority sets the price of one hour of care work and pays for the difference between the hourly rate and contributions of individual service users.

Table 11.1 displays the design of funding flows from the public sector to providers of LTC services for the nine Austrian provinces.

In the area of *institutional care*, provincial authorities provide subsidies for authorized (public or private) providers to cover parts of the building costs of private care homes. Providers that accept these subsidies pledge to care for clients who are not able to pay the user fee (for details on co-payments, see Section 3.4). Provinces (also) support persons in need of LTC living in an authorized care home if the care client's income/asset is not sufficient. The financial means come from the social assistance system (see Section 3.4).

The level of public funding varies, depending on the modes of calculating daily rates for care homes (Table 11.2). Again, provincial authorities may set – depending on the quality category of the care home – a daily rate or calculate daily rates based on specific types of operating costs of providers within their territory. As a consequence, the former mode leads to the same daily rate for all providers within the same quality category in a province; the latter implies that the daily rate relates to the specific cost structure of individual providers within the same quality category in a province; the daily rate may

Table 11.1 Funding models for domiciliary care, by province (Austria, 2010)

Provinces	Public payments per hour of care work...		Subsidy
	...are the same for all providers within a province	...differ between providers within a province according to the provider's cost structure	
Burgenland	Type 1		
Lower Austria		yes	
Carinthia	Type 1		
Upper Austria		yes	
Salzburg	Type 3		
Styria	Type 2		
Tyrol	Type 3		
Vorarlberg	Type 2*		yes**
Vienna		yes	

Note: *for home care only, **for health-related home care only.
Source: Trukeschitz and Buchinger (2007b, p. 150) updated.

Table 11.2 Models for determination of daily rates for institutional care, by province (Austria, 2010)

Provinces	Daily rates	
	...are the same for all providers within a province	...differ between providers within a province according to the provider's cost structure
Burgenland		yes
Lower Austria	yes	
Carinthia	yes	
Upper Austria		yes
Salzburg	yes	
Styria	yes	
Tyrol		yes
Vorarlberg		yes
Vienna	yes	yes

Source: Trukeschitz and Buchinger (2007b, p. 153).

therefore vary between providers. In any case, the daily rates refer to the residential costs; rates for personal care have to be added. These rates for personal care do not differ between providers of a province. Daily rates are subject to private payments of care home residents and can be subsidized by the provincial authorities in the case of insufficient income of care home residents (Trukeschitz and Buchinger, 2007b, p. 150).

3.4   Private co-payments for LTC services

In Austria LTC services are financed by private and public means. Private means (i.e., co-payments of service users) are essential for accessing most types of LTC services in Austria. Advice and information services are provided free of charge. In economics co-payments have been perceived as a means to contain public spending.

The agreement between the Federal State and the nine provinces on common measures for people in need of care stipulates that social circumstances of care clients have to be considered when the levels of co-payments are set (Article 3 (4)).

The rules for private co-payments for using professional LTC services differ again between home care and residential care and across provinces. For *home care*, user fees usually relate to the household income of the care recipient; some provinces explicitly take the level of care allowance into account. Maximum user fees are specified. There is substantial variation of user fees among the nine Austrian provinces. Accordingly, the shares of public and private expenditures on domiciliary care vary substantially by province (BAG, 2009, p. 68). Whereas clients need to cover only 19 per cent of total costs in one province, they pay for 50 per cent of total costs in another province.

A unique model of financing health-related home care can be found in Vorarlberg. People living in this province may join associations that provide health-related home care (*Hauskrankenpflegevereine*). Membership fees are usually paid for the entire family on a voluntary basis and are irrespective of current care needs. All members are then eligible for care services in Vorarlberg. The annual membership fee amounts to approximately €26. Donations are welcome if patients are in need of time-consuming care. Some associations have set private contributions to €6 per care hour. These contributions are treated as donations. Moreover, some family members donate a fair amount for the benefit of the health-related home care association once their relative has passed away (Trukeschitz and Buchinger, 2007b). In this funding model 40 per cent of total revenues are private payments (membership fees and donations) (Hauskrankenpflege Vorarlberg, 2011).

For *residential care*, direct public funding flows to service providers occur at the time of building the care home. Service users pay for residential care. Public funding connected with residential service utilization is only required if the service user does not have sufficient means. In this case social assistance steps in as a lender of last resort. Income and assets of the person in need of LTC are then administered by the provincial authority, only a small amount of money ('pocket money') remaining for their own use. Recipients of social assistance in general and people taking up residential care services whose financial resources do not cover care costs are obliged to refund benefits received from local authorities if their financial situation improves. Provincial authorities even have the right to claim refunds from family members. In 2009, all provinces decided to waive their right to reclaim benefits but refunds were still claimed from heirs and donees. In 2010, one province (Styria) reintroduced refunds from families and two more provinces (Carinthia and Tyrol) are likely to follow soon (Salzburger Nachrichten, 2010).

4 Analysis of the current Austrian LTC funding system

The 1993 Federal and provincial legislation on LTC established a legal right to LTC allowances for all individuals meeting eligibility criteria as specified by law. While payments made to individuals are limited to the amounts set forth for each of the seven dependency levels (see Section 2), total spending and hence the overall funding need for cash benefits is open ended. The absolute funding need derives from the number of beneficiaries and the share of beneficiaries in each benefit category (see Schick, 2009, pp. 27–28).

As a consequence LTC financing cannot easily be managed or restrained effectively. One way to limit the growth in LTC spending is quite explicitly via cutting benefit levels and/or changing eligibility criteria, which requires a change in legislation and implies that policy goals would have to be (partly) abandoned. Another choice is to implement and administer the benefit schemes in a tight-fisted manner. Or, as Schick (2009, p. 37) observed: 'In principle, entitlements are not compatible with budget control; in practice, the two must be reconciled'. In the Austrian case, legislators designed benefits parsimoniously from the start, at least when compared with health care benefits. Also, there is in fact evidence for tacit budget control which manifests itself in the administration of the benefit schemes.

In what follows, we will briefly illustrate both explicit (Section 4.1) and tacit budget control (Section 4.2) in Austria's LTC system.

4.1 Explicit budget control: Changes in eligibility criteria

As far as the explicit budget control of the programme is concerned, eligibility criteria target care allowances to individuals with substantial care needs. In addition, the entitlement laws stipulate as a very vague overall objective that benefits are to 'contribute' to meeting the additional cost of living that long-term dependency entails. The law does not specify the exact share of costs to be covered by the LTC allowance. In practice there is no tracing of out-of-pocket payments for individual beneficiaries in the course of the entitlement procedures (Rechnungshof, 2010, p. 54). Furthermore, payments to individuals are lump-sum, so that payments on the individual level are confined.

In the course of consolidating public budgets in autumn 2010, the Austrian Federal Government decided to change the eligibility criteria for LTC allowance. From January 2011 on, applicants for LTC allowance are required to be in an approved need of more than 60 hours of care per month, which lifted the threshold, by 10 hours of care need. In line with the increase of the eligibility threshold, the number of care hours required for entering the next benefit level was set to 85 per month (+10 hours). Interestingly, entry requirements for all other LTC allowance levels (3–7) remained unchanged. Having entered the system, the distance in terms of hours of care between levels 1 and 2 remain the same (25 hours of care), whereas the distance between levels 2 and 3 decrease from 45 to 35 hours of care as the change in care hours refers only to the first two levels of care dependency.

This very recent development not only implies that access to cash benefits is more restrictive; some provinces tie access to publicly co-financed social care services to the receipt of LTC allowance or a minimum level of LTC allowance. As eligibility criteria have been tightened, it is more difficult for dependent persons to access these services as well.

To complete the picture of recent changes in Austria in 2011, it has to be noted, however, that the benefit level of care allowance level 6 was increased to €1260 (+ €18) per month.

4.2 Tacit control of financial needs in executing the LTC cash benefit schemes

In addition to explicit budget control, various forms of tacit controls of programme spending can be observed. To begin with, adjustments of benefits for inflation have been made at inadequate intervals and in insufficient amounts. Between 1993 and 2009 benefits were adjusted four times (in 1994, 1995, 2005 and 2009) but the increase in benefits compensated for less than half of the increase in prices (Rechnungshof, 2010, p. 55).

Furthermore, the Austrian Court of Auditors (*Rechnungshof*) has repeatedly examined the administration of care allowance benefits in Austria. In 2010, it commented on findings from a 2007 audit covering 21 of about 300 administrative bodies involved in the administration of benefits. The 21 cases comprise all major entities such as the pension insurance and provincial administrative units. Looking at the routine administration of care allowances, it appears that a fair amount of discretion is used in approving benefit claims and in assigning claimants to one of the seven benefit categories. (Rechnungshof, 2010).

Another finding presented by the Austrian Court of Auditors points to delays in entitlement procedures. There are major differences between different administrating bodies in the time needed to verify claims. The duration of proceedings ranged from 40 to 137 days. The pension insurance, which is the biggest administrative body involved in handling care allowance applications, settled cases after 58 days on average, but 16 per cent of all cases took more than 90 days. A number of administrative bodies did not fix binding time lines for handling requests and some made it impossible to check the duration of procedures by simply not entering the necessary information in a central database (Rechnungshof, 2010, pp. 30ff.).

Furthermore, information on the approval or refusal of applications or on specific recommendations following the needs assessments could work as a set-screw in budget control. Providing less information to applicants may work to reduce the number of appeals – even if these appeals were justified to some extent. In its report, the Austrian Court of Auditors in fact criticizes several of the administrating bodies for providing insufficient information to (potential) beneficiaries. Official notification letters did not always specify the amount and type of help as recommended by the doctors conducting the assessments (Rechnungshof, 2010, p. 38). Furthermore, legislation is pending on narrowing the time limit for appeals in entitlement procedures for care allowances, from three months to four weeks.

Finally, cost containment may work through delays in benefit payments or demands for repayment. In Austria, more than 80 per cent of beneficiaries of the care allowance schemes receive payments at the end of the month (whereas pensions are usually paid at the beginning of the month). At least one of the administrative bodies reclaimed the benefits for a full month rather than allocating the amount to the exact day of death (Schick, 2009, p. 35; Rechnungshof, 2010, pp. 33–34).

In summary, there are some indications for 'tactical and behavioural features of budgeting to constrain expenditures' (Schick, 2009, p. 35) in the Austrian case. However, it is impossible to prove at this point that the patterns observed by the Austrian Court of Auditors are always intentional or that they all originate in a shared but unspoken strategy to curtail LTC financing needs.

4.3 Distributional effects of tax-based LTC funding

The Austrian public LTC system is financed by general taxes. Distributional effects of a LTC programme can be derived by analysing both who bears the funding burden and who receives the benefits from the LTC programme.

The overall budget of the state in Austria is built on the principle that public funds may not be allocated to specific purposes beforehand (*Non-Affektationsprinzip*). All revenues from taxes or duties are taken to cover any public expenses, one of them being public LTC expenditure. Under these conditions the financial burden of tax-funded LTC expenditures cannot be assigned to specific groups of Austrian society. Compared with systems mainly funded by premiums, all tax payers contribute to finance LTC-related public expenditures (Mühlberger et al., 2008a, p. 16).

Tax-funded systems draw on a set of various tax bases. Distributive effects are generated by the mix of tax bases. Value-added taxes and premiums to social insurance are known for their regressive distributive effects (i.e., redistribution from lower-income groups to higher-income groups). Income taxes show progressive distributive effects (i.e., redistribution from lower-income groups to higher-income groups). According to Mühlberger et al.

(2008a, p. 28), in total, the Austrian tax and duty systems have no vertica distributive effects.

With regard to the group of people who receive benefits from the LTC cash benefit programme, horizontal and vertical redistributive effects car be discerned: significant horizontal redistributive effects occur. In general the Austrian LTC system aims at redistributing resources from people whc are able to cope with activities of daily living to people in need of LTC Given that the risk of long-term dependency is clearly related to age, benefit for LTC imply redistribution between younger generations and the elderly (Mühlberger et al., 2008a, p. 80).

In addition, vertical redistributive effects (i.e., redistributive effects betweer different income groups) can be shown: primarily low-income groups benefi from the LTC cash allowance, although this benefit is not subject to means testing. Twenty-three per cent of all LTC cash allowance, recipients draw ε pension of less than €570 per month (before taxes). Half of the recipient have an income from pensions of less than €860 per month (before taxes (BMASK, 2010b, p. 11).

5   Future funding requirements and reform plans in Austria

5.1   Projection of funding requirements

Population ageing in Austria is far from ebbing away. As long-term depen dency risk is clearly age-dependent, long-term funding needs are expected tc augment in the decades ahead. Against the background of the financial crisi and general austerity policy this raises the question as to whether the cur rent financing system needs to be refurbished. This section presents finding from recent projections of LTC financing requirements for Austria, prepar ing the ground for a brief discussion of potential changes to Austria's LTC financing system.

In the past decade, a variety of projections of future funding needs for LTC have been conducted for Austria (Streissler, 2004b; OECD, 2006; Mühlberge et al., 2008b; European Communities, 2009; Buchinger and Schneider, 2010 Schneider and Buchinger, 2010). These projections use macrosimulatior approaches and most projections focus on estimating the costs of providing LTC to frail elderly people. In the following, we summarize findings from Buchinger and Schneider (2010) and Schneider and Buchinger (2010), whc present a very recent projection for Austria and the first to generate result disaggregated to the level of all nine Austrian provinces. This projection i based on a macrosimulation model along the lines of the UK Personal Socia Services Research Unit's LTC projection model (see Comas-Herrera et al. 2003). It spans the years 2008–2030 and delivers estimates for the future financing requirements in the care of persons age 65 and older.

A wide range of factors determine the amounts of public funds needed to cover the costs of LTC in Austria, for example demographic characteristics (like age or gender), health/morbidity of future generations of older persons, availability of other resources (like income, assets, family care), regional characteristics (like living in a rural or metropolitan area or a specific part of a country) and, not least, the design of LTC benefit programmes (e.g., eligibility criteria).

Thus, Schneider and Buchinger (2010) present cost estimates for three main scenarios which differ with regard to the specific assumptions concerning the health status of future generations of older people, the supply of informal care and the unit costs of care. The baseline scenario assumes that past trends in healthy ageing would continue in the future, that there is no change in the access to informal care and that costs increase by 2 per cent per year (Schneider and Buchinger, 2010).

The projection of elderly dependent persons in Austria yields an increase of 43.3 per cent (+426,053 dependent elderly individuals) in the baseline scenario. This rise in the number of older care recipients, in combination with the expansion of LTC services, entails an increase in the costs of LTC services of 122.9 per cent from 2008 to 2030. The largest part of LTC funding requirements can be attributed to residential care. As was the case in earlier projections (see Streissler, 2004b; Mühlberger et al., 2008b), findings are very sensitive to modifications in the underlying assumptions. In the best case scenario, funding requirements are estimated to rise by 70 per cent, whereas the worst case scenario delivers an increase in LTC costs of 240 per cent. The baseline estimate (122.9 per cent), according to Schneider and Buchinger (2010), falls between the projections of Streissler (2004a) or OECD (2006) (96 per cent) and that of Mühlberger et al. (2008b) yielding 160 per cent.

Schneider and Buchinger (2010) also find considerable variations in both the development of the frail older population and in LTC funding requirements between the nine provinces. Thus, the province of Vorarlberg faces the highest increase in costs (178.4 per cent) in the baseline scenario, whereas the smallest effects are projected to eventuate in Carinthia (81.9 per cent) and Vienna (96.3 per cent). These marked differences call into question the current division of financial responsibilities between the Federal State and the provinces, as it might overstrain several provinces.

5.2 Plans to establish a LTC fund (*Pflegefonds*) as a new financing platform

In November 2008, Austria's two biggest parties – the Social Democratic Party (SPÖ) and the Conservative Party (ÖVP) – decided to renew their coalition government. The grand coalition's political agenda for its four-year term includes plans for an overhaul of the country's LTC financing system. The aim is to create a nationwide and sustainable funding system with a special 'LTC fund' (*Pflegefonds*) as the preferred solution. This fund is to be established under the roof of the Federal Ministry of Labour and Social Affairs (BMASK). The Federal Government suggests the LTC fund is to deal with 'potential extra funding for care allowances', and (Federal) funding for grants which support investments in LTC infrastructure at the level of the provinces. The coalition agreement explicitly mentions subsidizing grants to provinces that would be tied to specific standards for access to LTC services, service quality and reporting (Regierungsprogramm für die XXIV. Gesetzgebungsperiode der Republik Österreich, 2008–2013).

Reforms along this line would mark the beginning of earmarked financing in the area of LTC. However, the changes that are envisaged by the Federal Government will not just be passed into law but call for a renegotiation of the existing 'Article 15a Agreement' with the provinces. A pre-existing working group on LTC reform (with representatives from both government levels, LTC care providers and social partners) is currently discussing how best to reform the Austrian LTC system but has not agreed on the specifics of a LTC fund to date.

Several revenue sources have been taken into consideration for the fund. It could be partly contribution-based and partly tax-based, as is the case with the family burdens equalization fund (*Familienlastenausgleichsfonds – FLAF*). As regards taxes, it has been put forward to raise existing taxes (e.g., VAT) or levy new taxes. Mühlberger et al. (2008a) advocate asset taxation. In Austria, asset taxation is low by European standards. The taxation of inheritances and gifts has been abandoned after a ruling of the Austrian Constitutional Court in 2008. Earmarking of revenues from asset taxation for LTC funding would be unusual in the Austrian context, where (as already mentioned in passing) all tax revenues generally furnish all types of spending needs. Mühlberger et al. (2008a, p. 46) also consider production taxes levied on the economic value added as a potential source of revenue.

Another option is to provide the fund with a stock of assets and hence a regular stream of income from assets (see Mühlberger et al., 2008a, p. 24). The problem with this latter option is that the stock of assets required to generate an adequate stream of revenues would be very substantial. To date, no such stock of assets has been identified that could be transferred to a LTC fund.

Mühlberger et al. (2008, p. 9) posit that *mixed funding* from taxes, contributions or income from assets facilitates adjustments to changing funding needs. Mixed funding also makes it easier to account for adequacy, volatility, distributional effects and other economic effects in the financing strategy.

The introduction of a LTC fund (*Pflegefonds*) could have long-lasting effects on the assignment of responsibilities across the three levels of government and on the organization and distribution of LTC services. It could make LTC financing and spending in Austria much more transparent (see Mühlberger et al., 2008a, p. 24). Notwithstanding that the Federal State and the provinces consented in their 1993 'Article 15a Agreement' (see Section 3.2) to establish a working group on LTC (*Arbeitskreis für Pflegevorsorge*),[6] which is to deliver a yearly report on LTC provisions, data on LTC financing are still very patchy. Not all provinces deliver adequate data on service provision. By contrast, the LTC fund would by design consolidate information on spending across all provinces timely, completely and accurately.

Establishing such a special fund also offers an opportunity to reduce the number of administrative bodies involved in implementing LTC legislation and to better integrate cash benefits with LTC services. With about 300 administrative entities working on claim proposals, the system is highly fragmented, entailing inefficiencies and inequality in access to benefits (Mühlberger et al., 2008a, p. 9; Rechnungshof, 2010). It also offers the opportunity to harmonize eligibility criteria and benefit as well as co-payment levels.

One step towards improving this situation was taken in spring 2011. The Federal State and the nine provinces agreed on concentrating legislative and administrative responsibilities concerning LTC allowances at the Federal Level, which will come into force in 2012. As a consequence, the number of administrative bodies dealing with the administration of the LTC allowance will be reduced from 303 to just 8. Funding of the LTC allowance will still be divided between the Federal State and the provinces. This regulation is temporary. The final solution to safeguarding LTC financing in Austria has been postponed. It will be negotiated in conjunction with the next fiscal equalization scheme in 2015.

6 Summary and conclusions

LTC dependency is one of the regular and major risks of life. This dependency risk does not only challenge dependent people, for example, by imposing high costs of care, but also their families, particularly their caring relative(s). Welfare States respond to this challenge by providing different sets of benefits and services for people in need of LTC. Varying models have been developed to fund this public support in Europe.

In this chapter we focused on funding modalities of LTC in Austria. We started out by briefly presenting the Austrian LTC system, including a sketch of major benefits. Against this background we discussed the roles and relationships of different funding agents and intricacies of LTC funding streams in Austria.

Austrian LTC policy has been built on major social policy principles dealing with the relationship between public and private responsibilities in providing for major risks of life. In Austria, the responsibility for covering the requirement for LTC is shared between the public and the private spheres, as well as between different government levels within the public sector. Two agreements between the Federal State and the nine provinces based on the Austrian Constitutional Act assure that central-level and provincial-level activities complement each other.

The Federal State is responsible for funding a Federal LTC cash benefit and for covering 60 per cent of public spending for an additional cash benefit covering '24-hour care' for certain groups of dependent individuals living in the community. The provinces are pledged to provide sufficient LTC services of adequate quality in their territory. They contribute to financing the LTC cash benefit and cover 40 per cent of public costs of a subsidy for 24-hour care. Tax deductions for people who face heavy financial burdens due to their physical or cognitive impairments should also be mentioned in passing. These tax deductions reduce tax revenues for all levels of government (see Section 3.2). Overall, the Federal State and the provinces currently contribute roughly in equal parts to public LTC funding.

The agreements between the Federal State and the provinces on LTC that are based on Article 15 of the Austrian Constitution provide provinces with discretion to implement efforts appropriate to their unique needs or political preferences and set the scene for a competition of differing policy models. The fact that about a third of provinces' social expenditure is related to care indicates that LTC indeed figures quite prominently in provinces' efforts to build profile. The provision of LTC services still varies substantially between the nine provinces. In some instances, provinces offer additional services or soften eligibility criteria for the financial support for 24-hour care.

At the same time, diversity presents challenges to (potential) claimants of benefits and questions the principle of equal opportunities and living conditions all over the country. Interestingly, initiatives and activities to collate the documentation of LTC regulation and service provision in the nine provinces do not seem to have succeeded. Official data on the provision of services by the provinces are still very sketchy for Austria, which inhibits benchmarking and policy learning, increases transaction costs and also makes it difficult to trace the exact amount, use and efficacy of LTC spending.

Funding for Austria's LTC system comes from general tax revenues, which is a classic design feature of Nordic welfare States but less common for Central European welfare States of the Bismarckian type. We have shown that tax funding of public support for people in need of LTC is an atypical funding mode for protection of major life risks within Austria's welfare system.

Looking at LTC funding from a fiscal federalism angle, it is important to note that both the Federal as well the provincial government levels hold legal competences in LTC care policy (Trukeschitz et al., forthcoming). All levels of government use their general tax revenues to finance LTC benefits, where the major part of provinces' tax revenues comes from the fiscal equalization scheme. The Federal State has not used subsidizing grants to provinces in the area of LTC policy.

In Section 3.3 we gave insights into the various funding models that provinces use to finance LTC services. Private co-payments are essential for accessing LTC services in Austria. The agreement between the Federal State and the nine provinces on common measures for people in need of care states that social circumstances have to be considered when levels of co-payments are defined. If dependent people still do not have sufficient means for purchasing residential services, social assistance steps in as a lender of last resort. Heirs and donees are obliged to refund these payments to the public budget. Furthermore, several provinces are about to return to reclaiming benefits from families of dependent persons who live in care homes – a policy which was abandoned only in 2009.

With a special emphasis on LTC cash allowances, we analysed the tacit behaviour of public authorities. Delays in entitlement procedures, insufficient information on the approval or refusal of applications or delays in benefit payments appear to be tactical and behavioural features of budgeting at all government levels used to constrain LTC spending.

The Austrian LTC system shows substantial horizontal and vertical distributive effects. Tax funding of LTC benefits seems to have no distributional effect in Austria. However, LTC care allowances inure to the benefit of dependent people and people with low income. The latter effect emerges even though the benefit is not means tested.

The benefit system as such works quite well in many areas but also faces substantial challenges to provide sufficient, equitable and sustainable support to dependent older people. One of the most urgent tasks to take up is to increase transparency in the provision of LTC services by provinces in order to promote policy learning, to control the flows of public funding and to improve budgetary performance.

Current projections alert policy makers to expected increase in the number of dependent persons, which would entail an upsurge in public spending under *status quo* conditions. Cost projections for LTC for persons age 65 and older estimate that funding needs might well double by 2030. Whether the current system of LTC funding is able to cope with these developments is subject to current discussions in the political arena as well as in academia. Most recent suggestions address new funding models, like a 'LTC fund' that could rely on various sources of revenues.

Acknowledgments

The authors wish to thank Dr Clemens Buchinger for helpful comments on Sections 3.3 and 5.1. We also thank the Austrian Federal Ministry of Science and Research and the Wiener Gesundheitsförderung GmbH for research funding.

Notes

*WU Vienna – Vienna University of Economics and Business, Research Fellow at the Research Institute for Economics of Aging, FLARE fellow 2008–2011 (European post doc programme 'Future Leader of Ageing Research in Europe (FLARE)', initiated by the ERA-AGE consortium and funded by the European Union Member States. Funding agent in Austria: Federal Ministry of Science and Research).

**WU Vienna – Vienna University of Economics and Business, Professor for Economics, Head of the Department of Socioeconomics, Director of the Institute for Social Policy and of the Research Institute for Economics of Aging.

1. The average old age pension in Austria amounted to €1223 per month in December 2008 (Hauptverband Der Österreichischen Sozialversicherungsträger, 2009), whereas the approximate cost of a nursing home is €2000–6000 per month depending on the care package included (Schneider, et al., 2006).
2. For a more detailed discussion of LTC benefits in Austria, see Schneider and Trukeschitz (2008); Hammer and Österle (2003); and Fernández et al. (2009).
3. In the case of dementia, the care client is eligible for support beginning with a placement in need category 2. One province (Lower Austria) waives the need to present a medical certificate on the need for 24-hour care.
4. Below the level of the provinces (*Länder*), districts (*Bezirkshauptmannschaften*), communities (*Gemeinden*) and other public bodies such as social insurance schemes or public associations of welfare agencies (*Sozialhilfeverbände*) are actors in LTC in Austria (Trukeschitz et al. (forthcoming)). Since there is limited space for discussion we will not detail the relevant funding streams in LTC for these levels of government but focus on the Federal and provincial levels.
5. Average across all provinces, excluding Vienna.
6. According to Article 12 of the 'Article 15a Agreement', the working group on LTC consists of three representatives of the Federal State, nine representatives from the provinces and representatives from a variety of social partners.

References

1196/AB (XXI. GP) (2000) Krankenversicherungspflichtige Beitragsleistungen für den Zeitraum 1.7.1993 bis 31.12.1999: Anfragebeantwortung durch den Bundesminister für soziale Sicherheit und Generationen Mag. Herbert Haupt zu der schriftlichen Anfrage (1191/J) der Abgeordneten Theresia Haidlmayr, Kolleginnen und Kollegen an die Bundesministerin für soziale Sicherheit und Generationen betreffend krankenversicherungspflichtige Beitragsleistungen für den Zeitraum 1.7.1993 bis 31.12.1999, Republik Österreich, Parlament.

Arbeiterkammer Wien (2005) '*Studie private Pflegegeldversicherungen. Durchgeführt vom Verein für Konsumenteninformation im Auftrag der AK Wien*', February.

BAG, Bundesarbeitsgemeinschaft freie Wohlfahrt (2009) 'Finanzierung der Pflege in Österreich. Fakten und Vorschläge aus Sicht der Trägerorganisationen innerhalb der BAG', in ÖKSA (ed.) *Finanzierung der Pflege in Österreich. Bedarf – Modelle – Perspektiven*, Wien: Österreichisches Kommitee für Soziale Arbeit, pp. 64–76.

Bergvall, D., Charbit, C., Kraan, D.-J. and Merk, O. (2006) 'Intergovernmental Transfers and Decentralised Public Spending', *OECD Journal on Budgeting*, 5(4), 111–158.

Bischof, S. (2009) *Das Pflegerisiko – private und staatliche Formen der Vorsorge. Wirtschaftsuniversität Wien*, Institut für Sozialpolitik, Diplomarbeit, October.

BMASK, Bundesministerium für Arbeit, Soziales und Konsumentenschutz (2008) *Österreichischer Pflegevorsorgebericht 2008,* Wien, Bundesministerium für Arbeit, Soziales und Konsumentenschutz.

BMASK, Bundesministerium für Arbeit, Soziales und Konsumentenschutz (2010a) 'Sozialbericht 2009–2010: Ressortaktivitäten und sozialpolitische Analysen', (Wien: Bundesministerium für Arbeit, Soziales und Konsumentenschutz).

BMASK, Bundesministerium für Arbeit, Soziales und Konsumentenschutz (2010b) *Österreichischer Pflegevorsorgebericht 2008 (Annual Report on Long-term Care in Austria)* (Vienna: Bundesministerium für Arbeit, Soziales und Konsumentenschutz).

Bonoli, G. (1997) 'Classifying Welfare States: A Two-Dimensional Approach'. *Journal of Social Policy,* 26, pp. 351–372.

BPGG *Bundespflegegeldgesetz, BGBl Nr 110/1993 i.d.F. BGBl Nr 147/2009.*

Bröthaler, J. (2008) 'Wandel und Beständigkeit. Eine Retrospektive des österreichischen Finanzausgleichs', in W. Schönbäck (ed.) *Sozioökonomie als multidisziplinärer Forschungsansatz: eine Gedenkschrift für Egon Matzner* (Wien (u.a.): Springer), pp. 171–190.

Buchinger, C. and Schneider, U. (2010) 'Projections of future long-term care expenditure in Austria (2008–2030) with special consideration of assistive technologies' in G. Geyer, R. Goebl and K. Zimmermann (eds) *Innovative ICT Solutions for Older Persons – A New Understanding. Proceedings of the Ambient Assisted Living Forum 09 Vienna, September 29–October 1, 2009* (Vienna: Österreichische Computer Gesellschaft), pp. 156–164.

Comas-Herrera, A., Costa-Font, J., Gori, C. et al. (2003) *European Study of Long-Term Care Expenditure: Investigating the Sensitivity of Projections of Future Long-Term Care Expenditure in Germany, Spain, Italy and the United Kingdom to Changes in Assumptions about Demography, Dependency, Informal Care, Formal Care and Unit Costs* (London: PSSRU, LSE Heath and Social Care, London School of Economics).

Eisenmenger, T. (2007) 'Private Pflegegeldversicherungen', in W. Pfeil (ed.) *Zukunft der Pflege und Betreuung in Österreich* (Wien: Manz), pp. 163–193.

European Communities (2009) *2009 Ageing Report: Economic and Budgetary Projections for the EU-27 Member States (2008–2060). European Economy 2|2009,* provisional version.

Eurostat (2010) Statistics Database.

Federal Ministry of Social Affairs and Consumer Protection (2008) *Austrian Report on Strategies for Social protection and Social Inclusion 2008–2010,* Vienna, September.

Fernández, J.-L., Forder, J., Trukeschitz, B., Rokosová, M. and Mcdaid, D. (2009) *How Can European States Design Efficient, Equitable and Sustainable Funding Systems for Long-term Care for Older People?* World Health Organization 2009 and World Health Organization, on behalf of the European Observatory on Health Systems and Policies 2009, Policy Brief No. 11.

Gruber, G. and Pallinger, M. (1994) *BPGG, Bundespflegegeldgesetz. Kommentar* (Wien: Springer).

Hammer, E. and Österle, A. (2003) 'Welfare State Policy and Informal Long-Term Care Giving in Austria: Old Gender Divisions and New Stratification Processes among Women', *Journal of Social Policy,* 32, pp. 37–53.

Hauptverband der Österreichischen Sozialversicherungsträger (2009) *Die österreichische Sozialversicherung in Zahlen. 23, Ausgabe,* August.

Hauskrankenpflege Vorarlberg (2011) *Hauskrankenpflege Vorarlberg,* http://www. hauskrankenpflege-vlbg.at/hauskrankenpflege.php, accessed 20 January 2011.

Mühlberger, U., Guger, A., Knittler, K. and Schratzenstaller, M. (2008a) *Alternative Finanzierungsformen der Pflegevorsorge. Studie des Österreichischen Instituts für Wirtschaftsforschung im Auftrag des Bundesministeriums für Soziales und Konsumentenschutz* (Wien: WIFO – Österreichisches Institut für Wirtschaftsforschung).

Mühlberger, U., Knittler, K. and Guger, A. (2008b) *Mittel- und langfristige Finanzierung der Pflegevorsorge. Studie des Österreichischen Instituts für Wirtschaftsforschung im Auftrag des Bundesministeriums für Soziales und Konsumentenschutz* (Wien: WIFO – Österreichisches Institut für Wirtschaftsforschung).

OECD (2006) *Projecting OECD Health and Long-Term Care Expenditures: What Are the Main Drivers?* Economics Department Working Paper 477.

Palier, B. (2008) 'The politics of reforms in Bismarckian welfare systems. A general presentation', in B. Palier (ed.) *A Long Good Bye to Bismarck? The Politics of Welfare Reforms in Continental Europe* (Chicago, IL: University of Chicago Press).

Rechnungshof (2010) 'Vollzug des Pflegegeldes', in Rechnungshof (ed.) *Rechnungshofberichte Reihe Bund*, (Wien: Rechnungshof), pp. 7–60.

Regierungsprogramm Für Die XXIV. Gesetzgebungsperiode Der Republik Österreich 2008–2013.

Schick, A. (2009) 'Budgeting for Entitlements', *OECD Journal on Budgeting*, 2, pp. 25–37.

Schneider, U. and Buchinger, C. (2010) *Projections of Future Long-term Care Expenditure in Austria (2008–2030)*, WU Forschungsinstitut für Altersökonomie, Working Paper (Wien: Wirtschaftsuniversität Wien).

Schneider, U. and Trukeschitz, B. (2008) *Changing Long-term Care Needs in Ageing Societies: Austria's Policy Responses* (Vienna: WU Vienna University of Economics and Business, Research Institute for Economics of Ageing).

Schneider, U., Österle, A., Schober, C. and Schober, D. (2006) 'Die Kosten der Pflege in Österreich – Ausgabenstrukturen und Finanzierung', *Forschungsberichte des Instituts für Sozialpolitik* (Wien: Institut für Sozialpolitik, Wirtschaftsuniversität Wien).

Streissler, A. (2004a) 'Geriatrische Langzeitpflege. Eine Analyse aus Österreichischer Sicht', *Wirtschaft und Gesellschaft*, 30, pp. 247–271.

Streissler, A. (2004b) *Geriatrische Langzeitpflege. Situation und Entwicklungsperspektiven* (Wien: Kammer für Arbeiter und Angestellte für Wien, Abt. Wirtschaftswissenschaft und Statistik).

Trukeschitz, B. and Buchinger, C. (2007a) 'Finanzierung mobiler Dienstleistungen der Altenpflege und –betreuung', *Kontraste*, 8, pp. 13–18.

Trukeschitz, B. and Buchinger, C. (2007b). 'Öffentliche Förderungen am Beispiel von Dienstleistungen der Altenpflege und -betreuung', in B. Trukeschitz and U. Schneider (eds) *Die Qualität arbeitsmarktpolitischer und sozialer Dienstleistungen im Kontext öffentlicher Beschaffungspolitik* (Baden-Baden: Nomos), pp. 127–165.

Trukeschitz, B., Schneider, U. and Czypionka, T. 'Federalism in health and social care in Austria', in J. Costa-Font and S.L. Greer (eds) *Federalism and Decentralization in European Health and Social Care: Competition, Innovation and Cohesion* (Cambridge: Cambridge University Press, forthcoming).

Vereinbarung gemäß Art. 15a B-VG – 24-Stunden-Betreuung, Vereinbarung gemäß Art. 15a B-VG zwischen dem Bund und den Ländern über die gemeinsame Förderung der 24-Stunden-Betreuung. *BGBl. I Nr. 59/2009.*

Vereinbarung gemäß Art. 15a B-VG – Pflegeversorgung, Vereinbarung zwischen dem Bund und den Ländern gemäß Art. 15a B-VG über gemeinsame Maßnahmen des Bundes und der Länder für pflegebedürftige Personen samt Anlagen, *.BGBl Nr 866/1993*.

VVO, Versicherungsverband Österreich (2008) *Pflegevorsorge statt Pflegelücke*, http://www.vvo.at/pflegevorsorge-statt-pflegelucke-2.html (accessed 26 March 2011).

12
Financing Long-Term Care in Germany

Andy Zuchandke
Institute for Risk and Insurance, Leibniz University of Hannover

Sebastian Reddemann
Center for Risk and Insurance, Hannover

and

Simone Krummaker
Center for Risk and Insurance, Hannover

1 Introduction

In 1995, after many years of public discussion dating back to the 1970s, mandatory social long-term care insurance (SLTCI) was implemented in Germany as the fifth pillar of the social security system. Prior to the introduction of mandatory SLTCI, acute care was covered by the mandatory health insurance programme while expenditures for long-term care (LTC) coverage were covered by the private income or private savings of the LTC-dependent individual or the individual's family. If these were exhausted, individuals in need of care could then apply for public welfare. These payments, however, were provided only for those identified as 'needy' by a community-based means-tested programme (*Hilfe zur Pflege*) under the aegis of Germany's social assistance programmes.

Private care insurance has been available in Germany since the mid-1980s. However, it played only a minor role in covering LTC cases as there were a maximum of only 250,000 private contracts purchased (Goetting et al., 1994, p. 289; Zweifel and Strüwe, 1998), despite the fact that the number of individuals needing LTC and applying for social assistance in order to get their expenses for LTC covered increased from 165,000 in 1963 to nearly 660,000 in 1993 (Statistisches Bundesamt, 2010). Further complicating the situation, German Reunification amplified the already problematic financing situation of LTC, which had become an enormous financial burden for the municipalities. Benefits for care as a component of the social assistance programme added up to €6.5 billion, more than one-third of the entire expenses for social assistance in 1991 (Statistisches Bundesamt, 2010, Table D6).

The goals behind the introduction of SLTCI in Germany were manifold. From a political perspective, it was believed that this new mandatory insurance would relieve the municipalities from having to increase expenses for health care under the social assistance programme, and it would allow for the necessary separation of social assistance and LTC risk coverage. Furthermore, the legislature intended to cover LTC risk as an existential risk, to protect the entire population against the financial risks of chronic illness and disability, to activate domestic resources for informal care, to enable the development of requisite infrastructure for LTC in a competitive market environment and to enhance the quality of ambulatory care (Geraedts et al., 2000, p. 395; BMGS, 2003, p. 186).

Though the implementation of SLTCI appeared to be dominated primarily by fiscal arguments, the majority of the identified goals were achieved. The benefits of LTC insurance are now paid as capped lump-sum payments depending on the severity of the chronic illness or disability. Even though the majority of the costs for LTC are covered by SLTCI, in many cases SLTCI benefits are not sufficient to cover all expenses, thus requiring many LTC individuals to exhaust their private savings and then turn to social assistance. Prior to the adoption and implementation of SLTCI in 1995, numerous suggestions were presented regarding social security LTC plans. Considering the demographic growth of German society and the current problem with the public pension system, many economists and politicians proposed a funded system to cover LTC risks. Moreover, they argued that the pay-as-you-go principle was unfair, as individuals in need of LTC at the date of the introduction of the new insurance would receive benefits without ever having contributed financially to the system. Others proposed a completely private mandatory insurance plan. Despite the arguments, the policy makers designed SLTCI as a pay-as-you-go system as this allowed for immediate relief of the municipalities' budgets.

Considering the ongoing demographic evolution of the German population, it is expected that the number of ageing individuals dependent on LTC will increase. Another important change occurring in the German population is that the number of one-generation households, as well as the number of females entering the job market, are increasing. In many cases, these previously unemployed female household members were able to provide informal care for an LTC family member. Once these informal caretakers became employed, the burden of care became an issue. The supply of needed supplementary institutional care to provide for individuals such as those in situations similar to the aforementioned has to be organized and paid for. Because SLTCI has been in a deficit for several years, and any reserves are forecast to be exhausted soon, the debate on how to reform SLTCI is once again heating up.

This chapter is organized as follows. In Section 2, we present an overview of the LTC system in Germany and discuss pertinent information regarding those individuals in need of care. Section 3 provides insights into the financing and expenses associated with SLTCI. In Section 4, we present the development of SLTCI as well as current discussions on several reform options.

2   Overview of long-term care in Germany

As mentioned in the introduction, the implementation of SLTCI as the fifth pillar of Germany's social security system represents a significant change for financing LTC in Germany. Even though SLTCI is connected to the existing statutory health insurance system, it is also an independent, self-governing corporation under public law. Long-term care insurance (LTCI) is compulsory; individuals covered by one of the statutory health insurance-funded programmes are automatically members of the respective LTC-funded programme. All such programmes are managed by special groups inside the health insurance system. Individuals with private health insurance are required to obtain private long-term care insurance (PLTCI).[1] Benefits and expenditures are the same for all LTC programmes, and there is an overall financial balancing among the LTC insurance providers. Because of these legal regulations, no competition among the LTC providers exists (Rothgang and Igl, 2007, p. 54).

SLTCI covers the vast majority of the population.[2] In 2008, 70.3 million individuals, approximately 86 per cent of the population, were members of SLTCI (BMG, 2010a). In that same year, an additional 9.4 million individuals, approximately 11 per cent of the population, were members of a mandatory PLTCI (PKV, 2009, p. 16).

With the introduction of SLTCI in 1995, a legal definition of LTC need[3] was drafted. This definition was marginally modified in 2001 (Rothgang et al., 2009, p. 41). According to the most recent definition, an individual is dependent owing to a physical, psychological or mental disease or handicap that requires a significant amount of assistance to carry out everyday life activities. The eligibility for LTC benefits from SLTCI depends on a medical examination and assessment of one's daily living capability. Benefits are differentiated into three degrees of need based on assessed limitations over a minimum period of six months. The needs assessed are the activities of daily living (ADL), such as eating, dressing, bathing, getting in and out of bed and toileting, and the instrumental activities of daily living (IADL), such as preparing one's own meal, doing the laundry, cleaning, shopping, managing money affairs, using the telephone and the Internet and mobility. The three levels vary by time, frequency and severity of needed assistance, not necessarily by the number of limitations (SGB XI Section 15, 1994).

1. Care level I: Needing assistance with hygiene, feeding or mobility for at least two activities from one or more areas at least once a day; dependent on help in the household several times a week for a minimum average of 90 minutes, with a minimum of 45 minutes devoted to basic care.
2. Care level II: Needing assistance with hygiene, feeding or mobility at least three times every day; dependent on help in the household several times a week for a minimum average of three hours, with a minimum of two hours devoted to basic care.
3. Care level III: Needing assistance with hygiene, feeding or mobility daily and throughout the day, including night time; dependent on help in the household several times a week for a minimum average of five hours, with a minimum of four hours devoted to basic care.

Every person with needs which meet the threshold established by the legal definition, regardless of age, wealth or income, is eligible for LTCI benefits provided that the individual contributed to the system for at least two years during the previous ten years. Hardship cases are defined as people in care level III with care needs of more than seven hours a day, including at least two hours a night, or individuals who require more than a single caregiver. Individuals applying for SLTCI benefits are assessed with regard to level of care by a medical review board (*Medizinischer Dienst*, MDK) for SLTCI. Medicproof assumes these responsibilities for those individuals insured by a PLTCI.

If an individual is eligible for LTC benefits, the dependent person can choose between informal (mostly in-family care) or formal care (professional institutions). If informal care is chosen, the recipient passes the paid (fixed and capped) benefits to the caregiver. To avoid moral hazard surrounding these payments, informal care has to be reviewed by a professional caregiver twice a year.[4] If formal care is chosen, SLTCI provides either home care or nursing home care services. In these instances, the institution or group providing the services receives the payments directly. In addition to LTC, SLTCI also provides short-term care and respite care (up to four weeks per year), part-time institutional care and benefits for consumable or technical aids.

SLTCI was initiated to provide basic coverage. This means that all benefits are capped and may be paid as a one-time lump-sum. The benefits, therefore, co-finance the total costs of LTC; they do not cover all LTC-incurred expenses. This is especially true in the case of nursing home care where the uncovered costs can be substantial (see Section 3), considering that the costs for boarding and lodging (so-called 'hotel costs') are not covered. These costs have to be covered by the dependant or the dependant's family.[5] If an individual is unable to cover the total costs by other sources (voluntary PLTCI, private income, savings or assets), access to the means-tested social assistance programme, maintained by the municipalities, is granted. All other sources of financing are described in greater detail in Section 3.

More than 2 million German citizens are currently in need of LTC and have access to monthly benefits from social and/or mandatory private LTCI. The majority of these individuals (1.5 million) receive ambulatory benefits; stationary care in nursing homes or institutions is provided to more than 700,000 people (Statistisches Bundesamt, 2008a[6]). Table 12.1 represents the number of individuals in need of LTC.

Table 12.1 shows that most of the individuals with LTC needs are classified as level I. In the event that the individual is receiving home care, the care is often provided by family members. This proportionate statistic, however, decreases over time and as care level increases (cf. Statistisches Bundesamt 2001, 2003, 2005, 2007, 2008a).[7] It is also worth noting that individuals with a higher level of care dependency are more likely to be in nursing homes.

The number of individuals requiring LTC, as well as the overall costs and expenditures for LTC in Germany, is increasing. Figure 12.1 represents the number of individuals who are LTC dependent and the total expenditures as well as the expenditures relative to GDP. There has been a slow but steady rise in the overall number of individuals dependent on LTC, with an average growth rate of 1.36 per cent. This increase can be observed specifically in care level I cases. The other two care levels have remained nearly constant over time. One factor of the overall rise is based on the demographic changes and growth in Germany (Rothgang et al., 2009, p. 53). When reviewing the data and considering various causes for the increase in care level I recipients during the period of the study, one must consider that the evaluations by the MDK may be stricter than they were in prior years (Rothgang and Igl, 2007, p. 58).

During the same period total expenditures grew, with an average annual growth rate of 2.51 per cent from €27.80 billion in 1999 to

Table 12.1   Individuals in need of LTC in 2007

	Care recipients	Level I	Level II	Level III
Home care thereof:	1,537,518	903,373	487,529	146,616
informal home care	1,033,286 (67%)	638,846 (71%)	308,997 (63%)	85,443 (58%)
formal home care	504,232 (33%)	264,527 (29%)	178,532 (37%)	61,173 (42%)
Nursing care	709,311	253,406	299,936	145,136
Total	2,246,829	1,156,779	787,465	291,752

Source: Statistisches Bundesamt (2008a).

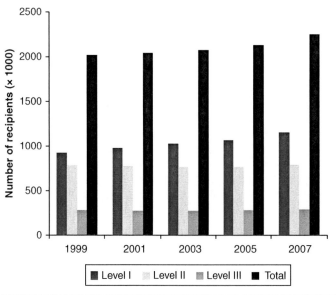

Total expenditures	1999	2001	2003	2005	2007
Absolute value (€bn)	27.80	29.42	31.30	32.27	33.91
Relative to GDP	1.38%	1.39%	1.45%	1.44%	1.40%

Figure 12.1   Individuals receiving LTC, by care level and total expenditures
Source: Statistisches Bundesamt (2001, 2003, 2005, 2007, 2008a).

€33.91 billion in 2007. As the average growth rate of total expenditure is higher than the average growth rate of individuals needing LTC, the increased expenditures can be only partially explained by this effect. The general technological advancements and increased wage rates, combined with a shift from informal to more expensive formal care, all contribute to that rise (Rothgang et al., 2009, p. 109).

3   Financing LTC in Germany

3.1   Social LTC insurance

3.1.1   *Earnings and Contributions*

As previously discussed, SLTCI, introduced in 1995, imposed mandatory coverage for a large part of the German population. Designed as a pay-as-you-go system, SLTCI is financed by income-related contributions, which are divided equally between employee and employer. The initial rate in 1995 was 1 per cent. As employers have to pay half of the contributions, one public holiday was abrogated to prevent an increase in labour costs.[8] Since

July 2008, the contribution rate has been 1.95 per cent of the gross labour income[9] (up to a contribution assessment ceiling in 2010 of €4162.50 per month). Childless members over the age of 22 have to pay an additional 0.25 per cent. Pensioners have been required to pay the full contribution rate by themselves since 2004, while the contribution rate for the unemployed is paid by the Federal Employment Office. Children up to the age of 25 years and spouses or life partners with monthly income below a certain level are co-insured.

The overall earnings of SLTCI are represented in Figure 12.2. Since the introduction of SLTCI, overall earnings have increased from €8.31 billion in 1995 to €19.61 billion in 2009. This represents an average growth rate of 7.6 per cent. The increasing contribution rates represent the major factor contributing to this positive growth. When examining the growth between 1997 and 2004, a period when the contribution rate remained constant, overall earnings increased only from €15.77 billion to €16.66 billion, which is an average growth rate of 0.78 per cent. This moderate increase resulted mainly from the labour market (i.e., a moderate increase in wage rates and stable unemployment rates), as earnings are dependent on the number of employed individuals as well as the amount of labour income. For a more detailed description, see Rothgang and Igl (2007, p. 73) and Rothgang and Dräther (2009, pp. 45–47).

Figure 12.2 Earnings, expenditures and balance of SLTCI
Source: BMG (2010b).

3.1.2 Expenditures and Benefits

SLTCI provides benefits for both home care and nursing home care in the case of medically approved need, providing that the insured has been a member of SLTCI for at least two years. The benefits are fixed to a monthly maximum per eligible person and are irrespective of age, income or wealth. The specific amount is determined by the level of LTC need (see Section 2) as well as the kind of care service (SGBXI Section 36 *et seq.*).

Table 12.2 displays the current benefits since 2010 for the major types of benefits (the figures in parentheses being projected benefits from 2012).

The table shows that for home care, benefits in-kind are approximately twice as much as the cash benefits. Additionally, benefits in-kind for nursing home care are higher than those for home care for levels I and II. The level III non-cash benefits for home and nursing home care are matched to prevent a shift from home care to nursing home care after the introduction of the SLTCI. It is worth noting that the beneficiary chooses the kind of benefit. It is also possible to combine cash and in-kind benefits. In addition to the above-mentioned major benefits, the SLTCI provides benefits for part-time institutional care (see Section 2). These benefits are equal to in-kind benefits for home care. If a family caregiver is on vacation or ill, the LTCI covers the costs of a professional caregiver for up to four weeks per annum and up to a maximum amount of €1510. Although SLTCI offers a variety of forms of benefits, the expenditures on home care and nursing home care make up approximately 85 per cent of benefit expenditures and approximately 80 per cent of overall expenditures (BMG, 2010b).

Figure 12.2 also depicts the increase in overall expenditures between 1995 and 2009. It illustrates that during the first two years (1995 and 1996), expenditures were steeply ascending. This rise was due to the payout of benefits for nursing home care implemented in July 1996. The average growth rate of expenditures between 1997 and 2009 was approximately 2.5 per cent, whereas the growth rates in 2008 and 2009 were approximately 4.4 and 6.2 per cent, respectively. The larger growth rates in those two years were caused by an increase in fixed benefits. Excepting these two years, the

Table 12.2 Expenditures per level of care (€)

	Home care		Nursing home care benefits in kind
	Cash benefits	**Benefits in kind**	
Level I	225 (235)	440 (450)	1023 (1023)
Level II	430 (440)	1040 (1100)	1279 (1279)
Level III	685 (700)	1510 (1550)	1510 (1550)

Source: BMG (2010c).

growth rates were relatively moderate, in some years less than 1 per cent. This corresponds to the constant benefit structure from 1995 to June 2007. The increased expenditures were driven by a higher number of individuals dependent on care, as well as by a shift from informal care to the more expensive professional care.

Examining the balance of the SLTCI funds (see Figure 12.2), it is apparent that expenditures have exceeded earnings in many years since 1999 (excepting 2006, 2008 and 2009). The surpluses in 2008 and 2009 were caused by the increased contribution rate from 1.7 to 1.95 per cent. The surplus in 2006 derived from the non-recurrent effect of contribution transfers being changed from the end to the beginning of the month. Therefore, the insurance fund received 13 instead of 12 monthly payments in 2006.

3.2   Mandatory private LTC insurance

Mandatory PLTCI is based on a funded system with average risk premiums as loadings for individual risks; differentiation by gender is not allowed. Additionally, the insurer has to accumulate age accruals. The private insurance industry has installed a clearing system to balance the unconsidered individual risks. As employers bear nearly half of the contribution rates for their employees in SLTCI, those who own a mandatory PLTCI receive a subsidy by the employer that equals the employer contribution for SLTCI. To level SLTCI and mandatory PLTCI, private insurance contracts are regulated. The following terms (among other) are taken into account by the insurer (SGBXI Section 110):

- No exclusion of previously ill or persons already needing LTC.
- The premium has to be independent of gender and current health status.
- The premium should not exceed the contribution assessment ceiling of SLTCI.
- Children have to be insured without extra premium.

The benefits paid for an insured person needing LTC must be at least equivalent to the SLTCI benefits (see Table 12.2) with respect to LTC level. This means that, like SLTCI, mandatory PLTCI does not offer full coverage.

Because of the small number of people insured under a PLTCI, the overall benefits and overall expenditures are much lower compared with SLTCI. Figure 12.3 shows the benefits and expenditures since 1995.

Whereas expenditures increased by about 50 per cent between 1997 and 2009,[10] overall premiums declined over the same period of time. As can be seen from the table, mandatory PLTCI posts a positive balance every year. A portion of that positive balance is put towards the required age accruals.

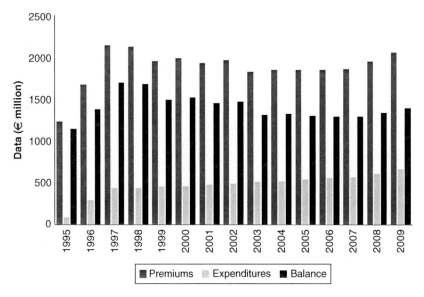

Figure 12.3 Contributions and expenditures of PLTCI
Source: PKV (2006, 2009).

3.3 Private insurance and social assistance

As both SLTCI and mandatory PLTCI do not offer full coverage, persons in need of LTC have to bear co-payments paid from their own income and assets. In the case of nursing home care, co-payments can be substantial. Table 12.3 shows co-payments for nursing home care in 2007 for each care level.

Co-payments comprise almost 50 per cent of overall costs, so even with LTCI coverage, individuals needing LTC have to pay a substantial amount 'out-of-pocket'. Due to the potential co-payments, private insurance

Table 12.3 Financing of nursing home care

	Costs for nursing home care			Components of financing	
	Nursing expenses	Costs for accommodation and fare	Total costs (without capital costs)	Payment of LTCI	Out-of-pocket payment
Level I	1307.20	608.00	1915.20	1023.00	892.20
Level II	1732.80	608.00	2340.80	1279.00	1061.80
Level III	2158.40	608.00	2766.40	1432.00	1334.40

Source: Statistisches Bundesamt (2008a) and BMG (2010c).

companies offer additional voluntary PLTCI contracts for both social- and privately insured individuals. Based on the benefit plan, the following various insurance contracts are provided (BMG, 2010c, p. 14):

- The insured person receives a constant pension in case the need for LTC arises.
- The insurer pays the residual costs fully or up to a certain ratio. The insured person has to provide evidence of the total costs.
- The insurer pays a fixed daily amount which is independent of the overall costs.

Despite the potential demand for additional LTCI and despite the fact that the number of insurance contracts tripled between 1995 and 2008, only about 1.3 million individuals owned a voluntary additional insurance contract in 2008 (GDV, 2009, p. 41). This represents only 2.2 per cent of all public and private LTCI members (excluding members not paying a contribution or premium). Thus, private co-payments cover only a small fraction and will therefore be neglected in our subsequent discussion.

If the personal wealth of the LTC individual or the LTC individual's relatives, who are potentially liable for support, cannot cover the costs for needed care after exhausting all other resources, the individual may apply for social assistance, called *Hilfe zur Pflege*. Although the eligibility for benefits is based on the legal definition for LTC need, there is one exception. People may access social assistance if they have been in need of LTC for less than six months. Like the rest of the social assistance programme, *Hilfe zur Pflege* is a tax-financed programme.

In Figure 12.4, the development of people receiving *Hilfe zur Pflege* is presented.

As pointed out in Figure 12.4, the number of people receiving social assistance decreased substantially with the introduction of SLTCI. This is especially true of home care, where the number of individuals receiving social assistance decreased by more than 65 per cent. Nevertheless, this figure indicates that about 284,000 individuals were still dependent on social assistance in addition to SLTCI benefits in 2008 and that three-quarters of these individuals were receiving nursing home care. When comparing the recipients of social assistance with the number of individuals receiving LTC benefits, it is clearly evident that, especially for individuals in nursing homes, people are financially strained under this system. While approximately 5 per cent of all individuals in home care received social assistance in 2007, almost 35 per cent of those individuals in nursing home care received social assistance (compare values in Figure 12.4 and Table 12.1).

The status of net expenditures (overall expenditures minus benefits[11]) is also represented in Figure 12.4. Net expenditures decreased by more than

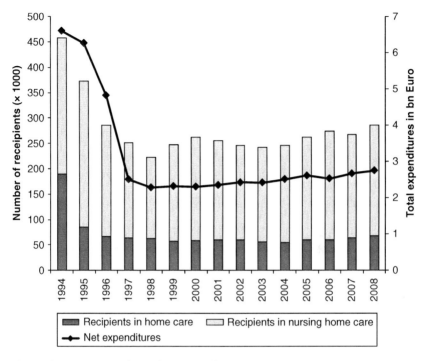

Figure 12.4   Payments of social assistance for LTC
Source: Rothgang et al., (2009), p. 108 and Statistisches Bundesamt (2010).

50 per cent, from €6.6 bn in 1994 (the year prior to the introduction of LTCI) to €2.7 billion in 2008, demonstrating the tremendous impact on expenditures for all municipalities. Note that expenditures were at a minimum in 1998 and slightly increased over subsequent years.

In addition to the social assistance financed by the municipalities, the federal states (*Bundesländer*) are obliged to support capital expenditures of nursing homes (investment costs). The federal states have two options to support these expenditures. They can either directly pay the constituted amount to nursing homes or support individuals in nursing homes who have to pay investment costs (SGBXI Section 9). Due to the different methods, financing investment costs differ greatly between the federal states (Schulz, 2010), thus making it difficult to quantify the expenditures. Schneekloth (2006, p. 29) estimated the average investment costs per month to be €376 per nursing home resident. These costs are only partly financed by the federal states; the uncovered costs again become the responsibility of the person receiving the benefits – the LTC individual. Multiplying this estimated amount by the number of individuals in nursing homes, the calculated total costs of capital expenditures in 2007 were €3.15 billion. Taking into account that investment costs are not completely financed by the federal states, the average monthly private costs for nursing home residents (see Table 12.3) are even higher.

After presenting information about the various sources of financing LTC expenditures, we will now calculate the remaining private costs. Unfortunately, the exact level of private costs is not calculable but rather has to be estimated. The estimation, based on Rothgang et al. (2009, p. 110), takes into consideration the direct costs.[12] Private expenditures have consistently increased over time, from €5.8 billion in 1999 to €9.21 billion in 2007, which represents an average growth rate of 5.88 per cent. Given the increasing costs for LTC combined with the rather stable benefits of LTCI, the increase in private costs to individuals is not surprising. The estimated levels of private costs do not consider the co-payments of capital expenditures, as there are no adequate data available to determine the amount of capital expenditures financed by the municipalities and thus the amount paid by the individuals in LTC.

3.4 Finance structure of overall expenditures

A brief overview of the finance structure of overall expenditures is worthy of consideration. As mentioned in the introduction, the overall expenditures increased over the last decade from approximately €27.8 billion in 1999 to more than €33.9 billion in 2007 (see also Figure 12.1). Concurrent with this increase in overall expenditures, all categories also increased during over the same period (compare the expenditures of each individual source). By examining Figure 12.5, we note that the ratio of overall expenditures varies among the sources.

Even though the expenditures of LTCI (social and private mandatory) make up the largest part of the total expenditures, the ratio decreased by more than 3 percentage points, to 54 per cent, in 2007. On the other hand, private costs increased from approximately 21 per cent in 1999 to 27 per cent in 2007. This effect was caused by the constant level of benefits in LTCI while the costs for LTC continually increased (e.g., wages). This additional financial burden for private households is one of the largest political issues for future reform options, negatively affecting the individual perception of financial security when LTC is required. Using data from the German Socio-Economic Panel (Zuchandke et al., 2010), it can be seen that the perception of financial security improved when SLTCI was first implemented. However, given the current situation of the increasing financial burden for LTC being placed on recipients, the perception of financial security in the case of LTC is likely to be a further blow to its image.

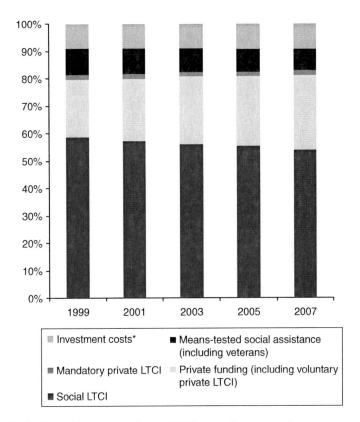

Figure 12.5 Financial structure of overall LTC expenditures

Note: *The investment costs are listed separately as we have no information about the extent to which these costs are financed by the Federal states and dependants.

Source: BMG (2010a, 2010b), PKV (2009), Statistisches Bundesamt (2010) and authors' own calculations.

4 Development and reform options of SLTCI

Prior to the SLTCI Act in Germany, the costs of care had to be financed almost entirely by individuals needing LTC and/or their families. Public support was only available for those who qualified under the means-tested social assistance programme. This situation changed substantially with the introduction of SLTCI. One aspect of the original insurance plan was to provide only partial coverage rather than full coverage, as detailed in Section 3. Currently, more than 50 per cent of the overall expenditures are covered by social and mandatory PLTCI. Nevertheless, the proportion of private costs compared with those financed publicly has increased over recent years (see Figure 12.5), and this trend will continue if the current system remains unchanged.

It is predicted that the overall costs of LTC will rise in the future, due to several factors. First, demographic change will increase the demand for LTC because of increasing life expectancy (Statistisches Bundesamt, 2008b). Various analyses are projecting a rise in benefit recipients. The estimated resulting costs differ among the studies, as each study is based on projected assumptions, such as age-specific care-risk, that vary. By assuming constant age-specific care-risk, Rothgang (2001) estimated that there will be between 2.9 and 3.3 million beneficiaries by 2040, whereas assuming a decreasing age-specific care-risk,[13] the number of individuals in need of LTC will be only 2.5–2.7 million by 2040. A recent study by Blinkert and Gräf (2009), also assuming a decreasing risk, forecasts 3.25–3.50 million beneficiaries by 2050. Quantifying the estimated higher demand for LTC to an increase in overall benefits, Pickard et al. (2007) estimate an increase relative to GDP from 1.24 per cent in 2000 to 2.72 per cent in 2050, an absolute increase of more than 70 per cent. These projections are based solely on the demographic impact of the respective age structure. Considering an adjustment to the legal definition of LTC dependence, more than 60,000 additional individuals will be in need of LTC and a significant shift to higher levels of care will be realized (Rothgang et al., 2009, p. 14), thus again resulting in increasing costs.

Another effect due to demographic change in Germany may be the transition from informal to formal care. Among other things, this is amplified by a decreasing number of potential caregivers as well as an increasing number of single households.[14] Other factors include the aforementioned technological advancements and the increasing wage rates (respectively, due to a positive rate of inflation). Pickard et al. (2007) also estimated the expenditures for LTC under the assumption of a switch from informal to formal care. By evaluating several scenarios, they predicted that expenditures will increase on average up to 3.24 per cent of GDP.

Considering the above projections, it is evident that a significant increase in overall LTC expenditures is on the horizon, and it must be managed. In the case of SLTCI benefits remaining constant, a relative change from public to private financing would continue much as it has for the last decade (see Figure 12.5). In other words, the purchasing power of LTC benefits would decline, as it did between 1995 and 2007 (Rothgang and Igl, 2007). Based on these facts, as well as on the recommendations of many scientists, the German government implemented a reform known as *Pflege-Weiterentwicklungsgesetz* (Bundesgesetzblatt, 2008). This reform has changed the benefit structure. In 2008 and 2010, the benefits were increased. They will be increased again in 2012 (all data are given in Table 12.2). In addition to the determined amounts, the government must also evaluate the necessity of increasing LTCI benefits based on the price, gross wage increases and the macroeconomic situation (see SGB XI Section 30). It is stipulated that this evaluation will be completed every three years, from 2015.

To the extent that the social security system and private LTCI only partially cover the overall costs of LTC, individuals must still rely on their own income and/or assets to finance the residual amount. If the individual is unable to cover the remaining amount, they can apply for assistance from the means-tested programme *Hilfe zur Pflege*. As shown in Figure 12.4, the number of individuals assisted by the social programme declined after SLTCI was implemented, but remains high with approximately 280,000 individuals receiving assistance in 2008.

Based on the increase in expenditures between 1995 and 2007 and recent projections, the *status quo* of SLTCI is not sustainable. To absorb the projected negative effects, several groups have proposed reforms to the present system. There are basically three options for large-scale reform under consideration (for detailed examination, see Rothgang, 2004). The options are the following:

1. Replacing SLTCI by a tax-funded means-tested system.
2. Converting the system into a capital-based (private) insurance.
3. Improving the pay-as-you-go system by indexing pensions to inflation, possibly by introducing tax-based or capital-based elements.

4.1 Tax-funded means-tested system

This proposal was introduced by a member of the Rürup Kommission and is characterized by a large number of goals (BMGS, 2003, pp. 210–212), most of which were found to be unachievable, thus leading to a rejection of the proposal.

For example, one of the major goals proposed under this plan was to reduce administrative costs. This goal was deemed short-sighted as the implementation of an administration capable of maintaining an efficient infrastructure for the care system is essential, and trimming costs would only overburden the municipalities once again. Another goal proposed under this plan was the reduction of non-wage labour costs. The argument against this reform basically claims that any relief granted under this plan must still be financed by someone. It is argued that this plan is little more than a change in names, as the additional costs would likely be tax financed. Other goals brought forth under this plan were also found to be unsustainable and, in some cases, counterproductive possibly leading to negative side effects.

4.2 Capital-based (private) insurance schemes

There has been much debate about whether a capital-based system can generate a higher return, whether it can actually strengthen intergenerational distribution and whether it is less prone to demographic change than the pay-as-you-go system. One way to transition to a capital-based system might be to extend the existing PLTCI to the entire population. However, as this system is not based on individual risk premiums, three other approaches for transitioning to a capital-based system are presented.

4.2.1   Instantaneous switch to a capital-based system

To simply abolish the pay-as-you-go system and replace it with a mandatory capital-based PLTCI would place a major burden on the current generation of insured individuals. Even though this system would be highly sustainable and would increase intergenerational justice once the transition is concluded, the excess strain it would place on the first generation is considered sufficient justification not to implement an instantaneous replacement of the old system, which is estimated to take at least 35 years to implement (Rothgang, 2004, p. 599).

4.2.2   Run-out option

The second possibility would be to gradually let the old system run out while concurrently creating a new capital-based system. Implementing the new system over a period of time would slowly reduce the spiking additional financing to zero, though this would take close to 40 years. Spikes in financing the new system may actually triple the current contribution. The Herzog Kommission (2003) recommends using this model while simultaneously capping the additional financial burden for the insured.

4.2.3   Freeze option

The last option is regarded as the most promising. It, too, proposes a switch to a capital-based insurance system; however, in this option, all benefits would be frozen at their current nominal level. The subsequent increasing gap would have to be absorbed by complementary private coverage. This gap would increase steadily over time until the frozen benefits are completely abolished, at which time the transition to a capital-based insurance system would be complete. This option complies with most of the self-imposed principles, and it is deemed the least disruptive. During this transition, the benefits would be dispersed only through the new private system, thus leading to possible diminished efficiency as administration costs and interface problems between the old and the new system are managed. For this reason, there are those who suggest an immediate and direct introduction of benefit dynamics into the current system after deliberating possible finance options.

4.3   Dynamization of benefits

The previous discussions indicate that an additional financial source for the adjustment of benefits to inflation and to increasing costs is inevitable. Following extensive discussions, this option drew the largest consensus. One major purveyor is the Rürup Kommission (BMGS, 2003). There are a number of options that would lead to an increase in supplementary funds:

- tax-based subsidies by the government;
- additional contributions by retirees;
- increased contribution rates; and
- the introduction of civil insurance elements.

To the extent that SLTCI is a prevention system, tax-based subsidies are an option that cannot be fully legitimated as they are, for example, in the case in the German pension system.

The second option seems the most feasible. The employed generation is not bearing a double-contribution, thus lowering the contribution rate to 1.2 per cent while investing the difference (0.5 per cent) in private provision funds would ensure that the system would remain stable until at least 2040 and equally distributing the burden over several generations of pensioners. These dynamics, however, will pose a problem after 2030, as, from then on, savings will build more slowly, diminishing considerably by 2040. Thus, a transition to a partial capital-based system seems to be the most sustainable.

This system could also be supplemented by a slowly rising contribution rate such that not only the retired but also the currently employed bear a part of the additional financing. Obviously, a rising contribution rate incorporates several flaws that bear careful consideration. Most importantly, it would raise non-wage labour costs unless the employer's contribution was to be fixed at its current level. This would subsequently result in increased monetary strain on the employed and should, therefore, be used in a restrictive way, but it should not be completely taboo.

Another possibility is to widen the clientele of SLTCI and impose a broader assessment base for the calculation of monthly contributions:

- include self-employed and civil servants;[15]
- raise or eventually abolish the limit for a voluntary switch to private insurance schemes to avoid the insured from switching to completely private insurance solutions;
- raise the contribution assessment ceiling; and
- include different sources of income.

Several calculations (Rothgang, 2001, p. 143) show that expanding SLTCI to the self-employed and civil servants would result in an improved risk structure and therefore lead to liquidity gains and additional receipts. Furthermore, the capital base established in private insurance could be absorbed into the SLTCI. This would require a legal assessment for usage restrictions, however.

The third and fourth options would directly result in additional funds without generating additional expenses. Having considered all the debating and research, it is evident that introducing elements of a civil insurance plan would provide a substantial contribution to the future financing of Germany's SLTCI, but it would not completely eliminate the financing gap. Practical problems pose the major hurdle for a successful implementation. Furthermore, an isolated introduction of these elements would not strengthen intergenerational equity.

5 Conclusion

The implementation of the mandatory SLTCI plan in 1995 led to a massive unburdening of municipal budgets, as well as private income and assets. The population was relieved of a substantial personal risk by a public insurance scheme upon the payment of contributions. The municipalities were relieved from financing costs that originally were not meant to be paid out of social assistance. While the implementation of SLTCI was certainly a positive step, the increase in contributions, benefits and co-payments since 1995 shows that the current system is not capable of successfully dealing with the health-care challenges of future ageing populations. The German government is aware of the impending need to reform the social security system as it pertains to LTC risk. Several reform options have been developed, evaluated, discussed and are still under consideration. It is interesting to note that only 15 years after the implementation of a new social insurance plan, the same design ideas for the newly reformed system were once again considered. The constraints of the existing system hinder the transition to an LTC insurance plan built upon a new financial base. The transition between systems must be accompanied by (tax-funded) transfers to the heavily loaded generation or into the new system itself.

The Minister of Health, Philipp Rösler, announced in October 2010 that he intends to implement a mandatory complementary capital-based insurance plan (BMG, 2010d). The details, however, have not yet been determined. Moreover, the political discussion about the possible reform options remains controversial. Considering the example of the reform needs of the German statutory pension insurance system, the evidence shows that problems with a system transition will worsen while inertia still holds sway.

Notes

1. Individuals with a labour income under a fixed contribution assessment ceiling (2010: €4162 monthly) are compulsorily insured in the statutory health insurance and in SLTCI. Individuals with a higher salary are voluntarily insured and can choose private insurance.
2. In 2008, the population was approximately 82 million.

3. As there did not exist a definition of LTC need before 1995, benefits were granted by social assistance authorities subject to their discretion.
4. If the dependent person does not request care advice, the cash payment can either be reduced or even interrupted (SGB XI Section 37, 1994).
5. In Germany, adult children are legally obliged to support their parents' costs of care if their financial means are exhausted.
6. There are no data for 2009 available yet. The publication 'Pflegestatistik 2009' will be available in December 2011. There are also data released on an annual basis by the Ministry of Health, but it does not provide data on private long-term insurance.
7. Compared with1999, the proportion of family caregivers decreased by approximately 5 per cent for each care level (see Statistisches Bundesamt, 2001, p. 7; Statistisches Bundesamt, 2008, p. 13).
8. One federal State did not abolish this public holiday, consequently requiring the employee to pay approximately three-quarters of the entire contribution rate.
9. Other income sources such as capital income are not considered.
10. The marked increase in expenditures between 1995 and 1997 was caused by a stepwise implementation of benefits.
11. As *Hilfe zur Pflege* is tax financed, benefits are represented by refunds of other social security institutions.
12. When taking into account intangible costs such as the opportunity cost of income, the overall costs would increase significantly.
13. The argument for taking into account the decreasing risk of needing LTC is due to increased life expectancy (Rothgang, 2001).
14. For a more detailed description, see Rothgang and Igl (2007, p. 60) and Rothgang (2001, pp. 28–36).
15. In the current insurance scheme, both groups are insured by mandatory PLTCI.

References

Blinkert, B. and Gräf, B. (2009) *Deutsche Pflegeversicherung vor massiven Herausforderungen*, Discussion Paper (Frankfurt am Main: Deutsche Bank Research).

BMG (Bundesministerium für Gesundheit) (2010a) *Long-term Care Insurance Persons Insured Under the Social Long-term Care Insurance*, http://www.bmg.bund.de/cln_160/SharedDocs/Downloads/DE/Standardartikel/P/Glossar-Pflegeversicherung/Long-term-care-insurance__Persons_20insured-4,templateId=raw, property=publicationFile.pdf/Long-term-care-insurance_Persons%20insured-4.pdf (accessed 28 September 2010).

BMG (Bundesministerium für Gesundheit) (2010b): *Finanzentwicklung der sozialen Pflegeversicherung – Ist-Ergebnisse ohne Rechnungsabgrenzung von 1995 bis 2009*, http://www.bmg.bund.de/cln_160/nn_1193090/SharedDocs/Downloads/DE/Statistiken/Statistiken_20Pflege/Finanzentwicklung-der-sozialen-Pflegeversicherung-Ist-Ergebnisse.html (accessed 28 September 2010).

BMG (Bundesministerium für Gesundheit) (2010c) *Ratgeber Pflege: Alles was Sie zur Pflege wissen müssen* (Berlin).

BMG (Bundesministerium für Gesundheit) (2010d) *Gesundheitsminister Dr. Philipp Rösler plant umfassende Reformen in der Pflege*, http://www.bundesgesundheitsministerium.de/cln_151/nn_1168762/SharedDocs/Interviews/DE/10-10-22-NOZ.html?__nnn=true (accessed 14 December 2011).

BMGS (Bundesministerium für Gesundheit und Soziales) (2003) *Nachhaltigkeit in der Finanzierung der Sozialen Sicherungssysteme*, http://www.bmas.de/portal/538/ property=pdf/nachhaltigkeit __ in__der__finanzierung_der_sozialen_sicherungssysteme. pdf (accessed 28 September 2010).

Bundesgesetzblatt (2008) *Gesetz zur strukturellen Weiterentwicklung der Pflegeversicherung* (Bonn).

Büscher, A. and Wingenfeld, K. (2009) 'Pflegebedürftigkeit und Pflegeleistungen', in H. Dräther, K. Jacobs and H. Rothgang (eds) *Fokus Pflegeversicherung. Nach der Reform ist vor der Reform* (Berlin: KomPart-Verlag), pp. 257–281.

GDV (Gesamtverband der Deutschen Versicherungswirtschaft) (2009) *Statistical Yearbook of German Insurance 2009* (Karlsruhe: Verlag Versicherungswirtschaft GmbH).

Geraedts, M., Heller, G.V. and Harrington, C.A. (2000) 'Germany's Long-Term-Care Insurance: Putting a Social Insurance Model into Practice', *Milbank Quarterly*, 78 (3), pp. 375–401.

Goetting, U., Haug, K. and Hinrichs, K. (1994) 'The Long Road to Long-Term Care Insurance in Germany', *Journal of Public Policy*, 14 (3), pp. 285–309.

Herzog Kommission (2003) *Bericht der Kommission 'Soziale Sicherheit' zur Reform der sozialen Sicherungssysteme*, http://www.sozialpolitik-aktuell.de/tl_files/sozialpolitik-aktuell/_Politikfelder/Sozialstaat/Dokumente/herzogkommission.pdf (accessed 28 September 2010).

Pickard, L., Comas-Herrera, A., Costa-Font, J. et al. (2007) 'Modelling an Entitlement to Long-term Care Services for Older People in Europe: Projections for Long-term Care Expenditure to 2050', *Journal of European Social Policy*, 17 (1), pp. 33–48.

PKV (Verband der privaten Krankenversicherung) (2006) *Zahlenbericht der privaten Krankenversicherung 2005/2006* (Köln).

PKV (2009) *Zahlenbericht der privaten Krankenversicherung 2008/2009* (Köln).

Rothgang, H. (2001) 'Finanzwirtschaftliche und strukturelle Entwicklungen in der Pflegeversicherung bis 2040 und mögliche alternative Konzepte' in Enquete Kommission 'Demographischer Wandel' des Deutschen Bundestags (ed.) *Herausforderungen unser älter werdenden Gesellschaft an den einzelnen und die Politik. Studienprogramm* (Heidelberg: R.V. Decker), pp. 1–254.

Rothgang, H. (2004) 'Reformoptionen zur Finanzierung der Pflegeversicherung – Darstellung und Bewertung', *Journal of Social Policy Research*, 6, pp. 584–616.

Rothgang, H. and Dräther, H. (2009) 'Zur aktuellen Diskussion über die Finanzsituation der Sozialen Pflegeversicherung', in H. Dräther, K. Jacobs and H. Rothgang (eds) *Fokus Pflegeversicherung. Nach der Reform ist vor der Reform* (Berlin: KomPart-Verlag), pp. 41–69.

Rothgang, H. and Igl, G. (2007) 'Long-term Care in Germany', *Japanese Journal of Social Policy*, 6 (1), pp. 54–84.

Rothgang, H., Holst, M., Kulik, D. and Unger, R. (2008) *Finanzielle Auswirkungen der Umsetzung des neuen Pflegebedürftigkeitsbegriffs und des dazugehörigen Assessments für die Sozialhilfeträger und die Pflegekassen* (Bremen).

Rothgang, H., Kulik, D., Müller, R. and Unger, R. (2009) 'GEK-Pflegereport 2009 – Schwerpunktthema: Regionale Unterschiede in der pflegerischen Versorgung', *Schriftenreihe zur Gesundheitsanalyse*, Band 73, Bremen.

Schneekloth, U. (2006) *Hilfe- und Pflegebedürftige in Alteneinrichtungen 2005* (München: TNS Infratest Sozialforschung).

Schulz, E. (2010) *The Long-term Care System in Germany*, ENEPRI research report No. 78.

Sozialgesetzbuch, Elftes Buch (SGB XI) (1994): *Soziale Pflegeversicherung* (last modification: Article 3 G v. 30.7.2009 I 2495).

Statistisches Bundesamt (2001) *Pflegestatistik 1999 – Pflege im Rahmen der Pflegeversicherung – Deutschlandergebnisse* (Wiesbaden).

Statistisches Bundesamt (2003) *Pflegestatistik 2001 – Pflege im Rahmen der Pflegeversicherung – Deutschlandergebnisse* (Wiesbaden).

Statistisches Bundesamt (2005) *Pflegestatistik 2003 – Pflege im Rahmen der Pflegeversicherung – Deutschlandergebnisse* (Wiesbaden).

Statistisches Bundesamt (2007) *Pflegestatistik 2005 – Pflege im Rahmen der Pflegeversicherung – Deutschlandergebnisse* (Wiesbaden).

Statistisches Bundesamt (2008a) *Pflegestatistik 2007 – Pflege im Rahmen der Pflegeversicherung – Deutschlandergebnisse* (Wiesbaden).

Statistisches Bundesamt (2008b) *Demografischer Wandel in Deutschland – Auswirkungen a. Krankenhausbehandlungen und Pflegebedürftige*, Heft 2 (Wiesbaden).

Statistisches Bundesamt (2010) *Statistik der Sozialhilfe – Hilfe zur Pflege* (Wiesbaden).

Zuchandke, A., Reddemann, S., Krummaker, S. and Schulenburg, J.-M. Graf von der (2010) 'Impact of the Introduction of the Social Long-Term Care Insurance in Germany on Financial Security Assessment in Case of Long-Term Care Need', *The Geneva Papers on Risk and Insurance – Issues and Practice*, 35 (4), pp. 626–643.

Zweifel, P. and Strüwe, W. (1998) 'Long-Term Care Insurance in a Two-Generation Model', *Journal of Risk and Insurance*, 65 (1), pp. 13–32.

13
Long-Term Care Financing in Central Eastern Europe

August Österle
Institute for Social Policy, Department of Socioeconomics, Vienna University of Economics and Business, Austria

1 Introduction

The Central Eastern European (CEE) region is no exception to the major challenges European countries are facing in the field of long-term care (LTC). Ageing societies and growing LTC needs, changes in the socio-economic context and their consequences for traditional modes of caregiving will further increase the pressure for ensuring sustainable funding for more comprehensive LTC systems. In the past two decades, LTC has become increasingly recognized as a social risk that will need substantial investment in publicly (co-)funded infrastructure and service provision. And many European countries have seen important reform steps in this respect. But tight budgets and forecasted large increases in public LTC expenditure have often limited the magnitude of reforms or have hindered the development and implementation of appropriate policies. CEE countries share the aforementioned challenges, but the *status quo* of the LTC systems is quite different in this region. Current levels of social protection beyond family or other informal networks and beyond social assistance are far less developed than in other parts of Europe.

This chapter explores CEE LTC systems with a particular focus on financing, analysing the *status quo* of funding regimes, on both the macro-level and on micro-level, and the trends and challenges arising in developing more comprehensive social protection schemes towards the risk of LTC. CEE countries that have joined the European Union (EU) in 2004 and in 2007 are at the centre of the analysis in this chapter. While the international comparative literature on LTC has been substantially growing in the past two decades, there is still very little coverage of CEE countries. The following section will start with an outline of the challenges LTC poses to societies in CEE. In addition, it provides a brief overview of how countries in this region are currently responding to these needs and of how people perceive LTC responsibilities.

After that, LTC financing will be studied from both a macro-level perspective (looking at the volume and the major sources of funding) and a micro-level perspective (analysing the ways in which funds are allocated in paying for services). An outlook and discussion of the perspectives for LTC funding in CEE will close the contribution.

2 LTC in Central Eastern Europe

LTC in CEE as compared with other European regions is faced with very similar trends in terms of ageing societies. At the same time, however, differences in the *status quo* and in the context create quite diverse challenges to the development of LTC systems and policies, not least for funding a growing future need for LTC. This section first introduces the broader demographic and socio-economic context for LTC in CEE. Then, it briefly depicts the *status quo* of LTC systems in this European region. Finally, the section studies the attitudes of CEE citizens towards public and private responsibilities in LTC, in particular perceptions and expectations with regard to funding LTC.

2.1 Demographic and socio-economic trends

Eastern Europe is no exception to a general European trend of ageing societies. According to Eurostat (2010) statistics, in the EU27, the proportion of those 80+ will increase from 4.66 per cent in 2010 to 6.93 per cent in 2030 and to 10.99 per cent in 2050, and the proportion of those 65+ from 17.38 per cent in 2010 to 28.81 per cent in 2050. In Eastern Europe, the current proportion of the older population is considerably lower, but will see even more significant increases in some of the countries as compared with Western European countries. The proportion of those 80+ will increase from between 2.73 per cent in Slovakia and 3.97 per cent in Estonia in 2010 to between 4.74 per cent in Slovakia and 6.68 per cent in Slovenia in 2030 and to between 9.04 per cent in Estonia and 11.96 per cent in Slovenia in 2050. The proportion of the population 65+ will exceed the European average in most CEE countries in 2050, ranging between 27.42 per cent in Estonia and 32.50 per cent in Slovenia in 2050 as compared with between 12.29 per cent in Slovakia and 17.47 per cent in Bulgaria in 2010 (Figure 13.1).

From a funding perspective, the old-age dependency ratio, those aged 65+ as a proportion of those 15–64 years of age, can give a preliminary indication of the economic pressures that ageing societies are facing. In the EU27 average, the old-age dependency ratio will change from 25.90 per cent in 2010 to 38.04 per cent in 2030 and to 50.42 per cent in 2050. The same trend is forecasted for CEE countries considered in this chapter. The old-age dependency ratio still is below the European average in 2010, but will be beyond the EU27 average in all these countries except for Estonia. The ratio will even increase to beyond 55 per cent in 2050 in Bulgaria (as compared with 25.29 per cent in 2010), in Poland (18.98 per cent in 2010), in

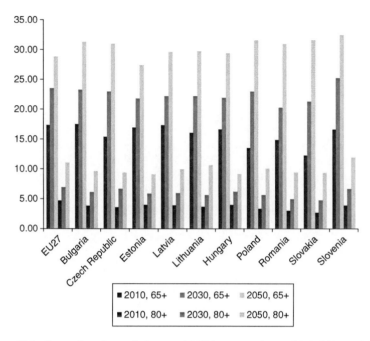

Figure 13.1 Share of total population aged 65/80 years and over, 2010, 2030 and 2050
Source: Eurostat (2008).

Slovakia (16.95 per cent in 2010) and in Slovenia (23.91 per cent in 2010) (Figure 13.2).

While ageing trends can give an initial indication of future LTC needs, changes in the prevalence of chronic illness and disability will have a major impact on the actual care needs. If, for example, healthy life expectancy increases faster than total life expectancy (a compression of morbidity), the length of periods of chronic ill-health and disabilities will decrease and will lead to a moderating effect on future LTC needs. According to European Commission (2009) forecasts, about 4.9 million older persons aged 65+ in the EU12, the countries joining the EU in 2004 and 2007, are dependent. For the period to 2060, in a pure demographic scenario, it is expected that their number will more than double (10.4 million in 2060, an increase of 114 per cent). Depending on the assumptions made – a compression of morbidity, an expansion of morbidity or a 'dynamic equilibrium' (an increase in light disabilities, but a reduction in severe morbidity) (Lafortune et al., 2007) – the increase in the number of people in need of care could be more moderate or even sharper. In the aforementioned projection, even when assuming constant disability (disability rates by age are assumed to shift in

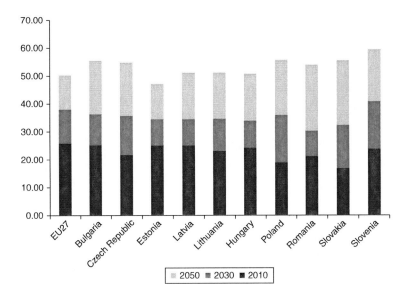

Figure 13.2   Old-age dependency ratio, 2010, 2030 and 2050
Source: Eurostat (2008).

line with life expectancy), the number of dependent older people in the EU12 will still increase by 95 per cent, with 9.5 million dependent older people in 2060 (European Commission, 2009).

As will be shown below, families are the main provider of LTC in CEE. But, similar to other European regions, family and other informal care resources are under increasing pressure (Mestheneos and Triantafillou, 2005; Lamura et al., 2008; Eurostat, 2010; Österle, 2011). The current context for informal long-term caregiving in CEE countries is characterized by employment rates for men and women in most countries below the EU27 average. At the same time, however, there also is a considerably lower proportion of part-time employment. Additionally, CEE countries display lower employment rates among older persons and a lower average exit age from the labour force. Current European economic policy orientation, as well as policies in single CEE countries, emphasize the need to increase employment participation and to delay retirement. This, however, will increase the pressure on traditional family-oriented care arrangements as many informal family carers are in their 50s and 60s. Further pressures arise from migration of younger generations within and beyond national borders. Taken together, these developments will change the arrangements families can make when care needs arise. And it might lead to changes in the perception of what is perceived as a family obligation (Österle et al., 2011).

2.2   LTC provision in CEE today

In a broader European perspective, LTC systems in CEE can be characterized by family-orientation, residualism, social assistance orientation and
comparatively low levels of service provision. The availability of services is
characterized by huge regional disparities and an almost complete lack of
services in many remote areas (Bettio and Plantenga, 2004; Chawla et al.,
2007; Pavolini and Ranci, 2008; Österle, 2010, 2011; World Bank, 2010).
In CEE, as in most other European regions except for the Nordic countries,
LTC does not have a long history as a separate field of social protection
(Österle and Rothgang, 2010). In fact, in most countries in this region it still
is not addressed as such. Existing social policy measures towards those with
chronic ill-health conditions or disabilities are found in different welfare
sectors – in the pension system, in disability policies, in the health care system or in social assistance schemes – in each of which eligibility criteria are
defined differently. As a consequence, access to social protection might differ
substantially for people with similar long-standing ill-health conditions.

Health care systems in CEE, from the early 1990s, have been transformed
from the previous Semashko model of the communist regimes towards social
insurance systems. The implementation of this policy development 'back
to Bismarck', however, shows considerable variation in the extent to which
it implements ideas of universal coverage and of liberal ideas of competition and market orientation (e.g., Marée and Groenewegen, 1997; Cerami,
2006; Nemec and Kolisnichenko, 2006; Kutzin et al., 2010). Health sector
provisions for LTC are found in both the inpatient sector (in specific institutions and in units in general hospitals) and the outpatient sector. Inpatient
health sector provisions, apart from acute care which is also a major source of
professional care for people in need of LTC, has come under increasing pressure for cost-containment considerations in the health sector. With these
considerations, the social care sector is seen as the appropriate context for
providing LTC, but the respective infrastructure in this sector is far from
adequately developed.

LTC in the social sector has been largely based on social assistance principles in CEE. Similar to the historical situation in many other European
countries and despite the differences in the predominant regimes until the
end of the 1980s, residential care has been – and often still is – the major public response towards the need for care if individuals and families are unable
to take care of a relative. The need for community care orientation has been
identified more prominently from the 1990s, and only in the past decade
have more systematic measures been taken to develop community care services. But, to date, service levels in the community care sector remained
very limited. In general, respective services are more developed in urban
areas, while many remote areas are highly deprived of provision. As a consequence, in many areas, home nursing provided by the health sector is the
only home care service available to people in need of LTC staying in their

private environment. These services, however, are strictly limited in terms of both medically defined eligibility and benefit periods.

With regard to the organizational structure, the communist legacy of State-run provisions still largely characterizes residential and community care provision in this region. The major institutional change from the early 1990s was decentralization. Earlier State responsibility was shifted towards regional and local authorities. A lack of experience in social care development and a lack of funding that would have supported decentralized responsibilities, however, have for years limited the modernization and extension of infrastructure and delayed the emergence of a broader welfare mix. In some countries, non-profit organizations became active in social care from the early 1990s, in particular church-related organizations, often reintroducing earlier activities as service providers. But public positions towards private providers entering social care provision have often been contradictory. On the one hand, despite a strong rhetoric of pluralization, many countries in the 1990s and into the most recent decade have discriminated against private providers in reimbursement principles. On the other hand, there are specific measures supporting non-profit initiatives. Countries like Hungary, Slovakia or Romania have, for example, a system where tax-payers can dedicate a small proportion of the personal tax payment to a non-profit organization, including organizations active in social care (e.g., Jenei and Kuti, 2009).

Apart from publicly (co-)funded service provision, CEE countries also have a history of care-related cash benefits. These benefits, mostly understood as an income supplement rather than cash for care, are paid either to the person in need of care or to the person providing care on an informal basis (Österle, 2011). Even if these allowances are mostly means-tested, they constitute a major financial resource for poor families and households. In the recent past, measures have been taken to develop such programmes beyond traditional income-supplement or income-replacement models. Examples include earlier means-tested benefits that have been transferred into more universal benefits for people with disabilities in Romania (Popescu, 2011), or the care allowance system introduced in the Czech Republic from 2007 (Barvikova, 2011).

In the past few years, there is a growing awareness of LTC as a social risk, driven by growing pressures arising from the aforementioned demographic and socio-economic trends, but also driven by processes of policy-learning in the EU, in particular in the context of the Open Method of Coordination. In many countries, proposals to establish novel and more comprehensive LTC systems have been put forward and have partly drawn on experiences in other European countries (Theobald and Kern, 2009). While CEE countries have seen major reforms affecting LTC, a paradigmatic change of the LTC system moving from social assistance orientation towards more universal benefits is the exception. Such a paradigmatic change has taken place in the

Czech Republic (Barvikova, 2010). With the 2007 reform, a tax-funded universal care allowance is paid to those in need of care at four different levels. Recipients are free in their decision on how to use the benefit, but funding of formal services is directly linked to that benefit. For different service categories, the State defines maximum rates for public contributions. Additional public subsidies can be provided to registered social service providers according to social service development plans through regional budgets. Subsidies are determined by the number and the amount of care allowances paid in the respective region and according to the number of registered social service providers and the capacities of residential facilities. In addition, financial support is given for nationwide activities, for development programmes or for training activities. Additionally, new regulations are being developed for accreditation of service providers. While implementation is still faced with difficulties, in the future this should also facilitate the entrance of private providers into the service market.

2.3   Attitudes towards LTC funding

According to a 2002 Eurobarometer survey, in most European countries a large proportion of the population (48.7 per cent) has a strong preference for a public responsibility in paying for taking care of older parents (Alber and Köhler, 2004). In Estonia, Latvia and Slovakia the respective proportion is even higher than the EU25 average (Table 13.1). A preference for family responsibility ('children should mainly pay for taking care of elderly parents') is supported by 18.0 per cent according to the EU25 average. In CEE countries, support for this answer ranges between 10.5 per cent in Slovakia and 45.6 per cent in Romania. All European countries where the relative majority sees children as responsible for paying for care of older parents are in CEE, namely, Bulgaria (33.8 per cent), Austria (44.0 per cent) and Romania (45.6 per cent).

Asking about expectations rather than preferences shows quite a distinct picture. In a 2007 Eurobarometer survey, respondents were asked 'If you were to need regular help and LTC that would require payment, who do you think will finance this?' According to the EU27 average, about half of the respondents expect that they would have to pay, while about one-third expect that public authorities or social security will pay (Table 13.2). While the option that the individual would have to pay is above the EU25 average in most CEE countries, the proportion of those expecting the State or social security to pay is below the European average. On the other hand, the expectation that a partner/spouse or another family member will provide the necessary care is significantly above the EU25 average, except for partner/spouse care in the Baltic States. These results can be seen as a reflection of predominant perceptions towards family care and the current level of public support for LTC, but might also be influenced by ongoing public debates in the period when the survey was conducted.

Table 13.1 Care financing preferences (%)

	State or public authority	Elderly themselves	Their children	All parties equally
EU25	48.7	14.5	18.0	17.0
Bulgaria	33.6	8.5	33.8	24.1
Czech Republic	34.4	8.9	18.1	38.0
Estonia	52.9	4.0	20.9	21.0
Hungary	29.8	4.6	29.6	34.8
Latvia	57.5	7.3	17.6	16.5
Lithuania	42.6	14.8	22.5	19.6
Poland	41.2	19.8	17.2	21.5
Romania	22.5	7.1	45.6	24.3
Slovakia	58.1	8.9	10.5	21.3
Slovenia	42.7	17.7	20.7	18.8

Note: 'Irrespective of your answer, who do you think should mainly pay for taking care of elderly parents? – The elderly parents themselves, their children, or the State or other public authorities (e.g. local government, Social Security, etc).'
Source: Alber and Köhler (2004).

Taking existing research on family values and attitudes together (e.g., Alber and Köhler, 2004; European Commission, 2007; Anderson et al., 2009), CEE countries are characterized by comparatively strong family orientation. And, given the limited availability of formal services and the income situation of the population, families and other informal networks are mostly left without any alternative but to provide the greater share of care work on an informal basis. In light of the aforementioned changes, however, there will be substantial pressure on developing more comprehensive LTC systems, ensuring availability and accessibility of basic care packages across countries, which will require substantial investment and increased public LTC expenditure. In the following section, how CEE countries address these challenges in their current and potential future funding regimes will be analysed.

3 Paying for LTC

This section will look at current funding regimes in CEE, the major sources of LTC funding, the ways in which public money is allocated in the LTC field and how public and private financial contributions come together in paying for services. Studying the structure of LTC funding on the macro-level has to consider the major potential sources of funding and, within the public sector, a potential division between different sectors (in particular, health and social care) and different federal levels. Models of financing care include unpaid private provision of care, private savings, private voluntary insurance, private insurance with public sector support or mandatory private insurance, tax-based funding and social insurance funding. (For a discussion

Table 13.2 Paying for LTC (expectations)

	Self	Partner/ spouse	Family: children, parents	Other relatives/ friends	Private insurance	Public authorities/ social security	Other	Don't know
EU25	48	19	18	2	15	32	2	7
Bulgaria	27	25	51	2	1	9	5	11
Czech Republic	65	22	22	1	18	32	3	4
Estonia	53	17	31	4	10	63	1	4
Hungary	51	24	31	1	6	15	4	5
Latvia	37	13	33	7	11	33	5	5
Lithuania	52	18	29	3	11	20	3	6
Poland	35	22	24	1	7	27	3	11
Romania	49	35	42	8	6	2	0	12
Slovakia	59	34	34	3	19	23	1	2
Slovenia	72	29	30	2	14	17	1	4

Note: 'If you were to need regular help and LTC that would require payment, who do you think will finance this? (multiple answers possible).' Other: You will not need any care that you have to pay for; Nobody; Other.
Source: European Commission (2007).

the options see Wittenberg et al., 2002.) On the micro-level, when paying for LTC, alternative payment models range between full public and full
private coverage, and – in between these alternatives – different modes of
defining public and private contributions.

In a very general depiction, CEE countries as compared with other
European countries are characterized by relatively low levels of public
expenditure and high levels of family or other informal care provision.
Public provision is divided between health sectors (funded by social health
insurance) and social assistance-oriented social care schemes. Additional programmes vary across the region, but might include specific provisions for
disabled people or care-related income supplements. While central regulation and central funding dominate the health sector, public funding in
the social sector is mainly a local and regional responsibility. Social sector
funding responsibilities at the State level are for cash-for-care schemes, for
infrastructure investment and for subsidizing pilot programmes. Very distinct principles also apply on the micro-level. Health sector provisions follow
the social insurance principle, with user contributions limited to – compared
with the social sector – small co-payments. In the social sector, instead, when
paying in residential care or when using community care, users are paying
a substantial share of total costs. Means-testing implies, for example, that
users of residential care have to spend most of their income (pension) on
residential care costs (or, at least, on the accommodation element of these
costs).

.1   LTC expenditure in CEE

Despite considerable limitations in the quality and the comparability of
LTC data (Huber et al., 2009), existing information on public LTC expenditure shows that CEE countries spend significantly less on LTC than most
other European countries (Table 13.3). According to Eurostat (2010) statistics, older-care expenditure ranges between 2.4 per cent of GDP in Sweden
and less than 0.1 per cent of GDP in Estonia, Bulgaria or Romania. In CEE,
the largest proportions are registered for Slovakia and the Czech Republic
(0.4 per cent and 0.3 per cent, respectively), while the European average is
0.48 per cent. Health care expenditure on LTC (services of long-term nursing
care) is between about 2 per cent of GDP in Denmark and Switzerland and
less than 0.1 per cent in Bulgaria (Eurostat, 2010).

According to Organization for Economic Cooperation and Development
(OECD) statistics, variations in public LTC expenditure are even more pronounced (OECD, 2010). Here, public expenditure on LTC as a percentage of
GDP ranges between more than 3 per cent in Sweden and the Netherlands
and less than 0.6 per cent in CEE countries. Only Slovenia, according to
this source, is on substantially higher levels than the other EU12 countries,
spending 1.1 per cent of GDP on LTC. Finally, according to the European
Commission (2009) projections on the budgetary implications of ageing

Table 13.3   Public LTC expenditure and expenditure projections (%)

Country	Elderly care expenditure (2006)[a]	Health care expenditure on LTC (2006/7)[b]	Public LTC expenditure projection[c]		
			2007	Pure demographic scenario 2060	AWG reference scenario 2060
EU27	0.48		1.2	2.5	2.4
EU15			1.3	2.6	2.5
EU12			0.3	0.8	0.8
Bulgaria	0.034	0.02	0.2	0.4	0.4
Czech Republic	0.326	0.26	0.2	0.7	0.7
Estonia	0.076	0.20	0.1	0.1	0.1
Hungary	0.292	0.22	0.3	0.6	0.6
Latvia	0.141	0.22	0.4	0.9	0.9
Lithuania	0.194	0.34	0.5	1.1	1.1
Poland	0.235	0.38	0.4	1.1	1.1
Romania	0.023	0.54	0.0	0.1	0.0
Slovakia	0.405	0.90	0.2	0.6	0.6
Slovenia	0.160	0.63	1.1	2.9	2.9

a. The percentage share of social protection expenditure devoted to old-age care in GDP. These expenditures cover care allowance, accommodation and assistance in carrying out daily tasks (Eurostat, 2010).
b. Health care expenditure on LTC: services of long-term nursing care (Eurostat, 2010).
c. Public expenditure on LTC as a percentage of GDP; pure demographic scenario: disability rates per age group are constant, no policy change; Ageing Working Group (AWG) reference scenario: combines a set of prudent assumptions including the assumption that half of the longevity gains to 2060 are spent in good health (European Commission, 2009).
Source: Eurostat (2010) and European Commission (2009).

societies, LTC spending according to the EU27 average was 1.2 per cent of GDP in 2006, ranging between 3.5 per cent in Sweden and less than 0.1 per cent in Romania. The EU12 average was 0.3 per cent, again with Slovenia as a major exception (1.1 per cent). Given the 2007 reform in the Czech Republic, one can assume that LTC spending in that country has also risen significantly in the past few years.

3.2   Paying for LTC in the health sector

In the health sector, in the 1990s, across the CEE region, countries established social health insurance systems (e.g., Marée and Groenewegen, 1997; Kutzin et al., 2010). To date, these systems also play an important role in the provision and funding of LTC, not least because of a lack of adequate provision in the social sector. The inpatient sector – intentionally or unintentionally – acts as a provider of LTC (including accommodation and treatment) in specific geriatric care units, in rehabilitation centres or in short-term intermediary units before transferring a patient back home or into a nursing home, but also in general units not specifically addressing the needs of chronically ill patients. A lack of service provision in nursing homes or in the community care sector often makes prolonged hospital stays or hospitalization of older people in need of LTC necessary, even though there is no acute health care need that would require a hospital stay. In addition to inpatient sector provisions, health care systems also finance nursing care in the outpatient sector. These services are strictly limited to medically defined nursing care, and limited both in the numbers of service units provided and in the length of the period of provision. Despite these limitations, nursing care provided by the health sector is often the only community care provision that is available across countries.

Health sector provisions have often been the only option to receive professional care when in need of LTC. Additionally, from a user perspective, health sector provisions usually are a much cheaper option than LTC provisions in the social sector. Compared with means-tested co-payments in the social sector, co-payments in the health sector are relatively moderate. Cost-containment concerns and stricter budget control in health care systems, however, have constantly increased economic pressure on the health care system in general, and on the hospital sector in particular. A reduction in hospital beds or a transformation of beds or entire units from health sector beds to social sector beds has been a prominent answer to these concerns, as, for example, in Hungary (Ersek et al., 2011). However, respective measures have rarely been accompanied by measures to develop an adequate infrastructure in the social sector.

3.3 Paying for LTC in the social sector

The second major branch of public LTC funding is the social sector. As outlined above, social service infrastructure in CEE – in a European comparative perspective – is at relatively low levels both in the residential care sector and in the community care sector (Huber et al., 2009; Österle, 2011). In general, urban centres provide a wider range of community care services, while these services remain limited or completely unavailable in many remote areas. With the decentralization of social assistance, regional and local authorities became the main players in the organization and funding of LTC services. Developments on these levels, however, have often been hindered by a lack of experience in the field of LTC and by budgetary constraints, leaving little room to move beyond already existing funding obligations (as for already existing residential care settings).

While many Western European countries in the past two decades have introduced more comprehensive LTC schemes, social assistance orientation remains the dominant principle in CEE countries. Access to services is, first of all, often limited by the simple lack of such services. This is still true in many rural areas in the region. Secondly, needs-testing and means-testing limit access to services. In the case of residential care, users' income or pension has to be used up to pay for a place in the respective institution (whereby there often is a differentiation between the costs of care and the costs of accommodation). Additionally, family members can be required to contribute to the respective costs. For community care services, co-payment regulations apply. These are income- and service-related contributions to be paid per service unit and not – as in the health sector – flat rate contributions. In addition, and again different from the health sector, there is in general no individual legal right to receive these services even if some countries have guidelines for the density of specific services. Many policy documents on the development of social sector provisions therefore explicitly refer to the requirement that – given limited budgets – services should be focused on the most needy population. Privately funded care services, for large parts of the population, are not an alternative given the low average or minimum pensions in the region.

Apart from funding services, cash for care is an important approach in CEE LTC systems, providing cash either to the person in need of care or to informal carers. Different from services, cash benefits are funded at the State level. The benefits are usually designed or understood as either an income supplement or an income replacement and are mostly means-tested. Individuals or families are financially supported when in need of care or when providing care. While these payments can become an important element of the disposable income in poor households characterized by unemployment or very low pensions, they are far from covering the huge amount of informal care provided by families in CEE. In the past few years, however, there has been a trend to abolish means-testing for some benefits. Most prominently, the Czech Republic has introduced a tax-funded cash-for-care system, where benefits are paid to those in need of care on four different levels (Barvikova, 2011).

3.4 Trends in LTC financing

Debates on the future of LTC, not least on its future funding, have intensified in the past two decades across Europe. In most CEE countries, these debates are in the earlier stages. Policy proposals have been developed by expert groups or have been put forward in strategy papers. Even if most proposals have often not been developed in detail, many related documents address social insurance as an option for establishing more comprehensive LTC systems. In Slovenia, a LTC insurance system has been specified in some detail and its implementation has repeatedly been announced. According to the draft, a person in need of care who meets the eligibility criteria could choose between a personal budget, the provision of services or a mix of cash and services (Flaker et al., 2011). Proposals for introducing LTC insurance have, for example, also been put forward in Slovakia, Hungary, Poland and

Romania. In the Hungarian case, there was a proposal to organizationally integrate LTC insurance into the existing social health insurance system.

Private insurance plays only a minor role in LTC funding in most European countries. Exceptions are Germany, where parts of the population (following the division in the health system) are covered via the private insurance system, or in France, which has recently seen a substantial growth in private LTC insurance (Le Bihan and Martin, 2010; Rothgang, 2010). Across the CEE region, the role of private LTC insurance is almost negligible. While the individual demand for private LTC insurance (as compared with, e.g., health insurance) is relatively low across Europe, the individual income situation in CEE countries additionally hinders the development of such a market. Private LTC also did not play any prominent role in proposals for LTC reform in this region. There have only been a few references to private LTC insurance as a potential source for LTC funding as, for example, in Poland (Kozierkievicz and Szczerbińska, 2007).

3.5 Future LTC expenditure

Future public funding requirements for LTC are influenced by a number of factors, including ageing and the development of morbidity and chronic illness, the role of families and other informal networks in LTC provision, changing divisions between private and public responsibilities and between informal and formal care provision, but also on account of the overall economic situation. According to European Commission (2009) projections, different assumptions on the aforementioned variables can have substantial budgetary implications for LTC expenditure, without changing the general picture of a significant increase in LTC expenditure in the coming decades. In a pure demographic scenario, with disability rates held constant by age group and with no policy change, LTC expenditure as a percentage of GDP will grow from 1.2 in the EU27 average to 2.4 in 2060. In the EU12 group, expenditure will grow from 0.3 per cent of GDP to 0.8 per cent in 2060. According to the 'Ageing Working Group' scenario, LTC expenditure as a percentage of GDP will at least double until 2060. In some of the CEE countries, in particular the Czech Republic and Slovakia, the proportion could even triple (Table 13.3).

Assuming some convergence across Europe in what materializes as public responsibility in LTC, the aforementioned increases could even be moderate projections. Convergence of CEE LTC systems towards standards in Western European countries (or even more so towards the standards in the Nordic countries) would imply a huge expansion in LTC infrastructure in CEE and, consequently, an even sharper increase in expenditure levels. According to OECD projection scenarios, public LTC expenditure was between 0.3 per cent and 0.4 per cent in Hungary, Slovakia and the Czech Republic in 2005. This could increase to beyond 2 per cent in 2050. Considering the demographic effect, LTC expenditure would account for 2 per cent of GDP in the Czech Republic, 1.5 per cent in Hungary and 2.6 per cent in Slovakia. An increase in dependency and, in particular, a more significant shift from informal care to formal care would even further increase LTC expenditure levels (Oliveira Martins and de la Maisonneuve, 2006).

4   Conclusion

With a macro-level perspective, residualism and social assistance orientation still is the dominant approach in most CEE LTC systems. Major macro-level changes have not specifically focused on LTC, but have been linked to the implementation of decentralization and pluralization principles. Other major reforms have taken place in the field of social assistance. These reforms have led to important changes on the meso- and micro-level of providing and funding LTC. But, in many of the CEE countries it is only very recently that LTC has been explicitly addressed as a separate particular field of social welfare.

In a number of recent policy documents, including national strategy reports in the context of the European Open Method of Coordination, there is a growing recognition for the need to transform a currently fragmented and residual LTC system into a more comprehensive social protection system, ensuring availability and quality of a predefined LTC services package for all citizens in need across the respective country. In the Czech Republic, following these objectives, the 2007 reform combines a tax-funded universal cash-for-care scheme with major changes in social service regulations. In other countries, social insurance has been proposed as the way forward. None of the countries so far has implemented a LTC insurance scheme, but a respective approach has been developed in detail in Slovenia. For Barr (2010, p. 371), there is a strong case for relying on public finance and for 'extending social insurance to provide mandatory cover for LTC'. Tax funding as a second public option is seen as more problematic, not least because of current and future competing fiscal demands. Others, emphasizing revenue collection, coverage rates and the labour market distortions that social insurance could create, have a more critical perspective on the revival of social insurance in many developing and transformation countries (e.g., Wagstaff, 2010).

Apart from the general design of a public LTC system between a safety net model and a universal model and the decision on tax funding or social insurance funding (Wittenberg et al., 2002), the mix between cash and in-kind orientation and the division of responsibilities between health and social sectors are major policy reform issues. In developing more comprehensive coverage for LTC, cash orientation has become an increasingly important approach in a number of European countries in the past two decades (e.g., Glendinning and Kemp, 2006; Ungerson and Yeandle, 2007). Cash orientation emphasizes objectives of choice and empowerment, but also employment and social service development, in particular where the use of care allowances or care budgets is linked to the consumption of formal services or to formal employment for carers. Even if not always explicitly mentioned, and especially where the use of the benefit is not strictly regulated, cash orientation also is favoured for cost-containment considerations. Similar paths have been taken in CEE countries and a number of reforms have recently intensified the role of cash for care. Investing in cash for care rather than services could, however, hinder the development of an adequate service infrastructure, in particular when cash payments are seen as an income supplement without contributing to a user-driven development of services. Another major issue for the future design of funding regimes is the division of responsibilities between health and social care sectors. To date, many changes in health care systems that had implications for those in need of LTC have not been driven by a broader LTC policy strategy, but mostly by cost-containment concerns. Hence, the financial pressure was shifted from the health sector to the social sector or – often in fact – to those in need of care.

Countries in CEE are faced with manifold developments challenging current ways in which LTC is organized, provided and funded. Given a forecasted growth in care needs, enormous financial burdens for those in need of care and enormous burdens for informal caregivers, the need for developing and adequate LTC infrastructure is pressing. Community care orientation, availability, affordability and quality of services are major objectives referred to in numerous policy documents. Achieving these objectives requires substantial investment in LTC infrastructure and new responses to ensure sustainable funding of the respective services.

Acknowledgements

This chapter is based on an international project on LTC in Central and South Eastern Europe. The project was funded by the ERSTE Foundation, whose support is gratefully acknowledged. A first version of the chapter was written while a Research Fellow at the HWK Institute for Advanced Studies in 2009/2010.

References

Alber, J. and Köhler, U. (2004) *Health and Care in an Enlarged Europe* (Luxembourg: European Foundation for the Improvement of Living and Working Conditions).

Anderson, R., Mikulič, B., Vermeylen, G., Lyly-Yrjanainen, M. and Zigante, V. (2009) *Second European Quality of Life Survey – Overview* (Luxembourg: Office for Official Publications of the European Communities).

Barr, N. (2010) 'Long-term care: a suitable case of social insurance', *Social Policy and Administration*, 44 (4), pp. 359–374.

Barvikova, J. (2011) 'Long-term care in the Czech Republic: on the threshold of reform', in A. Österle (ed.) *Long-Term Care in Central and South Eastern Europe* (Frankfurt: Peter Lang).

Bettio, F. and Plantenga, J. (2004) 'Comparing welfare regimes', *Feminist Economics*, 10 (1), pp. 85–113.

Cerami, A. (2006) *Social Policy in Central and Eastern Europe. The Emergence of a New European Welfare Regime* (Berlin: LIT Verlag).

Ersek, K., Meszaros, K. and Gulacsi, L. (2011) 'Long-term care in Hungary: between health and social care', in A. Österle (ed.) *Long-Term Care in Central and South Eastern Europe* (Frankfurt: Peter Lang).

Chawla, M., Betcherman, G., Banerji, A. et al. (2007) *From Red to Gray. The 'Third Transition' of Ageing Populations in Eastern Europe and the Former Soviet Union* (Washington, DC: The World Bank).

European Commission (2007) *Health and Long-term Care in the European Union*, Special Eurobarometer 283/Wave 67.3 (Brussels: European Commission).

European Commission (2009) *The 2009 Ageing Report: Economic and Budgetary Projections for the EU-27 Member States (2008–2060)*, Joint report prepared by European Commission (DG ECFIN) and the Economic Policy Committee (AWG). European Economy 2/2009, http://ec.europa.eu/economy_finance/thematic_articles/article14761_en.htm (accessed 12 July 2010).

Eurostat (2008) 'Ageing characterises the demographic perspectives of the European societies', *Statistics in Focus* 72/2008 (Brussels: European Commission).

Eurostat (2010) Eurostat database.

Flaker, V., Kresal, B. and Nagode, M. (2011) 'Needs and beads. The emerging long-term care system of Slovenia', in A. Österle (ed.) *Long-Term Care in Central and South Eastern Europe* (Frankfurt: Peter Lang).

Glendinning, C. and Kemp, P. (2006) *Cash and Care: Policy Challenges in the Welfare State* (Bristol: Policy Press).

Huber, M., Rodrigues, R., Hoffmann, F., Gasior, K. and Marin, B. (2009) *Facts and Figures on Long-term Care: Europe and North America* (Vienna: European Centre).

Jenei, G. and Kuti, É. (2009) 'The third sector and civil society', in S. Osborne (ed.) *The Third Sector in Europe: Prospects and Challenges* (London: Routledge).

Kozierkiewicz, A. and Szczerbińska, K. (2007) *Long-term Care in Poland: Assessment of Current Status and Future Solutions* (Poznań: termedia).

Kutzin, J., Cashin, C. and Jakab, M. (eds) (2010) *Implementing Health Financing Reform. Lessons from Countries in Transition* (Copenhagen: World Health Organization on behalf of the European Observatory on Health Systems and Policies).

Lafortune, G., Balestat, G. and the Disability Study Expert Group Members (2007) *Trends in Severe Disability Among Elderly People. Assessing the Evidence in 12 OECD Countries and the Future Implications*, OECD Health Working Papers No. 26 (Paris: OECD).

Lamura, G., Döhner, H. and Kofahl, C. on behalf of the EUROFAMCARE Consortium (eds) (2008) *Family Carers of Older People in Europe: A Six-Country Comparative Study* (Hamburg: LIT Verlag).

Le Bihan, B. and Martin, C. (2010) 'Reforming long-term care policy in France: private-public complementarities', *Social Policy and Administration*, 44 (4), pp. 392–410.

Marée, J. and Groenewegen, P.P. (1997) *Back to Bismarck: Eastern European Health Care Systems in Transition* (Aldershot: Avebury).

Mestheneos, E. and Triantafillou, J. (2005) *Supporting Family Carers of Older People in Europe: The Pan-European Background Report* (Münster: LIT Verlag).

Nemec, J. and Kolisnichenko, N. (2006) 'Market-based health care reforms in Central and Eastern Europe: lessons after ten years of change', *International Review of Administrative Sciences*, 72, pp. 11–26.

OECD (2010) *OECD Health Data 2010* (Paris: OECD).

Oliveira Martins, J. and de la Maisonneuve, C. (2006) *The Drivers of Public Expenditure on Health and Long-term Care: An Integrated Approach*, OECD Economic Studies No. 43, 2006/2 (Paris: OECD).

Österle, A. (2010) 'Long-term care in Central and South Eastern Europe: challenges and perspectives in addressing a "new" social risk', *Social Policy and Administration*, 44 (4), pp. 461–480.

Österle, A. (ed.) (2011) *Long-Term Care in Central and South Eastern Europe* (Frankfurt: Peter Lang).

Österle, A. and Rothgang, H. (2010) 'Long-term care', in F.G. Castles, S. Leibfried, J. Lewis, H. Obinger and Pierson, C. (eds) *The Oxford Handbook of the Welfare State* (Oxford: Oxford University Press), pp. 405–417.

Österle, A., Mittendrein, L. and Meichenitsch, K. (2011) 'The demographic and socio-economic context for long-term care in Central and South Eastern Europe', in A. Österle (ed.) *Long-Term Care in Central and South Eastern Europe* (Frankfurt: Peter Lang).

Pavolini, E. and Ranci, C. (2008) 'Restructuring the welfare state: reforms in long-term care in Western European countries', *Journal of European Social Policy*, 18 (3), pp. 246–259.

Popescu, L. (2011) 'Long-term care policy in Romania: a hesitant response to a pressing need', in A. Österle (ed.) *Long-Term Care in Central and South Eastern Europe* (Frankfurt: Peter Lang), pp. 189–205.

Rothgang, H. (2010) 'Social insurance for long-term care: an evaluation of the German model', *Social Policy and Administration*, 44 (4), pp. 436–460.

Theobald, H. and Kern, K. (2009) 'Elder care systems: policy transfer and Europeanization', in A. Cerami and P. Vanhuysse (eds) *Post-communist Welfare Pathways: Theorizing Social Policy Transformations in Central and Eastern Europe* (Basingstoke: Palgrave Macmillan), pp. 148–163.

Ungerson, C. and Yeandle, S. (eds) (2007) *Cash for Care in Developed Welfare States* (Basingstoke: Palgrave Macmillan).

Wagstaff, A. (2010) 'Social health insurance re-examined', *Health Economics*, 19, pp. 503–517.

Wittenberg, R., Sandhu, B. and Knapp, M. (2002) 'Funding long-term care: the public and private options', in E. Mossialos, A. Dixon, J. Figueras and J. Kutzin (eds) *Funding Health Care: Options for Europe* (Buckingham: Open University Press), pp. 226–249.

World Bank (2010) *World Bank Report. Long-term Care and Ageing. Case Studies – Bulgaria, Croatia, Latvia and Poland* (Washington, DC: World Bank).

14
Scandinavian Long-Term Care Financing

Martin Karlsson
Technische Universität Darmstadt, Germany

Tor Iversen
Department of Health Management and Health Economics, University of Oslo, Norway

and

Henning Øien
Department of Health Management and Health Economics, University of Oslo, Norway

1 Introduction

The Scandinavian countries – Denmark, Norway and Sweden – share a common history and common political traditions, which has led to very similar systems for social care being introduced in the three countries. This applies to the division of roles and responsibilities between different public bodies, as well as for the national policy objectives that have been laid down in various pieces of legislation. Thus, all three countries pursue the general goal of providing local care services free of charge to everyone in need, independently of their financial circumstances.

In this chapter, we describe the financing, governance and provision of long-term care (LTC) services in Scandinavia. The Scandinavian LTC systems have a common foundation in three important regards:

1. The system guarantees by law that every citizen in need, independent of socio-economic status and geographical status, is entitled to the necessary LTC services.
2. The LTC sector is predominantly funded by general taxes.
3. The responsibility of providing and financing the services is decentralized to local governments.

In order to provide the reader with a background of the universal, tax-financed and decentralized Scandinavian system, we open this chapter with a general overview of LTC systems in Scandinavia, starting with the history of the Scandinavian model of social care. This is followed by a discussion on whether these LTC systems could be classified as belonging to a distinct 'Scandinavian model'.

The Scandinavian countries have a long tradition of decentralizing the provision and financing of social services to the municipalities – the lowest government level. The strong local autonomy and the central position of local governments in the Scandinavian welfare States are illustrated in Figure 14.1. Even before the emergence of the welfare State, local government expenditure was above 40 per cent of total government expenditure, which is very high by international standards (Sellers and Lidström, 2007). Figure 14.1 shows that the relative importance of the municipal sector increased even further with the emergence of the welfare State. Beside LTC

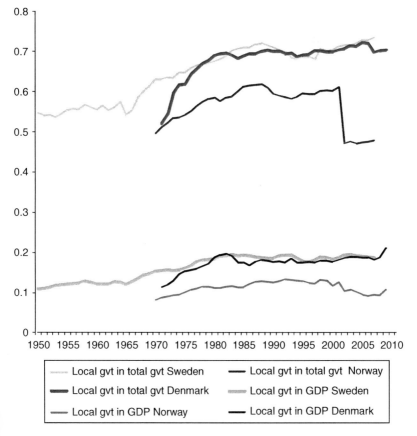

Figure 14.1 Proportion of local government consumption expenditure in total government consumption and GDP

Source: Authors' own calculations from national accounts.

services, health-care and child-care services contributed also to this general trend. In Section 2.3, we outline the governance structure of the LTC sector in Scandinavia, and point to differences in the degree of decentralization between the countries. In the remainder of Section 2, we discuss the overall size, services provided, volumes and trends and the element of private providers in the LTC sector.

The LTC sector is predominantly financed from general local taxes. The decentralized governance structure leads to local differences in LTC services offered (see Section 2.6), which violate the notion that service provision should be independent of geographical location. To smooth out local differences there is an income adjustment system which equalizes the tax bases of the municipalities. In Section 3 we discuss this system, local income taxes and other public sources of funding in the LTC sector. In addition to taxes, private co-payments finance a minor part of the LTC costs in Norway and Sweden. In Denmark, LTC services are provided on either a temporary or a permanent basis. Temporary services, which are only to be provided to the elderly who have a prospect of recovery, and are subject to income-dependent user charges. Permanent LTC services are provided free of charge, while users of both types of LTC must pay the full cost of housing and private services that are not regarded as LTC services. This is further discussed in Section 4. It should be noted that there are no private insurance policies for LTC costs available on the market in any of the countries, and hence taxes and out-of-pocket payments are exhaustive as sources of funding. In Section 5 we discuss the possible emergence of a private market of LTC insurance.

The final section concludes and provides a general discussion of the main features of the Scandinavian systems from an economic point of view, with particular emphasis on their efficiency and equity. Although the Scandinavian LTC sectors exhibit striking similarities, we will throughout this chapter discuss important differences, using Sweden as a base case and contrasting and comparing it with Norway and Denmark.

2 Overview of Scandinavian LTC systems

Up to the first half of the last century, LTC in all Scandinavian countries was provided almost exclusively by families. Only for those lacking family members and financial means, municipalities offered care in public poorhouses. Starting in the late 1940s, the public involvement in LTC evolved from being aimed at poor elderly to a more general approach. The pioneers were Sweden and Denmark, whereas Norway, which at that time was the poorest of the three countries, enacted reforms some years later (Daatland and Sundström, 1997).

In Denmark, nursing homes that were distinct from the traditional poorhouses started to appear in the 1920s, but the first piece of legislation that introduced universal principles for elderly care was passed in 1949. The main goal of the 1949 Act was to provide temporary home care for infirm house-wives; however, the scheme was extended to cover temporary needs of frail older people as well. In Sweden, municipalities were obliged to offer care in nursing homes starting in the late 1940s. This increased reliance on the public sector was confirmed by a revision of the law in 1956, after which adult children had no formal responsibilities for their parents. In Norway, a similar law was enacted in 1964 (St.meld. nr.25, 2005–2006).

Around 1950 the Swedish economy became overheated, and social reforms were brought to a standstill. Consequently, no further public nursing homes were built. To compensate for this, volunteer organizations started offering domiciliary care. This care was not means-tested, but offered to all elderly in regions where these organizations were operating. It soon turned out, though, that the volunteer organizations would not be able to carry out the expansion needed in domiciliary care. Thus, over the next decade, municipalities took on ever more responsibility – from volunteer organizations as well as from family members. After government grants for domiciliary care had been introduced in 1964, a rapid expansion of these services took place (Söderström et al., 2001). Also in Denmark and Norway, the 1960s and 1970s were characterized by a rapid expansion of formal LTC services (Daatland and Sundström, 1997).

During the first post-war decades, LTC services went through a gradual metamorphosis in all three countries. The traditional 'old age homes' became increasingly controversial, and ever more emphasis was put on dignity of the users and on the quality of care. Reformed care homes with a stronger focus on medical care were introduced. Also, there was a clear trend towards higher staff/user ratios, and the proportion of users with single rooms increased continuously from the 1960s to the 1980s in all three countries (Daatland, Platz and Sundström, 1997).

The public provision of domiciliary care in Sweden peaked in 1978, with 352,000 clients. The number of places in public nursing homes reached its peak at about the same time. In Denmark, the peak was also reached at around the same time, whereas in Norway, the number of beds in nursing homes continued to increase until the late 1980s (Daatland et al., 1997). Since then, the expansion of earlier decades has been reversed. In the 1980s, a retraction of public involvement in LTC was driven by a marked improvement in the health status of the elderly, improved living conditions as well as the awareness that there had been some oversupply in the 1970s.

In the 1990s, Sweden went through its deepest recession since the 1930s. The economic crisis caused severe financial problems in the public sector. As a consequence, the reductions in public provision of LTC continued, and care was concentrated on the neediest. At the same time, the Swedish model with public monopolies was challenged, and some municipalities introduced purchaser/provider organizations as well as voucher systems for domiciliary care. During the 1990s, the share of private caregivers doubled.

In Denmark, the long-term trend towards de-institutionalization has been almost as strong as in Sweden (Hansen, 2000), whereas in Norway only a small reduction in the number of nursing home beds has been observed (St.meld. nr.25, 2005–2006).

Since the late 1990s, the financial situation of local authorities in Sweden has been improving almost continuously, which has enabled them to halt some of the downward trends in the provision of LTC services. Some other trends from the 1990s have continued unabated, however, such as the ever-increasing market share of private providers. Indeed, the current national government actively supports the introduction of consumer choice models at the local level, and has provided earmarked funds for this purpose. In Denmark, the government introduced a uniform system for consumer choice in 2002 (Ministry of the Interior and Health 2005), whereas choice of provider continues being an exception in Norway, in particular for nursing services.

Other important innovations of the last decade include the tightened regulation of user fees and means-testing procedures in Sweden, and a cohabitation guarantee stipulating that spouses shall be offered institutional care in the same facilities. In Denmark, a radical restructuring of the municipal sector was undertaken in 2007, when the number of municipalities was reduced from 271 to 98. The main objective of this reform was to create units large enough to provide public services in an efficient manner. Furthermore, a major quality reform is under way in Denmark, which aims at strengthening the rights of individual users and provides extra funding for quality improvements (Schulz, 2010).

2.1   A Scandinavian model?

There is a long tradition in the social sciences of classifying different types of welfare regimes, such as Titmuss' (1974) distinction between *marginal* (Anglo-Saxon), *industrial achievement* (continental Europe) and *institutional* (Scandinavia) welfare States. The best known typology is probably that of Esping-Andersen (1990), which divides welfare States into *Corporatist, Liberal* and *Social Democrat*. A further typology was provided by Korpi and Palme (1998), who distinguish no less than five different types of welfare State regimes. No matter which typology is chosen, the countries covered in this chapter are always part of the same category, which is referred to as the institutional, Social Democratic, Scandinavian, universal or encompassing model.

The defining traits of this Scandinavian welfare model, according to Esping-Andersen, are, firstly, the existence of highly decommodifying and universalistic programmes; secondly, equal rights of blue- and white-collar workers; and thirdly, all strata are incorporated in one universal insurance system, but benefits are graduated according to earnings. Korpi and Palme (1998), on the other hand, define their 'encompassing' welfare State as a model that combines earnings-related benefits with universalism, providing basic security to all citizens and earnings-related benefits to the working population. Finally, Rothstein (1998) mentions the provision of publicly provided universally available services as one of three defining characteristics of the universal Swedish welfare State – the other two being a system of flat rate benefits tied to citizenship (e.g., basic pensions) and a mandatory social insurance system (e.g., sick pay).

Obviously, all these typologies represent ideal types, and it should be expected that each real-world welfare State will exhibit deviations from these criteria. As far as LTC is concerned, there are certainly some notable deviations from the principles of the 'universal' or 'encompassing' welfare model. Firstly, all the Scandinavian countries have elements of means-testing in the provision of care services: higher fees are charged from those who earn more, at least for some types of services. Secondly, only the *availability* of LTC services is universal, whereas there tend to be no universal principles for how needs assessment is to be carried out, how needs are mapped into care packages or for the quality of services. This is in clear contrast to the countries that have a social insurance system for LTC, and where all these issues are regulated by law (Wittenberg and Malley, 2007).

In an attempt to categorize European models for social care, Anttonen and Sipilä (1996) suggested a division into three different categories. According to this classification, the Scandinavian countries practise the *State responsibility model*, where local authorities are responsible for the provision of care services, which are universal and widely available. This model is contrasted with the *family care model* (Southern Europe) with families as main care providers and the *subsidiary model* (the Netherlands, Belgium, Germany and France), where the family also plays an important role but where substitutes for family care are available when necessary. However, the value added by this classification is questionable since it is based entirely on one single dimension of very complex systems for LTC; that is, who the primary provider of care is. Furthermore, it wrongly gives the impression that family care is of limited importance in Scandinavia, which is not correct in general.

2.2 Governance

In all three countries, municipalities have responsibility for financing and providing LTC, whereas the national government is responsible for overall control and for establishing the broad legislative and financial framework for health and social policy, including care for the elderly. The responsibilities of municipalities as regards LTC are regulated in Social Services Acts. They typically state that every resident who is in need has a right to home-based or institution-based care. Municipalities are further obliged to actively investigate needs in the local population, and to promote good living conditions in other ways. Furthermore, all three countries have the explicit objective to make it possible for older people to stay at home and live independently as long as possible (Socialstyrelsen, 2002a).

Although the structure of governance is almost identical in the three countries, there is nevertheless an important difference in the degree of decentralization of the local democracy. In Sweden, the emphasis has traditionally been on economies of scale, and in the post-war era there were several waves of restructuring of the municipal sector to create units large enough to be able to carry out their tasks effectively. Thus, the total number of Swedish municipalities has decreased by almost 90 per cent since 1950 (Daatland and Sundström, 1997). In Norway, on the other hand, the emphasis has been much more on local democracy and on keeping a high level of services in remote areas too. In Denmark, a major reform of the governance structure was undertaken in 2007, whereby the number of municipalities was reduced from 271 to 98. Consequently, Norway has the smallest municipality units (430 municipalities for a population of 4.9 million), Sweden is an intermediate case (290 municipalities for 9 million people) and Denmark has the largest units (5.5 million inhabitants are distributed over 98 municipalities).

2.3   The LTC sector

To get a picture of the size and importance of the LTC sector in Scandinavia, services of long-term nursing care are presented in Table 14.1 as a percentage of GDP. The numbers include expenditure on day care and in-patient care in nursing homes and long-term nursing care at home. In 2006, the Organization for Economic Cooperation and Development (OECD) average of LTC expenditure was 0.8 per cent, which puts Denmark and Norway way above the average and Sweden just below.

The most striking aspect of these findings is that Sweden on average lies approximately 1.35 percentage points below Denmark and Norway.

Table 14.1   Health-care expenditure on LTC as a percentage of GDP

Year	Denmark	Norway	Sweden
2003	1.96	2.37	0.72
2004	2.02	2.20	0.72
2005	2.07	2.14	0.71
2006	2.07	2.14	0.70
2007	2.00	n.a.	0.70

Source: EUROSTAT (2010). The figures are based on the System of Health Accounts (SHA), a system developed jointly by the OECD, World Health Organization (WHO) and EUROSTAT. The data include expenditure on day care and in-patient care in nursing homes and long-term nursing care at home. LTC is usually a mix of medical (including long-term nursing care) and social services. SHA includes only the medical part of LTC expenditure.

Although the SHA is the dominant source for comparison of health expenditure across countries within the OECD, there are several reasons why LTC expenditure numbers should be viewed with scepticism. According to Søgaard (2009), LTC expenditure is the least reliable component of the SHA. The reason is that the definitions and measurement instructions for LTC expenditure are so vague that they leave room for wide interpretations and, consequently, the numbers reported seem to be inconsistent across countries. Thus, the OECD average should be treated with caution. With regard to the Scandinavian countries, Søgaard (2009) classifies Denmark and Norway as using a broad definition focusing on care and personal assistance, while Sweden uses a narrow medical/nursing definition. Thus, there is a concern of underreporting by Sweden compared with Denmark and Norway. To compensate, we have also included numbers for Sweden from the Swedish Association of Local Authorities and Regions, which uses a broader definition of LTC expenditures in Table 14.2. The total cost for publicly financed LTC in Sweden was SEK 87 billion (€8.9 billion) in 2007, which corresponds to 2.8 per cent of GDP. In real terms, there was an increase of 1.7 per cent on the previous year (SALAR, 2009a). Over the past decade, Swedish public expenditure on LTC has fallen as a proportion of GDP and also as a proportion of total operating costs in the local authorities. This reduction in spending has occurred even though the proportion of older people in the population has increased somewhat. The share of local public expenditure devoted to LTC in Denmark is similar (Statskontoret, 2009).

Out of total LTC costs, the main part is made up by institution-based care (61.3 per cent); home-based care accounts for 37.1 per cent and preventive activities 1.6 per cent. Throughout the 1990s, the share of institution-based care increased (Swedish Ministry of Health and Social Affairs, 1999), but since 2002 this proportion has decreased (SALAR, 2009a).

Table 14.2 Trends in operational costs for local authorities in Sweden

Year	Costs at 2007 prices (€)		Elderly care as a share of	
	Total	**Elderly Care**	**Total Costs**	**GDP**
2000	41.76	8.97	21.5%	2.99%
2001	42.37	9.12	21.5%	3.07%
2002	43.24	9.24	21.4%	3.13%
2003	43.27	9.17	21.2%	3.11%
2004	43.72	8.75	20.0%	3.03%
2005	44.13	8.61	19.5%	2.94%
2006	45.13	8.73	19.3%	2.88%
2007	46.13	8.88	19.2%	2.84%

Source: SALAR (2009a).

2.4　Services provided

In Sweden, municipalities offer home help services, daytime community activities and similar social services to assist the elderly living at home. Since 1992, municipalities have also been responsible for local nursing homes and some other care institutions. At the same time, a new general term was introduced for all kinds of accommodating institutions under the responsibility of municipalities: 'special housing'. This term includes nursing homes, residential care facilities such as old age homes, service houses, group homes for people with dementia and so on. In Norway, institutions are categorized as either nursing homes or supported housing, the latter being housing rented or owned with care facilities attached or close by, but where there is no resident nursing staff (St.meld. nr.25).

In Denmark, the distinction between institutional and home care has become blurred in the last few decades. Since 1987 no conventional nursing homes have been built and housing arrangement is separated from service provision. Institutional care has been replaced by 24-hour health and social care supplied to all elderly in need, irrespective of housing. The 24-hour care is accessible every day for people in acute need (Colmorten et al., 2003). The municipalities are obliged to ensure that those who cannot remain at home are admitted to a nursing home or another care facility staffed around the clock. An admission board in cooperation with the home help, the home nurse and the local GP assesses whether an individual needs admission to a nursing home or increased services to stay at home. Denmark also has a more sophisticated and universal system for needs assessment than the other two countries. Everyone aged 75 and over is entitled to at least 2 preventative visits by a district nurse annually (Schulz, 2010). Since 1996, users of home-based services have also been entitled to a contract that states what services and how many hours the person is entitled to (Platz and Brodhurst, 2001).

Despite its high degree of reliance on formal care, the level of informal care being provided in Scandinavian countries is considerable. In Denmark, 60 per cent of older people receive some form of help from their spouse, or from relatives and friends (Schulz, 2010). For Sweden, it has been estimated that the level of help given by relatives to older people living at home is more than twice the amount provided by local authorities. According to one study, as much as 70 per cent of total service hours was provided by informal carers in 2000, and the share is likely to have increased during the last decade (Sundström et al., 2002; Sand, 2010). Over the last decade, the national government has started several initiatives to support informal carers. For carers who leave gainful employment in order to care for a severely ill family member, a family carer allowance can be applied for from the social insurance system (SALAR, 2009a). Similar grants also exist in Norway and Denmark (Helsetilsynet, 2009). The assignment is conditional on the carer being suitable for the tasks and that the arrangement is best for the care recipient. In Norway and Sweden, the systems are very similar. Carers receive a social security benefit from the central government and a rather modest care allowance from the municipalities. In Denmark the carer can claim compensation for foregone wages, and in this respect Denmark is fundamentally different from the other Scandinavian countries (Helsetilsynet, 2009).

2.5 Volumes and trends

In 2008, about 250,000 people 65 years of age and older received some kind of LTC in Sweden, corresponding to 15.3 per cent of the entire elderly population. It is apparent that the need for care is highly age-related even among older people: among those 80 years of age and older, 37 per cent received some kind of LTC in that year. The situation is similar in the other two countries, but in Norway, there has been a marked increase in the provision of services to people below the age of 67 years. During the last 10 years, the number of clients below 67 years of age has almost doubled and now accounts for approximately 25 per cent of the clients of LTC and for 37.1 per cent of total LTC expenditure (Huseby and Paulsen, 2009). This trend is related to the de-institutionalization of care for the young disabled. In Table 14.3, we have depicted recipients of home help and people

Table 14.3 Coverage of LTC services in Scandinavia, 2007–2008

	Institutional care (%)			Home help (%)		
	Denmark[a]	Norway[b]	Sweden[c]	Denmark[d]	Norway[e]	Sweden[f]
64–74	1.2	2.4	1.2	6.3	3.4	2.3
75–79	3.6	6.2	4.2	18.1	8.2	7.4
80+	14.1	23.7	16.6	42.9	24.9	21.9
Total 65+ years	5.0	10.8	6.4	18.1	12.1	9.2
N	48,921	66,528	106,163	154,571	74,423	n.a.

Notes:
a. Includes residents in nursing homes, sheltered housing, housing where care is provided and long-term stays in housing units. The figures for long-term stays in housing units are from 2008 and based on the age group 67–74 years.
b. Age groups 67–74, 75–79 and 80+ years.
c. Calculation as per 1 October 2006. The age group 65+ years furthermore includes people staying on a short-term basis and residents in service housing.
d. Home help to residents in their own homes with the exception of service housing.
e. Age groups 67–74, 75–79 and 80+ years, including residents in service housing who receive practical assistance (home help) and home nursing. Recipients receiving only home nursing are not included.
f. People who had been granted home help as at 1 October 2006 and who lived in their own houses or flats.
Source: Nordic Social Statistical Committee (2009), tables 6.2.12 and 6.2.13.

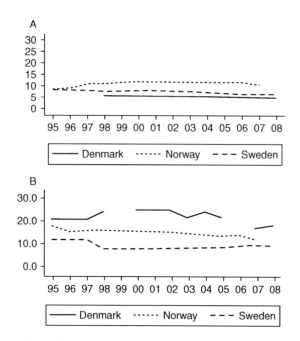

Figure 14.2   A. People living in institutions or in service housing B. People receiving home help, as percentages of the age group 65 years or more, 1995–2008
Note: Data for Denmark are incomplete.
Source: Nordic Social Statistical Committee (2009).

living in institutions as percentages of the respective age groups for all three countries.

The emphasis of care tends to change somewhat over time. The trends in provision of home-based and institutional care for the Nordic countries are plotted in Figure 14.2. As the figure shows, there is a trend to scale down institutional care. The policy objective behind this trend is to enable older people to stay at home as long as possible. The trend is particularly strong in Sweden but discernible also in Denmark, and this can be attributed to the Act on Housing for Older People (1987), which completely restricted the development of conventional nursing homes. Since 1987 no nursing homes have been built (Ministry of the Interior and Health, 2005).

The trends in Sweden over the last 20 years are shown in further detail in Table 14.4. It is clear that the trend to scale down public LTC continued during the 1990s, but that the pace of change has been considerably slower in the last decade. Furthermore, the share of LTC going to the oldest group has increased throughout the period, which can be seen by comparing the number of users amongst the 80+ group with the total number of users.

Table 14.4 Recipients of LTC in Sweden, 1993–2007

Year	Age 65+						Age 80+					
	Domiciliary care	%	Institution-based care	%	Total	%	Domiciliary care	%	Institution-based care	%	Total	%
1993	149,650	9.7	121,340	7.9	270,990	17.6	92,181	23.2	89,433	22.5	181,614	45.7
1994	145,034	9.4	128,553	8.4	273,587	17.8	90,665	22.2	94,855	23.2	185,520	45.5
1995	137,572	8.9	129,843	8.4	267,415	17.3	86,653	20.9	96,058	23.2	182,711	44.1
1996	129,543	8.4	127,012	8.2	256,555	16.6	82,956	19.7	94,509	22.5	177,465	42.2
1997	130,059	8.4	130,725	8.5	260,784	16.9	84,788	19.8	97,715	22.9	182,503	42.7
1998	126,049	8.2	118,715	7.7	244,764	15.9	84,253	19.5	90,787	21.0	175,040	40.5
1999	129,479	8.4	116,254	7.6	245,733	16.0	85,217	19.5	88,623	20.3	173,840	39.8
2000	125,324	8.2	121,305	7.9	246,629	16.1	86,070	19.0	93,717	20.7	179,787	39.7
2001	121,741	7.9	118,621	7.7	240,362	15.6	84,816	18.3	92,807	20.0	177,623	38.3
2007	153,700	9.6	95,232	6.2	248,932	15.7	110,700	23.0	76,100	16.0	186,800	39.0

Source: Socialstyrelsen (2002a) and SALAR (2009a).

In Swedish domiciliary care, a restructuring could be observed in the 1990s when efforts were concentrated on the most severe cases. Thus, the number of elderly with weekly services amounting to 1–9 hours per month decreased significantly, whereas those with services exceeding 50 hours increased. However, these trends have clearly been reversed during the last 10 years (Socialstyrelsen, 2001, 2008).

In Denmark, services are not as concentrated on severe cases as in Sweden. Amongst care recipients living in their own home, 62 per cent receive less than 9 hours of care per month, and only 3 per cent receive more than 80 hours per month. These figures reflect the fact that there is no minimum level of need that older people are required to meet to be eligible for home help (Schulz, 2010).

The figures presented so far conceal the fact that there is considerable variation between municipalities, in all countries, with regard to volume, composition and probably quality of LTC for the elderly. Table 14.5 shows the coverage of LTC in Swedish municipalities (out of 290 in total), with the highest and the lowest cost per elderly person. As may be noted, costs also vary significantly and the differences are not totally attributable to differences in the age structure in the elderly population (cf. Karlsson et al., 2004). In Huseby and Paulsen (2009), regression analysis on Norwegian data shows that – when controlling for morbidity and age structure – local revenue, municipality size and population density all explain parts of the variation in LTC expenditure between municipalities.

Table 14.5   Cost and coverage of LTC in selected Swedish municipalities, 2008

Municipality	Cost per person (€)	Home-based Care Share of 65+ Pop.		Institution-based Care Share of 65+ Pop.		Share of population
		Crude	Age Std	Crude	Age Std	65-w
Sorsele	8453	8	8	10	9	28.1
Berg	7931	14	13	7	6	24.7
Härjedalen	7816	10	9	8	7	25.4
Åsele	7804	12	11	8	7	28.4
Ragunda	7739	14	13	7	7	26.7
Nat. average	**3309**	**9**	**9**	**6**	**6**	**17.8**
Nykvarn	3625	5	8	3	5	13.1
Salem	3614	4	5	4	5	14.1
Håbo	3613	8	11	3	5	12.5
Vellinge	3542	12	14	3	3	18.1
Staffanstorp	3509	5	6	3	5	15.9

Note: 'Crude' refers to the actual proportion of individuals, whereas 'Age Std' provides figures which have been corrected for differences in the age structure within the older group.
Source: Socialstyrelsen (2009).

2.6   Private provision and consumer choice

Until the early 1990s, Swedish LTC was almost exclusively provided by local public monopolies. Private provision was limited to some complementary services like cleaning. There was also a broad political consensus that health and LTC should be publicly provided.

In the early 1990s, private entrepreneurs were allowed into the market for LTC. In the first few years, a rapid expansion of private care took place; the share of private entrepreneurs in the municipal budgets for LTC quadrupled. This trend continued at a somewhat slower pace throughout the 1990s (Söderström et al., 2001), and it appears to have continued unabated during the last decade (SALAR, 2009a; Socialstyrelsen, 2009).

The impact of this change becomes clear if the shares of clients who are served by private caregivers are considered. These figures, which are given in Figure 14.3, show that private caregivers have more than tripled their share since 1993.

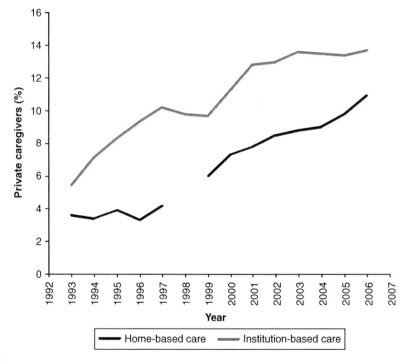

Figure 14.3   Proportion of clients assisted by private caregivers, 1993–2006
Source: Socialstyrelsen (2002b, 2008).

However, there are vast regional differences in this case. The emergence of private caregivers is restricted to some 40 local authorities in metropolitan areas and some larger towns. In some of these, the presence of private caregivers has emerged as part of a consumer choice model, where the individual user may choose between competing providers. In other cases, the private element is simply the result of procurement at the local authority level. The development of consumer choice models has been actively supported by the current centre-right national government, and several municipalities have applied for earmarked funds to develop their own models (SALAR, 2009a). A law regulating consumer choice models in public services was introduced in 2009, but even though a national system for consumer choice in primary care was introduced at the same time, it remains voluntary for the municipalities to introduce consumer choice models in LTC (SOU, 2008, p. 37).

In Denmark, on the other hand, consumer choice has been introduced universally by the national government. In 2002, a reform (the seniors' package) was enacted to secure the freedom of choice for the elderly. An older person who is eligible for subsidized housing is free to choose a nursing home or the special dwelling they prefer. Recipients of home-based care are also free to choose their preferred supplier. The local authorities must provide information on all providers that are approved to provide home-based services. The recipient can choose to have several providers: for instance, a public provider for personal help and a private supplier for practical help. Private suppliers within the LTC sector need to have contract with the municipality to have the right to provide their services. A majority of municipalities uses the 'approval model', according to which all providers that meet certain quality and price standards are approved as suppliers of home-based care services (Ministry of Interior and Health, 2005). However, the Danish movement towards private provision started from a lower level than in Sweden: before the seniors' package, there were no private providers of home care in Denmark. Private commercial providers of home care are gaining an increasing share of the market, but they are mainly in the field of practical assistance. Even today, the market share of private companies remains below 5 per cent in personal care, and the forthcoming quality reform will seek to improve older people's knowledge of their options to make an active choice in regard to a provider (Schulz, 2010).

In Norway, several municipalities have a tradition of contracting with non-profit nursing homes, even though public nursing homes dominate. Non-profit nursing homes are often owned and run by a religious or humanitarian organization. A contract with a municipality implies that their patients have been entitled to nursing home care similar to patients of public nursing homes. Apart from the city of Oslo, where some nursing homes have been put out to tender, there are no for-profit companies involved in publicly financed nursing homes in Norway. Also, within the home services, the proportion of private providers is a lot smaller than in Sweden and Denmark. For practical and personal home help only a few of the municipalities have introduced consumer choice between public and private providers. In Oslo, there is a consumer choice model of home services and in 2010 21.5 per cent of recipients chose a private provider. Regarding home nursing, in 2010 patient choice between public and private provider exists only in the city of Bergen. We conclude that both consumer choice and the combination of publicly financed and privately provided LTC is clearly more prevalent in Denmark and Sweden than in Norway.

3 Taxes and risk adjustment

A common factor in Scandinavian tax systems is the dual income tax structure, where capital incomes are taxed at a low and flat rate, whereas labour and transfer income is taxed progressively (Sørensen, 2009). However, the system for income taxation differs amongst Scandinavian countries in two important respects: firstly, the degree of progression is considerably lower in Norway than in Sweden and Denmark, and secondly, employers' social insurance contributions are much more important in Norway and Sweden than in Denmark, where marginal income taxes are correspondingly higher (OECD, 2009).

Swedish LTC is mainly financed from local income taxes, which make up around two-thirds of total revenue at municipality level. These general income taxes are charged by municipalities at a flat rate, averaging 20.74 per cent in 2010. The tax rates are determined by local politicians who have a considerable degree of autonomy (SCB, 2010). Although political preferences give rise to some local variation in tax rates (the span is currently between 18 and 24 per cent), the average level has been remarkably stable over the past 15 years. In Norway as well as in Denmark, the local tax base is broader than in Sweden, and also includes wealth and property taxes. Nevertheless, local taxes are slightly less important as a revenue source than in Sweden (Statskontoret, 2009).

In addition to local taxes and out-of-pocket payments, the central governments contribute to the financing of LTC through general grants paid to municipalities. In Sweden, such grants were introduced in 1993 and replaced a large number of earmarked grants. The current system consists of three main components: income adjustment, cost adjustment and structural grants. In total, SEK 58 billion (€5.90 billion) were transferred from the national government to local authorities in 2008, which corresponds to 17.6 per cent of their total revenues (SALAR, 2009b).

The overall objective of the government grants is to compensate for differences in tax bases and inherent differences in costs structures and thereby equalize the opportunities for local authorities to provide equivalent public services throughout the country. At the same time, local authorities shall not be compensated for differences in costs that are attributable to differences in service quality, user fees or productive efficiency. The systems are very similar in the three countries, so we report only the particulars of the Swedish system here. The Swedish system for government grants was reformed in 1996 and 2005, and smaller adjustments were made in 2008.

The *income adjustment* component in the system has the aim of equalizing the revenue side. The actual tax bases of the individual municipalities are compared with 115 per cent of the national average. Municipalities whose tax bases fall short of this benchmark level receive a payment from the national government equal to the shortfall multiplied by the regional average of local tax rates (Statskontoret, 2008). In order to avoid perverse incentives for municipalities with relatively strong tax bases, the fees levied on net contributors are calculated at a lower tax rate than the corresponding grant. In 2008, the national government paid SEK 52 billion (€5.30 billion) in income adjustment grants to the 279 net receivers, and 11 well-off municipalities contributed another 3.7 billion (€0.38 billion).

The *cost adjustment* component of the national grant is supposed to compensate for structural factors, such as demography, that are outside the municipalities' direct control. There are separate models for all different types of services that the municipalities are obliged to provide. For each such service, a 'standard cost' is calculated, and municipalities that exceed the standard cost receive a grant corresponding to the difference. This part of the system is symmetric, so municipalities with a favourable cost structure contribute the corresponding amount to the system.

In LTC, the standard cost is calculated using a partition of the older population into 240 different cells, based on age, marital status and ethnic background. To each of these cells a price tag is attached, which is based on the average costs of care at the national level. Not all components of this calculation are updated annually, however. Over and above the compensation for the standard costs thus calculated, there are special grants for institutional and domiciliary care in remote areas (Statskontoret, 2008). In 2008, the standard cost was SEK 8410 (€855) per inhabitant, and in total, SEK 6.50 billion (€661 million) were reallocated within the LTC system.

The third main component of the government grant system, the *structural grants*, was were introduced in 2005 with the aim of compensating municipalities that would otherwise have suffered considerable reductions in their grants due to the new system. Two further components are the *temporary grants* that were also introduced to compensate for changes to the system, and the *adjustment grants* (*regleringsbidrag*), which were introduced to allow the national government to transfer more resources to the local authorities than that stipulated by the system.

4   User contributions: Out-of-pocket payments, means-testing and personal needs allowances

In Sweden (as in the other two countries), only a small share of the expenditures on LTC is financed through out-of-pocket payments; according to the most recent estimates, this share was 3.7 per cent in 2007 (SALAR, 2009b), which is slightly less than the 5 per cent that was estimated ten years ago (Karlsson et al., 2004). Thus, out-of-pocket payments are less important for LTC than in the financing of child care (where the proportion is around 9 per cent) but nevertheless considerably higher than out-of-pocket payments in disabled care (at less than 1 per cent). Despite this, LTC fees of different kinds make up a considerable share of individual income for many older people.

In the early 1990s, municipalities were given considerable freedom in the design of the out-of-pocket payments. Some general principles were laid down in law. These principles are that fees should be *fair*, they may not exceed *production cost* and they must leave a *personal expenses allowance* ('pocket money'). As it transpired that the municipalities made use of this freedom – which resulted in a great degree of arbitrary variation in the levels and principles for calculating fees – some reforms to the system appeared to be necessary. Thus, in 2002 and 2003 the rules were tightened. Firstly, a national cap on out-of-pocket payment was introduced, stating that nobody shall have to pay more than a certain amount per month for personal services and for hotel costs, respectively. The caps are indexed to prices, and currently the cap for personal care is SEK 1696 (€173) per month, and for hotel costs the maximum is 1766 (€180) per month. Furthermore, the new law introduced a minimum personal needs allowance (currently SEK 4787/€488 for singles and SEK 4045/€412 per person for cohabiting partners). The reforms in 2002/03 also clarified how the user's income shall be calculated for means-testing purposes, and opened up a possibility to appeal against unfavourable decisions (Socialstyrelsen, 2007).

In Norway, the general principles for out-of-pocket payments are similar to those in Sweden. For nursing homes, the user payment depends on whether the stay is short term or long term. The user contribution for a short-term stay is independent of the resident's income. The municipalities can charge a flat rate per night and there is a maximum allowable rate set by central government (St-meld. nr.25). In 2010, the rate for a day and night stay was NOK 125 (€15.80; HOD, 2010). For a long-term stay the user payment depends on the resident's income. The municipalities are entitled to demand approximately 80 per cent of the resident's income above a certain lower limit. In addition, the municipality is not allowed to charge more than the actual costs of the service and the recipient must be secured a minimum amount of pocket money for personal expenses. The user contributions include boarding and lodging, and all health care services needed including medicines and physician services. The co-payment is not dependent on the level of services used by the individual resident.

For older Norwegians living in their own housing or supported housing, the system of user payment is very different. In general, the regulation of user payments for health and care services corresponds to the regulation that applies to the population at large. Older people living in supported housing, other than nursing homes, pay housing expenses from their personal income. Public support for housing expenses may be applied for according to similar rules applicable to the general population. Primary health services are provided under the regular general practitioner scheme. Co-payments for physician services and medicines are in accord with the general regulation, with an annual ceiling dependent on total co-payments and independent of an individual's income.

For home help, Norwegian municipalities can freely choose the user payment to be charged as long as this is not above actual cost and the recipient is left with a minimum residual income (St.meld. nr.25, 2005–2006). Many municipalities offer payment schemes with income-related ceilings.

We observe that there is far greater degree of income-dependent user payments for patients in nursing homes than there is for services to the elderly living at home. Hence, for older people with similar care needs it will be less costly for a municipality with provide nursing home care to a person with a high income compared to a person with a low income.

In Denmark, there is no distinction in financing arrangements between institutional and home-based care. Residents in nursing homes pay rents approximated at the cost of housing and must also pay for other services such as electricity, meals, hairdressing, shaving and so on, as for older people living in their own home. Permanent home help and home nursing are provided free of charge, irrespective of the type of housing (Colmorten et al., 2003). As of 1 July 2010, older people with a prospect of recovering from disability can be offered temporary home help and home nursing services. For these temporary services the municipalities are entitled to demand a fee per hour of received care that is dependent on the user's income. The design of the co-payment is regulated by central government – below a certain income level the co-payment is zero, and thereafter it is an increasing function of the user's income until it reaches a maximum admissible fee (Ældre Sagen, 2010).

5   Private LTC insurance

LTC insurance (LTCI) products are absent, or at least of very limited importance, in Scandinavia (OECD, 2004). The LTC sector is predominantly financed from general taxation, and private co-payments account for only a minor share of total LTC costs (see previous section). This does not mean that private LTCI will never be a reality in Scandinavia, as increasing demand for LTC services from an ageing population could be troublesome for public finances. In order to find out whether there is any evidence of an emerging market for private LTCI in Scandinavia, or whether there are at least products on the market that cover some aspects of LTC costs, we conducted a small survey by sending a questionnaire to five major insurance companies in each of the three countries. We asked the companies whether they currently have any products which cover some aspects of LTC costs and whether they have any plans to launch LTCI products. The general impression from this small survey is that there are currently no LTCI products on the market, nor are there any specific plans to develop such products in the near future. However, the companies recognize future challenges for the public system – an ageing of the population and growing expectations from the more affluent future elderly – that could increase the need for a private market.

Some of the companies emphasize that the future of this market is contingent on the possibility of designing viable products that can meet future LTC needs. This could be a significant challenge, considering experiences from the USA and the UK. Although the comprehensive public coverage in Scandinavia is bound to have a significant crowding-out effect on the demand for private LTC insurance, the market for LTCI is also limited in countries with systems that primarily rely on private funding (cf. Mayhew et al., 2010). The market for LTCI possibly suffers from common market imperfections in insurance markets – moral hazard and adverse selection. However, the inherently long planning horizon of these insurance policies is arguably of greater importance, and this probably makes LTCI one of the riskiest products insurers can sell (Wiener et al., 1994). In combination with these market imperfections, the large public element in Scandinavian LTC systems suggests that it will take some time before private LTCI will be funding a significant part of LTC costs in Scandinavia.

6   Conclusions: Efficiency and equity in Scandinavian LTC financing

The Scandinavian systems for financing LTC are remarkably similar. The institutional set-up is almost identical in the three countries: the local government carries the main responsibility for funding and provision of LTC, and the national government defines general goals and principles for locally provided services. These general goals and principles are also very similar between the countries. Differences between the three countries are notable only in the emphasis of different types of services, or in details concerning the design of schemes for user charges.

However, LTC is a sector where two fundamental principles of the Scandinavian model appear to collide: it is difficult to reconcile the universalism of the Scandinavian welfare State with the political tradition of strong local autonomy. Thus, the models practised for financing LTC seem to be a compromise between these two general principles: municipalities have some degree of freedom in designing local policies, but the national government intervenes to assure that the conditions are comparable throughout the country.

In recent years, there has clearly been a trend towards favouring universalism at the expense of local autonomy. This trend is discernible in all three countries, but interventions by the national governments take on different forms in the different countries. In Sweden, the current national government tends to promote change on a voluntary basis, by providing funds for which the local authorities can apply in order to introduce new governance models in LTC. In Denmark, on the other hand, much more emphasis has been on the rights of the individual user, and binding principles have been laid down in law. Clearly, the Swedish approach allows for more local experimentation, but it may also threaten universalism if other municipalities fail to follow successful pioneers.

Concerning the economic efficiency of the Scandinavian model, it is difficult to make a general assessment. Some aspects of the Scandinavian systems appear to further economic efficiency: first and foremost, the fact that there is one dominant payer that covers the bulk of LTC spending. This standardized approach should give rise to considerable efficiency gains in comparison with the fragmented systems in Germany, the UK or the USA, where the funding of LTC typically comes from several different sources. Furthermore, the Scandinavian systems entail, at least in principle, a considerable degree of institutional competition. Since municipalities are obliged to provide services to each resident in need, individuals have the option to move to municipalities that provide particularly good services. The national risk adjustment systems assure that the free movement of individuals does not give rise to financial problems in the receiving municipalities.

On the other hand, there are some aspects of the Scandinavian model that appear to be suboptimal from an efficiency point of view. For example, in none of the countries do municipalities carry the main responsibility for health care.[1] Since there are many situations where there is close substitutability between health and LTC, there is a risk that local and regional authorities try to dump costly cases on each other. There has been a tendency to integrate some aspects of the two systems (cf. Schulz, 2010), but the risk of cost shifting is always there as long as there are two different payers with partly different objectives. Furthermore, the user charges in health and LTC tend to be different, so there may also be an incentive on the part of the individual user to pick the most favourable system.

Moreover, the non-existence of private LTCI may be interpreted as an indication of inefficiencies in the design of the public subsidy. For some individuals, user charges may amount to a substantial share of their individual income (e.g., in Norway, as much as 80 per cent of an individual's income may be claimed as a payment for nursing home care). Risk-averse individuals would naturally wish to insure this risk, and thus it appears that the public sector crowds out the demand for private insurance, just as it does in the USA (cf. Brown and Finkelstein, 2007).This crowding out is generally expected whenever benefits from private insurance lead to a reduction in the public subsidy; that is, when insurance benefits count as income in the means-testing procedure. However, given that there is no requirement in Scandinavian countries to spend down assets before an individual becomes eligible for public support, the absence of private insurance might simply reflect that individuals put a low value on protecting their income in the contingency that they need LTC.

Concerning equity, there are many different dimensions of equity that need to be taken into consideration. Hence, an equitable LTC system should strike the right balance between those who need care and those who do not; between young and old (since otherwise the political sustainability of the system might be in peril); between poor and rich – which is a greater challenge than for income taxes in general, since there are important differences between rich and poor not only concerning resources available, but also in terms of care needs and life expectancy. Furthermore, equity between men and women has often been overlooked in discussions concerning LTC, but this issue is of tremendous importance, considering the fact that women provide the bulk of informal (i.e., unpaid) care to frail spouses or parents, whereas men tend to contribute more to the funding of public LTC services, but get less back from the system in terms of care. Thus, the design of an LTC system will inevitably have strong implications for discussions of gender equality (Karlsson, 2007).

The great regional variation in coverage levels, quality of services, eligibility criteria and consumer choice clearly seems to be inequitable, particularly in view of the Scandinavian welfare States' universalist ambitions. Another important issue is whether informal carers receive sufficient compensation: given that there are no legal obligations to care for a frail family member, it would seem inequitable if family carers do not receive full compensation for their work. On the other hand, the design of Scandinavian LTC systems appears to promote gender equality: the heavy reliance on public funding and formal care services implies that there is relatively low pressure on middle-aged females to give up gainful employment in order to care for frail family members, and furthermore, there is a considerable degree of redistribution from males to females in the systems.

The LTC sectors in Scandinavian countries will face important challenges due to changes in the composition of the population. One such change is that each country gradually becomes more heterogeneous due to immigration from non-European countries. Since the tradition that children take care of their frail parents is stronger in these countries, the willingness to pay for publicly financed LTC may decline. More important is perhaps the change in the age composition that is taking place. Contrary to health care, where remaining time to death seems to be the dominating demographic factor that determines expenditures, LTC expenditures seem to depend to a much greater extent on age. In Denmark the number of older people 80 years and above is expected to double from 224,000 to 457,000 by 2040 (De Økonomiske Råd, 2009). The expected increase is similar in Norway and Sweden. For Norway, it is estimated (assuming constant productivity) that the number of personnel in the LTC sector must double towards the middle of the century in order to maintain today's level of quality (St.meld. nr. 9, 2008–2009). Hence, demographic trends are likely to entail important challenges regarding both the number of personnel needed and the maintenance of public and universal funding of LTC.

Note

1. In Denmark, health care is the responsibility of the regional level of government, in Sweden health care is the responsibility of the county councils and in Norway, primary care is the responsibility of the municipalities and specialist health care is the responsibility of the national government.

References

Ældre Sagen (2010) *Varig og midlertidig hjemmehjælp – betaling,* http://www.aeldresagen.dk/Medlemmer/raadgivning/vaerdatvide/hjemmehjaelp/varig_og_midlertidig_hjemmehj%C3%A6lp/Sider/Default.asp, accessed 23 August 2010.

Anttonen, A. and Sipilä, J. (1996) 'European social care services: Is it possible to identify models?', *Journal of European Social Policy,* 6 (2), pp. 87–100.

Brown, J. and Finkelstein, A. (2007) 'Why is the market for long term care insurance so small?', *Journal of Public Economics,* 91 (10), pp. 1967–1991.

Colmorten, E., Clausen, T. and Bengtsson, S. (2003) *Providing Integrated Health and Social Care for Older Persons in Denmark* (Copenhagen: Danish National Institute of Social Research).

Daatland, S.O. and Sundström, G. (1997) 'Synsvinkel og tilnærming', in S.O. Daatland (ed.) *De siste årene. Eldreomsorgen i Skandinavia 1960–95* (Nova-Rapport 22/1997), pp. 102–126.

Daatland, S.O., Platz, M. and Sundström, G. (1997) 'Status og utviklingslinjer', in S.O. Daatland (ed.) *De siste årene. Eldreomsorgen i Skandinavia 1960–95* (Nova-Rapport 22/1997), pp. 153–171.

De økonomiske råd (2009) *Konjunkturvurdering – Sundhed* (København: De økonomiske råd).

Esping-Andersen, G. (1990) *The Three Worlds of Welfare Capitalism* (Princeton, NJ: Princeton University Press).

EUROSTAT (2010) *Data on Health Care Expenditure on Long-term Care,* http://ec.europa.eu/eurostat accessed 15 April 2010.

Hansen, E.B. (2000) 'Social protection for dependency in old age in Denmark', in *Modernising and Improving EU Social Protection: Conference on Long-term Care of Elderly*

*Dependent People in the EU and Nor*way, 17–18 June 1998 (London: Department of Health Publications).

Helsetilsynet (2009) *Omsorgslønnsordningen – en kunnskapsoppsummering. Internserien 7/2009. Statens helsetilsyn,* Oslo.

HOD (Helse- og omsorgsdepartementet) (2009) Rundskriv: *Endring av fribeløp og egenandeler for kommunale pleie- og omsorgstjenester,* Oslo.

Huseby, B.M. and Paulsen, B. (2009) SINTEF Rapport, *Eldreomsorgen I Norge: Helt utilstrekkelig – eller best i verden* (Trondheim: SINTEF).

Karlsson, M. (2007) 'Distributional effects of reform in long term care', *Ageing Horizons,* 6, pp. 133–141.

Karlsson, M., Mayhew, L., Plumb, R. and Rickayzen, B. (2004) *An International Comparison of LTC Arrangements. An Investigation into the Equity, Efficiency and Sustainability of Long-Term Care Systems in Germany, Japan, Sweden, the United Kingdom and the United States,* Actuarial Research Paper No. 156, Cass Business School.

Korpi, W. and Palme, J. (1998) 'The paradox of redistribution and strategies of equality: welfare state institutions, inequality, and poverty in the western countries', *American Sociological Review,* 63, pp. 661–687.

Mayhew, L., Karlsson, M. and Rickayzen, B.D. (2010) 'The role of private finance in paying for long term care', *Economic Journal,* 120 (534), pp. F478–F504.

Ministry of the Interior and Health and Ministry of Social Affairs (2005) *Report on Health and Long-term Care in Denmark* (Copenhagen: Ministry of the Interior and Health and Ministry of Social Affairs).

Nordic Social-Statistical Committee (2009) *Social Protection in the Nordic Countries. Scope, Expenditure and Financing 2007/2008* (Copenhagen: Nordic Social-Statistical Committee).

OECD (Organization for Economic Cooperation and Development) (2004) *Towards High-Performing Health Systems,* OECD health project (Paris: OECD).

OECD (2009) *Taxing Wages* (Paris: OECD).

Platz, M. and Brodhurs, S. (2001) 'Denmark', in T. Blackman (ed.) *Social Care and Social Exclusion. A Comparative Study of Older People's Care in Europe* (Basingstoke: Palgrave Macmillan), chapter 3.

Rothstein, B. (1998) *Just Institutions Matter* (Cambridge: Cambridge University Press).

SALAR (2009a) *Developments in Elderly Policies in Sweden* (Stockholm: SALAR).

SALAR (2009b) *Ekonomirapporten. Om kommunernas och landstingens ekonomi – oktober 2009* (Stockholm: SALAR).

Sand, A.-B. (2010) *Anhöriga som kombinerar förvärvsarbete och anhörigomsorg,* Kunskapsöversikt 2010:1, Nationellt Kompetenscentrum Anhöriga.

SCB (2010) *Kommunalskatterna 2010,* Statistiskt Meddelande SM1001 (Stockholm: Statistics Sweden).

Schulz, E. (2010) *The Long-term Care System in Denmark,* Working Paper, DIW Berlin.

Sellers, J.M. and Lidström, A. (2007) 'Decentralization, local government, and the welfare state', *Governance: An International Journal of Policy, Administration and Institutions,* 20 (4), pp. 609–632.

Socialstyrelsen (2001) *Nationell handlingsplan för äldrepolitiken. Lägesrapport 2001* (Stockholm: Socialstyrelsen).

Socialstyrelsen (2002a) *Socialtjänstlagen – Vad gäller för dig från 1 januari 2002?* (Stockholm: Socialstyrelsen).

Socialstyrelsen (2002b) *Nationell handlingsplan för äldrepolitiken. Lägesrapport 2002* (Stockholm: Socialstyrelsen).

Socialstyrelsen (2007) Uppdrag att följa upp och utvärdera socialtjänstlagens bestämmelser om avgifter inom äldre- och handikappomsorgen.

Socialstyrelsen (2008a) *Äldre – vård och omsorg 2007* (Stockholm: Socialstyrelsen).

Socialstyrelsen (2008b) *Vård och omsorg om äldre. Lägesrapport 2007.*

Socialstyrelsen (2009) Jämförelsetal för socialtjänsten år 2008.

Söderström, L., Andersson, F., Edebalk, P.G. and Kruse, A. (2001) *Privatiseringens gränser. Perspektiv på välfärdspolitiken* (Stockholm: SNS Förlag).

Søgaard, J. (2009) *International Reliability of SHA Total Expenditure on Health,* Working Paper, Danish Institute for Health Services Research.

Sørensen, P.B. (2009) *Dual Income Taxes: A Nordic Tax System* (Mimeo: University of Copenhagen).

SOU 2008:37, *Vårdval i Sverige* (Stockholm: SOU).

Statskontoret (2008) *Det kommunala utjämningssystemet – en förstudie* (Stockholm: Statskontoret).

Statskontoret (2009) *Kommunal utjämning i Danmark, Norge och Finland* (Stockholm: Statskontoret).

St.meld. nr. 25 (2005–2006) *Mestring, muligheter og mening. Framtidas omsorgsutfordringer* (Oslo: Det kongelige Helse- og omsorgsdepartement).

St.meld. nr. 9 (2008–2009) *Perspektivmeldingen 2009* (Oslo: Finansdepartementet).

Sundström G., Johansson, L. and Hassing L.B. (2002) 'The shifting balance of long-term care in Sweden', *Gerontologist,* June, 42 (3), pp. 350–355.

Swedish Ministry of Health and Social Affairs (1999) *Utvecklingen inom den kommunala sektorn* (Stockholm: Skr 1998:99:97).

Titmuss, R.A. (1974) *Social Policy* (London: Allen and Unwin).

Wiener, J.M., Illston, L.H. and Hanley, R.H. (1994) *Sharing the Burden: Strategies for Public and Private Long-term Insurance* (Washington, DC: The Brookings Institution).

Wittenberg, R. and Malley, J. (2007) 'Financing long-term care for older people in England', *Ageing Horizons,* 6, pp. 28–32.

15
Long-Term Care Financing in Switzerland

France Weaver
University of Geneva, Switzerland

Switzerland is a federal State with three levels of government: federal, 26 cantons and about 2600 municipalities. It counts nearly 8 million inhabitants (Table 15.1). In 1996, health insurance was made compulsory for all residents. The goal of this social health insurance is to enable universal coverage while providing freedom of choice in regard to insurance company and, to some extent, health care providers. The basket of covered services is determined at the federal level and cantons are in charge of ensuring a sufficient supply of health care services, including long-term care (LTC). The scope of services covered by social health insurance is large for acute and post-acute care, while it is partial for LTC.

LTC financing has two main features. First, it is decentralized into the 26 cantons, and in some cantons, it is the responsibility of the municipalities. Such decentralization results in variation in LTC use and financing structure across cantons and municipalities. Second, the share of private funding – that is, private household spending – is one of the largest among Organization for Economic Cooperation and Development (OECD) countries (OECD, 2010).

LTC represents one of the greatest financial risks faced by the elderly population, and in Switzerland, this risk is partially covered by social insurance and public payers. The three main payers for LTC services are: (1) the compulsory social health insurance through community-rated premiums paid by all residents, (2) private households through out-of-pocket expenditures, deductibles and co-payments and (3) the Confederation, cantons and municipalities through direct subsidies to providers, supplemental income to low-income individuals and allowance for impairment to individuals with limitations.

In 2008, LTC spending amounted to 1.7 per cent of the Swiss GDP; this proportion has been stable since 2002 and is in the middle of the distribution of European countries. It is lower than in some Northern European countries, such as Sweden, Finland, the Netherlands or Denmark, but it is

Table 15.1   Population, GDP and LTC spending
in Switzerland, 2008

Population	
Total	7,701,856
Proportion of 65+	16.6%
Proportion of 80+	4.7%
GDP	
Total (CHF billion)	542
GDP per capita (CHF)	70,300
Long-term care spending	
Total (CHF billion)	8.9
Proportion of GDP	1.7%

higher than in France, Austria or Germany (EU, 2006; OECD, 2006). House-hold spending on LTC amounted to 0.7 per cent, social health insurance 0.4 per cent and public subsidies 0.6 per cent of GDP. Thus, the combined share of social health insurance and public subsidies represents about 1 per cent of the Swiss GDP.

As in other countries, the ageing of the baby-boom generations raises concerns about the future funding of health care services in general, and LTC in particular. It is forecast that by 2030, LTC spending could represent between 2.5 and 3.0 per cent of GDP, mainly because of the increase in the number of LTC users (Weaver et al., 2008). The dependency ratio – that is, the proportion of individuals aged 65+ relative to those aged 15 to 64 – grew from 22.3 in 1997 to 24.3 in 2008. By 2030, it is forecast to reach 38.8, which is comparable to that observed in the EU15 (EU, 2006). In that context, the long-term financial sustainability of the Swiss LTC system is in question. In 2011, a new LTC financing scheme will be implemented. As a result, the repartition of spending between the three main payers is expected to evolve.

The aims of this chapter are to briefly describe the LTC system in Switzerland and to present its financing structure. Most results are provided for the entire country, with some being reported per canton to observe regional variations. Nursing home and formal in-home care are considered. The data sources are presented in Appendix A.1.

1   LTC use in Switzerland

Home care and nursing home care use are the two most prevalent types of formal LTC services in Switzerland. In 2008, the likelihood of home care use over a 12-month period was about 12 per cent among individuals aged 65 and over (Table 15.2). At age 80+, this proportion reached 27 per cent. From 1997 to 2008, home care spending expanded from CHF 0.8 to 1.4 billion, yet

Table 15.2 Home care and nursing home care use in Switzerland, 1997 and 2008

	Home care		Nursing home[a]	
	1997	2008	1997	2008
Costs[b]				
Total spending (CHF billion)	0.8	1.3	4.8	7.6
Share of total LTC spending	14.3%	14.5%	85.7%	85.5%
Share of GDP	0.2%	0.2%	1.2%	1.5%
Costs per hour (CHF)	72.3	100.7	n.a.	n.a.
Costs per day (CHF)	n.a	n.a.	234.0	246.0
Patients				
Number of patients	196,500	210,800	74,000[c]	134,400[d]
Share of patients aged 80+	42.3%	46.5%	75.0%[c]	75.6%
Share of patients using covered services[e]	48.2%	53.0%	n.a.	n.a.
Share of patients using non-covered services[e]	43.3%	36.4%	n.a.	n.a.
Likelihood of use over 12 months				
At 65+	13.3%	12.%	6.8%[f]	10.0%
At 80+	29.6%	27.0%	20.2%[f]	28.1%

Notes:
n.a. = not applicable.
a. The nursing home survey was revised in 2006; caution is needed when comparing 1997 and 2008 figures.
b. At constant 2005 prices.
c. Extrapolated from 1999 data.
d. Nursing homes and old-age houses.
e. The share of patients does not total 100 per cent because some patients rely on both covered and non-covered services, and other services are also provided by home health agencies, for example, meals.
f. 1999 figures.
Source: Spitex and Somed data (FSO, 2009a, b).

its shares of total health care expenditures and GDP have remained stable. Costs per hour of care have increased from about CHF 72 to CHF 101. An increasing proportion of patients rely on services covered by social health insurance and a diminishing proportion benefits from non-covered services, such as help with instrumental activities of daily living (IADL) limitations.

The likelihood of nursing home use over 12 months for individuals aged 65+ is one of the highest among OECD countries, at 10 per cent (OECD, 2005). In 2008, the institutionalization rate was 28 per cent for persons aged 80+ (Table 15.2). This age group represented 75.6 per cent of all nursing home residents. From 1997 to 2008, the costs per day increased slightly to reach CHF 246 (including board and food costs). The expansion in total nursing home costs is mainly driven by the increase in the number of residents.

There are large variations in home care and nursing home care use across cantons (Andreani, 2008; FSO, 2009a, b). The types of resident differ across regions. Nursing homes in the French- and Italian-speaking parts have heavier cases than nursing homes in the German-speaking part. Overall, regional differences in LTC use may be explained partly by differences in the age distribution and health status of the population, the cantonal LTC policy – that is, strategies in terms of supply of LTC services and subsidies to providers and patients – and the cultural and political differences impacting preferences of local populations.

In Switzerland, some LTC is still provided in acute care hospitals, mainly while patients are waiting for an alternative care arrangement, such as a nursing home bed. Non-acute care psychiatric and geriatric hospitals also provide some institutionalized LTC (Bayer-Oglesby, 2009). Intermediate care facilities, such as assisted living facilities or day care centres, are becoming more prevalent, but their number remains limited. No national data are currently available for these last two forms of LTC services. For illustration, some information on assisted living and day care facilities is provided for the canton of Geneva (see Table 15.5).

Additionally, non-governmental organizations (NGOs) play a role in the provision of LTC services. They are, for example, the Swiss Red Cross, Pro Senectute or the Alzheimer Association. They mainly provide help with IADL limitations, meals at home, temporary financial support, auxiliary equipment and social activities. These NGOs receive public subsidies and private contributions.

2   LTC spending in Switzerland

In 2008, LTC spending amounted to CHF 8.9 billion, which represented about 16 per cent of total health care spending and 1.7 per cent of the Swiss GDP. Since 1997, LTC spending has increased by more than 50 per cent, which is a faster expansion than for total health care spending (+42.3 per cent) or the Swiss GDP (+26.7 per cent).

As in most Western countries, nursing homes account for the largest proportion of LTC spending (Figure 15.1). However, this proportion is one of the largest with 85.5 per cent – versus 14.5 per cent for home care. By comparison, in Norway, Germany and the Netherlands, less than two-thirds of LTC expenditures are devoted to nursing home care and more than one-third to home care (OECD, 2005).

Over recent years, policy makers have argued that ambulatory care should be favoured over stationary care because the former is often less costly than institutionalized care. In terms of spending, there is no empirical evidence of a shift towards home care. For example, since 1997, the annual growth rates in home care spending have been fairly similar to those in nursing home spending (Figure 15.2).

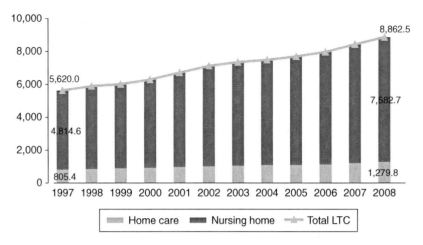

Figure 15.1 Home care and nursing home spending in Switzerland, 1997–2008 (in CHF million)
Source: FSO (2009a, b). At constant 2005 prices.

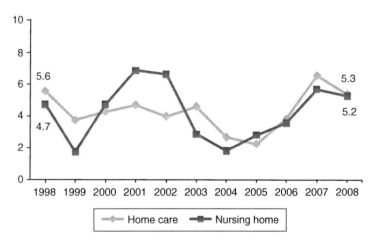

Figure 15.2 Annual growth in home care and nursing home spending (%) in Switzerland, since 1998
Source: FSO (2009a, b). At constant 2005 prices.

3 LTC financing structure in Switzerland

Like most OECD countries, Switzerland has a mixed financing of formal LTC services that combines public and private funding. The three major payers are compulsory social health insurance, private households and the different levels of government (Figure 15.3). Some other payers play a minor role

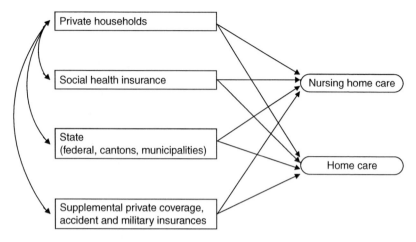

Figure 15.3   Overview of LTC financing in Switzerland

by comparison, that is, supplemental private coverage, compulsory accident insurance or military insurance.

The left side of Figure 15.3 shows the link between private households and the other payers. Private households pay premiums for social health insurance and other insurances, and they also pay taxes to the three levels of government. In addition, they pay for deductibles and co-payments. Inversely, households are reimbursed by social health insurance or other insurance if they have personally paid for LTC services. They may also receive direct subsidies from the State. The right side of Figure 15.3 shows that all groups of payers contribute both to nursing home and home care financing.

In Switzerland, there is limited financial support to informal caregivers. At the federal level, time devoted to caregiving of a relative can be taken into account in the determination of retirement and survivor benefits. The caregiver and care recipient have to co-reside and the care recipient has to suffer from moderate to severe impairment. In some circumstances, the retirement benefits and allowance for impairment (Section 3.3) can be paid directly to the co-residing informal caregiver. Respite care is available to some extent through the availability of short-stay nursing home beds and temporary help provided by NGOs.

3.1   Social health insurance

Since 1996, health insurance coverage has been compulsory for all residents. This insurance is individually contracted and is not employer-based. There are over 100 companies offering the same compulsory health insurance coverage. Premiums vary across insurers, regions (smaller than cantons), three age groups (0–18, 19–25, 26+) and types of coverage – for example, level of deductible, gatekeeping and health maintenance organizations (HMOs). In principle, premiums are independent of income, wealth or health status. Low-income individuals benefit from subsidies provided by cantons to pay for these premiums. Nearly 30 per cent of the population benefits from such premium reductions (Balthasar et al., 2008). Premiums have continuously increased over time. In 2008, the average premium amounted to CHF 315 per month for adults aged 26 and over. By canton, it ranged from CHF 219 in Nidwalden to CHF 419 in Geneva (FOPH, 2010).

Health services covered by social health insurance are defined at the federal level. Covered LTC services have to be prescribed by a doctor and include three categories of service (Article 7a, federal application law on health insurance services):

1. Evaluation of care needs and advice to patients and their relatives.
2. Medical care, such as diagnoses and treatments.
3. Basic care, mainly help with activities of daily living (ADL).

To synthesize, covered services can be viewed as 'medically related' care because they include medical care *per se* and support in ADL limitations that are due to health deterioration. ADLs are defined as activities required on an everyday basis: eating, dressing, transferring, taking a bath or shower and using the toilet.

When a person is considered permanently dependent, there is no time limit on the coverage of these services. According to federal law, such services can be provided in any setting – for example, at home or in nursing homes. However, other financial tools, such as supplemental benefits that differ by living arrangement, may impact the actual care setting (Section 3.3).

Until 2010, reimbursement rates were usually negotiated by the central association regrouping social health insurance companies and the cantonal home care or nursing home care providers, with the approbation of cantonal authorities. Tools used to define levels of care, and thus reimbursement rates, differ across cantons. For example, in four French-speaking cantons – Geneva, Vaud, Neuchâtel and Jura – nursing home care is measured by the instrument PLAISIR that is based on required minutes of care. Evaluation tools used in other cantons are based on effective minutes of care or on assessment-related grouping – that is, BESA and RAI/RUG.

As social health insurance is financed by individual premiums, some consider this payer as private. Others view premiums as a non-means-based tax and thus look at social health insurance as a public payer.

3.2 Private households

Two main types of LTC services are not reimbursed by social health insurance: food and board in nursing homes and 'non-medically related' home care, mainly support with IADL provided at home. IADL include the daily tasks that enable the patient to live independently, such as doing house-work, preparing meals, taking medications, shopping, using the phone and managing money.

In 2008, food and board represented more than 50 per cent of total nursing home costs and 'non-medically related' care amounted to 14 per cent of home care costs. These non-covered services are paid out-of-pocket by households, or are partly or totally subsidized for low-income individuals (Section 3.3). As for most types of care, individuals receiving covered LTC services face the deductible that they have selected – ranging from CHF 300 to 2500 per year – and a co-payment of 10 per cent, up to CHF 700 per year. The deductible level can be selected every year. Thus, actual or anticipated medical bills may lead insured individuals to modify their deductible choice over time and face variable out-of-pocket spending.

3.3   Public financing

Due to its federal structure, the Confederation defines the general principles relating to health policy and cantons are responsible for sufficient supply. Thus, LTC regulation and financing are decentralized into the 26 cantons.

Cantons have diverse LTC policies, resulting in a large variation in public spending (Table 15.3). For example, in some cantons, LTC policy is the canton's responsibility and in others it is the municipalities' responsibility. Cantons and municipalities can influence their spending through two main tools: the planning of supply and subsidies. Increasingly, contracts of services are established with home care agencies and nursing homes. These contracts allow the monitoring and rationing of supply and they also define the financial contributions of cantons and municipalities to LTC providers. For example, over the last decade, many cantons have had moratoriums on

Table 15.3   Overview of subsidies to finance LTC services in Switzerland

Government level	Subsidies to providers	Subsidies to individuals/patients	
		Direct subsidies	Indirect subsidies
Confederation*	To 2007, to home care agencies	Allowance for impairment	
		Supplemental benefits for low income	
Cantons and/or municipalities	Predetermined contributions Deficit coverage	Large diversity of subsidies	Means-tested rates for LTC services

Note: *Subsidies defined nationally, but partly financed by cantons.

nursing home beds. Due to demographic pressures and increasing waiting lists, these moratoriums are increasingly being suppressed.

Until 2007, a direct federal subsidy had been distributed to home care agencies through the federal retirement and survivor insurance. In 2008, it was suppressed because of a new financial equalization between the Confederation and the cantons. In the cantons, official lists of home care and nursing home care providers indicate which providers receive subsidies. Non-recognized providers can enter the LTC market, but usually they are not subsidized. Public subsidies to providers can be a predetermined financial contribution and/or the coverage of deficit.

Besides subsidies to providers, there are also direct and indirect subsidies to impaired individuals and LTC users. Two of the direct subsidies are defined at the federal level and are financed through the retirement and survivor insurance. The first of these is an 'allowance for impairment' for persons with moderate or severe disabilities. This allowance is not means-tested, as eligibility does not depend on income, demographic characteristics or cause of dependency. In 2010, the monthly allowance reached CHF 570 for moderate impairment and CHF 912 for severe impairment. It is provided independently of whether the person receives formal LTC. The second direct federal subsidy is the 'supplemental benefits' for low-income retired or disabled individuals. Such supplemental benefits are means-tested; they are provided when income from pensions and other sources does not cover basic living costs. They are not conditional on the use of health-care services, but LTC services that are not covered by social health insurance are taken into account in the estimation of these supplemental benefits. As a result, supplemental benefits contribute to the financing of nursing home care and they vary largely by individual.

Both types of direct federal subsidy have to be requested by individuals in need. As a consequence, some vulnerable individuals do not receive these benefits despite the fact they are eligible. Yet, some LTC providers encourage their patients to request these benefits as they contribute to paying for costs faced by home care beneficiaries and nursing home residents.

Numerous other types of direct subsidy are provided by cantons and municipalities. For example, the canton of Geneva provides additional cantonal 'supplemental benefits' and directly pays for some LTC services when other private and public contributions are not sufficient to cover a person's expenditures. A 'dignity lump sum' of CHF 300 per month is also available to nursing home residents. This amount is available for discretionary spending. The canton of Fribourg provides a lump-sum to impaired individuals residing at home (CHF 25 daily in 2008) and who receive formal or informal care (Bayer-Oglesby, 2009). These types of cantonal subsidies come in addition to federal contributions.

Beside direct subsidies, there is also indirect subsidizing of LTC patients. Prices of non-covered LTC services, such as help with IADL limitations, may depend on the patient's income, wealth or types of subsidies received. For example, rates may differ depending on whether the patient does or does not receive supplemental income.

As subsidies are financial incentives that influence both patients and providers, they are likely to impact the demand and supply of LTC services. The complexity of the financing scheme makes it challenging to disentangle the effects of specific subsidies or other public interventions on the LTC market.

3.4   Other payers

Besides social health insurance, two other social insurances cover LTC services: the compulsory accident insurance and military insurance. Compulsory accident insurance is financed by employers. It covers accident and illness related to work. Employees may also subscribe to optional non-professional accidents coverage. Military insurance covers professional and non-professional soldiers, social protection volunteers, Swiss Humanitarian Aid Unit employees and peace-workers of the Confederation. Both types of insurance provide more comprehensive coverage of LTC services than social health insurance. In principle, they cover all services, including help with IADL limitations, and coverage is comprehensive without co-payment or deductible.

Currently in Switzerland, there is no private market for LTC insurance devoted solely to cover the risk of dependency-related care. Some supplemental private plans provide daily lump-sums in the case of home care use or nursing home stays. However, such private LTC coverage is provided in plans that include more comprehensive coverage of acute care than social health insurance. The lump-sums do not fully cover LTC costs and are limited in regard to time. Other private plans partially insure disability by providing a small daily allowance in the case of impairment. Such daily coverage or allowance varies according to the level of coverage selected by the insured. No data are currently available on the number of beneficiaries and spending of these plans on LTC.

3.5   Main principles underlying LTC financing in Switzerland

Besides federalism, the financing of LTC services is based on three main principles: intergenerational transfers, means-based redistribution and private responsibility. At any point in time, the overall population contributes to the social health insurance through premiums and taxes, used to finance LTC services provided mainly by the elderly individuals. From a static perspective, solidarity between the healthy and unhealthy is a form of intergenerational transfer. In a dynamic perspective, the increases in health insurance premiums and taxes over the last 15 years have also generated intergenerational transfers: current LTC beneficiaries have paid lower actualized lifelong premiums and taxes than younger cohorts. In upcoming decades, the ageing of the baby-boom generations may increase such intergenerational transfers as the share of working-age individuals diminishes.

Means-based redistribution may be achieved through two mechanisms. First, public spending on LTC services is partly financed through progressive taxes – that is, some taxation rates increase with income and wealth. As a result, richer individuals contribute more to taxes used to finance LTC services than the poorer. However, the actual redistribution depends on the repartition of LTC use according to socio-economic status. If the richer use LTC services more than the poorer ones, there is no redistributive effect of non-means-based subsidies – allowance for impairment and subsidies to providers. The second redistributive mechanism is direct subsidies to low-income individuals, such as the federal supplemental benefits. Statically, this subsidy has a direct redistributive effect because it is based on income and wealth. Dynamically, it may not be the case if individuals spend-down their assets to become eligible.

In Switzerland, LTC remains largely a family responsibility. The provision of formal LTC is often viewed either as a complement to informal care as long as the dependency level remains moderate or as a substitute once the dependency becomes severe and requires institutionalization. Yet, no study has determined the actual causal relationship between informal care and formal LTC use in Switzerland.

On the formal LTC market, the main goal of private responsibility is to limit the risk of moral hazard – that is, covered and subsidized services may be overused because insured individuals are not faced with the actual price of such services. In the Swiss LTC system, reducing the risk of moral hazard is achieved by not covering some LTC services – that is, food and board in nursing homes, and 'non-medically related' home care – and by having deductibles and co-payments for services covered by social health insurance. The extent to which private responsibility limits the growth in LTC spending and impacts unmet needs with LTC are unknown.

4   LTC financing in 2008

The contributions of the three main payers of LTC services are different for home care and nursing home care services (Table 15.4). In 2008, social health insurance financed more than one-third of home care services, while it covered less than one-quarter of nursing home care spending. Private households directly financed a small share of home care services (about 6 per cent), but private contributions reached nearly 43 per cent of nursing home spending. This latter covers mainly meals and board. Public spending is estimated to cover more than half of home care costs and nearly one-third of nursing home costs. For home care, subsidies go mainly to providers, as they represented 47 per cent of home care spending. Direct subsidies to

Table 15.4   Repartition of LTC spending by payer in Switzerland, 2008

Payer	Home care		Nursing home care	
	CHF million	Percentage	CHF million	Percentage
Social health insurance	455	35.7	1808	23.8
Out-of-pocket	81	6.4	3106	41.0
Public subsidies	692	54.3	2395	31.6
*to individuals**	*92*	*7.2*	*1888*	*24.9*
to providers	*600*	*47.0*	*507*	*6.7*
Others	47	3.7	274	3.6
Total costs	**1275**	**100.0**	**7583**	**100.0**

Note: *Allowance for impairment, supplemental benefits in the case of nursing home stay, social assistance.

Source: FSO (2009a, b), Santésuisse (2010) and Retirement and survivor insurance (2010).

nursing homes are limited (nearly 7 per cent of spending). However, about one-quarter of nursing home spending is financed by subsidies to individuals, mainly through supplemental benefits to low-income individuals (CHF 1382 million) and allowance for impairment (CHF 334 million).

To summarize, social health insurance covers a larger share of home care services than nursing home care. Similarly, the share of public subsidies is larger for home care than nursing home care. As a consequence, private households bear a smaller proportion of home care spending than nursing home spending. However, a direct comparison of the financing structure of these two types of LTC services may be misleading because per-patient costs do not encompass the same array of services. Yearly per-patient costs are higher for nursing home than home care services, for two main reasons. First, institutionalized individuals usually have a higher level of dependency and require more intensive care and supervision than home care users (Jaccard-Ruedin et al., 2010). Second, nursing home spending includes food and board costs whereas home care does not. Thus, caution is necessary when comparing the financing structure of home care and nursing home care services.

Since 2001, the three main payers have faced an expansion in their LTC spending and their relative contributions have changed. The share of social health insurance has increased for both home care and nursing home care. For home care, it went from about 25 per cent in 2001 to nearly 36 per cent in 2008. For nursing home care, the progression has been slower as it went from about 19 to 24 per cent. Out-of-pocket spending has evolved differently for home care and nursing home care: it has remained stable for the former, but it has decreased for the latter (from 47 per cent to 41 per cent). Finally, the share of public spending on home care services has decreased over time from 62 per cent to 54 per cent, while it has remained stable for nursing home care at about one-third. These trends may have partly motivated the revision in LTC funding that will be implemented in 2011 (Section 5).

LTC spending and subsidies to providers in the canton of Geneva are presented as an illustrative case. It is one of the cantons that subsidize the most LTC services and information is also available for assisted living facilities and day care centres (Table 15.5). In 2008, subsidies to the home health care agency (CHF 112 million) were larger than to nursing homes (CHF 94 million). These subsidies are largely provided by the canton and to a lesser extent by the municipalities and some federal entities. In relative terms, subsidies to providers are the largest for ambulatory care – that is, home care and day care centres – than for residential care – that is, nursing homes and assisted living facilities. Overall, subsidies to providers supply one-third of total spending on the four types of LTC services (Canton of Geneva Office of Statistics, 2010a, b).

The relative contributions of the three main payers to home care and nursing home care services vary largely across cantons. In Figures 15.4 and 15.5, the grouping by payer differs from the grouping in Table 15.4: the figures show that, the contribution of private households includes both out-of-pocket expenditures and direct subsidies to individuals. As a result, only subsidies to providers appear as a distinct category. Cantons are ranked from the smallest to the largest in regard to relative public spending to providers.

In relative terms, cantons contribute more to home care than nursing home care spending. However, in absolute amounts, the reverse is true as subsidies to nursing home are often larger than subsidies to home health agencies, putting a heavier burden on the public budget. There is a clear linguistic divide, as Latin cantons have larger subsidies to providers than German-speaking cantons. Subsidies to home care providers are above 45 per cent in all Latin cantons (Neuchatel NE, Jura JU, Fribourg FR, Vaud VD, Valais VS, Ticino TI and Geneva GE), and only a handful of German-speaking

Table 15.5 LTC spending in the canton of Geneva, 2008

	Total spending (CHF million)	Subsidies to providers	
		CHF million	Percentage of total spending
Nursing home	446.8	93.6	21.0
Home care	166.6	112.4	67.4
Assisted living[a*]	11.8	1.4	12.1
Day care centres	6.2	4.7	76.3
Total	**631.4**	**212.1**	**33.6**

Note: *Including rents of CHF 10.8 million.
Source: Canton of Geneva, Office of Statistics (2010a, b).

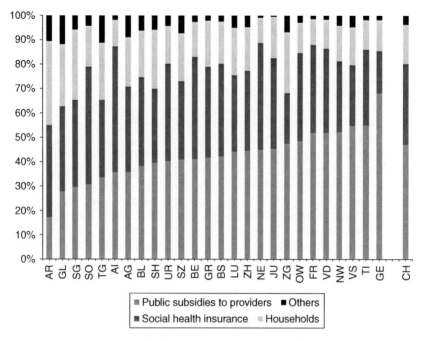

Figure 15.4   Relative contribution of main payers to home care spending by canton, 2008

Source: FSO (2010), Santésuisse (2010) and Retirement and survivor insurance (2010). Abbreviations explained in Appendix A.2.

cantons have such high subsidies (Zug ZG, Obwald OW and Nidwald NW). Subsidies to nursing homes also tend to be proportionally higher in the Latin cantons.

For both types of LTC, the cantons with the smallest relative subsidies are those with the largest relative contributions to social health insurance and, to a lesser extent, private households. Such findings may partially be explained by the type of home care services used by the population and the LTC policy chosen by each canton. In some cantons, patients rely relatively more on services covered by social health insurance – that is, medical care and help with ADL limitations – than in other cantons. Additionally, some cantons favour private responsibility and have limited their contributions in the LTC market.

Beside different financing structures in the Latin and German parts of Switzerland, there are numerous other differences in the LTC markets across regions, for example, in the types of providers, education level of employees, types of patients and intensity of care.

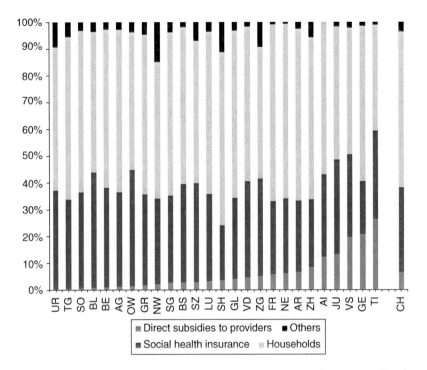

Figure 15.5 Relative contribution of main payers to nursing home spending by canton, 2008
Source: FSO (2010), Santésuisse (2010) and Retirement and survivor insurance (2010). Abbreviations explained in Appendix A.2.

5 Revised LTC financing structure

In January 2011, a new LTC financing scheme will be implemented. It provides a new repartition of the costs among payers for LTC services and it creates a new category of care – that is, transitory post-acute care – that is distinct from LTC. As these lines are being written, numerous aspects of these changes have not yet been finalized. Thus, only the main characteristics of the revision are presented below.

The new 'transitory care' includes medical care prescribed by a 'hospital-based physician of an acute care department' for a maximum duration of two weeks after discharge from a hospital. The goal of such care is to regain the autonomy that the patient had prior to hospitalization. It has to be provided in the home of the patient, which is either in her or his own apartment or in a nursing home for institutionalized individuals. Thus, it can be provided by a nursing home, home health care agencies or independent health professionals, such as nurses. The financing scheme is the same as for acute care: up to 45 per cent of the costs are charged to social health insurance, via a capitation payment scheme, and at least 55 per cent are charged to cantons. Transitory care cannot be cumulated with LTC and one challenge will be to distinguish between the two types of care. This new type of 'transitory care' is introduced to partly compensate for the reduction in length of stay, which is anticipated because of the 2012 introduction of a prospective payment system in all Swiss hospitals – that is, Swiss DRG.

For LTC services, the overall funding structure remains unchanged (Figure 15.3) but the relative contribution of each payer is expected to evolve. LTC services covered by social health insurance remain globally the same – that is, medical care and support with ADL limitations. The four goals of this revision are (1) to limit the future rise in social health insurance spending, (2) to introduce national rates for services covered by social health insurance, (3) to introduce a new contribution of private households with a uniform definition at the national level and (4) to define explicitly the financial role of cantons.

As before, LTC services covered by social health insurance are identified by federal law. The payment rates of social health insurance are now defined at the federal level. For home care, one rate per type of service has been determined: CHF 54.6 per hour of basic care and help with ADL limitations, CHF 65.4 for medical care and treatments and CHF 79.8 for evaluation of care needs and advice (Article 7a, federal application law on health insurance services). National nursing home rates depend on the required minutes of care, grouped into 20-minute categories. The minimum rate, up to 20 minutes of care, is CHF 9 and the maximum rate reaches CHF 108, for over 220 minutes of care. It is anticipated that these rates will not be automatically adapted to the costs evolution. As before, these reimbursement rates do not cover the actual home care and nursing home care costs.

A new *private contribution* is added to the existing deductibles and co-payments. This contribution is capped at 20 per cent of the maximum charges covered by social health insurance. For home care, as the maximum charge is CHF 79.8 per hour of care, the new out-of-pocket contribution is CHF 15.90. For nursing homes, the maximum daily reimbursement rate is CHF 108. Therefore, this out-of-pocket contribution is capped at CHF 21.60 per nursing home day or CHF 7884 per year. Cantons can decide not to enforce this 20 per cent out-of-pocket contribution for all patients or for some specific groups; this private contribution may therefore have lower caps in some cantons. As before, non-covered services are charged to private households. To partially compensate for the likely increase in out-of-pocket spending, supplemental benefits for low-income individuals and allowance for impairment will be expanded.

The cantons are in charge of the *residual costs*, defined as the difference between the costs of care and payments by social health insurance and private households. This residual financing is left to the cantons, which have to adapt their laws and define the costs of home care services and nursing home care by negotiating with providers (Article 25a, al. 1 federal law on health insurance). Some cantons will cover all the residual costs, others will delegate it to their municipalities and others will have a mix of both. The Swiss Association of Canton Health Ministers (GDK-CDS) anticipates an increase in canton and municipality subsidies of about CHF 350 million.

This revised scheme explicitly determines the additional maximum financial contribution of private households and makes clearer the contribution of cantons to the financing of LTC services, especially for cantons that have had limited involvement. It is anticipated that there will be a transfer of some LTC spending from social health insurance to cantons, particularly in cantons with limited public spending to date. It is hoped that the financing structure of LTC services will become more transparent and may converge across cantons over time.

As mentioned above, one challenge is the distinction between transitory care and LTC. The federal law has only broadly defined what the transitory care covers and the payment schemes differ: the former being a capitation system and the latter is a mix of capitation and fee-for-service. It may result in strategic behaviours from care recipients and providers. Additionally, the new private contribution implies that the most dependent individuals will face the largest out-of-pocket payments. If these individuals have limited financial resources, cantons will have to step in to provide subsidies. Finally, for nursing home care, there is a risk of underfunding for patients requiring intense care and supervision, because the social health insurance cap per day is set at CHF 108 for 220 minutes of care. This risk should be taken into account by cantons when determining the subsidized residual costs, and close attention needs to be paid to quality of care to ensure that care needs are met.

6 Discussion

Long-term financing is complex in most countries, and Switzerland is no exception. This complexity is due in part to federalism and to the mix of public and private payers. In Switzerland, out-of-pocket spending is among the largest of the OECD countries because private responsibility remains a core characteristic of social policy. The effect of the financing revision implemented in 2011 is difficult to anticipate. On the one hand, out-of-pocket expenditures may increase because a new private contribution is created. On the other hand, direct subsidies to individuals may increase if the share of individuals who are unable to cover their LTC spending augments.

In Switzerland, market mechanisms are limited because LTC services are regulated and cantons determine supply. Cantons ration the supply of LTC services to limit the rise in costs and the burden on public budgets. Waiting times are perceived as being long for nursing home care and also exist for in-home care services. However, the extent of such access constraints has not received much attention to date. The revised LTC financing scheme seems to emphasize regulation and direct subsidies to providers. Due to the lack of competition, providers may have limited incentives to improve quality and efficiency. As a result, cantons and municipalities must closely monitor the quality of care.

Two areas of LTC have been neglected to date in Switzerland: continuum of care and financial support to informal caregivers. The fragmented provision of LTC may reduce accessibility and lead to unmet needs for LTC. To address this issue, some cantons are starting to introduce the concepts of continuum of care and care management. The objectives are to coordinate the financing and delivery of acute and LTC services, to manage transfers between services and settings (home, hospital, nursing home), to make more efficient use of resources and to meet the patient's care and social needs.

As in other OECD countries, informal care remains one of the main forms of LTC. In 2007, it was estimated that nearly 12 per cent of the population aged 65 and over relied on informal care from family members, friends or neighbours (FSO, 2007). There is currently limited financial support to caregivers in Switzerland. As informal care plays an important role and the population prefers home care to institutionalized care, there is a clear need to develop financial and structural supports for informal caregivers. Supports emerge slowly in some cantons, such as counselling, respite care covered by social health insurance, financial subsidies, tax credits or work leaves.

Current and forecasted demographic changes, such as the increase in the proportion of childless individuals and one-person households, are likely to reduce the availability of family support. Such demographic pressure is anticipated to impact the use of formal home care and nursing home and the financing of these services. For example, the rise in the dependency ratio may undermine the principle of intergenerational solidarity.

In the upcoming decades, LTC policy will face substantial challenges to ensure that sufficient, equitable and sustainable care is provided to the ageing population. The LTC financing principles, presented in Section 3.5, may have to be rethought beyond what is included in the 2011 revision (Section 5). In addition, in Switzerland, more transparency is needed to observe the flows of public and private funding and to be able to determine the appropriate financial incentives to meet the care needs of the population at affordable costs for society.

Acknowledgements

Special thanks go to Blaise C. Martin (Deputy Chief Medical Officer, General Head Office of Health at Canton of Geneva). His expertise in LTC policy has noticeably contributed to this chapter. I also thank Peter Mosimann (the Geneva Foundation for Home Care Services) for insights on the 2011 revision, Anthony Francis and Nadia Borloz (Swiss Federal Statistical Office) for data and support, Hélène Jaccard-Ruedin (Swiss Health Observatory) and the editors of this book for comments.

Appendix

A.1 Data sources

Data on home care and nursing home care services come from two registries collected every year by the Swiss Federal Statistical Office (FSO): the *Statistics on In-Home Help and Care Services (Spitex)* and the *Statistics on social and medical institutions (Somed)*. The home care registry includes most public and private non-profit home care agencies, which include the vast majority of home care providers. Private for-profit organizations and non-governmental agencies that also provide home care services are not included in this data set. The nursing home registry is more comprehensive as it includes 98 per cent of all nursing homes (FSO, 2009a, b). Both data sources have been available since 1997; the latter was largely revised in 2006.

Two main kinds of financial contributions are not directly identifiable in these two data sets: out-of-pocket spending of private households for services covered by social health insurance – that is, deductibles and co-payments – and public subsidies to patients. As a result, data on home care and nursing home care providers are combined with data from social health insurance (Santésuisse, 2010) and federal retirement and survivor insurance (2010).

Data on supplemental benefits are available separately for nursing home residents and individuals living at home. All supplemental benefits for nursing home residents are taken into account in the estimation of direct subsidies to individuals. Supplemental benefits for persons living independently are not taken into account, as it is not possible to determine whether these persons rely on such supplemental income to finance home care services.

The allowance for impairment is allocated to individuals who need help to perform ADLs. This allowance depends on the level of impairment but not on the living arrangement. No information is available on the amounts paid to individuals residing at home or in nursing homes. Following recommendations from the Federal Office of Public Health that have been used in other studies (Weaver et al., 2008), 80 per cent of total allowances are allocated to nursing home residents and 20 per cent to home care beneficiaries.

A.2 Abbreviations of cantons by alphabetical order

AG	Aargau
AI	Appenzell Innerrhoden
AR	Appenzell Ausserrhoden
BE	Bern
BL	Basel-Landschaft
BS	Basel-Stadt
FR	Fribourg

GE	Genève
GL	Glarus
GR	Graubünden
JU	Jura
LU	Luzern
NE	Neuchâtel
NW	Nidwalden
OW	Obwalden
SG	St. Gallen
SH	Schaffhausen
SO	Solothurn
SZ	Schwyz
TG	Thurgau
TI	Ticino
UR	Uri
VD	Vaud
VS	Valais
ZG	Zug
ZH	Zürich

References

Andreani, T. (2008) *Indicateurs des institutions médico-sociales 2006. Résultats et analyses* (Neuchâtel: Federal Statistical Office).

Balthasar, A., Bieri, O. and Gysin, B. (2008) *Monitoring 2007. Die Sozialpolitische Wirksamkeit der Prämienverbilligung in den Kantonen*, Interface Politikstudien, BAG report (Luzern: Interface).

Bayer-Oglesby, L. (2009) *Bases statistiques pour la planification des soins de longue durée dans le canton de Fribourg à l'horizon 2010–2025*, sur mandat du Service de la prévoyance sociale du canton de Fribourg, Rapport final (Neuchâtel: Swiss Health Observatory).

Canton of Geneva, Office of Statistics (2010a) *Résultats statistiques: les établissements de santé à Genève. Données 2008*, http://www.ge.ch/statistique/statistiques/domaines/14/14_02_1/apercu.asp, accessed October 2010.

Canton of Geneva, Office of Statistics (2010b) *Résultats statistiques: Aide et soins à domicile, foyers de jour et immeubles avec encadrement social pour personnes âgées. Données 2008*, http://www.geneve.ch/statistique/statistiques/domaines/14/14_02_3/apercu.asp, accessed October 2010.

EC (European Commission) (2006) *The Impact of Ageing on Public Expenditures: Projections for the EU25 Member States on Pensions, Health Care, Long-term Care, Education and Unemployment Transfers (2004–2050)*, prepared by the Economic Policy Committee and the European Commission (DG-ECFIN), Special report 1 (Luxemburg: DG-ECFIN).

FOPH (Federal Office of Public Health) (2010) *Data Needed to Supervise the Compulsory Health Insurance 2008*, available in French or German, http://www.bag.admin.ch/themen/krankenversicherung/00261/05417/index.html?lang=fr, accessed October 2010.

FSO (Federal Statistical Office) (2007) *Swiss Health Survey 2007* (Neuchatel: FSO).

FSO (Federal Statistical Office) (2009a) *Statistique des institutions médico-sociales 2008 – Tableaux Standards* (Neuchâtel: FSO).

FSO (Federal Statistical Office) (2009b) *Statistique de l'aide et des soins à domicile (Spitex) 2007* (Neuchâtel: FSO).

Jaccard-Ruedin, H., Marti, M., Sommer, Heini, Bertschy, Kathrin and Leoni, Christian (2010) *Soins de longue durée – comparaison des coûts par cas dans le canton du Tessin,* Rapport 36 (Neuchâtel: Swiss Health Observatory).

OECD (2005) *Long-term Care for Older People* (Paris: OECD).

OECD (2006) *Projecting OECD Health and Long-term Care Expenditures: What are the Main Drivers?,* Economic Department Working Paper No. 477 (Paris: OECD).

OECD (2010) *OECD Health Data, Frequently Asked Data,* http://www.oecd.org/document/16/0,3343,en_2649_34631_2085200_1_1_1_1,00.html, accessed May 2010.

Retirement and survivor insurance (2010) *Statistique des prestations complémentaires à l'AVS et à l'AI – Tableaux détaillés* (Bern: Federal Office of Social Insurance).

Santésuisse (2010) *Base de données diagrammes: catégorie EMS /soins à domicile,* http://www.santesuisse.ch/fr/dyn_output_graphic.html? content.extdata[free1]= 18&short=0&detail=yes&navid=416, accessed May 2010.

Weaver, F., Jaccard Ruedin, H., Pellegrini, S. and Jeanrenaud, C. (2008) *Les coûts des soins de longue durée d'ici à 2030 en Suisse,* document de travail 34 (Neuchâtel: Swiss Health Observatory).

16

Long-Term Care Financing in Belgium

Peter Willemé and Joanna Geerts
Federal Planning Bureau, Belgium

and

Bea Cantillon and Ninke Mussche
Herman Deleeck Centre for Social Policy, University of Antwerp, Belgium

1 Overview of the system

Long-term care (LTC) in Belgium consists of a wide range of benefits in cash and in kind, organized at the federal, regional and municipal levels, and is related to health and social service provision.[1] The bulk of LTC services are provided as part of the federal public compulsory health insurance system, which is financed by social security contributions and general taxes. The main actors in the management of the system are the federal parliament (issuing the main laws governing the system), the Ministries of Health and Social Affairs, the National Institute for Health and Disability Insurance (NIHDI) and the sickness funds, which serve as intermediaries between the administration, the providers and the patients. Since public health insurance covers practically the whole population, LTC coverage is also nearly universal. However, since LTC services provided through the health insurance system cover only nursing care (as well as paramedical and rehabilitation care) and part of personal care to dependent persons, a whole range of services is organized and provided at the regional and local level. Indeed, while there is no specific LTC legislation at the federal level, the regional governments have issued decrees that regulate a wide range of issues related to LTC services: certification of facilities such as nursing homes and day care centres, integration and coordination of services at the local level, quality monitoring systems and so on. One community, the Flemish community, has set up a separate LTC insurance scheme, partly financed by a general contribution by the adult population and aimed at alleviating the burden of non-medical LTC expenses by means of a cash benefit. Generally speaking, the Belgian LTC system can be characterized as a mixed system with extensive publicly financed formal care services which are complemented by significant informal care provided mainly within the family. Compared with most other European countries, use of both formal home care services and residential care services is high in Belgium. The amount of public spending on LTC in Belgium is relatively high, while the role of private funding is modest (OECD Health Data, 2009; Kraus et al., 2010).

Belgian LTC policy aims at helping, supporting and nursing dependent persons. While public health insurance generally covers all age categories, many LTC services in Belgium are specifically targeted at the elderly dependent population. Separate regulations (not discussed in this chapter) exist regarding special provisions and benefits for disabled persons younger than 65 years.

1.1   LTC benefits

Formal LTC benefits consist of services 'in kind' and cash benefits. As a rule, the aim of LTC policy is to support dependent elderly persons in their own natural environment for as long as possible. If limitations in activities of daily living become too severe and adequate informal or professional support at home is unavailable or insufficient, the dependent person should have access to suitable and affordable residential care facilities. To achieve these broad policy goals, a range of residential and home-based LTC services has been developed.

1.1.1   Benefits in kind

In residential care, nursing and personal care is provided to mainly elderly patients with low to moderate limitations in homes for the elderly, and to patients with moderate to severe limitations in nursing homes. Eligibility depends on the severity and number of limitations, and is evaluated using the familiar six activities of daily living (ADL) items of physical limitations[2] augmented with a cognitive criterion (disorientation in time or space). Care in a semi-residential setting is provided in day care centres and 'short-stay' care centres. These are facilities providing nursing and personal care for patients with moderate to severe ADL or cognitive limitations who still live in their own homes, but (temporarily) lack adequate informal care or whose caregivers need respite time. The same eligibility criteria are used as in residential care. Short-stay centres provide residential services to patients for a limited time period in order temporarily to alleviate the burden of informal caregivers. In day care centres, elderly persons are taken care of during one or more weekdays, but they spend the night at home. Additionally, zero- or low-care elderly people, and moderately and severely disabled people having adequate informal care, can stay in 'service flats' and similar accommodation, which combine individual living arrangements with collective facilities (meals, home help and so on). Home nursing care is available for persons with mild to severe ADL limitations, irrespective of their age, their income and the availability of informal care. The eligibility for and intensity of care, and the corresponding level of financial intervention by the federal health insurance system, are determined using the same criteria as in residential care. Care provided by home nurses includes nursing care (e.g., wound dressing and administering medication) and personal care (mainly help with personal hygiene and dressing). This partly overlaps with home care services, which are subsidized by the regional governments. Home carers provide help with similar and other personal care tasks (e.g., help with eating or moving around), along with instrumental help (e.g., light housework, preparing meals). In Flanders, the 'First-line Evaluation' scale (BEL-*Beoordeling Eerste Lijn schaal*), which measures the severity of the patient's limitations in ADL (instrumental cctivities of daily living (IADL),[3] mental and social functioning, is used for needs assessment. Both in Flanders and Wallonia availability of home care services is limited by yearly quotas on the number of subsidized care hours. It is stipulated that care providers should give priority to persons with more severe care needs, with less financial means (Wallonia) and with limited informal care (Flanders). At present, however, there are no uniform standardized criteria determining the precise amount of help to which clients are entitled.

1.1.2 *Cash benefits*

There are two major cash benefits targeted at alleviating the financial burden of non-medical expenses incurred by LTC recipients. At the federal level there is an 'Allowance for Assistance to Elderly Persons' (*Tegemoetkoming voor hulp aan bejaarden* – THAB), which is part of several 'Allowances for the Handicapped'. It is a monthly allowance, allocated to persons aged 65 years or older who score a minimum of 7 points on a scale that includes ADL and IADL limitation items as well as a medical assessment. Eligibility for the allowance is means-tested, and the amount of the benefit depends on the severity of care needs and on the financial situation of the applicant, which takes into account current income, financial assets and non-financial assets. In 2008, 126,816 elderly persons received the THAB and the average monthly amount of the benefit was €274. At the regional level, Flanders has set up a separate LTC insurance scheme which pays a monthly allowance to patients who score at least 35 points on the BEL scale or who can prove their need for care by other means. The Flemish Care Insurance was established in October 2001 and was initially limited to home care. It was extended in July 2002 to residential care users. Both groups of beneficiaries currently receive €130 per month. The monthly allowance, which used to differ between home care and residential care recipients, is not means-tested. There is no age limit, but eligibility is restricted to Flemish residents and residents of the Brussels Capital Region (with some restrictions). The number of benefit recipients was 188,399 in 2008.

In Belgian LTC policy, special attention is being given to support informal carers, who play a pivotal role in enabling dependent elderly persons to stay in their own homes. This support takes the form of providing informal caregivers with information and social and psychological support to alleviate the physical and mental burden of prolonged caregiving. It also comprises a well-established system of paid leave schemes for employees: care leave schemes for medical assistance and for palliative care, and other, more general, leave schemes. In addition to the physical and psychological pressure, informal caregivers also face financial repercussions because of the extra costs of caring and the time needed to provide care. To address this problem, the federal and regional governments are currently studying the possibility of developing new tax benefits and social security measures aimed at reducing the adverse financial effects and disincentives faced by informal caregivers (Federal Public Service Social Security, 2009).

1.1.3   The Flemish Care Insurance – background

From the above it becomes clear that an asymmetrical LTC policy situation is developing in Belgium: whereas the federal 'Allowance for Assistance to Elderly Person' covers the entire Belgian territory, the other cash benefit is limited to the Flemish territory, with residents of the Brussels Capital Region being allowed to opt in. The Flemish Care Insurance is part of a relatively recent trend at decentralization of social policy. Whereas the Belgian welfare State has always developed at the national level, a process of 'deepening' of social policy in recent decades has gradually shifted the emphasis from the redistribution of income to the activation of benefit recipients, the creation of training and education opportunities and the introduction of provisions for older and younger families. The new approach entails a much closer alignment to local needs and requirements and consequently necessitates a more local implementation. In Belgium, as in some other countries, the decentralization trend is enhanced by the existence of significant social, economic, cultural and political differences between the sub-national entities (Cantillon and De Maesschalck, 2008). Moreover, as a result of successive institutional reforms, the regions and communities have acquired increasingly wide powers, sometimes extending to the realm of the federal social security system. This has given rise to areas of tensions, for example, between job placement and unemployment insurance, between prevention and insurance in health care, and in the fields of education and child benefits.

The Flemish Care Insurance scheme is yet another manifestation of the ongoing decentralization trend. In 1999, Flanders introduced an insurance scheme for care dependency. Even though the financial impact of this single programme is limited, it meant a fundamental change for Belgian social security: this was the first time a sub-national entity had supplemented the federal social security system with an entirely autonomous branch of social protection.

The following paragraphs give a brief sketch of the history of the Flemish Care Insurance. The concept of an insurance against care dependency was first floated within the *federal* government. In 1985, Jean-Luc Dehaene, the then Minister of Social Affairs, tabled the idea of an allowance towards the cost of home care. Five years later, his successor, Philippe Busquin, formulated a proposal for the introduction of a dependency insurance. In 1992, the next Minister, Philippe Moureaux, eventually included the idea in a policy document of the federal cabinet. Over the next few months, it would lead a life of its own, and come to be known under various names, including dependency insurance, independency insurance and self-sufficiency insurance (Rottiers, 2005).

Then, at the 1993 Flemish Conference on Wellbeing, the desirability of a care insurance was discussed at length:

> Many questions arise in relation to the management and regulation of services and benefits for care-dependent elderly persons. Should dependency be recognised as a new social risk and, if it should, then what is the competent level of government to address it? Should care insurance consist in services or should it be conceived as an allowance with which the recipient is able to purchase the necessary services, or perhaps a combination of the two? And in the latter case, how can the various measures be adequately coordinated? (Van Buggenhout and Sabbe, 1993, p. 788)

The response at the time was quite unanimous:

> In order for the general approach to succeed, it is necessary to elucidate the competences of the various policy levels, whereby the federal government should assume responsibility for the allowance policy, while the Flemish Community should organise the provision of services. Structural deliberation is required concerning the relationship and accumulation rules between the two kinds of interventions. (Van Buggenhout and Sabbe, 1993, p. 799)

In a similar vein, Pacolet and Spinnewijn (1993, p. 784) argued in favour of 'the restoration and maintenance or the further development of the social security systems of health care insurance and pensions'. The conference conclusions were therefore quite tentative in this respect. In the synthesis, it was asserted that

> as long as there are no unequivocal answers to the questions of whom the allowance should be granted to, how substantial the allowance may or should be, which care needs it should cover, and what the relationship

should be between the allowance and existing schemes, it would seem wise not to introduce mechanisms that might become uncontrollable. (Van Buggenhout and Sabbe, 1993, p. 155)

The then Minister of Wellbeing Wivina Demeester was also quite reserved:

It is far from clear whether a dependency or autonomy insurance will actually enhance people's autonomy. So is this kind of insurance necessary in order to make care affordable? This is probably not the right way to go...In my view, the best option is to enhance personal autonomy within the framework of existing provisions, without setting up a new insurance scheme. (Demeester, 1993, pp. 169–170)

Entirely in line with these viewpoints, the Dehaene government decided on 28 June 1995 to expand the THAB scheme with a system of service vouchers. However, the Flemish government responded by invoking a conflict of interest on the basis of the argument that service cheques are to be regarded as a service to persons, which – under the constitutional allocation of powers – is a Flemish area of competence. From that moment, Flanders took the lead in the design of a care insurance scheme. In 1997, Minister Demeester announced the introduction of the Flemish Care Insurance, a policy measure which was especially designed to gather new income for Flanders. Although the issues raised at the 1993 conference continued to cause concern, it soon emerged that there was a great desire on the Flemish side to take this opportunity to further expand the region's social competences. After some political tussling over various proposals – service cheques, cheaper elderly care, allowances for non-medical costs – a joint proposal of decree was approved as a compromise on 17 March 1999 and eventually published as the Decree of 30 March 1999 concerning the organization of the care insurance (Rottiers, 2005).

1.2 Formal and informal care

Formal LTC services are well developed in Belgium, with a diversified provision of residential, semi-residential, home nursing and home care services. Compared with most other European countries, use of formal care services by elderly persons is high in Belgium. The proportion of people older than 65 years receiving residential care in the European Union is on average 3.3 per cent (Huber et al., 2009), while it is double (6.6 per cent) in Belgium. Using data from the 2004 Survey of Health Ageing and Retirement (SHARE), Geerts (2009) showed that the share of users of both professional nursing care (13.4 per cent) and professional household help (16.6 per cent) in Belgium is among the highest in Europe. The average number of hours received per month by home care users, however, is rather low. Ample formal care provision notwithstanding, care-dependent Belgian elderly also receive substantial informal care by relatives and friends. For instance, SHARE 2004 data indicate that 45.2 per cent of moderately or severely care-dependent elderly persons living at home receive informal care from someone outside the household. Almost half (49.1 per cent) of these extra-residential caregivers are children or children-in-law, but friends, neighbours or other acquaintances (28.9 per cent) and other family members (14.5 per cent) are also frequently involved in providing extra-residential informal care.

The high share of both formal and informal care users places Belgium (together with France and Austria) somewhat outside the 'core' of European countries characterized by a trade-off between formal and informal care provision and use (Pommer et al., 2007).

2   Trends in LTC supply

As in many other European countries, expansion of home care services to postpone nursing home entry has become a priority goal in Belgian LTC policy. Home care services and public expenditures on home care have grown considerably. However, as will be discussed in Section 3.2, home care growth was not at the expense of investment in residential care facilities.

As Figure 16.1 shows, the supply of home care services and, in particular, of semi-residential facilities such as day care centres and short-stay centres, all intended to help elderly persons to live at home for as long as possible, has increased more than the supply of residential care services. Starting with the residential sector, there were some 119,000 mainly elderly persons living in homes for the elderly or nursing homes in 2007. Their numbers have

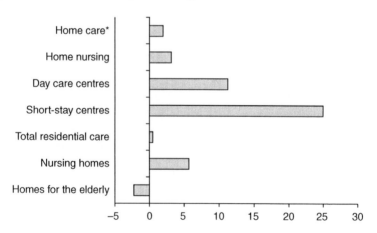

Figure 16.1   Average annual growth (%) of home and residential care facilities, 2002–2008

Note: *Data for Flanders only.
Source: NIHDI and the Flemish Agency for Care and Health (FACH).

increased steadily from around 90,000 in 1985, partly as a result of a gradual shift from hospital wards for LTC patients to dedicated care facilities for elderly persons with chronic care needs caused by age-related limitations.

The number of lower-care beds in homes for the elderly has decreased steadily in the last decade, from around 88,000 in 2000 to 66,000 in 2010, while the number of higher-care nursing home beds has almost doubled, from around 33,000 to 63,000 over the same period. The proportion of severely dependent residents, many of whom combine physical limitations with moderate to severe mental impairments such as dementia, has gradually increased accordingly. The share of severely limited residents (defined as having at least three physical limitations or one physical limitation combined with being disoriented in space and time, labelled 'High' and 'Very high' in Table 16.1), increased from around 58 per cent in 1998 to more than 63 per cent in 2007. The total number of beds in residential care facilities per 100 persons of 65 years and over has risen slightly in the past decade, from 6.8 in 1998 to 7.0 in 2008.

The availability of semi-residential facilities such as day care centres and short-stay centres increased substantially: from 241 to 1626 accredited beds in short-stay centres between 2000 and 2010; day care capacity increased from 713 to 1830 over the same period. As for home nursing and home care users, their numbers have increased steadily since the late 1990s, as shown in Table 16.2. In Flanders, the number of subsidized home care hours per 100 persons 65+ rose from 1273 in 1998 to 1374 in 2008.

Comparing Tables 16.1 and 16.2, the shift to providing care at home rather than in residential care facilities becomes apparent: home nursing care has grown by 30 per cent since 1997 and home care has even grown by 45 per cent, while residential care has increased by only 11 per cent over approximately the same period.

The apparent adequacy of current (aggregate) LTC provision provides no guarantee for the future. Indeed, with the possibility of a doubling of the dependent population by 2060 as a consequence of demographic ageing, maintaining current levels of care provision and quality standards will certainly be a challenge. It will require a sustained and increasing financial effort, as well as careful human resource planning, to ensure that the infrastructure and qualified nursing and caring staff will be in place when the share of the elderly in the population reaches its maximum.

3 Funding

3.1 Funding overview

Given the organization of the Belgian LTC system, with its division of responsibilities between the federal and the regional levels, it follows that the financial flows are rather diverse and complex. Very broadly speaking, that part of LTC covered by the universal health insurance system

Table 16.1 A breakdown of residential patients (N) by care level (selected years)

| | Homes for the elderly (Rustoorden voor bejaarden – ROB) | | | | Nursing homes (Rust- en verzorgingstehuizen – RVT) | | | Total |
| | Severity of limitations | | | | Severity of limitations | | | |
	Low to moderate	High	Very high	Total	High	Very high	Total	
1998	44,791	18,912	23,736	87,439	2,987	16,915	19,902	107,371
2001	45,521	18,130	17,988	81,639	7,512	30,103	37,615	119,359
2004	46,459	12,383	14,526	73,368	11,166	34,463	45,629	115,000
2007	47,011	11,858	14,277	73,146	14,761	34,950	49,711	118,840

Source: NIHDI. All data based on patient counts on 31 March.

Table 16.2   Number of home nursing and home care users, 1997–2004

	1997	2001	2004	2007
Home nursing care users	116,819	123,664	148,204	152,318
Home care users*	54,638	63,225	67,725	79,181

Note: *Data for Flanders only.
Source: Home nursing – NIHDI (all data based on patient counts on 31 March); home care – FACH.

(residential and home nursing care) is mainly financed by (non-earmarked) social security contributions paid by workers, employers and retirees, and to a lesser extent by taxes. Other LTC services and allowances are mainly financed by general taxes, collected largely at the federal level. Total LTC expenditures were approximately €5.7 billion in 2006[4] (1.8 per cent of GDP), of which almost 98 per cent was financed by a combination of social security contributions (59 per cent) and taxes (39 per cent). This figure does not include out-of-pocket payments for accommodation in residential care (approximately €2.3 billion).

Generally speaking, nursing and personal care services, both in residential care facilities and at home, provided via the federal health insurance system are financed by social security contributions (€3.3 billion) and taxes (€1.5 billion), while home care organized at the regional level is financed by taxes (€728 million), out-of-pocket expenditures ((€100 million) and specific contributions (approximately €54 million contributed to the Flemish Care Insurance scheme and allocated to home care). Table 16.3 gives a breakdown of total LTC expenditures in 2006 by care setting and funding source.

Board and lodging costs in residential care facilities are not covered by public health insurance. With an average pension of around €960

Table 16.3   LTC expenditures by care setting and funding source (2006, € million)

		LTC setting			
		Residential care	Home nursing care	Home care	Total
Source of funding	Contributions	2018	1295	54	3367
	Taxes	1505		728	2233
	Out-of-pocket	1	7.2	99.3	107.5
	Total	3524	1302.2	881.3	5707.5

Note: Excluding out-of-pocket expenses for accommodation in residential care and home care acquired with service checks.
Source: Update of the System of Health Accounts (SHA) data provided to the Organization for Economic Cooperation and Development (OECD). See http://stats.oecd.org/Index.aspx?DataSetCode=SHA.

per month in Flanders and around €940 in Wallonia (Rijksdienst voor Pensioenen, 2010, pension figures for 1 January 2009), many dependent elderly persons have insufficient recurrent income to pay their monthly nursing home bill, which was on average around €1250 in Flanders and around €950 in Wallonia (Federale Overheidsdienst Economie, 2009). As a result, elderly home owners sometimes have to sell their home when they move to a nursing home, while others have to rely on financial support from their children or on social assistance support. Social assistance agencies (the 'Public Centres for Social Welfare', abbreviated as OCMW in Dutch and CPAS in French) have the right to claim money from the children. The duty for children to support their parents, which is the legal basis for this claim, is currently being debated, with some political parties in favour of lifting the duty.

While for most outpatient health care services, patients are in principle required to pay the full fee up-front and then claim reimbursement with their sickness fund, regulations for nursing care delivery at home allow the third-party payer system (Sermeus et al., 2010). Patients pay only user charges, in principle amounting to around 25 per cent of the price. However, for some nursing interventions patients do not have to contribute and, in order to promote nursing care accessibility, many home nursing providers do not collect user charges (Sermeus et al., 2010). In 2006, the total amount of user contributions amounted to €7.1 million, and it declined even further to €6.9 million in 2008 (0.6 per cent of total home nursing care expenditures). Users of home care services are required to pay user charges. The hourly fee depends on the user's income and assets, the household composition and the severity and duration of care dependency. In Flanders, the total user fee amount was approximately €65 million in 2008, which is about 12 per cent of total home care expenditures. Co-payments are also charged for day care centres, short-stay centres and other publicly subsidized home and semi-residential care services.

Of the two major cash benefits for LTC aimed at alleviating the financial burden of non-medical expenses, the federal THAB is financed by general taxes, while the Flemish Care Insurance is financed by a combination of general taxes and a specific contribution paid[5] by every adult resident into a designated fund. The contributions make up approximately half of the annual budget.

Recently, specific measures have been taken to further improve access and affordability for LTC patients, which either takes the form of a monthly or annual allowance to cover non-medical expenses, or of a reduction in co-payments. An example of the former is the annual allowance for the use of incontinence materials; an example of the latter is the reduction in out-of-pocket payments for GP visits and home nursing care for severely limited patients, as well as for GP visits of palliative patients in nursing homes and homes for the elderly.

Nevertheless, in the case of severe care dependency, out-of-pocket expenses for LTC services can run high, in particular when a combination of different formal care services and/or very frequent or continuous care is needed. Highly subsidized public services and cash benefits do not prevent a considerable group of care-dependent persons from being confronted with high LTC costs (Pacolet et al., 2010). In order to improve the financial accessibility to LTC services, the Flemish government decided in 2009 to introduce a maximum billing system for home (and intermediate) care services. The system will place a means-adjusted maximum on clients' out-of-pocket expenses for home care, but has not been implemented at the time of writing.

It should be noted that not all out-of-pocket expenditures for home care are known, since elderly people who are not eligible for or who do not want to make use of subsidized home care can and do buy these services privately, mainly by using 'service cheques'. These are vouchers which can be purchased to pay for domestic services provided by public bodies or private firms who employ (usually low-skilled) personnel. The system was introduced in May 2003 in an attempt to regularize 'black economy' activities in the domestic services sector. The services provided under this scheme are paid in large part by government subsidies (around €13 per hour), with the balance paid by the user (currently €7.5 per hour). This amount covers the hourly wage of the employee, including social security contributions, and a profit for the employer. The money spent on service cheques is tax deductible by users up to a certain limit, implying that the government intervention is even greater than the subsidy. In 2008, the system cost around €1.3 billion. The amount spent on LTC is unknown, unfortunately, because the vouchers are used rather extensively to pay for domestic help other than help for elderly people with IADL limitations – for instance, by families with both spouses working full time.

3.2 The growth of commercial LTC provision

The care model as we know it in Belgium has traditionally been a balance between government initiative (such as public homes for the elderly organized by the social aid bureaux) and a sizeable private not-for-profit initiative. The commercial sector has had less of a presence in the field of LTC facilities, such as elderly homes.

The fact that the private – but not-for-profit – sector is very active in the field of care has everything to do with the way Belgian social security has its roots in private social initiatives rooted in the nineteenth century. At that time, next to local associations for leisure, adult learning and well-being, modest contingency funds, known as 'funds for mutual assistance', were established. Employers, for their part, united in so-called compensation funds, for the purpose of distributing the financial burden of child allowances for workers' families. After the First World War, the various branches of social insurance began to take definitive shape. And towards the end of 1944, the National Social Security System for Employees was introduced. The social organizations, such as the sick funds and the compensation funds, the labour unions and the employer organizations, remained part of the organization of the welfare State, hence also in the field of care. Social organizations, especially the Catholic ones, still hold a big share of the LTC field in Belgium. They are subsidized. When the Flemish Care Insurance was introduced, for example, sick funds as well as purely commercial insurers were allowed to offer this (obligatory) insurance to Flemish residents.[6] The sick funds took up almost the entire market share for Flemish Care Insurances. Today commercial care insurers' share of the Flemish Care Insurance market is minuscule.

In the course of the last years, however, there has been a sizeable increase in for-profit commercial initiatives, especially for elderly homes and child care facilities. Today one-third of elderly homes are run by not-for-profit organizations (usually Catholic), one-third by the State (mostly by the centres for social aid) and one-third by private commercial initiatives. In Wallonia and Brussels, the commercial initiatives hold a higher share (50 per cent) (ACV Konfederatie). It is highly likely that their share in the market will grow. Not only is commercial initiative being taken with regard to elderly homes, but also in the area of care at home: the introduction of service vouchers in 2001 gave rise to the offer of services by public institutions (e.g., centres for social aid), by not-for-profit organizations as well as by for-profit companies. In 2006, the for-profit companies created 58.5 per cent of service jobs in the framework of service vouchers system, while the not-for-profit sector accounted for 24.8 per cent of service jobs and the public sector 16.8 per cent. Again, we notice a sizeable share of commercial initiatives in this segment of the LTC field (Henry et al., 2008).

Finally, we should mention that private companies or self-employed nurses are increasingly involved in care at home.

Quite recently, a debate took place on the growing share of private companies buying or building elderly homes, or actually running elderly homes. Social organizations, such as the network of Catholic care institutions, expressed their concern and pointed to the risks of inequality of access and quality of care, as well as the risk of exclusion of vulnerable categories of elderly (Zorgnet Vlaanderen, 2009). Similarly, the union of elderly people (Okra) argued that in principle the logic of the market does not belong to the sector of health and well-being (Mooijman, 2010).

3.3 Cost-containment and adequacy

3.3.1 *Cost-containment*

The federal Ministries of Health and Social Affairs are, together with the NIHDI, responsible for the budget for care provision in residential care facilities and for home nursing care, which are part of the public health insurance system, and for overall capacity planning (mainly the number of beds in nursing homes), fees and levels of public intervention via negotiations with the providers' organizations. Responsibility for certification, monitoring and quality control of residential care services is mainly at the regional level. Home care capacity planning, budget, certification, monitoring and quality control are also a regional responsibility.

As part of health-care cost-containment measures, in 1997 a moratorium was agreed between the federal and the regional levels, limiting expansion of residential care capacity. Since 1997, successive protocol agreements between the federal and regional governments have aimed at progressively substituting nursing home beds for beds in residential care homes. In this way, policy makers aimed at guaranteeing a better financing of care-dependent residents, but within the margins set by the moratorium. A part of the budget corresponding to the maximum number of beds set at the federal level is allocated to the regions, which can decide on the allocation over services in different semi-residential and residential settings or to support home care.

Based on the observation that costs for home nursing were rising, various measures for controlling costs have been introduced since the late 1980s. For instance, a maximum day limit was fixed in the fee-for-service financing in order to limit supply-induced care provision, and rules were established to avoid double payments from a combination of nursing care delivery at home with care delivery in another setting (Sermeus et al., 2010). However, costs have continued to increase. In recent years, concerns have been raised on how to optimize financing in a growing home nursing sector. An advisory report by the Belgian Health Care Knowledge Center (KCE) recommended making a clearer distinction between acute care following an acute onset requiring hospital stay, and LTC for patients with chronic conditions and high levels of dependency. Another recommendation was to (partly) organize financing along the lines of a case-mix model. This will require a better delineation of dependency or resource utilization categories, minimizing cost variability between patients within the same category.

With regard to home care services subsidized by the regional governments, both in Flanders and Wallonia yearly quotas limit the volume of care hours that accredited organizations can provide.

3.3.2 *Efficacy, affordability and a need for policy coordination*

In view of the rising costs of LTC and the variety of policy instruments that address LTC needs, a higher degree of policy coordination is necessary. As mentioned, in Belgium, but especially in Flanders, the care-dependency risk is met by various policy instruments: social assistance (THAB), insurance (Flemish Care Insurance), cost control in residential elderly care, limitation of personal contributions for home care and (federal) service cheques. At the same time, issues of efficacy and affordability arise.

When we take a closer look at the Flemish Care Insurance, the scheme diverges in various ways from the national, Bismarckian social security system: it is a universal scheme, funded by means of a small individual contribution of €25 per year, supplemented by substantial government subsidies. Moreover, it consists in lump-sum allowances, irrespective of the beneficiary's income and degree of care-dependency. In other words, the system has characteristics of the Anglo-Saxon, Beveridgean social security system. Unlike under the federal system, eligibility for protection is not restricted to those over the age of 65, nor are private insurers excluded from its practical implementation.

So care insurance is designed to guarantee an allowance to anyone who is care-dependent, irrespective of their degree of care dependency and financial situation. It generates fresh revenue to cover the cost associated with population ageing and it reduces the financial insecurity of care dependent persons (Pacolet, 2008). At the same time, the lump-sum and universal nature of the insurance puts it at the limits of social efficacy and affordability. As under the old UK social security system, the lump sum contributions are too small to cover the rising cost of care. Moreover due to the universal nature of the allowance, the amount granted is inadequate for heavily care-dependent persons with a modest income. In their case, the selective and more generous allowances under the national system are indispensable. In other words, the two systems are complementary. However, even the combined allowances do not suffice to cover the cost incurred by the most severely care-dependent. Figure 16.2 illustrates how care allowances compare with care expenses. To this end, persons in a home care situation have been categorized in accordance with their expenditure level. We notice that, already from the fifth decile, care expenses exceed the Flemish Care Insurance allowance. If we add to this the maximum allowance under the THAB scheme, it becomes apparent that the cost of care for the most severely care-dependent is not covered by the combined allowances. Conversely, for about half of the chronically ill in a home care situation, the allowance exceeds the reported non-medical care costs.

As the intrinsic design of the Flemish Care Insurance scheme leaves little room for financial manoeuvre (i.e., the lump-sum contributions cannot be increased substantially), the Flemish Coalition Agreement of 2008 provides for measures to restrict the cost of care, by means of a maximum billing system for home care and through the introduction of a new system of cost limitation in residential elderly care. Hence, in Flanders the care-dependency risk is addressed by social assistance (THAB), insurance (Flemish Care Insurance), cost control in residential elderly care limitation of personal contributions for home care and (federal) service cheques.

Policy coordination clearly imposes itself here, not only with regard to the eligibility criteria and allowances under, respectively, the Flemish Care

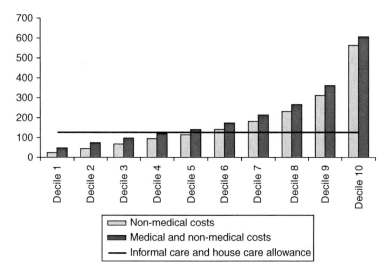

Figure 16.2 Monthly medical and non-medical costs (€, mid-2006) incurred by a chronically ill person in a home care situation in Flanders, compared with an allowance of €125
Source: Pacolet (2008).

Insurance and the THAB schemes, but also in relation to other provisions, not least the federal service cheques, which are often spent on domestic care services. With rising care expenses (even more so in Flanders than in Wallonia) and limited budgetary means, it is essential that the efficacy and efficiency of the totality of measures should be assessed and that coordination should take place between policy-making at the Flemish and the federal levels of government. This became quite apparent when the introduction of the Flemish Care Insurance scheme prompted a race-to-the-top between the two policy levels.

This race-to-the-top manifested itself three years after the introduction of the Flemish Care Insurance, when the federal government decided to substantially increase the generosity of the THAB scheme: in 2003, some 36,000 elderly persons were entitled to up to €170 extra per month, at an additional cost of €31 million. The dynamics of Belgium's federal political structure had apparently induced this move. A similar phenomenon was observed after the introduction of the Flemish school bonus: at the start of the following school year, a supplementary (national) child benefit scheme was introduced. Similarly, in the recent federal coalition agreement, it was announced that 'the government will, within the framework of the present federal schemes, evaluate and if need be increase the allowances for elderly persons'. The addition of the phrase 'within the framework of the present federal schemes' is quite telling: the evaluation of the totality of allowances provided by the various sub-national entities and hence any policy coordination are explicitly ruled out.

Apparently, then, a decentralization of social protection need not lead to negative social competition, as is assumed in the classical theory of fiscal federalism. However, in the context of the rising cost of population ageing and the absolute necessity of greater efficiency to maintain and enhance the effectiveness of the social protection system, the uncoordinated cost-increasing mechanisms between different policy-making levels raises serious longer-term sustainability questions.

3.4   Trends in LTC financing, 2003–2008

While in recent years availability and use of home care services increased at a faster rate than availability and use of residential facilities, the reverse was true for public expenditures for both care settings, as illustrated in Table 16.4. Between 2003 and 2005, the average annual increase in public expenditures (by NIHDI) on care in residential settings was 9.5 per cent, whereas public expenditures for nursing home care (also by NIHDI) increased on average by 7.2 per cent and the average annual growth of home care subsidies (figure for Flanders only) was 6.3 per cent. Apparently, expansion of home care services did not occur at the expense of public expenditures for residential care.

Table 16.4 illustrates another striking development in LTC financing: between 2003 and 2005, expenditures on cash benefits increased much more rapidly than expenditures on home and residential care services. Cash benefit growth slowed down in 2006, but it was again above the annual increase of in-kind benefits in 2008. As Pavolini and Ranci (2008) show, an increasing combination of monetary transfers to families with the provision of in-kind services is an important characteristic of LTC reforms in many European countries.

4   Critical appraisal of the system

The overall goal of Belgian LTC policy is to provide universal access to affordable and high-quality LTC, aimed, as in most European countries, at allowing elderly care-dependent persons to keep on living in their own homes as long as possible. This goal is primarily achieved by means of public health insurance coverage of nursing care and by a whole range of care services organized and provided at the regional and local level, and financed by general taxes.

Indeed, the targets of accessibility and affordability are at least partially met by the fact that nursing and personal care, both in residential care facilities and at home, are largely part of the public health care system, which combines universal coverage with relatively low rates of out-of-pocket payment. Furthermore, there are two major cash benefits targeted at alleviating the financial burden of non-medical expenses incurred by LTC recipients.

Table 16.4 Annual percentage growth in public LTC expenditures, 2003–2008

	2003	2004	2005	2006	2007	2008	Ave., 2003–2005	Ave., 2003–2008	Ave., 2006–2008
In-kind benefits									
Residential care	18.5	10.5	4.0	11.0	10.1	3.0	11.0	9.5	8.0
Home nursing	7.5	8.2	4.2	7.7	7.2	8.5	6.6	7.2	7.8
Home care (Flanders)				4.2	8.2	6.6			6.3
Total in-kind benefits				*9.1*	*9.1*	*5.0*			*7.7*
Cash benefits									
THAB	48.7	12.3	7.6	2.6	4.1	5.9	22.9	13.5	4.2
Flemish Care Insurance	85.9	26.4	9.9	6.4	9.9	12.9	40.7	25.2	9.7
Total cash benefits	*57.9*	*16.5*	*8.3*	*3.9*	*6.1*	*8.4*	*27.6*	*16.8*	*6.1*

Source: NIHDI, Flemish Care Fund (Vlaams Zorgfonds) and Research Centre of the Flemish Government (*Studiedienst Vlaamse Regering*).

At the federal level, there is the means-tested THAB. At the regional level, Flanders has set up a separate LTC insurance scheme. Recently, other specific measures have been taken to improve access and affordability for LTC users, for example, the annual allowance for the use of incontinence material. Nevertheless, the financial burden of medical and non-medical expenses caused by the chronic nature of the limitations and disabilities associated with old age can run high, especially in the case of severe care needs, resulting in an increased poverty risk among severely care-dependent elderly persons (Pacolet et al., 2010). In order to improve financial accessibility to LTC services, the Flemish government has decided to introduce a maximum billing system for home (and intermediate) care services. The system will place a means-adjusted maximum on clients' out-of-pocket expenses for home care, but has not been implemented to date. Compared with most other European countries, the amount of public spending on LTC in Belgium is relatively high, while the role of private funding is modest (OECD Health Data, 2009; Kraus et al., 2010).

With regard to service availability, it is probably fair to say that current LTC needs are relatively adequately covered by the provision of a diversified package of residential, semi-residential and home care services. The share of formal home care users among the 65+ population in Belgium is among the highest in Europe, but the intensity of care utilization is rather low. For several European countries there is evidence of greater targeting of services according to need. In Belgium, provision of publicly subsidized home care services is more indiscriminate, making it more difficult to effectively guarantee adequate support to the most severely care-dependent elderly persons or to persons with insufficient support from relatives or friends.

In the recent past, supply of residential and home care services in Belgium has more or less kept pace with the over-65 population. In the longer run, given the projected steep increase in the share of elderly persons in the population, the provision of sufficient services to meet demand and the overall financial burden of the system will become a major challenge. Moreover, the projected growing numbers of dependent elderly people will pose the problem of finding equally expanding numbers of informal and formal carers in order to maintain the current levels and quality of LTC in the future.

Another concern is the continued complexity and fragmentation of the Belgian LTC system. Despite several initiatives, both at the federal and the regional level, to improve care coordination, LTC service provision remains complex and fragmented, partly because of the division of responsibilities between the federal and the regional levels. As a consequence, elderly persons and their relatives may have a hard time to get the help they need, despite the relative abundance of its potential availability.

Additionally, the initiative of Flanders to introduce its own Flemish Care Insurance gave way to the development of a layered system of social protection, in which policy coordination between the various levels of government is entirely missing. We refer to the above-mentioned various policy instruments, which not only operate without coordination but which also caused a competitive spending increase, such as with the Flemish Care Insurance and the THAB schemes, but also in relation to other provisions, not least the federal service cheques, which are often spent on domestic care services. With rising care expenses and limited budgetary means, it is essential that the efficacy and efficiency of the totality of measures should be assessed and that coordination should take place between policy-making at the Flemish and the federal levels of government.

Acknowledgements

Part of this chapter is based on Willemé (2010), which is the Belgian contribution to Work Package 1 of the research project 'Assessing Needs of Care in European Nations' (ANCIEN). The ANCIEN project is funded by the European Commission under the 7th Framework Programme (FP7 Health-2007-3.2.2, Grant no. 223483).

Notes

1. The federal structure of the Belgian State results in a rather complicated division of power between the federal and the regional authorities. At the sub-national level there is a territorial division (the Flemish, Walloon and Brussels Capital regions) and a 'cultural' one (the Flemish-, French- and German-speaking communities, plus commissions responsible for the Flemish, French and bilingual institutions in the Brussels Capital region). While the organization of the social security system (of which public health insurance is part) is a federal responsibility, the Flemish-, French- and German-speaking communities are responsible for 'person-related matters', including some that affect health and LTC. As a result, most non-medical aspects of care for the elderly are community responsibilities. The Flemish- and German-speaking communities assume their responsibilities themselves, while the French-speaking community has devolved its responsibility to the Walloon region for matters relevant to the Walloon territory. Despite these institutional complications, we will use the generic term 'regional' in the rest of the text to designate the sub-national level of authority. Further, it should be noted that at the moment the division of power between the federal and the regional authorities is under discussion, and proposals have been made for a further decentralization of LTC responsibility.
2. ADL are bathing, dressing, transferring, toileting, continence and feeding.
3. IADL are house cleaning, washing clothes, ironing, shopping for groceries, preparing meals and general running of the household.
4. This figure is an update of the System of Health Accounts (SHA) data provided to the OECD. See http://stats.oecd.org/Index.aspx?DataSetCode=SHA, date accessed 14 September 2009.
5. Currently €25 per year (€10 for persons qualifying for lower co-payments in the compulsory health insurance system).
6. Both sick funds and private insurers charge the same insurance premium that is fixed by the Act introducing the Flemish Care Insurance.

320 *Models*

References

ACV Konfederatie (2010) *Je maakt geen winst op kap van kwetsbare zorgbehoevenden!*, http://www.acv-online.be/Actualiteit/Nieuws/Detail/Commercialiseringvanzorg. asp, date accessed 18 August 2010.

Cantillon, B. and De Maesschalck, V. (2008) *Gedachten over Sociaal Federalisme/Réflexions sur le fédéralisme social* (Leuven: Acco).

Demeester, W. (1993) *Ouderen in Solidariteit, Vlaams Welzijnscongres 1993*, Kluwer editorial.

Federal Public Service Social Security (2009) *Strategic Report on Social Protection and Social Inclusion 2008–2010*, Brussels.

Federale Oveheidsdienst Economie (2009) *Sectorstudie rusthuizen* (Brussels: FOD Economie).

Geerts, J. (2009) 'Gebruik van formele en informele zorg door ouderen. Vlaanderen/België in Europees vergelijkend perspectief', in Cantillon, C., Van den Bosch, K., Lefebure, S. (red.), *Ouderen in Vlaanderen en Europa. Tussen vermogen en afhankelijkheid* (Leuven/Den Haag: Acco), pp. 155–189.

Henry, A., Nassaut, S., Defourny, J. and Nyssens, M. (2008) 'Dienstencheques: Quasimarktmaatregel en vergelijking van prestaties van de dienstverlenende bedrijven', *B.T.S.Z.*, 2, pp. 145–174.

Huber, M., Rodrigues, R., Hoffmann, F., Gasior, K. and Marin, B. (2009) *Facts and Figures on Long-Term Care. Europe and North America* (Vienna: European Centre).

Kraus, M., Riedel, M., Mot, E., Willemé, P., Röhrling, G. and Czypionka, T. (2010) *A Typology of Systems of Long-Term Care in Europe – Results of Work Package 1 of the ANCIEN Project* (Vienna: Institute for Advanced Studies).

Mooijman, R. (2010) 'Zorg is geen koopwaar' Kunnen markt en zorg met elkaar verzoend worden?, *De Standaard*, 6 August, http://www.standaard.be/artikel/detail. aspx?artikelid=IV2TMOD9&s=1, date accessed 18 August 2010.

NIHDI – Statistics and trends of the residential care sector; Federal Public Service Social Security – Vademecum van de financiële en statistische gegevens over de sociale bescherming in België, 2007–2010; FACH (Flemish Agency for Care and Health) – Home care statistics.

OECD (2009) *Health Data 2009* (Paris: OECD).

Pacolet, J. (2008) *Afhankelijkheid en solidariteit: een impliciete of expliciete zorgverzekering* (Brussels: Colloquium of the Federal Public Service for Social Security), 1 October.

Pacolet, J. and Spinnewijn, H. (1993) 'Financiering van de verzorging van ouderen via de invoering van een afhankelijkheidsverzekering', in *Ouderen in Solidariteit. Vlaams Welzijnscongres 1993*, Kluwer editorial, p. 784.

Pacolet, J., Merckx, S., Spruytte, N. and Cabus, S. (2010) *Naar een verbeterde tenlastening van de kosten van niet-medische zorg thuis* (Leuven: HIVA).

Pavolini, E. and Ranci, C. (2008) 'Restructuring the Welfare State: Reforms in Long-Term Care in Western European Countries', *Journal of European Social Policy*, 18 (3), pp. 246–259.

Pommer, E., Woittiez, I. and Stevens, J. (2007) *Comparing Care. The Care of the Elderly in Ten EU-countries* (The Hague: The Netherlands Institute for Social Research).

Rijksdienst voor Pensioenen (2010) *Jaarlijkse statistiek van de uitkeringsgrechtigden* (Brussel: Rijksdienst voor Pensioenen).

Rottiers, S. (2005) *De weerbaarheid van de Vlaamse zorgverzekering: Waalse klachten en Europese bedenkingen* (Berichten/UA, Antwerp, Herman Deleeck Centre for Social Policy).

Sermeus, W., Pirson, M., Paquay et al. (2010) *Le financement des soins infirmiers à domicile en Belgique*, KCE Reports 122B (Bruxelles: Centre fédéral d'expertise des soins de santé (KCE)).

Van Buggenhout, B. and Sabbe, P. (1993) 'Afhankelijkheid en bejaardenzorg: een nieuw sociaal risico?', in *Ouderen in solidariteit, Vlaams Welzijnscongres 1993*, Kluwer editorial, p. 799.

Vlaams Agentschap Zorg en Gezondheid, Cijfers thuiszorg http://www.zorg-en-gezondheid.be/cijfers_thuiszorg/, date accessed 28 August 2010.

Willemé, P. (2010) *The Belgian Long-Term Care System* (Brussels: Federal Planning Bureau).

Zorgnet Vlaanderen (2009) *Zorg Te Koop? Standpunten van Zorgnet Vlaanderen over Privatisering, Commercialisering en Marktwerking.*

Index